RETHINKING

POWER

SUNY Series in Radical Social and Political Theory
Roger S. Gottlieb, editor

and

SUNY Series in Feminist Political Theory
Marion Smiley, editor

Rethinking Power

EDITED BY

Thomas E. Wartenberg

STATE UNIVERSITY OF NEW YORK PRESS

Published by
State University of New York Press, Albany

For information, address the State University of New York Press,
State University Plaza, Albany, NY 12246

Production by Christine M. Lynch

Marketing by Fran Keneston

Library of Congress Cataloging-in-Publication Data

Rethinking power / edited by Thomas E. Wartenberg.
        p.   cm. — (SUNY series in radical social and political
theory)
        Includes bibliographical references and index.
        ISBN 0-7914-0881-7 (acid-free). — ISBN 0-7914-0882-5 (pbk. : acid
-free)
        1. Power (Social sciences)   I. Wartenberg, Thomas E.   II. Series.
JC330.R47   1992
303.3—dc20   90-28586
                                                                      CIP

10 9 8 7 6 5 4 3 2

For Wendy

CONTENTS

ACKNOWLEDGMENTS

The following articles were originally published as indicated. I would like to thank both the authors and the publishers for their permission to reprint these essays.

"New Faces of Power," by Terence Ball, is a slightly revised version of Chapter 4 of Terence Ball, *Transforming Political Discourse* (Oxford: Basil Blackwell, 1988), reprinted with permission of the author and the publisher.

"Beyond the Three Faces of Power," by Jeffrey C. Isaac, originally appeared in *Polity*, volume XX, number 1 (Fall, 1987), pp. 4–30, and is reprinted with permission.

"Situated Social Power," by Thomas Wartenberg, is a revised version of an essay that originally appeared in *Social Theory and Practice*, volume 14, number 3 (Fall, 1988), pp. 317–43. It is also Chapter 6 of Thomas Wartenberg's *The Forms of Power: From Domination to Transformation* (Philadelphia: Temple University Press, 1990).

"The Critique of Impure Reason: Foucault and the Frankfurt School," by Thomas McCarthy, was first published in *Political Theory*, volume 18 (1990), pp. 437–69, copyright 1990 by Sage Publications, Inc. Reprinted by permission of Sage Publications, Inc.

"Five Faces of Oppression," by Iris Marion Young, was first published in *The Philosophical Forum*, volume xix, number 4 (Summer, 1988), pp. 270–90.

"Women and Power," by Jean Baker Miller, appeared in *Work in Progress*, number 82-01 (1982), pp. 1–5, published by the Stone Center for Developmental Services and Studies, and is reprinted by permission of the author.

"Gender and Sexuality: Masculinity, Violence, and Domination," by Nancy C. M. Hartsock, is a revised version of an article that appeared in *Humanities in Society*, volume 7, number 1-2 (Winter/Spring, 1984), pp. 19–45, and is used by permission of the author.

INTRODUCTION

Thomas E. Wartenberg

I

The title of this anthology, *Rethinking Power,* provides a key to understanding the context of the essays that are contained within it. As *rethinkings* of power, they presuppose a background of dissatisfaction with previously developed "thinkings of power." Their attempt to develop a theory of power is conditioned by a common recognition of the failure of those previous theories.

In attempting to rethink power, these essays agree that thinking about power is crucial for critical social thought and philosophy. They recognize the significance of power in the lives of human beings in contemporary society. Although the precise effects of power remain a subject of debate, these essays all acknowledge power as one of the fundamental realities of human social existence, a reality that explains the oppressive and demeaning nature of the conditions of human life. Power remains an important concept for explaining those conditions and for thinking of possible means of ameliorating them.

In addition, these essays all are critical of the failure of previous accounts of power to fully comprehend the role of power in the shaping of human life. The charge is that previous theories of power have failed to accord sufficient importance to power as a theoretical concept. As a result, these essays share a common desire to develop a theory that will accord power its rightful place among social phenomena.

Finally, these essays all situate the development of a more adequate theory of power within the general project of improving the lives of human beings. In this sense, they are examples of *critical* social thought and philosophy. They place the theoretical activity of developing a more adequate account of power and its effect in the social world within the more general practical context of overcoming the oppressive and demeaning circumstances that characterize much of human life today.

But no sooner do I point to a fundamental agreement among the contributions to this volume, than I immediately must correct the impression that these essays are written from a single theoretical perspective. For despite the general agreement among them, they come at the issue of power with fundamentally different commitments and methodologies.

The disparity that lurks beneath the appearance of unity among the essays in this volume reflects the fact that there is no single dominant paradigm in social theory today. With the decline of positivism and its specifically social theoretic counterpart, behavioralism, various other research programs have emerged as competitors in the struggle to succeed positivism.

Various factors led to the decline of positivism, the dominant paradigm in Anglo-American social theory during the 1950s and 1960s. Some were internal to positivism itself. The fundamental idea of positivism in social theory was to model social theory upon the physical sciences. The inadequacy of the account of scientific theorizing upon which this project depended, however, has generally been recognized, as both Ball and Isaac argue in their essays. As a result, even those theorists who accept the scientific status of social theory have been led to reject the particular form in which the positivists had cast it.

There are also many external factors that contributed to the demise of positivism. The recognition that gender and race had illegitimately been ignored by social theory led to the search for a mode of discourse that could incorporate such concerns. In addition, the reception within Anglo-American academia of poststructuralist French thought brought about a fracturing of the assumptions about the nature of social theory. In particular, poststructuralism challenged the idea that social theory should derive its own methodology from that of the natural sciences. As a result, social theorists no longer felt their own discursive possibilities limited by standards of validity imported from elsewhere.

Another important factor was the decline of Marxism as the dominant mode of critical social discourse. By stressing the centrality of class conflicts and economic factors to all social phenomena, Marxism exerted a unifying tendency upon divergent modes of critical discourse. The criticisms of Marxism by both feminism and poststructuralism resulted in a decline in its influence. Feminists asserted that the prioritizing of class over gender resulted in a one-sidedness in Marxist social thought. Poststructuralists, on the other hand, rejected the idea of a single overarching theory or 'metanarrative,' thus calling into question the fundamental stress of Marxism upon the economic.

Understanding the broader intellectual context within which these essays are situated allows us to see why, despite an agreement that an adequate conception of power is urgently needed, they develop their arguments so differently. Because they adhere to different theoretical paradigms that are struggling for ascendancy, the essays in this volume adopt different modes of discourse despite their focus upon a common object of study.

In order to see how these different theoretical commitments are reflected in the essays in this volume, consider the issue of whether it is appropriate to adopt a mode of discourse derived from natural science in addressing the issue of power. A number of the essays are united in their assessment of previous accounts of power as adhering to a view that social theory is amenable to scientization along the lines of behavioral sciences. However, their solutions to this commonly perceived problem move in fundamentally different directions. Some seek to develop theories that adhere to a more adequate philosophy of science, while others reject the language of science *tout court,* seeking to develop a different type of language necessary for social theory.

Similarly, although many essays are predicated on a belief that previous theories of power failed to detect power in all the different spheres of social relationships in which it actually is a factor, where and how they develop this insight differs radically. Bowles and Gintis, for example, in turning to the economy, rely on previous conceptions of power in order to show that the language of neoclassical economics has covered up its presence in the social realm. Airaksinen, Hartsock, and Gottlieb, on the other hand, attempt to demonstrate the presence of power in the sphere of sexuality by developing new vocabularies that allow that presence to emerge.

Some of the essays in this volume accept the idea that power is a constraint on the lives of human beings—an idea that previous theories of power had accepted—but seek to develop a more nuanced and sophisticated understanding of how such constraints are imposed. In their view, the failing of previous theories was their lack of sophistication. Others move in a fundamentally different direction by seeking to develop a positive notion of power, one that does not see power as fundamentally oppressive. In their view, the previous attempts at understanding power were hampered by their fixation on power as oppressive and coercive, thus missing the positive and empowering aspects of power.

So although all of these essays are *rethinkings* of power, they demonstrate the radically different manners in which such rethinkings are taking place. In responding to the failures of previous theories, these essays move in different directions, employing different modes of discourse, even as they all seek to advance our thinking about power.

II

One of the tasks that the reader of this volume faces is that of assessing the validity of the different analyses of power offered by the various essays. Having a sense of the complex structure of power relationships as they exist within contemporary society is a prerequisite for doing so. In order to aid the reader in this task, I will describe the presence of overlapping and contradictory power relationships as portrayed in a short episode that James Agee uses to open his classic study of tenant farmers in Alabama, *Let Us Now Praise Famous Men*.[1] At the same time, I will also demonstrate how complex a social phenomenon power is, thereby enabling the reader to see the need for the sorts of analyses of power as are contained within the essays in this volume.

Agee opens the main body of his book with an account of how he and Walker Evans—the photographer who accompanied him and whose photographs form the other half of the book—were taken by two white landlords to hear their African-American tenant farmers sing. Agee is unhappy about the disruption that this performance causes in the lives of these tenants on a Sunday morning: "They had been summoned to sing for Walker and for me, to show us what nigger music is like (though we had done all we felt we were able to spare them and ourselves this summons) . . . " [28–29] Once the singing has begun, however, Agee is deeply moved:

> It was as I had expected . . . in the style I have heard on records by Mitchell's Christian Singers, jagged, tortured, stony, accented as if by hammers and cold-chisels, full of a nearly paralyzing vitality and iteration of rhythm, the harmonies constantly splitting the nerves; so that of western music the nearest approach to its austerity is in the first two centuries of polyphony. But here it was entirely instinctual; it tore itself like a dance of sped plants out of three young men who stood sunk to their throats in land. . . . [29]

After being asked by their landlord, the African-Americans sing a second song for Agee and Evans, a slow one that is full of feeling. Again, Agee is deeply moved and his language now seeks to match that song in its evocative power:

> The tenor lifted out his voice alone in a long, plorative line that hung like fire on heaven, or whistle's echo, sinking, sunken, along descents of a modality I had not heard before, and sank along the arms and breast of the bass as might a body sunken from a cross. . . . [29–30]

At the end of this powerful rendition by the share-croppers, Agee reports ironically, "The landlord objected that that was too much howling and too much religion on end and how about something with some life to it, they knew what he meant, and then they could go" [30]. The African-Americans have some difficulty, Agee tells us, complying with this demand, but they do so, and sing their third and final song. At the end, Agee comments:

> Meanwhile, and during all this singing, I had been sick in the knowledge that they felt they were here at our command, mine and Walker's, and that I could communicate nothing otherwise; and now, in a perversion of self-torture, I played my part through. I gave their leader fifty cents . . . and he thanked me for them in a dead voice, not looking me in the eye, and they went away, putting their white hats on their heads as they walked into the sunlight. [31]

This episode reveals both the extent of and limitations to Agee's awareness of the moral complexity of his and Evans' intrusion into the lives of the tenant farmers about whom he is writing. After all, one of the flaws of *Let Us Now Praise Famous Men* is that, by focusing on three white tenant families, it fails to accord racism its rightful place among the sources that demean the lives of Southern tenant farmers. Despite his initial focus upon the lives of these African-American tenant farmers (and a black couple in a subsequent episode), Agee does not return to a consideration of the situation of African-Americans ever again in the book.[2] By using the suffering of the African-Americans as a means of entry into his "proper" concern—the situation of tenant farmers in the South—Agee neglects the importance of race to an understanding of tenantry.

To a certain extent, it might be thought that I am guilty of a similar failure, for the issue of race is one that is not faced as squarely as it might be in the essays in this volume. The failure is not, however, so much with the essays as with the state of contemporary social theory. There is a need for a more concentrated focus by theorists of power on the ways in which racism functions as a form of power and oppression. While class and gender have been the focus of the concerns of social theorists involved with the rethinking of power, the implications of race for theories of power has not received an equal amount of attention from social theorists.

With this in mind, let us return to the human social drama that Agee presents us with. There are three different groups of individuals that constitute the actors in this drama: the first group consists of the two educated strangers, the journalist Agee and the photographer Evans, in Alabama to report to a prestigious magazine on the status of sharecroppers; the second consists of the two landlords who take Agee and Evans to see their African-American tenants, somewhat fearful of what these strangers might report; finally, there are the tenants themselves, forced to perform for their bosses on their day of rest. In this seemingly simple setting, the power relations have a multiplicity and layering that is not clearly perceptible at first glance.

The economic dependence of the African-American tenants upon their white landlords is, of course, the power relationship that most immediately strikes the reader. Although this dependency is not the focus of the vignette, the very terms in which the actors are identified give primacy of place to their roles in an economic power relationship. Because their lives unfold within the context of an economic system of tenant farming, the African-American tenants are dependent upon their landlords, who thus have power over them.

But even this obvious power relationship has many nuances that require further elucidation. If one thinks of economic power as an ability to command someone else's labor in the workplace, then it becomes clear that the relationship between the African-American tenants and their white landlords is not simply one of simple economic dependency. The ability of the landlords to "summon" the tenants on a Sunday morning to perform for two strangers indicates that there are noneconomic forms of power in a relationship that many would classify as simply a form of economic oppression or exploitation. The lives of the African-American men are ruled by the whims of their landlords to a far greater extent than their simply having to deliver up to them a portion of their yield.

There are a variety of ways in which one could attempt to explain the more invidious nature of the oppressive power relationship within which these African-American men exist. One strategy would be to deny that the understanding of economic power that I have used in explaining the relationship is an adequate explanation of the economic system of tenant farming. Another would be to note that the economic power relationship between the African-American tenants and the white landlords coexists with a racial power relationship.

By a racial power relationship, I mean to indicate the ways in which African-Americans are oppressed within American society. In the South during the 1930s, African-Americans had to fear for their lives if they offended the white community in certain ways. Lynchings and terror kept African-Americans fearful of the consequences of their actions. As a result, African-Americans like the share-croppers were racially oppressed, since their racial heritage made them subservient to the whites around them, even if they had no other specific relationship with those whites.

As a result of the coincidence of racial oppression and economic oppression at the same site, Agee's African-Americans are even more powerless than they would be if they were merely subject to the economic oppression of sharecropping or tenant farming. This is because the white landlords are able to rely on assumptions about the proper place and mode of comportment of African-Americans to structure the context of their dealings with their tenants.

Agee's perception of the African-American tenant farmers themselves provides the key to another aspect of the power relations that structure this scene. Agee's text is structured by his desire to convey to the reader his acknowledgment of the power relationship that these African-American tenant farmers embody. Agee portrays himself as tortured by his relationship with these African-American men. His rhetoric establishes their ability to communicate with him and his ability to understand their music, to appreciate its technical and emotional accomplishments, something that is foreign to the crude and jagged landlords. Agee's use of the imagery of the deposition heroicizes the tenants, characterizing them as having a depth and nobility that far surpasses the nature of their supposed masters.

But this means that the manner in which we have so far understood the relationship between the landlord-masters and their tenant farmer-servants misses an important aspect of their relationship. Although there is a clear sense in which the landlords are masters and the tenant farmers servants, Agee's prose conveys the idea that this conception of their relationship is limited. His own Christian beliefs structure his portrayal of the tenant farmer-servants as "first in the kingdom of heaven." Agee perceives the African-American "powerless" tenant farmers as having a depth and nobility—a power—that surpasses that of their economic masters.

The importance of this point is that power relationships do not involve the simple, unidirectional hierarchy that the language of domination or oppression suggests. This point was first made by Hegel in his famous dialectic of lordship and bondage, for which he was duly subjected to ridicule by many philosophers. His insight remains true nonetheless: an understanding of oppression as consisting of a master who profits from the labor of his servants is simplistic and fails to provide an adequate characterization of the relationship between masters and their servants. A theory of power needs to recognize that those who are oppressed have different means of eluding the control of their masters that can even, in certain contexts, function as the basis for overthrowing them.

Despite the tendency to focus upon the relationship between the tenant farmers and the landlords as the central power relationship in this scene, it is important not to ignore the power relationship between Agee and Evans and the landlords. While there is nothing that Agee and Evans can do that will directly affect the life circumstances of either the landlords or their tenants, the landlords do recognize that Agee and Evans have power over them, even though they are not sure how or whether it will be manifested. Because of Agee's and Evans' ability to document the situation of the tenant farmers to the public as well as the government, the writer and the photographer have power over the landlords that makes the landlords view them with some disquiet and distrust. The landlords recognize that the public scrutiny to which Agee and Evans can subject them gives the writer and photographer power over them.

This power clearly shapes the interactions that Agee records. We should not, however, skip over the complexity of the phenomenon that this calls to our attention. The power Agee and Evans have over the landlords is the result of their ability to mobilize public opinion on behalf of the tenants, a power that the landlords recognize and fear. This power consists of a set of expectations on the part of the landlords about what might happen if Agee and Evans were to do certain things. The power that Agee and Evans have is constituted by the landlords' anticipation of actions that other people might undertake—people who are not directly present on the scene and are not known to any of the actual actors in the drama—as a result of the publication of Agee's and Evans' work.

We therefore must confront the fact that power has a more complicated mode of social existence than many theorists admit. Power is—at least some of the time and, as I argue in my contribution, much more frequently than is generally acknowledged—a factor in a social situation because of human beings' expectations about what might happen to them. Power can be a significant factor in social relationships even when it exists as a set of complex anticipated reactions to the assumed actions of remote social agents.

So even in an apparently simple incident like that narrated by Agee, power manifests itself as a complex social presence that exists in an intricate network of overlapping and contradictory relations. The task for a theory of power is to provide a conception of power that does justice to its tangled empirical reality while at the same time providing the social theorist with a precise tool for criticizing social practices and institutions. In particular, theories of power must explain the immersion of human beings in nets of power relations that constrain their possibilities while simultaneously uncovering the means by which human beings have the ability to resist and challenge those relations.

III

This volume collects a series of important contributions to the recent rethinking of power. Although they all reject received modes of thinking about power, they strike out in various directions in their attempts to develop understandings of power that are more adequate to contemporary social life.

The first contribution sets the stage for the reflections gathered in this volume by contrasting two different conceptions of power. Amelie Oksenberg Rorty imagines a dialogue on the nature of power between two characters, Buff and Rebuff. Buff is both a skeptic and a nominalist who argues that the standard social theoretical use of the concept of power depends upon an outmoded metaphysical framework. Rebuff, on the other hand, is a social theorist who comes to the analysis of power with a set of conceptual distinctions that she believes are sufficient to make sense of power. She claims that Buff's failure to attend to these crucial distinctions has led her to the skeptical position of denying the usefulness of power as an analytic tool for social theory.

Rorty not only succeeds in showing the need for a number of important distinctions in conceptualizing power, but by using the dialogue form, she also illustrates the contested nature of the concept of power itself. She demonstrates that theorists' defense of their own conceptions of power depend upon their interests and beliefs. Although she ends with an optimistic reconciliation between Buff and Rebuff, her dialogue exemplifies the basic dilemma of whether or not it is possible to reach such a consensus in theorizing power.

Terence Ball is also interested in the conflicts involving the concept of power within the work of social theorists and philosophers. In a sweeping survey of recent developments in theorizing power, Ball maps out the different directions that recent rethinkings of power have taken. He begins by discussing the dominant, behavioralist conception of power within Anglo-American social science, arguing that this view of power is based upon a "causal construal of power" that ignores the communicative aspect of human interactions. Ball goes on to categorize more recent investigations of power as falling into three distinct models, each of which moves beyond the confines of the behavioralist model: the communicative, realist, and deconstructionist models. After discussing the strengths and weaknesses of each of these models, Ball concludes by adopting a pluralistic attitude, claiming that we are not yet in a position to judge one model superior to the others.

Jeffrey C. Isaac defends the validity of the realist model of power in his contribution. Like Ball, Isaac rejects the behavioralist-influenced theories of power that have dominated much Anglo-American social thought. Isaac traces the shortcomings of these theories to their use of an inadequate empiricist philosophy of science, one that focuses upon the description of regularities rather than upon understanding the "real nature of things." He develops his realist theory of power on the basis of a more adequate philosophy of science, one that is "both essentialist and metaphysical" in that it posits entities as the bearers of causal properties or powers. By treating human beings as bearers of powers, Isaac is able to develop a notion of power that he believes will accord power its rightful status within social theory as a "structural determinant" of human behavior. By seeing power as a structural factor in such social relationships as that between a student and a teacher, the realist theory makes power an inherent feature of human social life.

For Wolfgang Balzer, the primary question concerning power is metatheoretical. Balzer is interested in defending research into the concept of power as a legitimate path for social scientific research. He does so by comparing my recent attempt to conceptualize power with game theory. His suggestion is that we should see these as two competing paradigms in social theory.

Balzer claims that game theory and power theory are different methods for analyzing social interactions. In order to make his case, he develops formal models of both game theory and power theory, models that clarify the assumptions made by the two competing theories. By displaying the assumptions of these two theories in this explicit manner, Balzer is able to show exactly where they conflict with one another. Employing recent ideas from the philosophy of science, he is able to show that attempts to conceptualize power are a legitimate path for social scientific research.

My own contribution to this volume puts forward a model that conceptualizes the presence of power in a social relationship as the result of a broad social field. I call this the "situated model of power" in order to indicate the role that the broader social context plays in the constitution of power relationships. Previous models of power, by focusing upon the two central actors in a power relationship, failed to understand the importance of a broader social context to the creation of a power relationship. The situated model of power corrects this failing, using the concept of a social alignment to indicate the role of the social context in constituting power relations. After developing the basic elements of this model of power, I turn to a variety of power relationships in contemporary society in order to show how the situated model of power illuminates their nature.

Timo Airaksinen's essay moves in a different direction by emphasizing the rhetorical component in domination. Many theorists conceive of domination as simply a brute fact, a form of social relationship that is instituted once the attempt to cooperate has failed. After exploring a variety of forms of domination, Airaksinen argues that there is a rhetoric of domination, i.e., that a domination relationship takes place by means of a particular conceptual understanding shared by the dominating and dominated agents. In particular, Airaksinen looks at various attempts by both the dominating and the dominated to describe their respective situations, arguing that, while the dominant always try to mask the domination in a rhetorical appeal, the dominated have the ability to reveal what the dominator wishes to conceal. Drawing on the writings of the Marquis de Sade, Airaksinen shows the problematic nature of such appeals, arguing there is no neutral audience to whom the dominated may appeal in an attempt to undo their domination. In making his argument, Airaksinen notes certain similarities between his work and that of Michel Foucault.

The next two contributions focus directly upon Foucault's work. In a number of daring and innovative studies, Foucault argued that philosophers and social theorists had misunderstood the nature of power. According to Foucault, such theorists had conceived of power according to a "juridical" model in which power was localized as the possession of the strong and then used to repress and control the weak. In contrast to this view of power, Foucault argues that power is both "relational" and "capillary," something that permeates every aspect of the social world. There are no agents who are simply the possessors of power and who can use it to dominate others. Rather, power is itself something that permeates all social relationships and that constitutes all human beings. Foucault developed this way of thinking about power by showing how this type of power came into existence in modern Europe. Many theorists think that Foucault's writings have revealed important new ways to think about power's presence in the social world.

Thomas McCarthy assesses the significance of Foucault's work for critical social theory. He begins by arguing that there has been too great an emphasis on the divergences between Foucault's standpoint and that of the Frankfurt School. However, this is only the prelude to McCarthy's central argument, which seeks to show that Foucault's understanding of power and its role in the constitution of the human subject is inadequate for the purposes of a critical social theory. Tracing Foucault's understanding of power from his major works on the prison and sexuality to his later attempt to describe an ethics of the self, McCarthy argues that there is an important transformation in Foucault's understanding of power and its effect on human beings. Whereas Foucault began, according to McCarthy, with a conception of power that made it virtually coextensive with the social—a view that identifies power with domination—he ends up completely sundering power (now understood in the sense of self-creation or "power to") from domination. In both cases, McCarthy argues, the fundamental framework that Foucault employs is inadequate to the complexities of human social life. McCarthy suggests that the work of Jürgen Habermas, the contemporary standard bearer for the Frankfurt School, offers a more adequate model of the ways in which power structures the social world.

Gayatri Chakravorty Spivak also focuses upon Foucault's understanding of power. She does so by comparing his view to both the ideas of Derrida and the novels of Mahasweta. Spivak worries that Foucault's "nominalist" account of power has been too easily taken up by social theorists and assimilated as either a pragmatic epistemology or a feminist political project. By demonstrating affiliations between the positions of Foucault and Derrida, Spivak seeks to show the impossibility of such patronymic appropriations of Foucault's work. In particular, Spivak points to Foucault's understanding of power as based upon relations of force, an understanding that has eluded even his sympathetic interpreters. Finally, Spivak turns to the writings of the Bengali novelist Mahasweta, arguing that Mahasweta's writing shows that the difficult problem of a colonized society cannot be readily conceptualized within a narrative constructed elsewhere, thus illustrating the importance of the claims made in common by Foucault and Derrida.

Iris Marion Young seeks to make issues of power central to questions of justice in society. The primary concern of contemporary philosophical accounts of justice has been questions of distribution, i.e., the just mode of distributing the benefits of social association. Young thinks that such a focus misses the primary thrust of many new left social movements that have sought to bring about a more just society. Her claim is that such movements are more concerned about power than distribution and that an adequate theory of justice needs to incorporate this fact. Young develops an account of oppression that links issues of justice with those of power. Employing the metaphor of power's multiple faces, Young argues that oppression has five different faces: exploitation, marginalization, powerlessness, cultural imperialism, and violence. By arguing that questions of power are intimately related to questions of justice, Young confronts in a fundamental way the liberal political theorist's blindness to issues of power. She shows that issues of power are among the most fundamental in assessing the validity of human social arrangements.

Just as Young argues that there is a need for philosophical theories of justice to incorporate questions of power, the economists Samuel Bowles and Herbert Gintis argue that economists need to develop a theoretical framework that acknowledges the role of power in economic transactions. Relying on an interest-based notion of power, Bowles and Gintis criticize the idea that economic exchange takes place in a power-neutral context. Within neoclassical economics, the wage contract between a worker and an employer has been treated as an instance of a free exchange. Bowles and Gintis argue that such a view of the labor-capital relationship ignores the presence of a power relationship. Specifically, the ability of the capitalist to fire a worker who does not perform at a high-enough level gives rise to a power relationship that neoclassical economists have ignored. As a result of this feature of the labor-capital exchange, Bowles and Gintis call it a "contested exchange," i.e., one whose terms are determined by a power relationship between the two parties.

Howard McGary pursues the relationship between knowledge and power in a somewhat different direction than that taken by Foucault.

McGary is concerned with the power that scientists have in contemporary society because of the assumption that they are the producers of knowledge. He criticizes the idea that such research is pure and thus not liable to restriction for moral reasons. Focusing upon the case of I.Q. and intelligence research—research that has been used to further racial oppression—McGary makes a case for limiting the research of scientists in light of the power that the knowledge they produce can bring. Like the two preceding contributions, McGary's questions the dominant assumption that power can be excluded from a specific domain. His claim is that knowledge is fraught with power and that this needs to be taken account of in our social policies concerning its production.

Feminist theorists have developed one of the important lines of research in contemporary rethinkings of power. Jean Baker Miller's essay, "Women and Power," explores the need for a feminist conception of power. Miller's basic thesis is that theories that describe women as powerless in male-dominated society misrepresent women's lives, experiences, and capabilities. She claims that women have historically been powerful, only that their manner of possessing and exercising power is different than that recognized by traditional theories, themselves largely the product of men. According to Miller, within their traditional roles women have developed their power to empower others in such roles as mothers and teachers. She argues that this is a form of power central to the existence of society, but one that social theorists have failed to accord a significant theoretical role. She begins to develop a conception of this type of power, one that she urges social theorists to adopt.

The final two contributions to this volume extend the exploration of power and gender to the realm of sexuality. While sexuality is a domain in which power has always been exercised, it is one that traditional social theory has treated in remote ways, at best. At least since Freud, however, we have had to acknowledge the fact that sexual practices are an important factor in our understanding of society as a whole.

Nancy C. M. Hartsock's essay is a contribution to the debate among feminist theorists about the nature of sexuality and pornography. Hartsock argues that power plays an important role in the constitution of sexuality. Asserting that what is usually referred to as sexuality is really male sexuality, she explores the association of male sexuality with hostility, violence, and domination. Drawing on the work of Robert Stoller, Hartsock shows how the dominant understanding of sexuality within our culture makes it impossible for women to experience a form of sexuality that is uniquely their own. As a first step in creating this possibility, she puts forward the concept of *eros* as a more general understanding of the human capacity for union, sensuality, and competence. Hartsock's essay shows that it must be recognized that power permeates even the most intimate and private aspects of our lives.

Roger S. Gottlieb also argues that power structures our lives in ways that previous theorists have ignored. In his essay, Gottlieb focuses upon one of the most serious threats to human existence in this century: the possibility of nuclear war. Gottlieb's thesis is that the possibility of a total destruction of human life stemming from a nuclear war is the result of a particularly masculine understanding of power. While the competitive determination to prove oneself superior to others has been seen as a component of a male identity that attracts men to war as a form of testing, Gottlieb argues that the form of power in modern society has given rise to a new type of desire for war. Positing rationalization, professionalization, and commodification as three aspects of modern power, Gottlieb attributes a desire for war to males whose identities have been constituted by these modern forms of power. He thus sees the possibility of the destruction of human life as stemming from the particular modes of power through which males are constituted in contemporary society and posits the need to understand the role of power in society as a necessary task in averting the danger of nuclear war.

IV

In closing, let me return to the African-American sharecroppers standing before Agee and Evans at the demand of the white landowners. I used Agee's description of that episode to demonstrate the difficulties involved in understanding the precise manner in which power structures human social interactions. As Agee's description makes clear, the reality in which he found himself was a complex and differentiated one, one that will not easily yield itself to the analysis of the theorist.

The problem of finding an adequate theoretical vocabulary for describing a scene as rich as the one Agee presents can stand for the quandary of the contemporary social theorist. In recent years, we have had our eyes opened to a complex social reality. The goal of a critical social theorist is to provide a language that can adequately conceptualize the newly discovered complexity of the presence and workings of power in society.

The essays assembled in this volume provide a good means for beginning the task of understanding the complex, multiple, overlapping, and contradictory forms of power that structure our lives. By focusing on such factors as the context within which a power relation is constituted and the diversity of the faces of oppression, these essays provide an important framework for understanding what power is and how it works.

I have invoked Agee's writing once again to remind the reader that the goal of a theory of power is both to understand the ways in which the lives of human beings are constricted as well as to reflect upon the possibilities for eliminating such constriction. Rather than trying to define reality within a set of rigid categories, these essays reflect the desire to accommodate theory to the richness and complexity of social reality while still maintaining a critical stance. They show a concern for developing a theory that will be socially useful but that will not achieve its utility by illegitimately simplifying the reality it seeks to comprehend. These "rethinkings of power," therefore, have an important role to play in a critical social theory that seeks to give human beings greater control over the circumstances of their own existence.[3]

Chapter 1

Power and Powers: A Dialogue Between Buff and Rebuff

——————————————— *Amelie Oksenberg Rorty*

Not long ago, I was asked to participate in a conference on POWER. In despair at not knowing what power—its sources, rights, and limits— might be, I went to the Schlesinger Library and rummaged aimlessly through a file marked "Unclassifiable." I came across an ill-scrawled manuscript, a dialogue between what appeared to be two cantankerous characters, Buff and Rebuff. The ink was faded; the handwriting was spidery and jagged. While there seemed to be two distinct scripts, they were nevertheless close enough that they might have been written by a person with a divided mind and shifting moods. To my astonishment and relief, the subject—if one can speak so confidently about *the* subject of such an odd assortment of observations—was, of all things, power.

Buff: I've just come from a dreadful committee meeting on the redistribution of power in the university. I don't even know what *power,* as such, is, let alone what constitutes its fair distribution. I get bills from Electric Power and Light. I have heard about the power of the purse, the power of ridicule, nuclear power, moral power. Whatever all these, and many other, notions may have in common seems far too general to be useful. The attribution of power simply indicates an active capacity to bring something about. But how is it characterized? Is it simply a space holder for a set of specific causes? It has all the earmarks of being a remnant of much ridiculed occult causes: "opium induces sleep by virtue of its dormative powers." But is it *power* that brings about effects? Or is it rather the detailed, specific properties of a network of causes? Shouldn't we distinguish varieties of power? After all, Germans distinguish *Macht* as forceful might and

Kraft as carrying some connotation of power guided by skill or intelligence. In Latin there are further important distinctions among *vis* (force or energy, the source of our word, *vitality*), *dominatio* (domination), *potestas* (might), and *potentia* (potentiality). All these uses have very little in common, and each has its complications.

Rebuff: Come off it, Buff. You know very well that some people, some groups have power, and others don't. Some are in a position to define the conditions of their lives—to control resources and command cooperation in such a way that they can secure the satisfaction of their desires or realize the programs that are important to them. Others have to take a much longer and more indirect road to negotiate their interests, and they have a much lower rate of success. You can afford the luxury of not knowing what power is. The dispossessed cannot. How about this as an initial, highly provisional definition of power? Power is the ability—probably many abilities are required—to define and control circumstances and events so that one can influence things to go in the direction of one's interests.

Political power is whatever it takes to get one's way. It rests on four independent factors that assure control: first, *potentia*, potentiality, a set of capacities and abilities, a combination of *Macht* and *Kraft*; second, *vis*, access to raw material and the technological capability to transform the raw material into marketable goods; third, *dominatio* and *potestas*, politically and socially institutionalized control, formally or informally legitimized to command (and sometimes to coerce) obedience; and fourth, to my mind most significant, the intellectual and imaginative power to define the terms in which others regard their own interests and desires, so that their support is assured without coercion or the overt exercise of material or political power. It is this power—the power to control the concepts in which the social and political world is constructed—that transforms the mere exercise of force into effective power. The most powerful form of power is that of so defining people's conceptions of priorities, interests, and desires that they acknowledge force as a rightful form of power.

[Like those in the grip of *furor definiensis*, Rebuff appears to be a bit of a windbag. She continues:] Even the exercise of power over material conditions requires cooperation; the primary power of the visibly powerful is usually hidden, and indeed it is often deliberately hidden. Wise parents do not show their ultimate latent power. Real power, real *Kraft* is silken: the power to elicit cooperation without commanding it, without even raising suspicion or resistance. It is the power to disarm the kind of opposition which, if it were allowed to come to self-consciousness, would set severe constraints on the primary exercise of power. But this characterization—we won't pretend it is an adequate definition—also shows the hidden power of the relatively unempowered. As Hegel so vividly demonstrated, the primary step in empowering the unempowered is bringing them to the realization that the overtly empowered require their cooperation. The second step is bringing them to the awareness that they have the negative power of limitation, of blocking, of destroying the interests of the overtly empowered.

We need a battery of distinctions for types of power. First, there are overt and covert forms of power. Because the overt power of the dominant usually, but by no means always, requires the cooperation of subordinates with their own forms of power, the attribution of power is always the attribution of relative, marginal power. No Pope without the faithful, no lords without peasants. Second, there is also a distinction between manifest and latent power. Even when it is manifest, overt power requires more than the cooperation of subordinates; it also requires the latent power necessary to assure that cooperation. For instance, the Pope's overt power depends on the recognition of the faithful; his manifest power is secured by his latent power: whatever it is that wins him the obeisance of the faithful. "How many legions does the Pope have? Are the keys to heaven in his hands?" Similarly, no lords without peasantry, but no relation between lords and peasantry without the lords' control of a cultural, social, and economic system that creates a cooperative peasantry.

Subordinates—the faithful in the Church, the peasants in a feudal system, servants in an aristocracy, students in a university—also have both manifest and latent power. Their manifest power is *potentia* and *Kraft*; it consists of the skills and resources that they exercise both on their own behalf and in the service of the overtly empowered. Hidden within their manifest power is their power to accord cooperation or to subvert the interests of the dominant. The latent power of subordinates is the power of resistance, destruction, noncooperation. This resistance can take two dramatically different forms: without questioning the initial terms and assumptions of the relation, it can attempt to become the dominant party, or it can attempt to transform the character of the relation by denying the assumptions upon which it rests. Because it undermines the terms of the continuing struggle for ascendancy, the second alternative seems the more powerful. But it requires and presupposes the power to effect a dramatic reorientation on oneself as well as on others. The more central the issues in a power relation, the more difficult it is for the subordinates to free themselves of their old assumptions, and the more difficult it is for them to change the conditions that reinforce old practices.

Of course, none of this is news to anyone who has read Hegel on the master-slave relation.

Buff: Whew! I didn't follow all of that when I first tried to read Hegel, and I don't follow it now in your version of Hegel. Sounded to me like "the jug with the mug has the brew that is true." You made too many distinctions within I don't know what. You have talked about types of power, the need for cooperation as setting limits on power, systems and relations of power. But you still haven't said what you are talking about. And I put it to you that in each case you have presupposed the very thing we are supposed to understand. Your discussion bears all the marks of circularity. You have spoken of *control, influence,* and *ability.* All those things involve the very thing we are trying to understand, *power.*

Your provisional definition links *power* to the satisfaction of interests and desires. That seems much too narrow and tendentious a definition. To begin with, those with political power, particularly those with the power to control the mass media, can strongly influence the range of a population's desires. Conceptions of interests, therefore, already reflect existing power relations. You claimed that "power is whatever it takes to get one's way." But that is ambiguous. If it means "getting what one *thinks* one desires," then strong empowerment can be dangerous to those with malformed desires who misconceive their interests.

Second, and even more important, a good deal of power is simply directed to the active exercise or expression of ability or talents independent of the satisfaction of desires. A painter can have great power without having any desire to paint or any interest in becoming a painter. Not all abilities are directed to the satisfaction of desires, nor do they all define a field of interests. I always quote Spinoza whenever I can. "By virtue and power I understand the same thing: virtue insofar as it is related to man, is [his] very essence insofar as he has the power to bring about certain things which can be understood through the laws of his own nature alone."[1] Growth expresses, *is* the power of a plant. No desires come into play.

Power is a mote in the eye of the perceiver. Like freedom, power is most acutely seen and most perceptively understood by those who lack it. Those who (for any number of reasons or causes) can't satisfy their desires, or can't develop and exercise their potentialities, invent this idea of power, which they project on those whom they imagine more fortunate than themselves. But we all are empowered: we all have capacities, traits, skills. And we are all unempowered: we all are unable to assure the satisfaction of our desires and are limited in the expression of our natures. There are limits and constraints on our capacities, and sometimes those limits are other people. Because we are focused on what we are trying to do, on the details before us, rather than on ourselves as active, we are generally less aware of our power than of our limitations and constraints. In thinking of what we are trying to do, we focus on the cooperation we require, on how others block us. We naturally tend to be more aware of the power that limits us than we are of ourselves as limits to the power of others. The dominant are at least sometimes perfectly sincere when they bemoan their dependent powerlessness. For instance, presidents of universities are perceived as being at the center of power; but in fact such officials are constrained on all sides. They are held accountable for finances over which they in fact have no control, are made responsible for educational policies that they can only formulate and implement through faculty consensus. Any initiative they attempt requires the approval and the cooperation of a large and extremely heterogeneous range of factions and interests.

Rebuff: Maybe one of the reasons that we are having so much trouble with these definitions is that power is relational and marginal: it is exercised in a field of counterforces. In a way, Buff, you are right: there is no such thing as power in and of itself. To assert that X *has power* is absurd in physics, and it is absurd in the political world and the social and psychological world. And for all I know it is also absurd in the spiritual world, whatever that is. In truth, X always has marginal power in comparison to Y, to do Z at time t, in a situation where M, N, O, and P are also contributory causes, causes which (by virtue of their also being necessary to the satisfaction of X's interests), also have latent power. If X has marginal power over Y to do A at time t, nothing follows about whether X will have the power to do A at time t+1, when M and N, but not O and P are contributory; nor does anything follow about whether X has the power to do B, even at time t. Marginal power is always highly specific, relative to a situation and to an outcome. But of course X may have the kind of power conducive to her retaining her marginal advantage over Y, even over changes in time and circumstances.

Buff: Why is it that when you talk to me it always sounds like *noblesse oblige,* but when I disagree with you, it always sounds like *lèse magesté?* Aren't we here manifesting the various forms of power? Here I am, cast as straightperson, able to act only by setting limits to your airy and arid theories. I put it to you that this stuff about relational power is, like all cliches, true enough. But it is wholly uninformative. If it is not nonsense on stilts, it is nevertheless nonsense in high heels. You have not helped me with your X, Y, Z. Power is relational in that is it marginal and its exercise requires a set of necessary further conditions. But so described, what is *not* relational? The activities of a grandmother, a university, an organism are all relational in that trivial way. I can't take a step without being related to the ground, nor sing without air. My grandmother and my department chairperson are each related to me in that they have, each in a distinctive way, some clout over me: they can put me in a position in which I pretty much have to do things I don't really want to do because the cost of refusal is, by my own lights, too great. Different relations, different clouts. Sometimes I have put the clout they have over me in their hands. And sometimes I continue to put them in a position to command me because they formed me and my desires.

On the other hand, sometimes, perhaps often in the case of effective power, the cooperation of subordinates is required. But not always. Sometimes power creates a relation, rather than presupposes it. Initially colonial powers were acquired by invasion, before there was any background of a relation or acknowledgment. The sense in which all power presupposes a relation may sometimes turn out to be quite trivial. An invading colonial force may be related to the people it invades only in their relative *Macht* over the same terrain. They needn't initially understand one another's language, let alone one another's culture or desires. In such cases, the power of force or might creates, rather than presupposes, a relation.

Rebuff: Here are some things that might be meant by insisting that power is relational. Anyone—an individual, a political party, an ethnic minority, a nation, an age-group—who is empowered always and only has power relative to someone else's lack of power and to someone else's complicit cooperation. The attribution of power is typically the attribution of marginal power, "more power than Y, or even power over Y, to bring it about that he does something." But even that is not enough, because unless we specify what kind of action is in question—to bring about *what*—the attribution of power is empty.

The attribution of power is usually made against the background of expectations about the normal course of events in the absence of intervention. Power is furthermore exercised in a field of counterforces. We focus on the active cause that made the difference in what would have happened, other things being equal. The powerful intervening cause requires the background of standard operating causes: it could not do its special thing without them. Power is attributed to the cause that made the difference between what normally would happen and what did happen. In speaking of power in this way, we assimilate it within causation: in identifying a cause, we focus on the differential and distinctive, rather than on the range of necessary contributory factors. The cause is identified against the background of working assumptions about the normal directions of a range of interactive forces. It presupposes the contributions of a whole field of aligned and countervailing forces.

Buff: Well, look what has happened. You have described several ways that power appears within a field of relations. But you still haven't really told us what power *is.* There are a lot of things that are relational in just the way you observed; utility, for example. X isn't useful as such: it is useful *to* someone *for* something, in contrast to the other things that might be available. Come to think of it, your half-baked attempt to give a definition of power—the one that was so hopelessly circular, you remember—made reference to utility. There is suspicious circularity: political power is whatever one has that is useful in serving interests or expressing vital potentialities (sic!); but whatever is useful in serving interests will be accounted among one's powers.

I return to my previous point: sometimes, to be sure, overt power can only be successfully and effectively exercised in a genuine system of interdependence. But that is not always true: the brutality of unknown assailants, common robberies, and violent attacks do more than constitute force. They not only coerce compliance; they have the power to change a person's whole mode of life. Withdrawal and retreat— living in a boarded-up apartment, moving away from cities—are hardly the exercise of counterpower. Don't forget that even if power exists in a field of forces, even if every power implies a relative dependence, there are still radical inequalities in the distribution of force. Perhaps an army depends on the peasantry for its food; but if the army has weapons, it can coerce the peasantry. Perhaps a dictatorship depends on the cooperation of the mass media; but if it has an armed secret police, it can usually control the press.

Rebuff: I can see you are being obstreperous, exercising negative power. The kinds of cases you are talking about constitute force, rather than complex power. Let's try another tack. "Power," Hobbes says, "is a person's present means to obtain some future apparent good."[2] He goes on to distinguish natural powers—strength, eloquence, intelligence—from instrumental powers—wealth, reputation—which can be acquired by natural powers and then, as he puts it, invested to acquire yet more power. Random acts of violence aren't exercises of power because their effects are only incidentally connected with the intentions of those who exercise the power. Robbers don't want city people to change their modes of life; they just want money. And they only want money to get something else.

Buff: And what about political tyrants, colonial invaders, harsh overlords who do not stand in a direct relation to their slaves, whom they see as cheap to replace? If, as Hobbes says, "power is a person's present means to obtain some future apparent good," then anything goes. Sometimes a person succeeds in getting what appears good to her by silence, illness, or debility. Are these then her powers? You need an ad hoc distinction between *force* and *power* to prop up your claim that power is always relational.

Rebuff: That's by no means an *ad hoc* distinction. But I don't need it to make sense of the idea of marginal power, which is always relational. You know very well that there are those who can, and those who cannot, bring about the conditions that satisfy them; those who can, and those who cannot, freely express their natures. Look, I want to return to your own observations that we are most acutely aware of power when we feel powerless. We know, or at any rate believe, that some people can satisfy their desires, and others cannot; some are free to be themselves, and others are not. Nevertheless, because both the dominant and the subordinate naturally focus on what they are trying to do, they both generally focus on their relative powerlessness, rather than on the manifest exercise of their powers. The experienced sense of powerlessness is vivid; but power is rarely experienced as such because it is being exercised in a way that requires attending to the details of what one is doing.

Buff: You are being too sophistical by half. Why don't you just admit that the idea of power generates conflicting intuitions? On the one hand, there really is such a condition as being relatively powerless, and we better not forget it. Many are so situated that they cannot reasonably hope to get or to do what seems good to them, to satisfy their manifest desires. Yet at the same time, we'd better not forget the immense power of those who may think themselves powerless. They have covert, latent power over the overtly empowered. It was Meredith who said that the satirist has the power to overthrow the most ruthless tyrant, and Shelley who said that the poets are the unacknowledged (but true) legislators of the world.[3]

The disempowered have their own hidden power: since power and powerlessness are always a function of desire—the desire for some apparent good and the ability or inability to satisfy it—the powerless can, in principle and within severe limits, detach themselves from their experienced powerlessness by transforming their desires. This is the strategy of Stoics: to assure freedom from any form of dependence: they move to detach themselves from the field of powers and counterpowers. The argument of the Stoic is that the apparent freedom that power secures is severely limited: it is contingent, uncertain, vulnerable. By contrast, detachment from issues of power is autonomous and secure. And isn't it *that,* they ask, perhaps rhetorically, that we want when we want power? We want freedom from the perpetual dissatisfaction of limitations and unsatisfiable desires; and a detached identification with the laws of nature is the way to get it. The Stoic is, of course, right.

Strangely, the easiest and most readily available power is the power of imaginative nihilism. Anyone can bring New York City to a screeching halt by dressing as a construction worker, moving a few manhole covers near the major tunnels and bridges, and putting up barriers rerouting traffic. The Manhattan police would probably move in to help. Anyone can set Wall Street in utter confusion with a set of well-placed pseudonymous phone calls or computer bugs. But then what?

Every manifest power is matched by a hidden powerlessness, the powerlessness of being dependent on cooperation and sanity. Every manifest powerlessness is matched by a hidden power, the power to withhold cooperation. Consider hidden forms of power: sullenness, failing to carry out what is required, silence, total zaniness. At rock bottom worst, we all have the power of stubborn, noncooperative ridicule, and destruction. The subordinate have the power of exit: either nihilistic, inventive destruction or Stoicism.

But of course both of these powers—the power of detachment and the power of imaginative destruction—are themselves dependent on insight. Since the subordinate can only realize their power, and the ability to act from that realization, if they are already imaginatively and intellectually enabled, the true latent power of the dominant is that of forming the mentality of subordinates and their capacity to develop Stoic insight or a wild imagination. The Stoic and the destructive options already presuppose a kind of power, even if it is only the power of negativity or detachment.

Rebuff: To be sure, the Stoic and nihilistic options are sometimes genuinely liberating. They sometimes enable us to realize that our desires are irrational and that we have mistaken and malformed conceptions of ourselves and our basic abilities. But the rhetoric of Stoicism and nihilism can sometimes also be used to support malformed and even dangerous illusions. They can encourage inappropriate detachment from legitimate but unsatisfiable activities and desires. Unjust political systems often benefit from—and attempt to encourage—the Stoic outlook. And they can direct the nihilistic movement to harmless, diverting aestheticism.

There are times, too, when the Stoic and the nihilistic options are only notional. They are constrained by the power that comes out of the barrel of a gun. When brute force and violence control basic necessities—food, work, shelter, communication, and affection—Stoicism and nihilism must work against the ground-floor operation of natural physical and psychological directions. It is not only lunacy but also offensive to offer the Stoic or nihilist solution to battered children and to inmates of concentration camps.

I should never have fallen in with your relentless nominalism, with your individualistic premises. Of course, if we focus on the actions of individuals—whether individual persons, classes, subcultures, or institutions—*power* fragments and disperses. To understand power, we need to consider the ways that structures constrain and direct individuals, the ways that political and economic structures define interactions among individuals and groups. That is why power is often invisible; it is not lodged in any individual person or institution. The structures of institutions determine the flow of authority; the structure of an economy determines access to goods and services; the structure of social arrangements determines the legitimacy of voice. It is through and in these that power is exercised, as enabling or limiting interests and their satisfaction. It is these that construct the mentality that forms a culture's conceptions of its interests.

Buff: In a way, I see the truth of that. But I am afraid that my relentless nominalism, as you call it, needs more. First of all, how does this structuring work? Surely structures are only expressed through and in the actions of individual institutions—the courts, the tax office, the schools, the family—and eventually through the individuals who are serving as officials in these institutions—the judges, the tax assessors, the principals. Second, rather than defining the power of social and political structures, you've merely claimed that power is exercised through such structures. In the course of your description, which rings true enough, you've again illicitly introduced the very notion we are trying to understand. You've said structures determine authority, enable or constrain satisfactions; but these are just different ways of referring to the exercise of power. You are moving in circles, and the déjà vu is giving me vertigo.

Nominalist that I am, I am cheered by your remarks about the power of the imagination. For it is, after all, the imagination that groups and regroups our experiences, that constructs what you so pompously call *structures*. But you must remember that the "power of the imagination" is in itself not just *one* disposition or trait. It is a vast network of relatively independent constitutional and educable abilities and skills. There is no one faculty called *the imagination*. We now stress the ability to "think differently," to question dominant assumptions about what is supposed to be natural or necessary, to envisage new possibilities, to analyze and restructure experience. But the exercise of the imagination in all these enterprises involves a number of quite distinct abilities. A person can be good at analysis, at separating the variables of complex and compounded wholes, without being good at synthesis, recombining them to form novel structures. Someone can be good at constructing new syntheses without being good at constructing them in such a way that they seem vivid, viable, and available. The separable skills of "the imagination" can involve adding details to pre-existing options, filling out a bare schema, improvising and constructing variations on a set theme, redescribing variables or situations, tracing remote and distinct consequences, drawing inferences from merely hypothetical considerations, rearranging and revising priorities, introducing new, visionary values. The talents for developing, improvising, reconstructing, revising, and creating are related but distinct—oops, *powers*.[4]

Rebuff: We might come closer to agreement if we agree to differ. Perhaps the word "power" just designates several radically distinct concepts that have been confusedly merged. The terminology and issues of the Aristotelian notion of *dynamis* are based on a conception of natural species and natural kinds with nonrelative capacities, abilities, potentialities. The satisfaction of desires is only one, and by no means the most important, measure of an individual's power, which is primarily directed to activity, to the expression and exercise of abilities in action. *Dynamis* is fundamentally a metaphysical and biological notion whose application to political theory has radically different implications from those derived from Hobbes' materialistic mechanics. Hobbesian power is extensionally identified, relativised in a field of forces, directed to the satisfaction of desires.

We can compromise in this way: I will agree to there being quite distinct conceptions of power, some of which may satisfy your nominalist conditions, if you will agree that some other conceptions of power are open to essentialist and structuralist analyses.

Buff: I have no trouble in agreeing that there are numerous conceptions of power, but in all consistency I can't accept the view that any of them postulate anything like irreducible essences or structures.

But I am tired of our discussion. It seems clear that we shall not convince one another. Let me end by summarizing my view:

1. Power exists in a field; its attribution is always specific, marginal, and dynamic. X has marginal power, in comparison to Y, to bring about or to do Z, in situation M, N at time t, when there are specific contributory and oppositional forces.

2. The power of the dominant depends on the *Kraft* of subordinates, whose cooperation is often assured by the latent power of the dominant. Since the consent of subordinates is often manipulated or coerced, dominant power includes the capacity to control the cooperation of the subordinates.

3. The manifest power of subordinates consists in the talents and skills that make their cooperation necessary to the dominant. Their latent power lies in ridicule, noncooperation, destruction, Stoic detachment, or nihilistic blockage.

4. All forms of power reside in and are exercised by individuals. But the range and strength of an individual's power, her conceptions of her interests and options, are affected by the groups with which she is associated. Individual agents are frequently unaware of the structured patterns of their actions. Groups, patterns, and structures are not, however, agents in themselves: they are not entities with actions or powers of their own. Although they are modes of organization, they are not organisms with an internal principle of motion. They represent relations among forces without themselves having any quantity or direction of force. It is therefore misleading to speak of groups or structures as "constraining and directing." Nevertheless, structures and institutions that define lines of authority, legitimation, and access to information, goods, and services effectively channel and limit options open to individuals. Precisely because they are not entities with

discernible directions and because they articulate the terms for legitimation, structures and institutions are often more difficult to discern and reform than are specific oppositional forces.

5. Because powerlessness is more vividly experienced than empowerment, because power tends to be more visible to those who believe themselves to lack it, the sense of power—the phenomenology of the subject—is not an adequate guide to its analysis.

6. Imagination is the key to power: it expands or limits the control of material resources; it determines the direction of desires. As Shelley knew, poets, visionaries, and varieties of rhetoricians have the greatest power. At least in her own lifetime, a poet's power to persuade depends on her relative political power, as well as her own imaginative power.

7. The imagination is not itself a dynamic force; it is composed of a vast array of constitutional and acquired skills, abilities, and operations.

The manuscript breaks off here. I am unable to judge whether its author or authors considered it finished, or whether in having the last word, Buff had the final say.[5]

Chapter 2

New Faces of Power

——— *Terence Ball*

I

The "scandal of philosophy," Kant once remarked, was its failure to address and resolve the problem of our knowledge of the external world. The scandal of social science—or perhaps only one of its several scandals—is that it has so far failed to arrive at a satisfactory understanding of power. This is all the more remarkable when we consider that power is arguably the single most important organizing concept in social and political theory. On this much, at least, behavioralists and their critics agreed. As Herbert Simon noted during the heyday of the "behavioral revolution" three decades ago, the definition and measurement of power "is clearly a central problem of political science. Indeed, until it is solved, political science, defined as the study of power, cannot be said to exist."[1] Anthony Giddens has written more recently, "The study of power cannot be regarded as a second-order consideration in the social sciences. Power cannot be tacked on, as it were, after the more basic concepts of social science have been formulated. There is no more elemental concept than that of power [which is] one of several primary concepts of social science. . . ."[2]

Of what, then, does this purportedly primary concept consist? To begin with, it is apparently a "relational" concept, in that it refers to some sort of relation between social agents or agencies. Power is, further, a relation in which one agent or agency somehow affects the attitudes or actions of another. But this only complicates instead of clarifying the question. What kinds of entities count as agents or agencies? Do only individuals count, as methodological individualists maintain? Or is power properly located at the level of legal and political institutions or social structures? Do the intentions of individual agents

14

matter in ascribing power, or do only consequences count? And, not least, what kind of "affecting" is involved in ascriptions of power: does any kind of affecting count, or only that which is in some sense normatively noteworthy?

These are by no means the only, but are among the most important, questions around which theoretical, methodological, and conceptual controversies have centered since mid-century. They, along with other allied issues, are addressed afresh by other contributors to the present volume. My own aim in the present essay is more modest. I shall try to look in two directions at once. I want to begin by looking backward at relatively recent attempts to construct the concept of power, and forward to present and possible future reconstructions. The first of these is the debate over the three dimensions or faces of power; the second, a series of attempts to transcend the confines of the behavioralists' "causal" construal of power in order to expose still other faces of power to clearer view and critical scrutiny.

II

"For we all of us, grave or light," wrote George Eliot in *Middlemarch*, "get our thoughts entangled in metaphors, and act fatally on the strength of them."[3] The history of the concept of power, as I have tried to show elsewhere, suggests that philosophers' metaphors have a way of becoming behavioral scientists' models.[4] If nothing else, an examination of the discourse of behavioral political science in the third quarter of the twentieth century suggests that the rule of metaphor is likely to be most powerful when it is least apparent. By looking closely at the behavioralists' treatment of power, we can see how concepts that had formerly functioned in one discourse spilled into and transformed the language of another. This episode also allows us to see how the contradictions and limitations inherent in the newly transformed discourse were exposed and criticized, thereby preparing the way for alternative discourses' reconstruction of power.

The debate about power might best be narrated as a tale of conceptual transfers and transformations from one face or dimension to another. Put briefly, it began with the equating of power with cause, the latter being understood as an observable constancy of conjunction between contingently related events. This empiricist equation, which can be traced back through Hume to Hobbes, was willingly if perhaps unwittingly revived by behavioral political scientists in the mid-1950s. Recalling the route by which he came to view political power in mechanistic-causal terms, Herbert Simon says that he turned

> to the task of defining political power, only to find myself . . . unable . . . to arrive at a satisfactory solution. The difficulty appeared to reside in a very specific technical point: influence, power, and authority are all intended as asymmetrical relations. When we say that A has power over B, we do not mean to imply that B has power over A. . . . When I had stated the question in this form—as a problem of giving operational meaning to the asymmetry of the relation between independent and dependent variable—it became clear that it was identical with the general problem of defining a causal relation between two variables. That is to say, for the assertion, 'A has power over B,' we can substitute the assertion, 'A's behavior causes B's behavior.' If we can define the causal relation, we can define influence, power, or authority, and vice-versa.[5]

Apparently unaware that this solution was already three centuries old by the time he proposed it, others were quick to follow Simon's lead.[6] Robert Dahl, for example, acknowledged that his "way of thinking about power or influence is analogous to the concept of force in mechanics. In mechanics object A exerts a force on object B if A produces a change in the velocity of B." While warning that "we ought not to push such analogies very far," Dahl nevertheless insisted that "our ideas about underlying measures of [power or] influence rest on intuitive notions very similar to those on which the idea of force rests in mechanics." The "underlying idea in both cases" is essentially the same.[7]

But perhaps, *pace* Dahl, we do not ordinarily push our analogies and metaphors so much as they push us.[8] The early behavioralists' attempt to transfer the language of mechanics to the description and explanation of political phenomena raised a host of further questions. Among the more difficult of these is the question of interdiscursive translation, which arises in the following way. If one wishes to employ the discourse of mechanics to talk about politics, then one must find conceptual equivalences for translating between discourses. Hence Simon's equations of 'power' with efficient causation. We see this also in the tendency of behavioral political scientists to treat 'power,' 'influence,' and 'authority' as synonyms.[9] Still other concepts, such as 'communication,' are relocated in conceptual space and made to do new work. For example, Simon, working backward from the newer idiom into the old, asks, "What corresponds, in the social sciences, to the postulate of 'no action at a distance?' " The "direct analogue," he answers, "is 'no power or influence without communication.' " Although " 'communication' cannot be taken quite literally as 'verbal communication,' " he adds, "the principle remains an important and probably indispensable tool for the identification of power or influence mechanisms."[10] Once again, Simon's lead was followed by others whose shared view is succinctly summarized by Dorwin Cartwright. "Communications," he says, "is the mechanism by which interpersonal influence is exerted."[11]

One of the difficulties that arises in talking about communication in purely mechanistic terms stems from the fact that human beings, unlike billiard balls, are language-using creatures. To put the point crudely, human beings do not ordinarily exercise power by bumping into other human beings but by communicating with them through a system of signs or gestures or words. And behaviorally oriented political scientists acknowledged this by referring to the "mechanism" of a "preference communication" or a "persuasive communication" between agent A and patient B. A exercises power over B if and only if A communicates a preference to B and B complies with A's expressed preference. The paradigmatic power-wielder thus becomes the police officer directing traffic, and the paradigmatic preference (or persuasive) communication the police officer's command. If police officer A succeeds in getting motorist B to do what A commands, e.g., stop (or go), then A has exercised power over B.[12]

Early behavioralists further stipulated that A and B be individuals and that A's action and B's response must be observable events isolated in space and time, with A's preference communication preceding B's response; there must, that is, be a "time lag" between the two events.[13] Thus, an exercise of power can be said to have occurred only if A makes an observable attempt to cause B to do something that A intends but that B would not otherwise do. If A's "power attempt" succeeds, then A is said to have power over B with respect to the particular "issue area" over which they openly disagreed.[14]

During the second phase of the debate the behavioral construal of power was criticized less because it is mistaken than because it is partial and one-sided or "one-dimensional." According to the "two-dimensional" account advanced by Peter Bachrach and Morton Baratz, political power is Janus-faced. They readily concede that the pluralists were right in viewing power as a causal relation between individual actors that is sometimes exercised in an overt and observable way. Sometimes, but not always; for power has another, hidden face. Power may in some instances be exercised covertly and in ways that are not directly observable but indirectly inferable. For instance, A might exercise power by controlling the agenda, thereby limiting discussion, debate, and decision-making to supposedly safe issues that do not threaten A's interests. Or A might be able to take advantage of biases built into the political system that tend to favor A's interests over B's. Or again B, anticipating defeat or reprisal, might be unwilling to challenge A on a particular issue. The fact that there is no observable conflict—no direct challenges or overt "power attempts"—does not necessarily mean that no power is being exercised. On the contrary, it may well mean that a dominant person or group is exercising power in a particularly efficient and effective way.[15]

Although an improvement over its predecessor, the two-dimensional critique and alternative, Steven Lukes argues, does not go far enough. While Lukes agrees that "The absolutely basic common core to, or primitive notion lying behind, all talk of power is the notion that A in some way affects B," he adds that "in applying that primitive (causal) notion to the analysis of social life, something further is needed—namely the notion that A does so in a non-trivial or significant manner."[16] The sort of significant affecting specified by the concept of power involves one agent's ability not only to affect another, but to do so in a way that adversely affects the other's interests. Lukes' "three-dimensional" alternative accords a central place to the concept of interest. "A has power over B," Lukes contends, "when A affects B in a manner contrary to B's interests." Of course the one- and two-dimensional construals of power also, as Lukes notes, presuppose some conception of interests.[17] But defenders of the one- and two-dimensional views are alike in sharing an unduly narrow and naive understanding of "interest." Specifically, both simply assume that would-be challengers do in fact know what their real interests are, simply because they know what they want or prefer. One's interests are, in short, reducible to one's preferences, whether revealed through participation (as in the one-dimensional view) or known by B but concealed from A (as in the two-dimensional view).

This, Lukes claims, will not suffice. For interests, unlike preferences or wants, are such that one can be mistaken about them. One may have mistaken beliefs about what is and is not in one's interests. Indeed, the most effective way in which A can exercise power over B is to shape B's very beliefs about what is and is not in B's interest. To the degree that A can instill in or take advantage of B's false or mistaken interpretation of B's interests, A's power is well-nigh complete and all the greater for being virtually invisible to those over whom it is exercised. Is it not, Lukes asks, "the supreme exercise of power to avert conflict and grievance by influencing, shaping, and determining the perceptions and preferences of others?"[18]

Lukes' emphasis on "objective" interests is reminiscent of the Marxian notion of "false consciousness." Someone suffering from false consciousness labors under the illusion that his subjective or perceived interests—those instilled by and benefiting a ruling class, caste, or group—are in fact his real or objective interests, and more especially the economic interests of the class to which he belongs. But there are also, Lukes insists in a manner more reminiscent of Kant than of Marx, interests that we all have simply by virtue of being human. Whether aware of it or not, each individual human being has an interest in being or becoming an autonomous agent. Thus, the slave who sees his lot as normal and natural, or the wage-laborer who is utterly uncritical of the capitalist system, or the Indian Untouchable who accepts his lowly status within the Hindu caste system, are arguably unaware of their objective interests.[19]

Although Lukes' three-dimensional view of power has led to some interesting and important research,[20] it has come under sharp attack from several directions. Some critics have charged that in equating "exercising power" with "causing harm" Lukes has unduly restricted the range of power, ruling out instances in which power can be exercised through rational persuasion and even in beneficial or benevolent ways.[21] Other criticisms have centered upon his defense of the concept of objective interests, either because one has no way of knowing what those interests are or because the analyst's belief that he knows what they are leads to "paternalism" or "vanguardism."[22] Other critics focused on his claim that power is an "essentially contested" concept. They contended that Lukes cannot coherently claim that power is essentially contestable and that his three-dimensional view is conceptually and analytically superior to alternative conceptualizations.[23] For our purposes, however, the more interesting challenges are those directed against the very discourse in which the "three faces of power" debate was framed in the first place.

III

The challenges to which I refer have come from several quarters. These include, to mention only a few, critical theory, realist metascience, neo-Marxist theories of the state, structuralism, deconstructionism, and feminist theory.[24] Since the last of these is treated elsewhere in this volume by Jean Baker Miller, Nancy Hartsock, and Iris Young, I shall not dwell on the contribution of feminist theory to the reconstruction of power. Instead I propose to consider only three of these attempted conceptual reconstructions, which I call the communicative, the realist, and the deconstructionist. Despite their differences, all are alike in expressing profound dissatisfaction with the way in which social scientific discourse has heretofore constructed, analyzed, and applied the concept of power. It is as yet too early to tell whether these alternative discourses will remain distinct or whether they might yet prove to be mutually compatible and capable of merging.

The Communicative Model

Let us consider first the challenge posed by the communicative construal of power. We saw earlier how the concepts of power, cause, and communication were linked by behavioralists (and their philosophical forebears): Before A can be said to exercise power over B (i.e., cause B to do something that B would not otherwise do), A must have communicated something—a "motion" or a preference—to B. If B, having a different motion or preference then changes in the wake of A's communication, A can be said to have exercised power over B with respect to the content of that communication. Early behavioralists were wont to illustrate the point by referring to colliding billiard balls or, in the case of human agents and patients, to policemen and motorists.

A communicative perspective on power invites us to look at what is being presupposed in such exercises of power. In order to exercise power, two conditions, neither of which was central to the behavioralist account, must already have been satisfied. The first is that the power-wielder must be capable of communicating certain things in certain ways; he or she must, in short, be a competent speaker. The second is that the recipient of such a "persuasive communication" be capable of understanding it and knowing what kind of speech-act it is. The motorist must, for example, know that a particular communication from a policeman is an order or a command rather than, say, a suggestion, a plea, or a request.[25] Both must possess a common stock of concepts, such as "command" and "obedience," which are partly constitutive of their discourse and are the precondition of their being able to communicate and thus to be members of the same community. As Peter Winch observes,

. . . it does not make much sense to suppose that human beings might have been issuing commands and obeying them before they came to form the concept of command and obedience. For their performance of such acts is itself the chief manifestation of their possession of those concepts. An act of obedience itself contains, as an essential element, a recognition of what went before it as an order.[26]

Both must, in short, have power of a certain sort, namely the power of speech. From a communicative or linguistic perspective, then, a "power relation" can best be characterized, *pace* Hobbes, not as an agent-patient but as an agent-agent relation. In this respect, at least, relations of power are relations between (ontological) equals.

This can be seen even more clearly if we look not at the power of policemen but at the power of agents acting in a political capacity. For it is in the role of citizens, Hannah Arendt argued, that people act as free and equal agents who create power collectively through their communicative action and interaction. In order to make this case Arendt had to begin by remaking several crucial distinctions. Above all, political power had to be carefully distinguished from force, violence, coercion, authority, and other concepts that behavioralists had told us to treat as synonyms, inasmuch as each ostensibly refers to some sort of causal relationship. Such conceptual conflation represents a politically disastrous loss of precision:

It is, I think, a rather sad reflection on the present state of political science that our terminology does not distinguish among such key words as 'power,' 'strength,' 'force,' 'authority,' and, finally, 'violence'—all of which refer to distinct, different phenomena and would hardly exist unless they did. . . . To use them as synonyms not only indicates a certain deafness to linguistic meanings, which would be serious enough, but it has also resulted in a kind of blindness to the realities they correspond to.

Theirs is not, however, a naive or innocent blindness, but has at its base a particular and historically specific conceptual-cum-political reduction:

Behind the apparent confusion is a firm conviction in whose light all distinctions would be, at best, of minor importance: the conviction that the most crucial political issue is, and always has been, the question of Who rules Whom? Power, strength, force, authority, violence—these are but words to indicate the means by which man rules over man; they are held to be synonyms because they have the same function.

But, she adds, "It is only after one ceases to reduce public affairs to the business of dominion" (i.e., of "power over") "that the original data in the realm of human affairs will appear, or, rather, reappear, in their authentic diversity."[27]

According to Arendt, political power is a potentiality or capacity for acting that arises when equals come together. This mode of mutual empowerment is the medium of political action. For politics is acting with words; it is the communicative activity that constitutes and sustains political communities. And communication is necessarily two-way, requiring that speakers and listeners engage in mutually meaningful conversation, debate, and dialogue.[28] Through speech we communicate our views and coordinate our activities. It is people coming together for this purpose that makes power possible and necessary. "Power," writes Arendt, "corresponds to the human ability not just to act but to act in concert. Power is never the property of an individual; it belongs to a group and remains in existence only so long as the group keeps together." Her point is that groups or communities, acting in concert, have the capacity—the power—to empower their members and/or leaders. So, for example, "When we say of somebody that he is 'in power' we actually refer to his being empowered by a certain number of people to act in their name. The moment the group, from which the power originated . . . disappears, 'his power' also vanishes."[29] "All political institutions," she says, "are manifestations and materializations of power; they petrify and decay as soon as the living power of the people ceases to uphold them."[30]

Like the communities out of which it arises, power is communicatively constituted:

> . . . the public realm, . . . because it ultimately resides on action and speech, never altogether loses its potential [i.e., power-generating] character. . . . Power is actualized only where word and deed have not parted company, where words are not empty and deeds not brutal, where words are not used to veil intentions but to disclose realities, and deeds are not used to violate and destroy but to establish relations and create new realities. Power is what keeps the public realm, the potential space of appearance between acting and speaking men, in existence.[31]

Power is no more and no less perishable than the communication community that brings it into being. And if that community conflates the concepts constitutive of its discourse—'power' and 'violence' among them—then its common speech is impoverished and its very existence threatened.

Arendt's critics have found her account of power peculiar, to say the least. Even one as sympathetic as Steven Lukes calls hers "an interestingly idiosyncratic concept of power."[32] But when seen from the vantage point of conceptual history, her concept of power, although arguably archaic, is hardly idiosyncratic. Indeed, it harks back to the classical concept of power captured in the Ciceronian maxim, *potestas in populo,* which she translates as, "without a people or group there is no power."[33] And it has affinities with Hegel's master-slave dialectic, with Marx's account of proletarian revolution, and with Heidegger's notion of ontological empowerment, all of which point to the kind of power possessed *in potentia* by those who are supposedly powerless.[34]

A more recent variant of Arendt's communicative concept of power can be found in contemporary critical theory and in the program for a critical social science. Brian Fay, for example, argues that political power is a "dyadic" or two-way relationship "rooted in part in the reflections and will of those interacting, both the powerless as well as the powerful." Because people have the capacity to reflect critically upon their situation, that self-understanding—and the relations of power predicated upon it—is subject to change. Power can, in short, be a relation in which people are not dominated but empowered. The task of a critical social science is to discover the conditions under which the powerless can empower themselves:

> For critical social science, power exists not only when a group is controlled but also when a group comes together, becomes energized, and organizes itself, thereby becoming able to achieve something for itself. Here the paradigm case is not one of command but one of enablement in which a disorganized and unfocused group acquires an identity and a resolve to act in light of its new-found sense of purpose.

Thus, for example, education, understood as a critical practice, "is in part a process of empowerment in which a group of people who do not understand themselves to be such a group gradually discover that they are and gain the will to act in concert." A critical social science sees people "as creatures actively involved in creating and sustaining all their forms of social life, including their relations of power."[35]

Jürgen Habermas elucidates the communicative concept of power by contrasting Weber's views with those of Arendt. Weber "defined power as the possibility of forcing one's own will, whatever it may be, on the conduct of others. . . . Arendt, by contrast, understands power as the capacity to agree in uncoerced communication on some community action." Although both are alike in "discuss[ing] power as a potency realized in actions," Habermas notes, "each relies on a different model of action"[36] (and thus, I would add, on ontologically different models of agency as well). Weber subscribes to a "teleological model of action in which an individual subject or a group has a set purpose and chooses the means suitable for realizing it." To the degree that this requires the assent or actions of other human beings, 'power' refers to the means by which their compliance is secured. Power, for Weber, is essentially instrumental or "manipulative." Weber's "teleological model of action," Habermas contends, "considers only agents who are oriented toward their own success and not toward agreement."[37]

Arendt's "communicative model of action," on the other hand, is predicated upon the idea that "the basic phenomenon" of political life is not "the instrumentalizing of another's will for one's own purposes but the formation of a common will in a communication aimed at agreement." Power arises out of communal deliberation and decision. It therefore "rests on conviction and hence on that peculiarly coercion-free force with which insights prevail." In short, "the communicatively engendered power of common convictions goes back to the fact that the parties are oriented toward agreement and not just toward their own respective success. . . . Power is formed within communicative action; it is a group effect of speech in which agreement is an end in itself for all parties."[38]

Habermas's recasting of Arendt's analysis of power in the terms of Austinian speech-act theory and of his own counterfactual ideal speech situation need not detain us here. Of greater interest are Habermas's reasons for believing Arendt's communicative concept of power to be in need of updating. The "few weaknesses" in her concept of power stem, he says, "from the fact that Arendt remains bound to the historical and conceptual constellation of Aristotelian thought," which, Habermas holds, is anachronistic within the setting supplied by the modern nation-state.[39] Within a progressively "rationalized" society "the elements of strategic action" described by Weber and decried by Arendt "have increased in scope and importance." Although Arendt is right to say that political communities and institutions "live not by violence but by recognition," Habermas nevertheless maintains that "we cannot exclude the element of strategic action from the concept of the political." For 'politics' means something different in our time than it did in Aristotle's. Politics for us is an activity from which force and violence are not conceptually or categorically excluded. "Political violence" is no longer an oxymoron but a "means for acquiring and holding onto power." And insofar as the strategic "struggle for political power has . . . been institutionalized in the modern state"—via interest groups, political parties, and other organized associations—"it thereby becomes a normal component of the political system." Moreover, as critical theorists and as citizens we need to be aware of the ways in which violence is used by some individuals or groups "to keep other individuals or groups from perceiving their interests."[40] A concept of power that fails to recognize these developments is inadequate.

Of what use or relevance, then, is the communicative concept of power? It is useful, Habermas maintains, insofar as it supplies a standard or criterion for assessing the legitimacy of political actions and practices. For "it does not make good sense that someone should be able to generate legitimate power just because he is in a position to keep others from perceiving their interests. Legitimate power arises among those who form common convictions in communication free from coercion."[41] In Habermas's hands the communicative conception of power becomes a counterfactual ideal or standard to which action should aspire, even though it is incapable of being achieved in the modern world. It is, in short, the kind of power present in the ideal speech situation, in which discourse is free from domination and "the forceless force of the better argument" reigns supreme.[42]

The Realist Model

A second and equally fundamental challenge to the heretofore dominant understanding of power comes from metascientific "realism."[43] At first a dissident movement within the philosophy of the natural sciences, realism has been among the postpositivist challengers to the reigning empiricist orthodoxy. More recently, the discourse of realism has been transferred to the social sciences, where it is altering the meaning of the terms constitutive of its discourse, including 'power.' As a philosophy of social science, realism is a species of naturalism; that is, realists hold that there are no differences in principle between the methods and explanatory practices of the natural sciences and the social sciences. At this abstract and programmatic level realists and empiricists are in agreement. But this increasingly influential philosophy of science holds that the empiricist tradition's understanding of science in general, and its conception of causal explanation in particular, is radically flawed. Instead of viewing causal relations in contingent Humean terms, realists speak of "intrinsic natures," "causal powers," and "natural necessity." For example, one of the causal powers of copper is the power to conduct electricity, and one of the causal powers of glass is the inability to do so.[44]

The realist maintains that human beings have "powers" in the social world in much the same sense that copper, glass, and other substances do in the natural world. People possess these powers not as individuals but by virtue of occupying certain socially structured roles and being in certain socially defined and relatively enduring relationships.[45] A teacher, for example, has the power to teach and examine students; a policeman the power to direct traffic; a legislator the power to legislate; and so on. Realism's rejection of empiricism and its understanding of power provides the basis for its critique of behavioralism's understanding of power.

Defenders of the realist revision of power maintain that the "three faces of power" controversy was a tempest in the old empiricist teapot. Lukes, no less than the proponents of the first and second faces, remains committed to the ontology and epistemology of empiricism. Realists propose, accordingly, to reject the behavioralist understanding of power by undermining its empiricist foundations and to revise that concept in the light of a rival philosophy of science. Several points about that exercise in conceptual revision are worth noting.[46]

The first is that power remains, for the realist, a causal relation; but realism's ontology and its understanding of causation differ from that of the empiricist tradition. Whereas empiricists were ontological (and methodological) individualists, realists are ontological (and methodological) relationalists.[47] That is, realists hold that power is possessed and exercised not by individuals as individuals but by people in their capacity as socially situated role-bearers possessing certain intrinsic characteristics or "natures." As Jeffrey Isaac notes, in speaking of "the intrinsic natures of social agents" the realist refers "not [to] their unique characteristics as individuals, but [to] their social identities as participants in enduring, socially structured relationships."[48]

Second, causal powers are viewed by realists as capacities or dispositions to act that are actualized in, but not exhausted by, their exercise. The possession of such powers is socially and logically necessary, but their successful exercise is not. "The possession of these powers in the performance of social activities," writes Isaac, "is necessary to these activities; but the successful exercise of these powers is contingent."[49] Thus, realists insist upon distinguishing, as Hume and modern behavioralists did not, between the possession and the (successful) exercise of an agent's power.

Third, such social and political power is not equivalent to or translatable as "power over" or domination, but as "power to"—the power to engage in certain sorts of socially defined practices (e.g., teaching) and to exercise the powers that are constitutive of those practices. And even when it is appropriate to talk about "power over" (as in the master's power over the slave), such power is nevertheless parasitic upon a socially given "power to" act in certain ways.

Fourth, power is necessary inasmuch as human societies would fall apart without the kind of capacity for coordinated action that we call power.

Fifth, for the realist the concept of interest has no necessary connection with the concept of power. The teacher's possession and exercise of her power, for instance, need not imply any disregard of the student's interests; quite the contrary, in fact.

Finally, following from the aforementioned features of realist discourse, power is not a normatively negative concept. Power is not necessarily evil; it is, rather, a necessary and indispensable feature of social and political life.

This is not to say, however, that the realist understanding of power and its place in social-scientific inquiry is wholly without normative import. On the contrary, as Jeffrey Isaac notes,

> The concept of power . . . figures in contemporary debates regarding class structure, gender relations, the nature of the state, [and] nuclear arms. . . . To locate the sources of power in society is to locate the enablements and constraints that operate on all of us . . . To locate power is to fix moral responsibility, both upon those who exercise power illegitimately and upon those social structures that make this power available.[50]

The upshot is that the realist revision of the concept of power is itself empowering: it enables social agents armed with it to see, and to act in, the social world in a new way.

The Deconstructionist Model

Yet another attempt to revise the concept of power has been undertaken by Michel Foucault. His understanding of power, he admits, has undergone a radical change. He writes that until 1970 or so, "I accepted the traditional conception of power as an essentially judicial mechanism, as that which lays down the law, which prohibits, which refuses, and which has a whole range of negative effects: exclusion, rejection, denial, obstruction, obfuscation, etc. Now I believe that conception to be inadequate." It was, he says, "in the course of a concrete experience that I had with prisons . . . [that] convinced me that the question of power needed to be [re]formulated. . . . "[51]

Foucault's reformulation of power *(le pouvoir)* proceeds along the following lines. He begins by suggesting that the "force model" implicit in the concept of repression—that is, of domination or "power over"—"is a wholly negative, narrow, skeletal conception of power . . . which has been curiously widespread." Far from simply "carrying the force of a prohibition," power is productive; i.e., it is implicated in the production and reproduction of social practices:

> If power were never anything but repressive, if it never did anything but to say no, do you really think one would be brought to obey it? What makes power hold good, what makes it accepted, is simply the fact that it doesn't only weigh on us as a force that says no, but that it traverses and produces things, it induces pleasure, forms knowledge, produces discourse. It needs to be considered as a productive network which runs through the whole social body. . . . [52]

The crude force model might in some respects have been suitable for characterizing premodern power, which tended to be exercised sporadically, overtly, and often brutally.[53] But this model hardly suffices to capture and describe the ways in which, and the means by which, modern power is possessed and exercised. The productive power that makes modern society possible is, Foucault insists, a new kind of power, exercised in new ways.

Modern power, Foucault contends, takes the form of "disciplinary power." By this he means not simply the power to punish, but the power to "transform human beings into subjects" that has been generated by the various "disciplines" that belong to what we call "the human sciences," including medicine, psychiatry, penology, criminology, and the various social sciences. These disciplines have helped to create and maintain "a society of normalization," in part through their specialized discourses employed at socially specific sites—hospitals, asylums, prisons, etc.—and in part through their employment of the "apparatuses of knowledge" *(savoir)* peculiar to those disciplines and their discourses.[54] The human sciences are, or at any rate purport to be, caring and humane, their practitioners to be the bearers of a new kind of power that Foucault calls "confessional" or "pastoral power." This is the supposedly solicitous power to extract confessions, to pry into the innermost secrets of the subject, and to persuade the subject to participate in his own subjection.[55]

Historically, this change in the meaning of power was in part made possible by, and went hand in hand with, new techniques of administration and surveillance:

. . . from the seventeenth and eighteenth centuries onwards, there was a veritable technological take-off in the productivity of power . . . [A]bove all, there was established at this period what one might call a new "economy" of power, that is to say procedures which allowed the effects of power to circulate in a manner at once continuous, uninterrupted, adapted, and 'individualised' throughout the entire social body. These new techniques are both much more efficient and much less wasteful (less costly economically, less risky in their results, less open to loopholes and resistances), than the techniques previously employed. . . . [56]

Among these new techniques was the institutionalization of "the gaze" *(le regard)*, not only in prisons—several of which were actually modeled on Bentham's plan for a "Panopticon"—but in asylums, hospitals, schools, and other sites. Aware that they were under surveillance, patients, inmates, and pupils became obliged to watch themselves, to examine and scrutinize their own conduct, and thereby to participate in the process of their own normalization.

Modern power in Foucault's account is allied as never before with knowledge, or rather with discipline-specific 'knowledges' consisting of specialized skills, techniques, schemes of classification, etc. What is thereby created and sustained is a system in which power and knowledge are inseparable; in short, a *regime du savoir* or "regime of power/ knowledge."[57] This is not, however, a centralized or state-centered regime but consists instead of a highly decentralized array of "local" discursive practices operating in unsuspected and subtle ways in everyday life to produce "normal" subjects and, in so doing, to reproduce itself. This sort of "bio-power" or "micro-power" penetrates and circulates through the very "capillaries" of the social body.[58]

Foucault's revised understanding of power is in several respects novel and unique. But it also shares several affinities with the communicative and realist views examined earlier. The following list, though hardly exhaustive, might suggest some points of contact among apparently disparate perspectives. Like the realists—and like Marx, who may be read as a realist of a certain sort[59]—Foucault's focus is not upon isolated individuals but upon individuals as role-bearers implicated in the production and reproduction of relatively enduring and systematically structured social relations. And like Arendt, Foucault insists that power relations are discursively or communicatively constituted by and between free subjects. Thus violence, being mute—or at least not needing speech—must be sharply distinguished from power. Far from being power's "primitive form, its permanent secret and its last resource," violence works in a very different way. "A relationship of violence acts upon a body or upon things; it forces, it bends, it breaks on the wheel, it destroys, or it closes the door on all possibilities." A relation of power, by contrast, "can only be articulated on the basis of two elements which are each indispensable if it is really to be a power relationship." The first is "that 'the other' (the one over whom power is exercised) be thoroughly recognized and maintained to the very end as a person who acts," and not as a passive object or lifeless thing—or "patient," if you like—upon whom others act and who can in turn only react.[60] "The term 'power,' " he writes, "designates relationships among partners," adding that "relationships of communication . . . by virtue of modifying the field of information between partners, produce effects of power."[61] The second feature of a power relationship is that it necessarily implies choices and options: "faced with a relationship of power, a whole field of responses, reactions, result, and possible interventions may open up."[62]

In a manner reminiscent of but not identical with Arendt's, Foucault links power with the freedom to choose and to act:

> Power is exercised only over free subjects, and only insofar as they are free. By this we mean individual or collective subjects who are faced with a field of possibilities in which several ways of behaving, several reactions and diverse comportments may be realized. Where the determining factors saturate the whole there is no relationship of power; slavery is not a power relationship when man is in chains. (In this case it is a question of a physical relationship of constraint.) Consequently there is no face to face confrontation of power and freedom which is mutually exclusive . . . but a much more complicated interplay. In this game freedom may well appear as the condition for the exercise of power (at the same time its precondition, since freedom must exist for power to be exerted, and also its permanent support, since without the possibility of recalcitrance, power would be equivalent to a physical determination). . . . At the heart of the power relationship, and constantly provoking it, are the recalcitrance of the will and the intransigence of freedom.[63]

Insofar as human beings remain free they retain a capacity for acting and thus the power to resist. There is, he adds, "no relationship of power without the means of escape or possible flight. Every power relationship implies, at least in potentia, a strategy of struggle. . . . It would not be possible for power relations to exist without points of insubordination which, by definition, are means of escape."[64] The task of the theorist, Foucault maintains, is to participate in the politics of everyday life by clarifying the nature of the micropractices that constitute modern power, thereby disclosing points of possible intervention and resistance and thus helping to empower others to take advantage of them.

Although there appear to be several points of tangency among the three aforementioned attempts to reconstruct the concept of power, it would be claiming too much to suggest that they are compatible in any, much less all, essential respects. And whether or how they might comport with a feminist understanding of power remains an open question. I leave it to the reader of this and the following essays to decide whether some sort of rapprochement among such diverse perspectives might yet be reached.

Chapter 3

Beyond the Three Faces of Power:
A Realist Critique*

───────────────── *Jeffrey C. Isaac*

A great deal of ink has been spilled debating the meaning of the concept of power. In Anglo-American political science the fulcrum of the debate is what is sometimes called "the three faces of power" controversy. There is an air of scholasticism surrounding this debate, and there is thus a healthy skepticism among many about the usefulness of yet another intervention. This paper, however, is not simply another entry in the debate. It is a critique of the debate itself.

The debate about the term *power* rests on the misconception that the purpose of social science is to document empirical regularities. I will label this view empiricism and suggest that the behavioral revolution in political science is responsible for it. This misconception has led many to think of power as a behavioral concept, referring to the conjunction of the behaviors of two parties, such that "A has power over B" means that in some sense A does something to get B to do something. I will argue that this view is doubly confused. First, it is limited to situations of "power over" and fails to see that "power over," or what I will call domination, is parasitic upon a "power to." Second, it fails to distinguish between the possession and the exercise of power.

I will argue that none of the three faces of power is able to recognize this because of their commitments to behaviorism. I will propose

*The author wishes to thank the following people for their help in preparation of this chapter: Terence Ball, Robert Dahl, Peter Manicas, Roy Bhaskar, Erik Olin Wright, David Mayhew, Burt Zweibach, Mike Krasner, Ian Shapiro, and Debra Kent.

that another, increasingly accepted philosophy of science—realism—enables us to think better about power. Moreover, I will propose that power be conceived in structural rather than behavioral terms or, to be clearer from the outset, in terms of the structures within which behavior takes place. In conclusion, I will suggest some of the implications of this argument for research, specifically as it regards theorizing about the state.

Behavioralism and the Faces of Power

The behavioral revolution in political science has, unsurprisingly, had important and long-term effects on the practice of political research. These effects, however, have been much less innocent than the revolutionary vanguard believed. Robert Dahl, in his famous "monument to a successful protest," wrote: "The behavioral approach is an attempt to improve our understanding of politics by seeking to explain the empirical aspects of political life by means of methods, theories, and criteria of proof that are acceptable according to the canons, conventions, and assumptions of modern empirical science."[1] This quotation gives something of the flavor of the intellectual moment—optimistic, naively self-assured about the nature of the scientific outlook that was to be emulated. But as Dahl himself unwittingly makes clear, the success of this protest movement represented in fact much less the triumph of scientific methods than an emerging hegemony of an empiricist view of science. Dahl quotes an early prescriptive tract, which he presents as simply and matter-of-factly scientific:

> [We favor] a decision to explore the feasibility of developing a new approach to the study of political behavior. Based upon the study of individuals in political situations, this approach calls for the examination of the political relationships of men . . . by disciplines which can throw light on the problems involved, with the object of formulating and testing hypotheses concerning uniformities of behavior. . . . [2]

This view of scientific explanation as the documentation and prediction of empirical uniformities was a central tenet of the behavioral movement. A theory, David Easton wrote, is "any kind of generalization or proposition that asserts that two or more things, activities, or events, covary under specified conditions."[3] A more recent work asserts: "Science is concerned with the explanation (and prediction) of specific events by means of statements which are invariantly true from one set of circumstances."[4]

This understanding of science is what I, following Roy Bhaskar and Rom Harré, will call empiricism. It takes the empirical world, the world of experienced occurrences, to be the object of scientific investigation and eschews any appeal to underlying causes and natural necessities as unscientific "metaphysics."[5] This view extends beyond the positivist claim that theories are verifiable in experience and refer to unproblematic and unmediated observables. Empiricism hinges primarily on an ontology, or theory of reality, which is Humean, namely that there is nothing but a flux of events whose only relationship is one of contingent conjunction. This view is widely accepted by philosophers and social scientists who are otherwise critics of Humean bedrock empiricism. Thus Karl Popper, arguably the most important postpositivist philosopher of science, distinguishes between scientific method, which he calls "methodological nominalism," and "essentialism." "Instead of aiming at finding out what a thing really is, and at defining its true nature," he writes, "methodological nominalism aims at describing how a thing behaves in various circumstances, and especially, whether there are any regularities in its behavior."[6]

Like Hume, Popper associates any attempt to provide real definitions and analyze causal necessities with medieval scholasticism and unscientific metaphysics. Also like Hume, he construes causality as constant conjunction. Popper writes:

> To give a causal explanation of an event means to deduce a statement which describes it, using as premises of the deduction one or more universal laws, together with certain singular statements, the initial conditions. . . . The initial conditions describe what is usually called the "cause" of the event in question.[7]

Thus, because any talk of natural necessity is derisively branded metaphysics and because the only meaning that can thus be given to causality is as empirical regularity, the task of scientific explanation becomes deductive-nomological—the formulation of generalizations about empirical regularities that enable us to predict that "Whenever A, then B."[8] This ideal of scientific explanation, once dominant within the philosophy of science, has been subjected to much criticism in philosophy. But just as it took some time before political scientists were willing to adopt this ideal, there has also been a lag between its abandonment by philosophers and its rejection by political scientists. One consequence of this is its continuing influence on the debate about power.

The First Face of Power

This understanding of scientific explanation shaped a new and rigorous effort to formalize the concept of power. A number of articles were published, all variations on the same theme—power is a causal relation between the behaviors of two agents, causality being understood as constant conjunction.[9]

This approach was taken up by Robert Dahl, one of the most important figures in the three faces of power debate. Dahl, in a series of articles, argued the need for a definition of power amenable to the kind of empirical research envisioned by behavioralism. Thus he wrote: "Power terms in modern social science refer to subsets of relations among social units such that the behavior of one or more units (the response units, R), depend in some circumstances on the behavior of other units (the controlling units, C)."[10] Power, then, is an empirical regularity whereby the behavior of one agent causes the behavior of another. Dahl is explicit about this, noting that:

> For the assertion "C has power over R" we can substitute the assertion "C's behavior causes R's behavior" . . . the language of cause, like the language of power, is used to interpret situations in which there is a possibility that some event will intervene to change the order of other events.[11]

That this notion of power rests on a Newtonian analogy seems obvious. We are all naturally at rest or at constant velocity, until our movement is altered by an external force. Power is that force whereby social agents alter the behavior of other agents or, as Dahl puts it, get them to do what they would not otherwise do.[12] True to his empiricism, Dahl insists that there are no necessary relationships between the behaviors of agents, writing that "the only meaning that is strictly causal in the notion of power is one of regular sequence: that is, a regular sequence such that when A does something, what follows, or what probably follows, is an action by B."[13]

These remarks may sound unexceptionable, but their force must be emphasized. Dahl is insisting here that his notion of power smacks of no metaphysics, that its assertion involves nothing that is not empirically evident. This view of power is the basis of the entire three faces of power debate. All of the contestants agree that power is an empirical relation of cause and effect, and none of them conceives of power as involving any necessary connections, or what I will later call structural relationships. This is not to say that the reason for this is that subsequent contestants consciously wished to endorse the Humean view. It is, rather, that they simply failed to challenge it, most likely because they failed to recognize it—an interesting example of the power of a view that is neither asserted nor recognized as such.

The controversy about power does not revolve around this major premise. It revolves, instead, around the following question: How do we identify those instances in which A gets B to do that which B would not otherwise have done? As Steven Lukes points out, this question hinges on the question of a counterfactual: What would B have otherwise done? Dahl's answer to this is that B's revealed preferences indicate this.[14] Thus, "A has power over B" means that A's behavior regularly causes B to do something that B does not *want* to do. This has been called the "first face of power" insofar as it involves manifest instances of conflict and compliance. It has also been called the "decisionist" view insofar as it is limited to instances of actual decision-making or choice in action.

It is on the basis of this interpretation of the counterfactual that Dahl and his student Nelson Polsby insisted that any scientific claims about power must focus on instances of manifest conflict. In this insistence, they employed their understanding of scientific method in order to delegitimate radical critics of American society who wrote about power without referring to regular sequences of the above-mentioned sort. Thus Polsby, in his *Community Power and Political Theory*, chastised what he called "categorialism," categorical claims such as "A has power over B," which refuse to specify the empirical conditions, the causal behaviors, under which B can be predicted to act (note the similarity of this criticism to Popper's invidious distinction between methodological nominalism and essentialism). Thus Polsby writes about the claim that there is a dominant class:

> For this latter statement to mean anything in a scientific sense, we must, according to the formal requirements postulated above, make reference to specific decisions in which particular outcomes are affected by members of the classes into which we divide the population, and secondly, we must state the conditions under which we can take it as demonstrated that the upper class does not have more power than the lower class.[15]

Ascriptions of power, then, are falsifiable predictions about the stimuli of the powerful and the responses of the powerless. Similarly Dahl, in his now-classic "Critique of the Ruling Elite Model," criticized C. Wright Mills by asserting that "I do not see how anyone can suppose that he has established the dominance of a specific group in a community or nation without basing his analysis on the careful examination of a series of concrete decisions."[16]

It is important to see what these criticisms accomplished, for doing so will clarify exactly what this chapter is criticizing. On the one hand, some very sensible and plausible points are made regarding the importance of empirical evidence and the possibility of theoretical criticism. On the other hand, the whip hand of science is deployed to question the very meaning and reference of claims about power that do not conform to Dahl's decisionist perspective. It is not Dahl's emphasis on the empirical, but his reliance on empiricism, on the Hume/Popper view of causality and scientific explanation, that is the problem with his view of power.

The Second Face of Power

The Dahl-Polsby view of power was challenged by Peter Bachrach and Morton Baratz, who introduced the notion of a "second face of power."[17] Their criticism rests on two points. The first is that Dahl and Polsby sometimes write in a naively positivist vein, as though the location of power were unproblematic and simply a question of observation. Bachrach and Baratz insist that this is mistaken, that all science involves the making of judgments of significance that are derived from a theoretical perspective. Their second objection is that Dahl's formulation misses a crucial feature of power—the suppression of conflict. In criticizing Dahl's decisionist focus on actual conflict, Bachrach and Baratz develop the concept of a nondecision, which they define as "a decision that results in suppression or thwarting of a latent or manifest challenge to the values or interests of the decision-maker."[18]

The point of this argument is that power entails not simply interaction, but limitations on interaction. Yet their formulation is also ambiguous and open to the charge that it is little different from Dahl's. On the one hand, Bachrach and Baratz suggest a structural formulation, conceiving power as implicated in institutionalized practices. It is in this regard that they refer to Schattschneider's concept of the "mobilization of bias," writing that:

> Political systems and sub-systems develop a "mobilization of bias," a set of predominant values, beliefs, rituals, and institutional procedures ("rules of the game") that operate systematically and consistently to the benefit of certain groups and persons at the expense of

others. Those who benefit are placed in a preferred position to defend and promote their vested interests.[19]

This formulation, however, comes dangerously close to postulating underlying structural relations as determining behavior, risking the essentialism so scorned by properly trained scientific theorists. Polsby makes the point:

> The central problem is this: Even if we can show that a given status quo benefits some people disproportionately (as I think we can for any real world status quo), such a demonstration falls short of showing that the beneficiaries *created* the status quo, *act* in any meaningful way to maintain it, or could, in the future, *act* effectively to deter changes in it.[20]

Once again, the mark of science is the examination of behavior, but a given status quo, in and of itself, holds no interest for the theorist of power.

In the end, Bachrach and Baratz sacrifice their interest in structure to the interest of science. They say explicitly that power involves actual compliance and go so far as to assert that "it cannot be possessed," only exercised.[21] Conceding to behavioralism, they hold that "although absence of conflict may be a non-event, a decision which results in prevention of conflict is very much an event—and an observable one, to boot."[22] By admitting this, Bachrach and Baratz expose themselves to a criticism made by Geoffrey Debnam—that implicit in their formulation is an important distinction between power as nondecision and power as mobilization of bias. The former refers to behavioral regularities, differing from the first face only insofar as it includes covert instances of suppression as well as overt instances of compliance.[23] The latter is an unexplicated and ultimately nonbehavioral phenomenon. Polsby's criticism is thus decisive: "How to study this second face of power? To what manifestations of social reality might the mobilization of bias refer? Are phenomena of this sort in principle amenable to empirical investigation?"[24] Bachrach and Baratz never explicitly answer this question, but instead sacrifice their insight about the institutional basis of power to the scholarly "mobilization of bias" that I have labeled empiricism.

The Third Face of Power

Steven Lukes, in his *Power: A Radical View,* picks up where Bachrach and Baratz left off. He applauds their "two dimensional view" of power as an advance over Dahl's "one dimensional" perspective. He agrees that the study of power involves interpretative questions about which phenomena to study, but he also believes that Bachrach and Baratz's critique of Dahl's behaviorism "is too qualified." As he writes of their formulation:

> It gives a misleading picture of the ways in which individuals and, above all, groups and institutions, succeed in excluding potential issues from the political process. Decisions are choices consciously and intentionally made by individuals between alternatives, whereas the bias of the system can be mobilized, recreated, and reinforced in ways that are neither consciously chosen nor the intended result of particular individuals' choices. . . . Moreover, the bias of the system is not simply sustained by a series of individually chosen acts, but also, more importantly, by the socially structured and culturally patterned behavior of groups, and practices of institutions which may indeed be manifested by individuals' inaction.[25]

Lukes thus proposes that if the concept of power is to take account of the way in which interaction is itself shaped and limited, it cannot limit itself to instances of behavioral compliance as the one- and two-dimensional views do. He asks, "Is not the supreme exercise of power to avert conflict and grievance by influencing, shaping, and determining the perceptions and preferences of others?"[26]

Lukes submits that his view of power, along with those of Dahl and Bachrach and Baratz, all "can be seen as alternative interpretations and applications of one and the same underlying concept of power, according to which A exercises power over B when A affects B in a manner contrary to B's interests."[27] It is Lukes who makes the concept of interest central to the debate, yet it is important to see how much his similarities with his predecessors outweigh his differences. Lukes agrees that power is a causal concept denoting behavioral regularities. He agrees too that "A has power over B" means that A's behavior causes B to do something that B would not otherwise do. As Lukes puts it, "any attribution of the exercise of power . . . always implies a relevant counterfactual."[28] In the cases of the first two faces of power, the counterfactual is provided by the existence of empirical conflict between the revealed preferences of A and B. Lukes differs from these views in insisting that preferences can themselves be the effect of the exercise of power. He thus insists that what B would do otherwise cannot be gauged properly by B's preferences, but rather by B's *interests*. Lukes, then, defines power as follows: "A exercises power over B when A affects B contrary to B's interest."[29] The concept of power can thus refer to relations between A and B even in the absence of empirical conflict.

Lukes contends that this view captures the essence of power as an empirical relation between A and B and that the sole difference between this view and those articulated by his antagonists is that "those holding the three different views of power I have set out offer different interpretations of what are to count as interests and how they may be adversely affected."[30] Lukes' view is that the concept of interest, or what has been called "objective interest," refers to what an agent would do under ideal democratic circumstances. It thus follows that if it can be plausibly argued that A affects B in a manner that limits B from doing what B would do under ideal conditions, then it can be properly said that A exercises power over B.[31]

This notion of objective interest has been subjected to a great deal of criticism, some of which will be discussed below. But regardless of the merit of Lukes' understanding of interests, the importance of the concept for him is grounded in his commitment to viewing power as an empirical regularity. Despite his criticisms of his antagonists, he is explicit that he is merely interpreting a shared concept. Insofar as this is true, Lukes' formulation, like that of Bachrach and Baratz, is ambiguous regarding the "socially structured and culturally patterned" dimension of power.

In a later essay, "Power and Structure," Lukes seeks to clarify this, arguing that structural and empirical approaches must be synthesized and suggesting that there is a "dialectic of power and structure."[32] Social structure limits action, and power, being an event-like phenomenon, is discernible empirically. Power, he says, is an "agency" concept, not a "structural" one, yet he writes that it "is held and exercised by agents (individual or collective) within systems and structural determinants."[33] This clarifies somewhat the relation between power and structure—social structure provides the limits within which power is exercised. But it also leaves unanswered the problem posed by Lukes' earlier discussion of power in structural terms. In other words, what is the nature of these structural determinants of power? How determining are they? If power is an agency concept rather than a structural one, and if it denotes behavioral regularities, then what precisely is the difference between Lukes' third face of power and the view of Bachrach and Baratz? Is it simply a focus on a different class of events, those that involve the transgression of objective interest rather than simply compliance? If Lukes' view is different, his bifurcation of power and structure does not go far in showing us how. In short, Lukes seems unable to articulate the structural nature of social power which, he rightly notes, is so important.

In the end, Lukes leans toward a view of power differing little from that of his predecessors. Like them, he views power in terms of behavioral regularities rather than their structural determinants. And like them he conflates the possession of power with its exercise, insisting that power is an agency concept rather than a structural one. Lukes explicitly rejects the locution "power to" and instead accepts an exclusive emphasis on "power over." For him, power is exhausted in interaction, in the regularity with which A can get B to do something, thus having power over B. His formulation leaves no room for consideration of the enduring powers to act that are possessed by A and B and that are brought to bear in interaction. He justifies inattention to the locution "power to" by arguing that it is "out of line with the central meaning of power as traditionally understood and with the concerns that have always preoccupied students of power."[34] But it is precisely this traditional idiom that I wish to question. An adequate formulation of the concept of power must recognize that the power one agent exercises over another agent in interaction is parasitic upon the powers to act that the agents possess.

The purpose of the above discussion has been to demonstrate some root similarities among the contestants of the three faces of power controversy, and to point out that the debate about power has been conducted within rather narrow parameters. Nonetheless, within these parameters, some serious problems are left unresolved. And while the irresolution of conflict is not always a signal of something awry, in this case it may indicate the need to broaden the parameters of debate, and in fact to free the discussion from its behavioralist legacy.

The major unresolved difficulty of the debate concerns the problem of the limits within which interaction occurs, or what I have called the structural nature of power. This problem has proved inarticulable within the confines of the debate, in virtue of the shared premise, established by the behavioral revolution, that power is the empirical causation of one actor's behavior by that of another actor. Bachrach and Baratz, as well as Lukes, have failed to develop the structural dimension of power to which they rightly point. This is not a problem for Dahl, who never raises this issue, and in this respect Dahl's view is the most consistent.[35] However, its consistency is purchased at a price— its inability to conceptualize the way power is implicated in the constitution of the conditions of interaction. Dahl's critics insist, rightly, that A can have power over B without it being the case that B resists in any way, in fact in virtue of B's quiescence. However, it does not seem that the critics have been able to formulate a clear alternative conception.

To take an example, it seems reasonable to claim that the Soviet Communist Party apparatus has power over Soviet workers and peasants even though it clearly does not prevail over them in situations of actual conflict of revealed preferences, but Dahl's view would prevent us from claiming this (I do not mean, and do not believe, that Dahl would deny this, only that the logic of his articles about power would deny it). Yet, to stick with this example, is it necessary to argue about the objective class interests of the workers and peasants in order to say this? I should think not. There is of course another possibility, one which appears startlingly commonsensical but which violates the basic premise of the three faces debate—that the CPSU has power over the Soviet masses by virtue of the structure of Soviet society in which political power is monopolized by a single party. This claim is, however, clearly essentialist in Popper's sense, in that it is interested in the nature of Soviet society rather than in the search for behavioral uniformities. Such theoretical interests, therefore, require more than going beyond the three faces controversy; they require rejecting the empiricism that is the controversy's foundation.

Realism and Social Science

As I have emphasized, the empiricism which is at the root of the debate about power is primarily an ontological doctrine about the nature of causality and the aim of scientific explanation. Few social theorists would deny what contemporary conventionalists like Thomas Kuhn have taught us—that science is irreducibly interpretative, the scientist's access to the world being mediated by the conceptual and theoretical frameworks of his or her science.[36] However, through behavioralism, political scientists have accepted this without questioning the ontology of empiricism. Realist philosophy of science involves a critique of this ontology.

Contemporary realists reject the understanding of natural laws as contingent empirical regularities and of causality as regular sequences of events.[37] They defend the concept of natural necessity, that scientific laws explain the properties and dispositions of things that are not reducible to their empirical effects. The physical properties of copper (malleability, fusibility, ductility, electrical conductivity) are, for example, not contingent effects caused by antecedent events; they are the enduring properties of copper as a metal, which can be accounted for by its atomic structure. In this view, causality is understood as the actualization of the properties of real natural entities with causal powers.[38] Scientists develop theories to explain the phenomena of experience, like the fact that copper conducts electricity and string does not, by an appeal to the structures that generate them.

In the realist view, the world is not constituted such that it can be explained by subsuming events under covering laws of the form "whenever A, then B." Rather, it is composed of a complex of what Harré calls "powerful particulars," or causal mechanisms, which operate in an unpredictable but not undetermined manner. As Roy Bhaskar writes in his influential *A Realist Theory of Science:*

> The world consists of things, not events. . . . On this conception of science it is concerned essentially with what kinds of things there are and with what they tend to do; it is only derivatively concerned with predicting what is actually going to happen. It is only rarely, and normally under conditions which are artificially produced and controlled, that scientists can do the latter. And, when they do, its significance lies precisely in the light that it casts on the enduring natures and ways of acting of independently existing and transfactually active things.[39]

This understanding of science does not eschew empirical evidence, but construes this evidence as the means by which scientists explain underlying causes. In the realist view, this understanding is implicit in what scientists actually do, in their classification schemata, in their experimentation, and in their development of causal concepts. Stephen Toulmin writes of the scientist:

> He *begins* with the conviction that things are not just happening (not even just-happening-regularly) but rather that some fixed set of laws or patterns or mechanisms accounts for Nature's following the course that it does, and that his understanding of these should guide his expectations. Furthermore, he has the beginnings of an idea what these laws and mechanisms are . . . [and] he is looking for evidence which will show him how to trim and shape his ideas further. . . . This is what makes "phenomena" important for him.[40]

Science is thus both essentialist and metaphysical in Popper's and Polsby's invidious sense. But it does not therefore presume any immutability or teleology about the world, nor does it presume that it can be unproblematically rationally perceived. It presumes, instead, that the world exists independently of human experience, that it has certain enduring properties, and that science, through the development and criticism of theoretical explanations, can come to have some knowledge of it. No greater testimony can be provided on behalf of this view than that of the mature Albert Einstein who, in a 1931 letter to the positivist Moritz Schlick, wrote:

> In general your presentation fails to correspond to my conceptual style insofar as I find your whole orientation so to speak much too positivistic. . . . I tell you straight out: Physics is the attempt at the conceptual construction of a model of the real world and its lawful structure. . . . In short, I suffer under the (unsharp) separation of Reality of Experience and Reality of Being. . . . You will be astonished about the "metaphysicist" Einstein. But every four- and two-legged animal is de facto this metaphysicist.[41]

In the realist view, social science would be similarly concerned with the construction of models of the social world and its lawful structure. The primary object of theoretical analysis would not be behavioral regularities, but the enduring social relationships that structure them.[42] This approach need not result in a form of hyperdeterminism that reifies social structure. Indeed, the idea of social structure developed by realists is based on a categorical rejection of the bifurcation of structure and human agency.[43] Anthony Giddens has argued that there is a "duality of structure."[44] He proposes that social structures are both the medium and the effect of human action. As such, they exist neither apart from the activities they govern nor from human agents' conceptions of these activities. At the same time, they are also a material condition of these activities. Giddens uses the analogy of language to illustrate this: there would be no language without speakers speaking, and yet language is at the same time the medium of speech. Language has structural properties on which agents draw in order to perform communicative acts. The major point of this approach is that purposive human activity has social preconditions, which are the relatively enduring relations (e.g., husband/wife, capitalist/worker, citizen/ representative that constitute the complexity of any given society. Individuals and groups participate within these conditions, reproducing and transforming them in the course of their ordinary lives.[45] As Giddens writes: "In respect of sociology, the crucial task of nomological [i.e., theoretical] analysis is to be found in the explanation of the properties of structures."[46]

The Concept of Power Revisited

We are now in a better position to appreciate the limitations of the three faces of power debate and to reformulate the concept of power.

The behavioralist foundations of the debate constrained its participants from conceiving power as anything more than a behavioral regularity and prevented them from seeing it as an enduring capacity. To do so, of course, risks presupposing what Nagel has called "objectionable metaphysical implications." But, as I have suggested, in the realist view of science, presuppositions about the enduring nature of causal mechanisms are the essence of actual scientific practice. It is only at great cost that the discussants of power have eschewed such premises.

Pitkin has rightly pointed out that empiricist theories of power have abused language in their inattention to linguistic complexities and to questions of meaning.[47] Witness, for example, Jack Nagel's observation:

> Words, as Humpty Dumpty observed, can mean anything we choose them to mean. Why bother to dispute definitions? I do so precisely because definitions are merely arbitrary, whereas hypotheses are potentially subject to agreement producing tests. Therefore, the most useful definitions are those which direct efforts to empirical research.[48]

This was, as we have seen, the attitude of the behavioralist innovators regarding the concept of power—that the concept should acquire a formal definition amenable to their notion of scientific explanation and falsification. The first thing to note about this, however, is that this effort was a striking failure in its own terms. If the most useful definitions are those that direct efforts toward empirical research, then the three faces of power debate can only be adjudged fruitless, as it has resulted in a dearth of research that actually conforms to the methods prescribed by the debate.[49] The empiricist view of definition is simply wrong, but it is mistaken in a way that sheds light on the theoretical sterility of the debate over power.

Words can only be intelligibly used in the context of their previous usage. Empiricist power theorists have confined themselves to one particular locution, "power over," corresponding to their belief that a proper social science is a science of behavioral regularities. What is crucial is that they have all failed to provide a *real definition* of power,[50] substituting instead an operational definition of the form, "A has power over B means that. . . . " Power, a potential word, becomes redefined to describe not potentialities but actual events.[51]

"Power" derives from the Latin *potere,* meaning "to be able." It is generally used to denote a property, ability, or capacity to affect things.[52] The attribution of properties or capacities is a common feature of everyday life, e.g., "that car is fast." This does not mean that ordinary ascriptions constitute valid scientific explanations, but it does indicate the congruence of the ordinary sense of the term with the arguments developed here.

According to the realist philosophy of science outlined above, powers are a central subject matter of natural science. As Harré writes: "To ascribe a power to a thing or material is to say something about what it will or can do . . . in virtue of its intrinsic nature."[53] To use an earlier example, to say that conductivity is a power of copper is to claim that copper possesses an enduring capacity to conduct electricity that is intrinsic in its nature, in this case its atomic structure. I want to argue that social science should be similarly concerned with the ascription of powers to social agents, and with the explanatory reference of these powers to agents' intrinsic natures. By the intrinsic natures of social agents I mean not their unique characteristics as individuals, but their social identities as participants in enduring, socially structured relationships. Theories of power, then, should be conceived as interpretative models, developed by social scientists subject to the rigors of critical consideration, about the social structures that shape human action. To speak in this way of the social structures that account for power is no different from speaking of the atomic structure that accounts for conductivity. Both sorts of claim are equally fallible, equally subject to theoretical and empirical criticism and equally concerned with underlying, and nonobservable, causal mechanisms.

Power, Structure, and Agency

Social power should be understood relationally, by which I mean in terms of the underlying social relations that structure behavioral interaction and not in terms of the contingent regularities in the behaviors of discrete agents who may have no necessary relationship to one another.[54] The relation between teacher and student, for example, is not a contingent relation between two parties who happen to engage in interaction. It is an historically enduring relation, the nature of which is precisely that teachers have students and vice versa. It is the nature of these social identities to be in relation to one another. As such, it is their nature to possess certain powers, powers that simply cannot be conceived as contingent regularities. The teacher possesses the power to design the syllabus, direct classroom activities, and give and grade assignments. The student possesses the power to attend class, to do the schoolwork, and to evaluate the teacher's performance. These powers to act are part of the nature of the relationship. They are not regularities, strictly speaking, but are routinely performed and purposeful activities. The possession of these powers in the performance of social activities is necessary to these activities, but the successful exercise of these powers is contingent. Thus, the teacher may not succeed in directing the classroom's activities, and the class may be unruly. But the teacher's power is not thereby nullified. Any particular teacher's consistent failure to direct the classroom is a different story, and it may well nullify his or her power. However, we would then likely say that he or she is a bad teacher, unsuited to the role of teacher and personally unable to exercise the social powers associated with the role. More generally, the persistent inability of teachers in general to direct their classrooms successfully may well indicate that the teacher-student relation is in crisis, and that students are exercising their powers to contest their subordination.

I will thus define social power as *the capacities to act possessed by social agents in virtue of the enduring relations in which they participate.* Giddens distinguishes between a broad sense of power as the capability of an actor to intervene, and a narrower sense, as "the capability to secure outcomes where the realization of these outcomes depends on the agency of others."[55] What I have defined as social power is the latter. Thus, while the term power is properly used to describe many situations, as for instance my neighbor's persuasive ability that resides in his .45 Magnum, the term social power is intended to call attention to the way the capacity to act is distributed by generalized and enduring social relationships (is it the case that my persuasive neighbor is also a policeman?). In this sense, social power involves what Giddens calls relations of interdependence. The teacher's power entails the student's presence and requires that the student act in a certain way.

This relational understanding of power clarifies the distinction between "power to" and "power over," or what I would call relations of domination and subordination, a distinction ignored in the three faces of power debate. I have suggested that social relations distribute power to act in certain ways to those who participate in them. Insofar as this is true, it is these relations, rather than the behaviors that they shape, which are the material causes of interaction. To return to the teacher-student example: the teacher's behavior does not cause the student's behavior in this sense, and the student's behavior is not simply a response to the teacher's stimulus. Rather, the teacher-student relationship provides the teacher with the power to give homework assignments, which is successfully or unsuccessfully exercised in interaction with the student. The relationship is the material cause of interaction, the specific ways in which the teacher and the student, who is equally a purposive agent, act as the efficient cause.

This sort of structural determination of power is precisely what Bachrach and Baratz and Lukes gestured at but failed to articulate. They were interested in the reason why the student is subordinate and saw rightly that this subordination is not properly conceived as simply a contingent regularity. They suspected that there was some necessary institutional cause of this subordination but, because they lacked a capacitative concept of power, they could not clarify this. I want to suggest that a theoretical explanation of the subordination of students must analyze the structure of education and the way power is distributed by this structure. Whatever regularities exist in behavior must be explained with reference to the structural relations of power.

To propose this is not to detach the concept of power from human agency. As I defined it, social power refers to the capacities to act that are possessed by agents in virtue of their social relations. But what are these relations but idioms of human conduct? To say that teachers and students are in a certain structural relationship is only to say that there are people called teachers and students who characteristically do the things that the relationship involves. If social power is never exercised, it can hardly be said to exist. But its exercise is always shaped and constrained by certain enduring relations. I am going to school this afternoon to give a lecture on Dahl, and in doing so, however unintentionally, I am exercising the power of a teacher. The sorts of structurally distributed powers that I have discussed are constantly exercised in the course of ordinary life, at home, at work, at school, at the tax collector's office, and the exercise of them is always contingent. Bosses by nature have the power to supervise production, but tomorrow the workers may strike. Teachers by nature have the power to conduct class lessons, but tomorrow the students may boycott class and conduct their own teach-in. It is a necessary feature of the existing structure of education that teachers are dominant and students subordinate. But the exercise of these powers, the way this relationship is worked out in concrete practice, is contingent, determined by the way particular individuals and groups choose to deal with their circumstances.

The contingency of the exercise of power is, ultimately, connected to another important reality—the openness of history, and the fact that social structures are only relatively enduring, not immutable. Insofar as the exercise of power is always contingent, it is constantly negotiated in the course of everyday life. Thus, not only the exercise of power, but also the very existence of relations of power themselves, can become objects of contention and struggle. In such struggles subordinate groups will obviously be at a disadvantage. But they never simply respond to the behavior of the powerful. The reproduction of the relationship always involves their agency, which can be mobilized as well to transform the relationship itself. Power relations approximate less a model of stimulus and response, and more a model of endemic reciprocity, negotiation, and struggle, with both dominant and subordinate groups mobilizing their specific powers and resources. A theory of power must analyze structural relations and the way they are worked out concretely by socially situated human beings. To think of the latter apart from the former is mistaken. But it is equally mistaken to ignore the way people make their own history, even if they do not do so under conditions of their own choosing.

Power and Interest

Lukes, we may recall, introduced the concept of interest into the three faces of power controversy. While a full treatment of the concept would go beyond the scope of this chapter, some comments about the connection between power and interest are in order.

For Lukes, the concept of interest is necessary to the discussion of power insofar as it answers the question of the counterfactual: What would B do were it not for A's behavior? I have argued that this way of thinking about power is mistaken and that rather than treating A's behavior as the cause of B's behavior, we should focus on the structural relations that bind A and B together, viewing these as the material cause of both A's and B's conduct. In this sense, Lukes' counterfactual question does not figure in my account, because I reject the Newtonian premise on which it rests. Rather than A getting B to do something that B would not otherwise do, social relations of power typically involve both A and B doing what they ordinarily would do. The structure of education, not teachers, causes students to act like students, just as it causes teachers to act like teachers. Teachers and students, given their social identities, would not otherwise do anything but what teachers and students regularly do. And neither a conflict of revealed preferences, nor of objective interests, must be discovered in order to attribute power to these roles.

As Lukes recognizes, a relation of power can exist even in the absence of an empirical conflict of revealed preferences. However, contrary to Lukes, a relation of power can also exist in the absence of a conflict of objective interests. It may well be the case that my power over my students is in their best interest, but the relationship is not for that reason any less one of domination and subordination. Lukes' own formulation would seem to deny this, opening him up to the charges of vanguardism.[56] However, to say that the use of the concept of power does not logically require recourse to the concept of interest in the way Lukes argues is not to deny that the idea of interest has a role to play in the analysis of power. As power is determined by social structure, so too is interest.

We must be clear about what interest means, for it has at least three meanings that must be distinguished. The first meaning refers to the revealed, or subjective, preferences actually held by individuals. In this sense, as I have suggested, the concept is not epistemically necessary to claims about social power. Different individuals have different preferences. Some may like their social role. Some may not. Some may not and yet prefer to do nothing about it. We can talk about the structure of power in the classroom without reference to the preferences of the students, who are subordinate even if they prefer to remain so. This is not to deny that people's preferences are causally important, only to question Dahl's view of why they are.

The second meaning is Lukes' idea of objective interest, i.e. what really is in the interest, or good, of an agent whether he thinks so or not. I have argued that we need not have recourse to this concept in order to locate a relation of power, for the peasant with a gun to her head is subordinate even if collectivization is in her interest. While I believe that we can thus talk about power independent of the issue of objective interests, I do not believe that the concept is unintelligible or irrelevant, as many of Lukes' critics have claimed.[57] We will return to this issue.

These two usages have preoccupied theorists in the debate about power, but the idea of interest may also be understood in a third way. I will call this "real interests" and define it as those norms, values, and purposes implicit in the practice of social life and associated with social roles as principles of action.[58] So understood, interests are real because they are causally effective in practice in a sense in which objective interests are not. To return to the teacher-student example: Professor X may have a preference for extreme discipline in her class; she may have an objective interest, as a pedagogue, in teaching a seminar; but as a college English teacher she has a real interest in teaching a particular body of work within the guidelines of the university (grades, exams, schedules, room assignments, etc.). This is the interest that is shared by college English teachers in the university system as such. Similarly, her students may prefer to read *Rolling Stone* magazine; they may have an objective interest in reading Shakespeare; but as students in the university system they have a real interest in going to class, somehow fulfilling the course requirements, and getting college credit.

What I have called real interests obviously play a central role in the constitution of social power. They are the practical norms that justify and legitimate power relations. The rationality that characterizes the role of the university students, in this example, sustains their subordination. Similarly, while the proletarian may prefer to make more money and may have an objective interest in the transformation of capitalism into socialism, he has, in a capitalistic society, a real interest in finding and keeping a job. The satisfaction of his preferences must be tailored to this and thus despite his objective interests, he is unlikely to challenge the system. Once again, the rationality that characterizes the role of worker in a capitalist society sustains the structure of power.[59]

The analysis of power thus requires an analysis of the real interests and of the ideologies that sustain it. The analysis of ideology and its connection to power played a central role in what Mills called "classical social theory,"[60] and yet ideology has received very little attention in debates among political scientists about power.

I would, at the same time, argue that the analysis of power also requires, in a different sense, an analysis of objective interests. This of course hinges on the question of the relationship between fact and value, and of description versus evaluation, in social analysis. Many of Lukes' critics, particularly Polsby, ridicule any attempt to move from an analysis of social reality to a critique of it. However, many contemporary philosophers have argued that it is both possible and necessary to do so.[61] There are two ways in which writers dealing with power have dealt with this and while both are problematic, there is merit in their interest in an analysis of power with practical, emancipatory intent.

The first strategy is that of Lukes and, more generally, of Habermas, which may be called the neo-Kantian approach. In this view, the analyst of power must judge empirical reality against a postulated ideal condition of autonomous agency. Habermas' ideal speech situation, in which individuals could hypothetically engage in "undistorted communication" about what to do, is paradigmatic.[62] The problem with this approach is not that it enjoins the theorist to make normative judgments about the actions of others. All normative theory, from Plato to Dahl's *A Preface to Democratic Theory*, does this. The problem is that it detaches the analysis of objective interest from the analysis of actual power relations. As in Kant, this view seems to rest on a sharp dichotomy between the real world of causal relations and an ideal world of autonomy. How those subject to relations of power might identify with this ideal condition and be inclined to bring it about is left problematic.[63]

The second strategy is that most often associated with Lukácsian Marxists. If the first strategy fails to bridge the gap between the real and the ideal, the second obliterates it. It does this by positing a teleology whereby those in a subordinate position are either actually or immanently in opposition to the existing system of power.[64] One consequence of this is that discrete acts of resistance, and more ordinary forms of negotiation and conflict, are inaccurately interpreted as signs of a movement toward social transformation. This mistake leads to the moralizing of theoretical analysis and a failure to recognize the coherence and stability of social forms. A second consequence of this is an inattention to real normative questions. Insofar as change is seen as immanent, it becomes less imperative to figure out why change is justified and how the future should be better organized.[65]

Somewhere between the idealism of the first strategy and the historicism of the second lies the terrain within which the analysis of power can properly broach the question of objective interest. Normative theory, as an analysis of what forms of social life are just and legitimate, must always address questions of actual social practice and historical possibility, yet it can never be reduced to a mere corollary of descriptive analysis. And it is only at the limiting case that the conclusions of normative theory become causally effective as the objective of a real social group.

Conclusion

I have argued that the three faces of power debate falters on its shared premise of behavioralism and that social power is better conceived as those powers distributed by the various enduring structural relationships in society and exercised by individuals and groups based on their location in a given structure. I would like to conclude by suggesting some implications of my argument for empirical research.

First, the argument of this chapter is a critique of a metatheoretical debate about the concept of power, not of the actual research done by the participants in the debate. It seems clear that the debate has failed as a methodological agenda for empirical research. More interesting is the possibility that the participants themselves, in their own empirical analyses of power, did not strictly employ their formal concepts. Books such as Dahl's *Polyarchy* and his more recent *Dilemmas of Pluralist Democracy* do not conform in any obvious sense to the canons of behavioralism. And even *Who Governs?* talks about the power of Mayor Lee of New Haven in terms much closer to the view I have developed in this essay.[66]

Second, there is a great deal of empirical and theoretical analysis that already presupposes the view of power I have developed. Debates in contemporary feminist theory about patriarchy, for example, center around the structural relations of gender and how they distribute power and opportunities between men and women.[67] Marxism as a theoretical tradition has always treated power in structural terms. "Capital," as Marx puts it, "is a social power."[68] In their analyses of the labor process and changing forms of capital accumulation, contemporary Marxists have emphasized the structural dimensions of class domination, focusing particularly on the question of ideology. Moreover, the traditional Marxian emphasis on class struggle involves a view of the contingency and negotiation of the exercise of power akin to the one I have suggested.[69]

I would also suggest that Mills' *The Power Elite* can be seen as presupposing a realist view of power. Mills insists throughout the book that the power of the elite is structurally determined, that they are a group "in positions to make decisions having major consequences" and that "behind such men and behind the events of history, linking the two, are the major institutions of modern society. These hierarchies of state and corporation constitute the means of power."[70] This is not to endorse Mills' theory or to paper over the kinds of evidentiary weaknesses that Dahl and others have pointed out. But it is to suggest that to dismiss it as meaningless and metaphysics, as the behavioralist critics did, does not do it justice. There is a difference between questionable science and nonscience, a difference ignored, all too often self-righteously, by behavioralists.

In terms of contemporary debates within political science, the theory of the state is that area that is most illuminated by the realist view. The advent of behavioralism led to the decline of the state as an object of theory (the real state, of course, grew into, among other things, a massive financial supporter of behavioral research). Lasswell and Kaplan, advocating behavioralist approaches, insisted on seeing "such political abstractions as 'state' and 'sovereignty' in terms of concrete influence and control."[71] David Easton, in *The Political System* and other works, unleashed an assault on the metaphysical connotations of the concept of the state, preferring instead the concept of the political system as one more amenable to the development of empirically deductive theories.[72] It is common knowledge that the concept of the state is experiencing a renaissance. Political economists, democratic theorists, and theorists of international relations are all discovering that there is some overarching coherence to the institutions of government that is obscured by the concept of the political system. In the face of this renaissance, Easton has reiterated the behavioralist critique in a recent issue of *Political Theory*. The specific target was the Greek Marxist, Nicos Poulantzas, but the enemy was really the concept of the state. As Easton argued, either the state is the empirical behaviors of government officials, "or it is some kind of undefined and undefinable essence, a 'ghost in the machine,' knowable only through its variable manifestations."[73] This argument should sound familiar. It forms the basis of Popper's critique of Marxism and of Polsby's book on power. Easton is clear that the validity of the concept of the state rests on questions about the nature of science.

But what Easton fails to see is that all science is based on reasoning from empirical phenomena to their causal mechanisms. In this respect, the concept of the state is no different from the concept of a magnetic field—we cannot observe such a field, and yet the concept has definite meaning and denotes a hypothetically real structure with real effects. Theorists of the state have begun to recognize that conceptual issues of the sort raised in this article are central to their own research. Thus Bob Jessop, in *The Capitalist State,* discusses the state as a set of structural relationships that distribute power to government officials. As he writes: "The state is a set of institutions that cannot, qua institutional ensemble, exercise power." The powers of the state are, rather, exercised separately, by specific officials, occupying specific institutional roles. But, he insists, a theory of this power must be a theory of the structural relations that distribute the power so exercised.[74]

No metatheoretical analysis of the sort presented here can ever decide substantive questions in social theory. The belief that such an analysis could so function was one of the great mistakes and great tragedies of behavioralism. In its empiricist zeal, it stigmatized a great deal of valuable substantive work on purely formal grounds. The point of this paper is not to repeat this error by once again providing an, albeit different, litmus test with which to judge who deserves the badge of scientific approval. It is, rather, to expose some fundamental weaknesses in the prevailing debate about power, in the hope that social researchers can now proceed to examine social structure uninhibited by the stigma of metaphysics. In exposing the mobilization of bias underlying the three faces of power debate, I hope, in some small way, to empower those theorists who have been constrained by the power of empiricism.

Chapter 4

Game Theory and Power Theory:
A Critical Comparison

 *Wolfgang Balzer*

The last decade has witnessed the application of game theory to social science. Created by abstracting from social games like chess and bridge, von Neumann's model was seen to be applicable to more "serious" social phenomena as well: to situations with two or more agents with conflicting goals and with the ability to influence each other. Starting essentially from prisoner's dilemma (see below), research focused on models capturing "socially rational" behavior. After Michael Taylor's demonstration that such models were possible in terms of super-games,[1] a veritable explosion took place in sociological research using game-theoretic models.[2] By now it seems fair to say that those branches of social science that deal with interaction and conflict in exact ways are dominated by the game-theoretic approach.

On the other hand, studies of power continued to develop with the same slow pace they had for centuries, articulated mainly by practitioners of politics and by philosophers, and more recently by more professional scientists.[3] In contrast to the flourishing of game theory, however, no comparable evolution took place in models of power. Only recently, an account by Thomas Wartenberg opened a broader perspective that may be said to combine more operational approaches (like Dahl's) and "internal" conceptual analysis with comprehensive views of social reality.[4] Wartenberg's account can be shown to combine most other approaches to power and to provide a frame in which all other special forms of power can be defined.[5] In addition, it is presented in a conceptually clear, analytic form. For these reasons I will take his approach as *the* representative of power theory.

My aim in this paper is to analyze and compare the two approaches—the game-theoretic and that of power—from the perspective of applications in social science. The result of comparison will be stated in the form of a somewhat provocative thesis of incommensurability, and the analyses performed will be used to justify that thesis.

My account of both approaches will concentrate on the *basic* models (or most general theoretical assumptions) used on each side. It is not possible to consider all the specializations that have developed. This will not affect my results, however, because the two approaches may be conceptualized as *theory-nets* in which more special models, assumptions, or "pictures" are all built on one fundamental, basic model such that most questions of comparison between the full theory-nets in a precise sense reduce to questions of how the basic models are related.[6]

Game Theory

The classical social application of game theory is the prisoner's dilemma. Two individuals, p_1 and p_2, are arrested, say for the illegal possession of guns. The district attorney believes that they robbed a bank the other night, but he has no evidence. Both are put into jail in isolation and accused of bank robbery. The district attorney proposes the following deal to each p_i individually. If p_i confesses the bank robbery and p_j does not confess, p_i will get the preferred status of a chief witness and go to jail for one week. If p_j does confess, p_i will go to jail for five years; if neither confesses, they will both go to jail for one month for possession of a gun. Thus, each prisoner p_i is faced with the following dilemma. If his friend (p_j, $j \neq i$) confesses, p_i is also inclined to confess, otherwise he alone will get five years while his friend gets by with one week. If the friend does not confess, then p_i is still more inclined to confess for this will get him the minimal punishment. So whatever his friend may do, p_1 is inclined to confess. The situation is completely symmetric, so p_j has the same inclinations. If both of them follow this line of reasoning dictated by individual rationality in the state of isolation, both of them will confess. This, however, leads both of them to the *worst* result they can achieve in that situation. So the dilemma is that applying the principle of individual rationality obtains the worst result, while a better result can only be obtained at the cost of "irrational" behavior.

In order to analyze this situation, game-theoretic apparatus uses the notions of *individuals,* of *strategies* or *alternatives,* and of *preference* or *utility.* We will not deal here with iteration of moves or with "mixed strategies." For each individual p_1 there is a set of alternatives (moves, actions, courses of actions, sequences of moves) comprising exactly those that are entertainable by p_i in the situation to be modeled. It is not necessary to spell out precisely what is meant by entertainable here. Usually, the set is larger than the set of alternatives actually entertained, but smaller than the set of physically possible ones. It is usually restricted by the social and institutional frame in which the individual finds himself.[7] In the example above, p_1 and p_2 both have two alternatives: to confess or not to confess.

Each choice of an alternative by actor p_i amounts to some action of p_i that leads to subsequent events or states causally determined by this action. Out of the sequence of subsequent events, one distinguished event or state is picked out and made the subject of an evaluation by actor p_i; we call it the *resulting state.* So each choice of an alternative by p_i leads to some resulting state that is then evaluated by p_i; p_i reflects, or is assumed to know anyway, how much the resulting state is worth to her. In other words, there is a utility function for each individual p_i that assigns some value to each state resulting from p_i's choice of any alternative and the corresponding action.

The crucial point is that p_i's choice and action do not *fully* cause the resulting state; p_i's action is only a partial cause, that is, one event among others, which only *together* cause the resulting state. Because of the interactive nature of the situation, different moves of other agents will lead to different resulting states for a given individual p_i even though p_i sticks to his choice. In other words, one alternative chosen by p_i will lead to different resulting states, depending on which alternatives are chosen by the other agents.

The example cited makes this very clear. If p_1 chooses the alternative to confess, the resulting state that he evaluates depends on the choice of p_2. If p_2 also chooses to confess, then the state resulting for p_1 from his choice is five years in jail. But if p_2 chooses not to confess, the state resulting for p_1 from p_1's action (to confess) is very different, namely one week in jail. The same holds for p_2, of course.

As the resulting state is (assumed to be) uniquely determined by the sum of all the individual's actions, game theorists assign utilities to the sums of such actions rather than to the resulting states. Once each individual has made his choice and taken the corresponding action, the resulting state will evolve "automatically" (causally). If there are n ($n \geq 2$) individuals, the "sum" or combination of their choices is represented by an n-tuple, $\langle a_1, \ldots, a_n \rangle$, each a_i representing the choice of individual p_i. Formally, then, the arguments of the utility functions are taken from the space of all such n-tuples. For each individual p_i and each combination $\langle a_1, \ldots, a_n \rangle$ of choices there is a utility value $U_i(a_1, \ldots, a_n)$ expressing the utility that individual p_i has from the state resulting for him from combination $\langle a_1, \ldots, a_n \rangle$. In the cited example, we may take the lengths of the periods in jail as indicators of (inverse) utility values: the longer the period in jail, the smaller the utility of that resulting state. In general, however, the utilities of one common resulting state need not be the same for different individuals.

In summary, a basic *model* of game theory is made up of the following items:

1. a set of individuals $p_1, \ldots, p_n$
2. n corresponding sets $A_1, \ldots, A_n$ of alternatives, one for each individual
3. n utility functions $U_1, \ldots, U_n$, which are all defined on the set of all n-tuples $\langle a_1, \ldots, a_n \rangle$ of elements of $A_1, \ldots, A_n$, and which all take real numbers as values.

This material has to have a special form in order to pass muster as a proper model. In game theory the basic assumption of form is that the individuals choose rationally, in some sense. There is no unique explication of what a rational choice for p_i is in a frame given by items 1–3. The general idea is that the individuals choose such that the resulting states (or rather the corresponding n-tuples $\langle a_1, \ldots, a_n \rangle$ of actions, choices, or alternatives, as just explained) have some kind of "equilibirum property." The notion of equilibrium, in turn, may be defined along different lines, which in general are not equivalent. The most commonly used notion is that of *Nash equilibrium*. A combination of choices $\langle a_1, \ldots, a_n \rangle$ is a point of Nash equilibrium if and only if for any $i \leq n$, any deviation $\langle a_1, \ldots, a_i^*, \ldots, a_n \rangle$ with $a_1^* \neq a_1$ would result in some decrease of utility for p_1:

$$U_i(a_1, \ldots, a_i^*, \ldots, a_n) < U_i(a_1, \ldots, a_n)$$

One way to formulate the axiom of rationality is to say that each individual should choose, or will choose, an alternative that belongs to some point of Nash equilibrium, provided the game has such a point. In order to turn this into a more descriptive form we might add to the model, for each individual p_i, one alternative $a_i0 \in A_i$ which is interpreted as that alternative which p_i actually chooses when the game is played. Collecting all these distinguished alternatives we obtain an n-tuple $<a_10, \ldots, a_n0>$, and the axion of rationality basic in game theory says that this n-tuple *is* a point of Nash equilibrium. It should be noted that game theorists usually do not make explicit this move from the rule of behavior to a descriptive formulation.

Instead of going into details of refinements, we have to concentrate on a more fundamental feature inherent explicitly or implicitly in the basic models described above, namely the status of the utility functions. Utilities are difficult to determine. It seems fair to say that up to now there is not a single method for a practical determination of utilities in "real-life" situations. There are some experimental determinations in laboratory situations, but it is not clear in what way these can be made to function in real-life situations without substantially changing such situations.[8] Moreover, it is common sense that utilities are not stable over time: people may change their taste, and thus their utility.

In game theory utilities are assumed to be given and stable. In the light of the previous considerations these assumptions are rather strong and unrealistic. We may rephrase the assumptions in terms of the notion of the *rules of the game*. Each game essentially is given by its rules; the only possible variations of a game are who participates and how many participate. In the conceptual frame of a simple game as described above there are two components that together make up the rules of such a game.

Let us look at these components first in the special case of social games. Here, we first have the different alternatives open to each individual as determined by the rules of the game. If a player had some alternative not allowed by the rules, we would not say that she plays according to these rules or that she plays the game given by these rules. Second, there are the utility functions telling how much the players get out of the game. In the case of social games, game theorists often speak of *payoff functions* instead of utilities. Each player's payoff is determined by the rules of the game, so the payoff functions are part of, or constitutive of, the rules of the game. Since there are no other components in the basic models, we may say that the sets of alternatives together with the utility (or payoff) functions in social games make up the rules of the game. This analysis is by no means forced. It makes precise our intuitive notion of the rules of the game in a natural way.

If we pass from social games to games in general, this definition of the rules of the game no longer seems self-evident, and thus needs further explanation. To see that the rules of the game may be identified with the sets of alternatives and utility functions also in the general case, we have to further reflect on the notion of the rules of the game. What are the rules of the game on a more informal level? They are *rules*, of course, but this is a difficult concept, and we have nothing to say about it. Second, they determine the procedure of the game. This does not mean that once we know the rules we know precisely how the game will proceed. Certain choices can be made at every step. But the set of possible alternatives from which one has to choose is determined by the rules of the game. Moreover, the rules tell who wins and how much. Again, this is not determined a priori but depends on the actual course of the game. For a given course, however, the rules determine the gains and losses in a strict sense. Now if, in a general model of game theory, we look for the components that determine the course of the game, we find those already mentioned: alternatives and utilities. These two components work together to determine the course of the game, and there is no further component in the model with such an effect. This justifies identifying the two components as the rules of the game even in those general cases in which ordinary language would not apply the term. In the prisoner's dilemma, the rules of the game are given externally. They consist of the possible choices (to confess or not to confess) and the different lengths of the periods in jail. Sometimes one normally speaks of rules of the game also in such contexts, but this is metaphorical. Note that the prisoners do not participate in the game voluntarily.

For the justification of our final claim it will be important that game theory assures that the rules of the game are given and must not be changed by the players while the game is continuing. This has to be stressed because game theorists, when confronted with this line of reasoning, tend to belittle the assumption that the rules are given and to give an image according to which the rules of the game have a weaker and more flexible status. We have to be aware of the kind of evidence relevant for deciding such an issue. The evidence here cannot consist of a statement of one single game theorist who imagines a new theory having some notions in common with game theory, and who for whatever reason wants to call it "game theory." The evidence here can come only from historical and metascientific studies of the literature and self-representation of the whole group of game theorists. On such a basis we may claim that the rules of the game in fact have the status of being given externally, or in advance. Game theory presupposes these rules; it does not aim at introducing, defining, or giving meaning to that notion. There is no space to argue for this in metascientific detail; we will only cite some authorities: "The rules of the game, however, are absolute commands. If they are ever infringed, then the whole transaction by definition ceases to be the game described by those rules."[9] "A game is distinguished from a real situation of conflict by being performed according to completely determined *rules*. . . . In order to make the game accessible to mathematical analysis the *rules of the game* have to be formulated exactly."[10] "The general concept of a game therefore comprises the following three elements: (1) the sequence of steps decided on by persons or by chance; (2) the level of information of the players; and (3) a payoff function."[11] These citations show that the rules of the game are essential to the game's identity: to change the rules means to change the game, that is, to play a *different* game.

There is another allied assumption of game theory that usually is also ignored. To see this assumption, let us look at the typical case in a social game in which all the players accept the rules of the game before they start playing. This is a voluntary act on the part of each player. If a player is forced to participate, the payoff values derived from the rules of the game may be quite different from her "real" utilities. For instance, it may be of highest utility for her to lose the game if she knows her opponent has executed other winners in the past. To accept the rules of the game voluntarily is an indication of independence and of being roughly at the same level as the other players. As soon as one player is dependent on, or much inferior to, the other player, there is some probability that her utilities are not adequately represented by the payoff function determined by the rules.

These considerations suggest the following broad corollary. The rules of the game will be respected in greater degree the more equal and independent of each other the participants are. We can express this in the form of a slogan: Given utilities indicate equality and independence. This is admittedly a very vague formulation. There is no space here to argue in detail for the connection between given rules and equality and independence. We have to leave the issue with the status of intuitive plausibility. To give it more force, the point may be illustrated by the flexibility of individual utilities. A person's utility function may change for various reasons, among which we certainly must include emotions. A player recognizing that the rules of the game are very (un)favorable to her may change her utility function just for emotional reasons. Such emotions need not, but may, indicate strong dependencies or strong inequalities. Conversely, the presence of inequalities or dependencies may indicate that utilities are not given and stable, but may quickly change.

If this analysis is correct, the assumption of givenness of the rules of the game indicates another, more implicit, assumption: that the different players in a game are independent of each other and are roughly of equal status with respect to the game. Of course, the notions of independence and equality of status have here a large degree of variability and are further complicated by being relative to the particular game. A master may play a game of chess with his slave. However, we think that these assumptions have an important role in delineating the intended applications of game theory from other, contrived applications. For example, it seems beside the point to analyze a fight for life or death as a game (though this is conceptually possible and is even done by game theorists).

Theory of Power

In order to describe Wartenberg's theory of power,[12] let us also begin with an example. Consider some individual p_1, a politician, whose history includes a dark side. Another individual, p_2, coming to know about this talks to p_1, threatens to tell the story to the local newspaper and in this way manages to get a job in the city administration. Clearly, this is an instance of p_2 exercising power over p_1—though perhaps not of the most brute kind.

As in game theory, each of the two individuals has a set of possible alternatives before him, any one of which he may choose to the exclusion of the others. It is difficult to characterize such a set *in abstracto*. Certainly, any alternative has to be physically feasible; given the individual's means, we may imagine all possible causal consequences following from any action made possible by these means. However, the difficulty then is pushed back to determining what are an individual's means. To allow for any physically possible means would be unnecessarily general. In the example, p_2 might be much stronger and thus able to beat p_1. However, because of their social context this would not increase his probability of getting a job and therefore such an alternative need not be considered from the beginning. In general, a characterization of the alternatives open to an individual will be strongly theoretical and will require consideration of the social system and the individual's special manner of socialization.[13] In the example the politician's space of actions may be taken to consist of four alternatives. First, he might do nothing and act as if no threat had been made. Second, he might wait but start preparing some campaign for survival in case the thing gets published. Third, he might behave "cooperatively," and use his influence to get p_2 a job in the city administration. Fourth, he might try to retaliate and threaten p_2 in some way. It is clear that many other possibilities might be considered, but the level of detail and of relevance depends on the concrete case.

As a second theoretical component there is an *assessment* of the respective situation by that individual. Assessment has two components. First, it consists of an *understanding* of the situation and of the different alternatives on the individual's side. This is a basic term from the hermeneutic tradition, and a difficult one. It reflects at least two major human properties: intentionality and the ability of interpretation. Any understanding of a situation depends on the interpreter's intentions. If I am in a hurry to reach a plane, my understanding of getting stuck in the subway is likely to focus on the incompetence of the workers, while in another situation I might see the incident as caused by a technical mistake, such as a short circuit. Similar differences of understanding result from differences in interpretation. As a scientific interpretation my understanding of a rain dance is one of an exotic, esthetic cultural event, whereas as a magical interpretation, the event becomes a major social and political issue. Interpretation may depend on intention, and vice versa. Usually, however, interpretation further varies with other parameters, in particular with knowledge and special forms of socialization. Whether the same holds for intentions is less clear, and in our opinion very doubtful. Technically, the effect of understanding is to filter out a subset of alternatives from the set of all possible ones as those that are relevant and seriously considered by the individual. In the example, we may assume that the politician's intention is not so friendly that he would get p_2 a job without the threat. Positively, his intention by and large may be to have an efficient administration in which performance is the major criterion for getting a job or losing it. His understanding of the situation is also influenced by this intention. He interprets p_2's approach as a threat, which he might not if p_2 were a close relative or if the whole administration were known for being completely corrupt. In such an environment, the publication in the newspaper probably would not create any problem for him. We will not attempt to analyze more formally the notion of understanding in the following.

The second component of assessment consists of a *valuation* of the given, understood alternatives. Formally, a valuation may be represented by means of a utility function. Each alternative gets assigned some numerical value. On the basis of these numbers, comparisons can be made of alternatives that by themselves are hard to compare, and rational decisions may be made by applying one or the other formal criteria of rationality. As was pointed out above, numerical representation of values or utilities is difficult to achieve in practice. If two numbers have been assigned, then the difficulty must have been overcome in the way in which these numbers were assigned. Since no real-life methods exist here, the real difficulties cannot be said to have been solved. In the example, the politician's valuation is hard to tell because this amounts to determining which of the four alternatives he prefers. If he is an active, aggressive character, alternative four (retaliation) might be his preferred reaction; if he is lazy, alternative one (do nothing) might be preferred; and so on.

In the context of the present stage of power analysis, there is no need for quantitative analysis. However, in order to facilitate comparison we take each individual p_i's valuation as represented by a function V_i that maps alternatives into real numbers. We require V_i to be a partial function only, so that some alternatives may pass unevaluated.

Following Wartenberg, the three components, alternatives, understanding, and valuation, may be said to form an individual's *action-environment*. An action-environment then has the form

$$<p,A,UN,V>$$

where A is individual p's set of alternatives, UN p's understanding, and V p's valuation of a given situation.

In general, the action-environments of different individuals may be rather different; it would be too unrealistic to require them to be very similar or even identical for similar individuals. However, some weak form of similarity constraint seems realistic and appropriate. If individuals have been brought up in the same social group under very similar conditions and have acquired similar social positions and roles, there is some plausibility to the idea that their action-environments will have some similarity, just as in microeconomics the use of such "stability assumptions" is important because it yields strong empirical claims (at the risk, of course, of being too idealized or "false").

We now may describe the basic model of power theory. It captures situations in which one person exercises power over another person. The fundamental axiom characterizing such a model says that one of the individuals exercises power over the other. This informal requirement may be made precise in the conceptual frame outlined in the following way:

p *exercises power over* p* if and only if p intentionally changes p*'s action-environment in a fundamental manner.[14]

Basically, therefore, to exercise power means to change some action-environment. Any change consists of a transition from one state to another, so we arrive at a quasistatic representation in which change of an action-environment is described by two succeeding action environments $E(b)$ and $E(a)$ (b and a as in before and after) such that the latter is different from the former. For given individual p_i let us write $E_i(b)$ and $E_i(a)$ to denote p_i's action-environments before and after some change. We may identify the two action-environments with that change itself, provided they are different from each other. So we define a *change of action-environment* to be a pair $<E(b),E(a)>$ of two different action-environments of one individual such that $E(a)$ follows after $E(b)$ in time. Using this ontology, a model of power theory consists of a set $\{p,p^*\}$ of two individuals and four action-environments $E(b),E(a),E^*(b),E^*(a)$:

$$<\{p,p^*\},E(b),E(a),E^*(b),E^*(a)>$$

where $E(b)$, $E(a)$ are the two succeeding action-environments of individual p, $E^*(b)$, $E^*(a)$ are those of individual p^*, and $E(b)$, $E^*(b)$ are simultaneous. In order to be a proper model, such an entity has to satisfy the above-stated axiom of change, i.e., one of the individuals exercises power over the other. If, for instance, p exercises power over p^* this means that p intentionally changes p^*'s action-environment in a fundamental manner, the change being represented by $<E^*(b),E^*(a)>$.

The requirement of the change being fundamental can be read in two ways. It may be read as a threshold for degrees of change to be overcome in order to constitute an exertion of power, or it may be read as making the definition fuzzy. We do not prefer either of these options. The question may be a matter of further development of the theory. "Intentional" is necessary to exclude unintended changes from counting as exercises of power. If I injure somebody by crashing into her car unintentionally, we do not say that I exercised power over her though the result may be a very fundamental change of her action-environment.

On the basis of the defined notion of exercising power it is easy to introduce the notion of *having power* by means of counterfactuals. *p has power* over p^* if and only if there exist situations in which p could exercise power over p^* by acting accordingly.

"Change" may occur in one of three types or combinations, depending upon the three components making up an action-environment. First, the set of alternatives may be changed, existing alternatives may be taken away, new alternatives may be added, or both possibilities may occur in the same step. Second, the understanding of the situation may be changed. And third, the valuation may be changed. Each of these changes may occur in isolation, but mixed cases also are possible: if a new alternative is added, it may be valuated in the same process. This amounts to a simultaneous change of the valuation function. In the above example, the politician's set of alternatives may be seen as being enlarged. Though this sounds counterintuitive at first sight, we think it is the correct way to see the situation. The "new" alternatives coming into play are those different from the first one, those in which he reacts to the threat in some way. Though these alternatives were physically possible to him even before the threat was made, it is unlikely that he would have thought of them or would have taken them into account in his actions. Of course, the situation may also be described by including those alternatives in the set of alternatives from the beginning and assuming that the politician did not understand them or, if he did, did not evaluate them. The most natural description, however, seems to be one in which they do not occur originally.

The models introduced capture the most basic form of exercise of power. Other interesting forms are obtained by adding further, special requirements, for instance on the particular way in which the action-environments are changed. In this way, the most important *forms of power*, force, coercion, influence, manipulation, may be characterized.[15]

A final remark about the model is that the axiom of change essentially is antisymmetrical. Only one of the two individuals, the so called *superordinate agent* (formally it does not matter which one) exercises power, and in this case the action-environment of the other individual, who is called the *subordinate agent*, is changed. The model does not specify the superordinate agent's action by which she causes the subordinate agent's action-environment to change. The superordinate agent's action-environment does not play any role in this formulation.

In formal terms, however, symmetry is not excluded. In a model of the theory of power it may well be the case that one individual p exercises power over the other individual p^*, and simultaneously p^* exercises power over p. Such kinds of symmetry in real applications usually reveal different forms or kinds of power exercised in the two directions. For instance, p may exercise power in the form of coercion over p^*, while p^* at the same time manipulates p (stupid master p and clever slave p^*). Inclusion of the superordinate agent's action-environment in the models provides a frame for insertion of the items just mentioned.

Comparison

There is not enough space here for accounts of both theories' historical developments, which certainly would further the comparison. We will confine ourselves to the systematic level on which there are different criteria of comparison: formal structure, method of application, nature of objects, problems, problem-solving capacity, empirical content, success. This list is certainly not complete, and it must be admitted that the theory of power described in the previous section does not yet have the status of a generally acknowledged theory. This, together with the fact that it is not completely formalized, suggests relaxing the standards of comparison as far as formal structure is concerned. At the present stage, results of comparison that can be logically proved would not be ultimately convincing because one always might try (and succeed) to escape by changing the power theory. Nevertheless, formal comparison is the most important dimension of comparison we have, so it will be discussed first.

Consider two models of the respective theories, a model of game theory of the form $<\{p_1, \ldots, p_n\}, A_1, \ldots, A_n, U_1, \ldots, U_n>$, and a model $<\{p,p^*\}, E(b), E(a), E^*(b), E^*(a)>$ of power theory. In the light of the interpretations of the different components of these models, some formal identifications are possible. First of all, the individuals in both models can be the same. The possible difference in number of individuals is not essential; for the sake of comparison we may restrict ourselves to models consisting of just two individuals on either side. Next, let us look at the sets of alternatives attached to the individuals. The alternatives themselves may be compared without difficulty. Any alternative open to an individual in game theory may be taken as an alternative for the same individual in a model of power theory, and vice versa. However, in the model of power theory each individual has two sets of alternatives, one before and one after power is exercised. The game-theoretic model, on the other hand, does not contain a distinction of before and after. Starting from the game-theoretic model, we may try to build up a power-theoretic model by taking over the individuals and by taking the game-theoretic sets of alternatives to be the power-theoretic sets of alternatives present *before* power is exercised. The problem then is how to fix the sets of alternatives *afterward*. Of course, simple identification would not work, for in power theory, the two sets of a person's alternatives before and after may be different.

However, formal comparison is not restricted to a term-by-term identification. It may involve further constructions using the full theoretical pictures of either theory to be compared. In the present case, it seems possible to construct reasonable sets of alternatives before and after out of one game-theoretical set of alternatives by using the additional structure of the game-theoretical model. Consider first the case in which individual p_i's set of alternatives after power is exercised is smaller than that before; i.e., the effect of exercising power was to eliminate one or more of p_i's alternatives (by force, for example). In this case the following kind of identification suggests itself. We may look for a game-theoretic model in which the sets of alternatives are just those occurring in the power-theoretic model "before." Now for any alternative to be eliminated and for any state resulting from that alternative in the sense of the section on game theory, p_i's utility should be smaller than that for any alternative not to be eliminated and for any state resulting from the latter. In other words, the states resulting from those alternatives to be eliminated have minimal utility for p_i irrespective of what the other individual chooses to do. Taking such a model of game theory (which can be easily defined), we may identify the sets of alternatives "after" in the power-theoretic model with the sets obtained by taking away the minimal alternatives just described in the game-theoretic model. If we manage to find a game-theoretic model in which those minimal alternatives are uniquely determined (which we always can find), we can construct the power-theoretic sets of alternatives out of the sets of game-theoretic alternatives in the way just described. A similar kind of construction may be performed in the second possible case in which exercise of power leads to an extension of the set of alternatives present before.

These constructions show that different power-theoretic sets of alternatives can be obtained out of one set of game-theoretic alternatives if we choose appropriate models possessing further properties on the game-theoretic side. Of course, the construction cannot succeed for *any given* pair of models. Nevertheless, the method provides rather strong identifications: For any given game-theoretic model (with two individuals), we may trivially find some power-theoretic model such that the sets of alternatives "before" in the latter are identical with the sets of alternatives in the former. Conversely, for any given power-theoretic model we may find a game-theoretic model with additional special properties such that the sets of alternatives of the first model before and after can be constructed out of those of the second model as described above.

A third component of the two models that might be seen as a candidate for formal comparison consists of the utility functions and valuation functions. Here things become difficult. Purely formally, the problem is this. If alternatives are identified along the lines just considered, then the arguments of a game-theoretic utility function and a power-theoretic valuation function are different. Whereas the valuation function takes a single alternative as argument, the utility function needs a resulting state in the technical sense, i.e., an n-tuple of alternatives. If the alternatives are identified one by one in two corresponding models, such identification is impossible for utility and valuation functions. Still, we may try to construct one from the other as we previously did for the alternatives themselves. Starting from a power-theoretic model, we might construct a corresponding game-theoretic model as follows. Individuals and alternatives (before, say) are taken over as above. We define each p_i's utility function, U_i, as being independent of other individuals' choices; i.e., if $<a_1, \ldots ,a_n>$ and $<a_1^*, \ldots ,a_n^*>$ are resulting states such that $a_1=a_1^*$, then $U_i(a_1, \ldots ,a_n)=U_i(a_1^*, \ldots ,a_n^*)$. A simple way to achieve this is to define $U_i(a_1, \ldots ,a_n)=V_i(a_1)$. In the game theoretic model thus constructed, the utility functions cannot be strictly identified with those of the power-theoretic model. They can be regarded, however, as inessential formal variants of the latter. Intuitively, the utility p_i gets from a list of choices $<a_1, \ldots ,a_n>$ is just the value V_i that p_i attaches to the alternative a_i from her own set of alternatives. For this value the choices of other individuals do not matter. It seems possible to obtain game-theoretic "descriptions" of every power-theoretic model in this way. Conversely, if we start with a game-theoretic model, we can get a power-theoretic "image" by giving up a one-by-one identification of alternatives and simply taking the power-theoretic alternatives to be the n-tuples of alternatives from the model of game theory. This yields a straightforward identification of utilities and values by defining the valuation functions to be the same as the utility functions.

In summary, there are quite substantial possibilities of formal comparison and identification between models of game theory and power theory. They indicate that both theories have the same or very similar applications and objects. The meanings of the terms "individual" and "alternative" may be kept unchanged, and the meanings of "utility" and "valuation" may be identified to a large extent. These facts agree with the informal observation that both theories deal with similar kinds of phenomena—at least in a large area of overlap. This may be expressed by saying that there are many real situations or systems that can be captured simultaneously by models of game and power theory. The situation of the prisoner's dilemma gives rise to a power-theoretic model if we concentrate on the district attorney's exercise of power over the two criminals, and the politician's blackmail may easily be analyzed to yield a model of game theory.

On the other hand, it is difficult to obtain a satisfactory, complete comparison that would show that one theory can be completely "reproduced" in the other. The previous discussion was "local," i.e., two corresponding terms were considered without looking at the impact of their comparison on the other parts of the models. We did not take into account whether the identifications considered are all compatible with each other and did not ask whether they are compatible with the basic axioms characterizing the models on each side. A full intertheoretical relation would imply that not only one theory's terms can be matched with, or constructed out of, those of the other theory, but also that the basic axioms are related by implication, at least in addition to some translation or identification of the terms involved. It is obvious that neither theory is a specialization or a theoretization of the other. It is less clear whether one of them can be reduced in a precise sense to the other.[16] This would require, among other things, a relation of derivability of the axioms. It is far from clear whether the basic axiom of rationality characteristic of game theory as formulated above implies, or is implied by, the basic axiom of change in power theory, even if appropriate constructions of the kind discussed earlier are inserted. Intuitively, this does not seem possible as long as natural kinds of translations of the terms are used. However, it is not easy to say which kinds of translations of one theory's terms into terms of the other are natural.

It is not our aim here to show that one of the theories is fully reducible to the other. This would show that the reduced theory in some sense is more restricted and "poorer" than the other, and in this sense could be replaced by the other one. Rather, the aim of the previous formal comparison was to show that both theories have very much in common: terms, meanings of terms, and a large overlapping set of applications. If this is so, if both theories' models are sufficiently different and if neither theory can be reduced to the other, they are rivals, at least in their domain of overlap. We state this result for later reference:

(1) *Game theory and power theory are rival theories in a large domain of common applications. There are many ways to establish or construct identities between models of the two theories.*

Having stressed these identities, we may now turn to the differences. Clearly, the basic axioms of both theories are rather different from each other, not only in formulation but also in spirit. The game-theoretic axiom of rationality requires that all individuals choose alternatives that make up a point of equilibrium, i.e., alternatives that under the constraints of the game for each individual yield utilities that in some sense can be called maximal. In Nash equilibrium, for instance, they are maximal because any deviation from the chosen alternative would yield a decrease in utility for the individual who deviates. This axiom requires behavior disciplined by the rules of the game: reflection on what the other individuals' alternatives and utilities are and a kind of calculation of one's own best (equilibrium) choice from a rather complicated range of choices. The power-theoretic axiom of change is very different. It cannot be regarded as a rule of behavior; it is purely descriptive. It just states that one individual changes the action-environment of the other. It does not have any implications of rationality or maximization of utility. An exercise of power can be entirely irrational in the sense of yielding utilities that, for both the subordinate and the superordinate agent, are much lower than those resulting from a choice of other alternatives. The axiom of change implies neither strategic consideration of the possibilities of the other agent or agents nor evaluation of one possibility against another. It does not rule out such behavior, of course, but it also does not require it.

It seems difficult to draw some natural link between those two requirements. No translation of either axiom that would turn the translated statement into one derivable from, or implying, the other axiom seems possible. On the other hand, in the light of statement (1) above, there has to be some connection. We may get a better understanding by trying to add each axiom to the frame or surrounding of the other one. First, what would it mean to add the axiom of rationality to that of change? In the model of power theory, there are two places where the axiom of rationality could be added. First, it could be added on the superordinate agent's side, so that her action that causes the change of the other agent's action-environment is rationally chosen, i.e., in a way to maximize her own valuation. Second, the subordinate agent might be required to change her action-environment in a rational way, namely such that the changed environment yields better courses of action than were previously available given the superordinate agent's action. Although it is not clear whether the second possibility still falls under the established paradigm of rational behavior, it is still a genuine possibility. Both these extra assumptions would amount to an additional feature not present in the original models. So power theory might be enriched by assumptions of rationality.

Conversely, there is no clear way to add the assumption of a change of action-environment to those of game theory. If we try to construct something like an individual's action-environment in a given game-theoretic model, we are bound to fail. On the one hand, in a given model there are no means to identify an individuals' valuation of his alternatives. Utilities are given only for resulting states, and from these there is no general way to obtain a valuation of single alternatives. On the other hand, the idea of change is alien to the game-theoretic model, as we argued earlier. Game theory assumes that the rules of the game, including utilities and alternatives, are given and stable.

The two possibilities of adding the assumptions of one theory to those of the other show a certain asymmetry. It is easily possible to add assumptions of rationality to those of power theory, but it is difficult to add assumptions of changes of action-environments to those of game theory. This indicates that power theory starts from a more fundamental level. By adding rationality, we ascend to the higher level of game theory. Conversely, to ascend from game theory to power theory in this way is difficult, as just discussed, and there is no way to descend from game theory to power theory by omitting the assumption of rationality.

This leads to a fundamental difficulty: by adding an assumption of change to game theory, we obtain a set of assumptions that contradicts the basic *presupposition* of game theory, namely that the rules of the game are given and stable. This is a situation whose significance can be seen by reflection on other episodes in science. Feyerabend proposed that two theories related in this way are *incommensurable.* According to his proposal, two theories are called incommensurable if and only if the meaning of their essential descriptive terms rests on contradictory principles.[17] Now principles on which the meaning of a theory's essential descriptive terms rest have traditionally been called presuppositions. So Feyerabend's characterization amounts to saying that the theories' presuppositions contradict each other. By a slight liberalization—allowing for presuppositions as well as for axioms— we obtain the case before us. Two theories are incommensurable if and only if their axioms or presuppositions contradict each other.[18] Of course, this stipulation makes sense only in the presence of a strong overlap of applications of the theories in question as guaranteed by (1) above.

So we have finally arrived at the thesis mentioned in the introduction: game theory and power theory are incommensurable. They are rival approaches to a large array of common phenomena, they have many features (terms and meanings) in common, but their models and basic assumptions are distinct to an extent that makes full comparison difficult if not impossible. Further, the axioms of power theory contradict the presuppositions of game theory. The first three points have emerged in this section. The contradiction of basic axioms and presuppositions is justified by our earlier elaboration of those axioms and the game-theoretic presupposition.

Some objections that rest mainly on misunderstanding may be dealt with right away. A first objection consists in pointing out that game theory can describe exertions of power. This is acknowledged. The point, however, is that it can do so only *in the given frame* of the rules of the game. Since the essence of power consists in changing these rules, game theory fails to grasp the essential feature of power. A more subtle version of this objection refers to forms of influencing each other's choices, in particular in connection with supergames. The tit-for-tat strategy mentioned above, for instance, may be seen as a means by which player p tries to influence her opponent to play cooperatively. Again, the objection does not take into account the presupposition of game theory that the rules of the game are given. In the present example this means that every player's *supergame* strategies are fixed before the game begins and are known to each player. The opponent p^*, therefore, will *not* see tit-for-tat as a means to coax her to play cooperatively. She chooses her strategy in the light of all given strategies of p, one of which is tit-for-tat. If p^* in fact chooses some strategy that takes into account p's playing tit-for-tat, we cannot say that p changed p^*'s action-environment by playing tit-for-tat. p^* chooses her alternative *before* p's move, not knowing which strategy p actually will play. p^*'s only "reaction" (the term is not really appropriate) is a reaction to the given set of p's strategies. Still, it may be said that the existence of suitable strategies or alternatives in a game changes the players' action-environment, for if they were not present, the players would choose differently. This is correct, but in this form the statement is no longer an objection. For now it is not the other player that induces a change, but the existence of certain strategies, i.e., the rules of the game. The initial objection confuses behavior caused by the rules of the game with behavior caused by the other player's behavior. In game theory the latter *cannot* occur.

A second objection is that the theory of power presented here is inadequate because it completely neglects rationality. A "good" theory of power, it is held, should incorporate rational agents from the beginning. To this there are two replies. First, as mentioned already, we easily may add features of rational behavior to the model of power theory. So the present theory may serve as a basis on which a fuller theory of "rational power" may be erected. Second, by not incorporating those features in the basic models, we have a much more general point of departure. Humans may *be* rational, but we certainly do not always *behave* rationally. So the theory of "rational power" envisaged is not a theory more adequate than the one considered here, but only a special case of the latter, or more technically, a theoretization.

A third objection holds that the phenomena of exercising power and of playing games are disjoint, so that the two theories presented here are as well. In other words, the phenomena both theories deal with are different, so the theories have no common applications. If this were so, a claim of incommensurability would make no sense, for incommensurability presupposes that the two theories are rivals and have many common applications. We have to be careful here to make clear what we mean by the phenomena studied by a theory. This term may be used with two different meanings. It may refer to the brute facts, the real systems as given completely independent of the theory in question. But it also may refer to the facts or systems as seen from the point of view of that theory. The brute fact of a man knocking down another man under ordinary conditions is one phenomenon, the situation seen as an exercise of power is another phenomenon, and the situation seen as a scene played realistically for the camera installed further away is a third phenomenon. We admit that a real situation as seen from the point of view of power theory and a real situation as seen from the point of view of game theory may be different. Nevertheless, there is some real situation giving rise to the two interpretations, though we cannot say much about it. But the claim that power theory and game theory have overlapping domains of application is meant in the sense that there are common brute facts or real systems in the first sense just mentioned. By "application" we mean a process starting at a level independent of the theory in question, a process including conceptualization in a first step. A real system may be conceptualized in different ways and thus may give rise to the application of two different theories. In these meanings of "phenomenon" and "application" our assumption of an overlap between game and power theory is rather trivial. Examples of systems to which either theory can be applied have been mentioned already, and the reader can easily come up with others.

The theme of incommensurability has been much discussed recently, and several definitions have been proposed. Kuhn has linked it to more comprehensive entities like *Gestalt,* world-views, and sociopsychological features. Cases of incommensurable theories can be identified at the sociopsychological level by continuous unproductive discussions by proponents on both sides in which no real arguments are advanced and propagandistic elements are substantial. The transition from one such theory to the other, or from one theory's model to a model of the other theory, involves a *Gestalt*-switch, a radical and deep reinterpretation or reorientation. Finally, the two theories are closely associated with different comprehensive views about the world or substantial parts of it.[19]

These further characterizations of incommensurability may be used to further justify our hypothesis. All three features are present in our case. First, there is little communication between scholars of the two camps. I have myself experienced rather emotional and bitter discussions when the comparison was brought up. Second, the transition from one model to the other involves something like a *Gestalt*-switch. Game-theoretic individuals are independent of each other as far as the game is concerned, they are equal to each other as far as the game is concerned, they are free to play the game, and they stick to the rules of the game. The picture usually associated with the notion of power is one of everyone being everyone else's enemy. Individuals are neither independent nor equal. Exercise of power is the open expression of dependence and inequality. The subordinate agents are not free to leave the situation captured by a model of power theory. There are no rules of the game, there is only the rule of the stronger. Third, these strong contrasts point to more comprehensive views about humans and society. Game theory is in line with Hobbesian ideas of social contract as a means to establish social order, while power theory looks at social order essentially as a means to stabilize social stratification.

I do not want to close with passages that give the impression of a political fight rather than of a scientific study. If my analysis is correct, then both theories are rivals insofar as they have a large array of common applications and their models are quite different from each other (perhaps irreducibly). Furthermore, the basic axiom of power theory contradicts the basic presupposition of game theory, which according to Feyerabend means that both theories are incommensurable. However, in contrast to the situation in the natural sciences, incommensurability here does not mean that both theories or their proponents have to fight until one approach is eliminated and replaced. This pattern may be typical for physics, but it is not typical for social science. In physics, incommensurabilities are rather small, and the victorious theory usually incorporates all or most of the achievements of the losing theory. In our case, this is quite different. If one of the two accounts were to replace and eliminate the other one, this would mean a substantial loss. If power theory were simply replaced by game theory, the axiom of change would get lost. In game theory, there is nothing to indicate that individuals try to change each other's action-environments. Conversely, if game theory were given up in favor of power theory, the assumption of rationality inherent in game theory would no longer be made. In this case, one might enrich power theory by such an assumption, but the point is that mere replacement (without enrichment) would not save the basic assumptions of the replaced theory. This situation is not found only in the case of the two theories considered here, it also obtains for other pairs of theories in social science, such as microeconomics versus game theory, microeconomics versus power theory, or Marxian value theory versus any of the other three.

The significance of incommensurability in the social sciences must not be judged by means of its significance in the natural sciences, namely that one of the two rival theories will ultimately replace the other one. But then incommensurability loses its frightening aspect. If we imagine incommensurable theories in peaceful coexistence, another term seems appropriate: *complementarity*. Each theory focuses on one particular side or dimension or surface of the common real systems, and though the picture obtained is in some sense a complete description of the systems, it is incomplete insofar as there are other sides or dimensions or surfaces of the same systems that, when described in terms of another theory, make them look quite different. Game theory and power theory, in fact, are complementary in this sense. Game theory focuses on the rational, calculating aspect of human beings, while power theory concentrates on the inherited *Wille zur Macht.* These are two sides of human existence that perhaps cannot be united without residue, and so each of them becomes important as a branch of social scientific research.

Chapter 5
Situated Social Power

Thomas E. Wartenberg

A central problem with many theories of power developed by theorists in both the Anglo-American and continental traditions is that power is conceived in too static and objectivized a manner. In this chapter, I shall focus upon one such problematic feature of theories of power, the assumption that power is dyadic. According to this assumption, power is located within a dyad consisting of a dominant agent who wields power over a subordinate agent. The salient feature of this conception of power is its localization of power in a sphere of existence made up of the two social agents who constitute the central actors in the power relation itself. The power that exists between them can then be understood by simply considering their relation without reference to their wider social context.

This model is a feature of the discourse of many social theorists even though they often do not specifically acknowledge it. Brian Fay, on the other hand, has recently argued that a critical social theory must work with a dyadic conception of power. His argument for this view is that only the dyadic conception of power gives both the dominant and the subordinate agents a degree of responsibility for the existence of the power relation between them:

> Something as crucial in social life as power must involve the activity of those being led or commanded as much as those leading or commanding. Power must arise out of the interaction of the powerful and powerless, with both sides contributing something necessary for its existence. *Power must be dyadic.*[1]

Fay argues that only the dyadic conception of power does justice to the fact that power arises out of the interaction of the powerful and the powerless. Without a dyadic conception of power, Fay implies, the role of the disempowered would not be recognized, making it impossible to articulate strategies by which the disempowered could seek to change the power relationships within society. Fay claims that, as opposed to a model that conceives of power as something that can be possessed by a dominant agent, the dyadic conception of power stresses the fact that power results from the social interaction of two parties. His dyadic conception of power stresses the relational nature of power, the fact that power is always the outcome of a social relationship.

While Fay is right to stress the role of the disempowered in constituting the very relations in which they lack power and to stress the contested nature of power relationships, it is a mistake to see this as legitimating the dyadic conception of power. The problem with the dyadic conception of power is that it abstracts from an important aspect of power relations, namely that they come into being as the result of the actions of agents who do not themselves figure explicitly in the power dyad itself. I shall argue that in the central relationships involving social power, it is precisely the role of "social others" that needs to be highlighted if one is interested in both understanding and criticizing such power relationships. Those social theorists who, like Fay, ignore these peripheral social agents fail to provide a model of power that can fulfill the task they are interested in, namely that of illuminating strategies for social change.

In this chapter, I shall develop a conception of power—the situated conception of power—that rectifies this shortcoming of the dyadic conception. The situated conception of power, while acknowledging the role that the disempowered play in the constitution of power relations, nonetheless also conceptualizes the role that "peripheral social others" play in their constitution. By calling this account of power *situated,* I stress that the power dyad is itself situated in the context of other social relations through which it is actually constituted as a power relationship.

The situated conception of power replaces a model that treats power as an agent's possession by a model of a social field. By viewing the power that the dominant agent has over the subordinate agent as the result of the actions of peripheral social agents, the situated conception of power treats an agent's power over another agent as a result of the social field within which the two agents are themselves located. Only in the context of a social field constituted by agents external to the power dyad is that dyad itself constituted as a power dyad.

Grading and the Teacher-Student Relationship

As a first step in my argument that the situated conception of power illuminates some fundamental aspects of power that have been overlooked by many social theorists, I shall analyze the specific power relation that exists between a teacher and a student. I have chosen this example to highlight the nature of situated power for a number of reasons. Foremost among them is the familiarity and simplicity of the idea that teachers exercise power over their students. Although this idea is quite obvious, I shall show that its very obviousness allows us to see the need for using the situated conception of power in order to analyze it. In later sections of this chapter, I will go on to apply the situated conception of power to other, more controversial examples.

The teacher-student relationship is extremely complex and is constituted by a multiplicity of overlapping and conflicting tendencies. I shall focus solely upon the role that grading plays in the constitution of the relationship between a student and a teacher as a power relationship.[2] I shall not attempt to develop a theoretical model that describes the actual structure of power in the relationship between students and teachers, but shall concentrate on the specific role that grading plays in the constitution of the relationship between a student and a teacher as one in which power is a factor.

While it can be argued that evaluation is necessary to the practice of teaching—for it is the means whereby the teacher is able to communicate to the student his success in acquiring knowledge or skills—grading does not have such a status; it is simply a particular means whereby such evaluation is accomplished. Within American education, assigning a student a grade has become the general way in which a teacher evaluates the student's performance.[3] It involves giving a particular mark to a student, a mark that places that student's accomplishments in some comparative relation to the accomplishments of other students. Grading is thus the specific form that evaluation takes within American higher education, but it is not a universal feature of teaching itself. It is also a feature of the teacher-student relationship that helps constitute it as a power relationship. The question that I shall pose, then, is this: How is a teacher constituted as having power over her students by virtue of the fact that she grades them?

Let us consider how the dyadic conception of power would analyze a teacher's power over her students. Fay presents the following definition of power:

> A exercises power with respect to B when A does x a causal outcome of which is that B does y which B would not have done without the occurrence of x.[4]

According to this definition, an agent exercises power over another agent only when the dominant agent does something that results in a change in what the subordinate agent does. A teacher's power over her student is seen as the result of actions that she performs. For example, if a student is not doing the work required of him, his teacher could attempt to get him to do the work by threatening to lower his grade significantly if he did not work harder or by assigning him extra work to do to pass the course. In such a case, the teacher would be trying to get the student to work harder by threatening him with a lower grade or even failure for not complying with her demands.

While the dyadic conception of power may be able to give an account of how the teacher exercises power in such disciplinary situations, it is not able to give an account of a more basic aspect of the power inherent in the teacher-student relationship. Students routinely act as they do in a classroom because of the power that teachers have, even though teachers themselves do not do anything special to cause students to alter their actions. The mere fact that a teacher will grade her students gives her power over them.

The point I am making is that the power a teacher has as a result of grading her students is not simply *interventional,* i.e., something that occurs as a result of actions that a teacher performs; a teacher's power over her students is *structural,* i.e., a feature of the structure of their relationship that is constituted by the teacher's evaluation of the performance of her students by means of a grade. Fay's definition does not acknowledge such structural aspects of power relations; the ongoing structuring of the behavior of a student by the teacher's grading him cannot be accommodated within Fay's definition, which conceptualizes power as resulting from the actions of the empowered agent.[5]

This example suggests that a more comprehensive conception of power is required, one that recognizes not only particular interventions as instances of the presence of power in society, but also ongoing structural features of social relationships as similarly constituted by the presence of power. The situated conception of power recognizes power as a factor in ongoing social relationships, the sorts of situations in which, according to the dyadic conception, a dominant agent does not exercise power at all.[6]

According to the situated conception of power, one needs to move beyond the classroom itself in order to gain an adequate understanding of the power of a grade, for the teacher's power over the student is constituted by the actions of social agents *peripheral* to the central dyad. The question that needs to be clarified is precisely how the actions of these "social others" constitute the relationship between the central actors as a power relationship.

In order to explicate the role that agents external to the power dyad play in the constitution of a situated power relationship, I shall ask why a student is harmed by receiving a grade that he perceives to be low.[7] There are, of course, many reasons why a student might be harmed by receiving such a grade. For example, a student who thought that she had written a good paper might be hurt because she would take that low grade to signify the teacher's belief that she had not succeeded in doing so. Another student might be hurt because she wanted to please her teacher and took the low grade to mean that she had not done so. There are, therefore, various reasons why a student might be harmed by a low grade.

For the purposes of my discussion, however, I shall bracket all such factors and ask, leaving to one side all the effects that can be localized to the dyadic relationship itself, whether there is not another important dimension to the harm done to a student by a low grade. To see that this is so, consider the following situations in which a low grade has an adverse effect upon the welfare of a student. A student's parents might punish him for receiving a low grade; an honors society might not admit him because of the low grade; a principal might expel him for receiving the low grade; a law school might use the low grade as a means to weed out the student; a firm might reject the application of the student because of the low grade. All these are examples of agents external to the power dyad whose actions are dependent upon the grade that the student receives from the teacher and who harm the student because he received a low grade.

In all of these examples, it is obvious that the grade itself, being by nature a sign, does not have an adverse effect on the well-being of the student. Rather, it is the way in which social agents peripheral to the teacher-student relationship react to the grade that constitutes its negative effect.[8] A student's well-being is affected by the grade only through the mediation of human beings situated outside of the classroom who use the grade as a sign that results in their administering harm to the student, e.g., by denying him access to the opportunity to further his education. Because the ability of students to realize many of their plans and projects is predicated upon their achieving a certain level of success as measured by their grades, a low grade may affect a student's ability to realize her plans. To use a familiar example, a student who wishes to attend medical school but who fails organic chemistry will have that option foreclosed. To attend medical school, she needs to attain at least a certain proficiency in organic chemistry.

Although these facts are familiar enough, they cannot be accommodated within the dyadic conception of power. The situated conception of power, on the other hand, acknowledges that power relationships are constituted by the presence of social agents peripheral to the central power dyad and whose treatment of the disempowered agent is regulated by certain features of the empowered agent's relation to that agent. It posits a structure of *social mediation* that is essential to the constitution of social power relationships, for without the "cooperation" of social others with the "intent" of the teacher's grading, the student would not be harmed by the low grade.[9] Only because these others do cooperate with the teacher's intent does the student have an interest in receiving a high grade from her teacher, a grade that will result in others having a positive assessment of her abilities and achievement, thus allowing her access to the item over which they have control. It is the presence of these others, as the conduits through which the teacher's act is transformed into a set of social realities affecting the student's access to various things that constitutes the relationship between the student and teacher as one involving social power.[10]

This is not to say that a student who receives what she takes to be a low grade from a teacher does not feel hurt. My account merely claims that one aspect of the hurt that the student experiences when she receives the low grade is an anticipation of the actual harm that the grade will do to her. In this sense, I want to suggest that social theorists need to recognize that an individual's experience of the world has an explicitly social content in that an agent's actual subjective experience is a reflection of the social structure of that agent's world.[11]

The account that the situated conception of power gives of a teacher's power over a student is made more persuasive by observing that, if a student can be sure of never encountering an individual who will use a low grade as a basis for her treatment of the student, the fact of grading will not result in the teacher's having power over the student. In actual social situations in which parental authority has broken down and young people have little hope of being in a position in which a grade might function as a means of access to a decent job, discipline has become a major educational problem. One reason for this is that the power of the teacher has been eroded by the dyadic relationship between the student and the teacher, which is no longer situated upon a field of social relationships that are structured in such a way as to constitute that dyadic relationship as a social power relationship.[12]

The example of the teacher-student relationship, then, shows that agents peripheral to the power dyad play a constitutive role in the formation of a social power relationship between two social agents. In such cases, an agent's power over another is determined by the use that the peripheral agents make of the empowered agent's actions and decisions. This *differential structure of orientation* that the peripheral agents have in regard to the dominant and subordinate agents is the crux of the social power that the dominant agent possesses. The actions of other social agents constitute a broad social field that both structures and conveys power between the two agents who form the central dyad in a situated power relationship.

Advantages of the Situated Conception

The example of grading and the teacher-student relationship shows that a central aspect of the power that exists in that relationship is best explained by the situated conception of power because of its stress on the role of peripheral social agents in the constitution of a power relationship. Although power has often been seen as dependent solely upon the actions of the dominant and subordinate agents, such is not the case in situated power relationships. Situated power relationships are not constituted by threats that a dominant agent makes to a subordinate agent, but first make it possible for the dominant agent in a situated power relation to make an effective threat to a subordinate agent. To choose a slightly different example, when a teacher threatens a student with lowering her grade unless she has sexual relations with him, the effectiveness of such a threat can only be understood against the background of an already established situated power relationship, one which is itself not constituted by such a threat. It is the background field constituted by such relations that I have analyzed by means of the concept of situated power. Situated power relations are structural in nature, and thus are more independent of the particular volitions and decisions of individual social agents than can be accounted for by using the dyadic model of power.

The situated conception of power also denies the claim that power is really a form of social agreement or consent among social agents. Though the subordinate agent certainly submits to a situated power relation, such submission cannot adequately be characterized by the notion of an agreement. To speak of an agreement, both parties to the agreement must have roughly equal ability to affect each other. But this is precisely not the case in relationships of situated social power. The subordinate agent faces a situated power relationship as a given over which he can have little effect but which will have a significant effect upon him. He encounters such situations much as he does natural necessities, as things to which he must submit in order to realize his own desires and intentions.

In order to have a clear understanding of the situated conception of power, it is important to distinguish it from the contextuality of power attributions, i.e. the claim that all attributions of power to an agent depend on the context within which they are made. This is a point that David Hume makes in the following quotation:

> But according to common notions a man has no power where very considerable motive lie betwixt him and the satisfaction of his desires, and determine him to forbear what he wishes to perform. I do not think I have fallen into my enemies power, when I see him pass me in the streets with a sword by his side, while I am unprovided of any weapon. I know that the fear of the civil magistrate is as strong a restraint as any of iron, and that I am in as perfect safety as if he were chain'd or imprison'd. But when a person acquires such an authority over me, that not only there is no external obstacle to his actions; but also that he may punish or reward me as he pleases, without any dread of punishment in his turn, I then attribute a full power to him, and consider myself as his subject or vassal.[13]

Hume points out that an inequality that allows one agent to harm another without being harmed by that agent is not in itself sufficient to constitute the relationship between them as a power relationship. The presence of the magistrate functions in Hume's example as an equalizer, keeping the armed agent from harming the unarmed agent with impunity. The relationship between the two agents is not a power relationship precisely because of the effect that the social context has on their dyadic relationship. All attributions of power to a social agent are contextually dependent.

From the perspective of the contextuality of power attributions, much of the recent theoretical discussion of power has focused upon a mistakenly abstract conception of power in that it has treated power as residing in social agents independent of the broader social context. The contextuality of power attributions shows that power does not work in this abstract way. We attribute power to an agent only when there are no countervailing social factors that would keep her from exercising her power should she choose to.

The contextuality of power attributions is certainly an important point that any theory of social power needs to acknowledge. Nonetheless, the situated conception of power, in that it claims that there are certain relationships of power that would not be power relationships were it not for the social context, asserts the converse of the point made by the contextuality of power attributions. According to the contextuality of power attributions, power is attributable to an agent only when there are no social factors that would keep her from exercising her ability to affect another agent. Only in the absence of such countervening social factors is a difference in abilities or possessions sufficient to constitute a power relationship between the two agents.

The situated conception of power operates at a different level of analysis than this. It claims that certain power relationships exist only by means of the actions of social agents who simultaneously empower and disempower other social agents by means of their differential responses to them. It thus posits a particular structure of social mediation external to the power dyad that is essential to its constitution as a power relationship. In a different context, Hume recognizes the importance of such structures of social mediation:

> The mutual dependence of men is so great in all societies that scarce any human action is entirely complete in itself, or is performed without some reference to the actions of others, which are requisite to make it answer fully the intentions of the agent.[14]

The situated conception of power is a specific manner of understanding the nature of power relationships that involves such a view of human action. Its specific claim is that social power relationships require a social field that goes beyond the two central agents.

The situated conception of power thus agrees with the contextuality of power attributions in stressing the importance of the social context in constituting the power relationship between social agents. However, it makes a more specific claim about how power relationships are constituted. It asserts that many relationships of social power are constituted *in the first instance* by the way in which peripheral social agents treat both the dominant and the subordinate agents. As such, it claims that a particular type of social context can constitute a power relationship between two social agents. The situated conception of power differs from the contextual view in that it posits a particular form of social power relationship as important for understanding the nature of power in contemporary society; it does not simply make a general point about the importance of the social context in assessing who has power over whom. As such, the situated conception of power functions at a more basic ontological level than the contextuality of power attributions, positing a specific structure of social relationship as the basis of social power.

The Concept of a Social Alignment

In developing the situated conception of power, I have argued that the relationship between the two agents who form the power dyad is constituted by a basis of peripheral social relationships. Not any set of peripheral social relationships, however, is sufficient to constitute a relationship between two agents as a power relationship. It is therefore necessary to develop a more specific model of the structure of social relationships through which situated power relationships are constituted.

The concept that I shall use to refer to the specific structure of social mediation through which situated power relationships are constituted is that of a *social alignment*. *Webster's Dictionary* defines the term "align" in the following manner: "to bring into line; to array on the side of or against a party or cause; to be or come into correct relative position." "Alignment" is then defined as "the act or state of being aligned; esp. the proper positioning of parts in relation to one another."[15] By using the term *alignment* to refer to the structure of social relationships that are necessary for constituting a situated power relationship, I am emphasizing the "relative positioning" of social others that is necessary for the constitution of a situated power relationship.

In order to justify my use of this term, let me consider two contexts in which the word *alignment* normally occurs. Nations are spoken of as being *aligned* or *nonaligned* with one of the two superpowers. In this use, the term indicates that each superpower has a certain set of policies around which the aligned nations orient themselves. The superpower is a focus for the activities and policies of its aligned nations. In this use, "alignment" indicates a center for the *orientation* of the actions and positions of other nations.

The second use of "alignment" is one that has to do with cars. We speak of the *alignment* of the front wheels of a car, a structure in which the front wheels are parallel with one another and perpendicular to the body of the car. In this use, "alignment" refers to a geometrical distribution of the parts of a car, a *coordination* of two parts of the car that enables the entire car to run smoothly.

By using "alignment" to refer to the structure of peripheral social agents through which a situated power relationship is constituted, I am drawing on both of these ordinary uses of the term. The behavior of the agents external to the power dyad can be seen as *oriented* around the actions of the dominant agent, for it is his actions that they use to structure their treatment of the subordinate agent. Furthermore, their *coordinated* actions are needed to create a power relationship as a smoothly functioning one, even though they are not the central location of the relationship itself.

A *situated power relationship* between two social agents is thus constituted by the presence of peripheral social agents in the form of a *social alignment*. A field of social agents can constitute an alignment with respect to a social agent just in case their actions in regard to that agent are coordinated in a specific manner. To be an alignment, however, the coordinated practices of these social agents need to be comprehensive enough that the social agent facing the alignment encounters that alignment as having control over certain things that she might either need or desire. In cases in which this coordination of the actions of the peripheral social agents is used to determine the access that an agent has to certain desirable items, these peripheral social agents constitute a social alignment.

The concept of a social alignment thus provides a way of understanding the "field" that constitutes a situated power relationship *as* a power relationship. In the grading example, I argued that students face a whole set of possible consequences contingent upon the grades they receive from their teachers. I am now claiming that this set of contingencies is best conceived of by means of the concept of a social alignment, for the contingencies consist in the differential treatment that the subordinate agent will receive from others as a result of the dominant agent's action. Because these social others *align* their treatment of the subordinate agent around the actions of the dominant agent, the relationship between these two agents is constituted as a social power relationship.

A social alignment is thus a quasimonopolistic structure through which individuals gain access to things they wish to have. It is the fact that a social agent's access to many different desirable items is controlled by the peripheral social agents that constitutes a social alignment. I earlier mentioned the question of getting into medical school. Because such things as the opportunity to study medicine are desirable and controlled by the grading alignment, the grading alignment is actually able to function as a social alignment.

Let me note in passing that alignments need not be fixed institutional structures. To see this, consider a group of businesses that decides to boycott all the products of a certain country. In that case, the country is being treated in the same manner by all these social agents (the businesses), so that these businesses form one crucial aspect of an alignment with respect to that country by structuring their purchasing practices in a coordinated manner. If the businesses are an important, irreplaceable outlet for the products of that country, then they have a second characteristic necessary for them to function as a social alignment: They control an important item the country desires, namely a market for the goods of that country. If they have this sort of monopolistic control over the purchase of these products, then the businesses form an alignment by coordinating their purchases in a systematic manner. By boycotting the goods of that country, they are able to create a situated power relationship with that country.

This example shows that alignments are not limited to permanent and fixed modes of social interaction; they can come to exist for specific purposes and for limited amounts of time. In such cases, alignments may function in an interventional rather than a systematic manner.

My discussion of the nature of a social alignment shows that situated social power is not easily constituted: An entire set of social practices has to be coordinated in certain very specific ways in order for such power to exist. If the "backups," i.e., aligned social practices, are not in place in specific sorts of ways, there will be a means for the subordinate agent to escape the power that the dominant agent has over her.

I shall refer to this aspect of a situated power relationship as its *heterogeneity*. By that term, I refer to the fact that situated power does not reside exclusively in a single site or institution of society. The situated conception of power shows that social power is a heterogeneous presence that spreads across an entire field of agents and practices, although its exercise depends upon the decisions of the dominant agent. Such heterogeneity is constituted by a complex coordination among agents located in diverse sites and institutions, all of whose presence in a social alignment is necessary to constitute a situated power relationship.

This general account of the role of alignments in the constitution of situated social power relationships will be strengthened by considering an example of how, in the absence of such an alignment, the power of an agent will be severely limited. Consider a situation in which a city passes a law that requires businesses to meet new pollution standards. The law states that businesses have to make certain investments in their physical plants in order to conform with the new code. Suppose further that a large firm threatens to move out of the city if it is forced to comply with the new code. As a result of this threat, the city allows the firm to retain its old plants in the condition they are presently in and to disregard the newly passed law.

In this example, the local government is not able to use its power to get the large corporation to comply with its wishes. We can understand why the government is unable to get the corporation to comply with the law once we realize that the two alignments are competing with one another for power. The governmental alignment acts through a variety of social institutions including the legislature and the police. It seeks to force the corporation to accept its demands as binding on its actions. If it were successful, the governmental alignment would have power over the corporation. The corporation, on the other hand, employs many of the government's citizens in its productive activities. It also generally complies with certain governmental regulations and is a source of government income. Because the corporation is able to relocate, it can threaten to take an action that would adversely affect the local government. Not only would such an action cause unemployment and loss of essential revenues, it might even cause voter unrest and lead to an adverse election result. Because of these possible results, the business's threat is likely to succeed and keep the local government from enforcing stricter pollution requirements than are generally in force in other locations to which the corporation could move.

My analysis makes clear that the reason that the local government is unable to succeed in its attempt to get the corporation to comply with the law is that it lacks a broad-enough governmental alignment to back up its efforts. Although the local government has a judicial and police branch with which to enforce its legislative decisions, the ability of the corporation to simply relocate gives it a simple means of avoiding compliance with those strategies and tactics. Only if other local governments were prepared to back up the decisions of a single government would that government's coercive power be truly effective in relation to large, relatively mobile corporations. That is, the local governments would have to have some mechanism for creating an alignment with regard to decisions made about regulating corporate practices. From such a point of view, we can see exactly the role played by more comprehensive governmental structures: they play precisely the role of alignment structures that coordinate decisions of more local governments.

This scenario also reveals a serious problem with the demand made by both conservatives and progressives for local government control. The problem with such an idea is not simply that the local governments are more corrupt or susceptible to extrapolitical pressure, as many have suggested, for such problems are, at least in principle, soluble. The real problem is the lack of an alignment structure. With local autonomy, a structure is created that would allow businesses to evade measures passed in the social interest, since there would be no alignment structure to help guarantee a means of forcing the businesses to abide by local governmental decisions.

Some Consequences for Social Theory

In order to illustrate how social theory will benefit from adopting the situated conception of power, I will outline four specific applications to problems in social theory. First, I will show that the situated conception of power provides the means for understanding institutional power and expertise. I will then demonstrate how it gives an account of how "macro" phenomena like the male domination of women come to be factors at the "micro" level of individual social interactions. I will also show how the relationship between a capitalist and a worker can be analyzed by means of the situated conception of power. Finally, I will present the situated conception of power's explanation of processes of subjection, i.e., of how individual social agents are constituted by the presence of power in society.

Institutional Power and Expertise

In order to show that the situated conception of power provides a clear manner of conceptualizing the power that agents have within social institutions, I will consider the example of a judge. In so doing, I will show that the account of power that I developed in the context of the teacher-student relationship can be generalized to provide a means of understanding the structure of institutional power.

Clearly, a judge has power over a defendant in that his decision about the guilt or innocence of the defendant, as well as about the severity of the punishment, has a significant effect on the defendant's well-being. If a judge declares the defendant to be guilty, then the defendant is placed in prison; if a judge declares him innocent, then he is freed.[16] This aspect of the judge-defendant relationship makes it similar to that of the teacher-student relationship explored earlier in that the dominant agent makes a decision that affects the well-being of the subordinate agent.

The conception of a situated power relationship will allow us to explain how the judge's power over the defendant is constituted. The judge's declaration of guilt or innocence, or of pronouncing sentence, is used by other agents to determine the manner in which they will treat the prisoner. The various agents who comprise the judicial and penal systems—from lawyers and bailiffs to police and prison guards— all structure their relation to the defendant around the pronouncement of the judge. As such, the future well-being of the defendant is determined by means of the judge's pronouncement. It is this structure of differential relation that constitutes the power that the judge has over the defendant.

This example shows that positions of power within specific social institutions can be explained by means of the situated conception of power. Such positions can be seen as a limiting case of this conception of power, in which the social alignment that constitutes the power is a single social institution itself and the social practices located within it.

The example of the judge also shows how the situated conception of power makes sense of the idea that expertise is a prevalent form of power in contemporary society, one that has many pernicious results. Although many social theorists have objected to the rise of experts in contemporary society, they have failed to provide a sufficiently material (i.e., social) analysis of what such expertise amounts to. The situated model of power shows that the rise of expertise in contemporary society corresponds to the development of a specific social structure that allows the expert to wield power.

Once we recognize the existence of a situated power relationship behind the power of an expert, we can see that the normal legitimation of such expertise obscures the structure of power that constitutes expertise as a specific form of social practice. When thinking about why an expert is given power, we tend to focus upon the dyadic relationship between the expert and the social agent over whom he has power. Because the expert has more knowledge than other social agents, we assume that the expert's power is legitimately held. Thus, a teacher is given the power to grade the student because of the belief that the teacher is an expert by virtue of her possession of a certain amount of esoteric knowledge. As a result of this expertise, it is thought that the teacher has the ability to discriminate among different levels of performances by the students. The teacher's assigning of grades is taken to be a rational means of assessing the students' abilities. Similarly, in the case of the judge, his expert knowledge in judicial matters is the justification for placing him in a situated power relationship with those accused of criminal offenses.

Although the expert's possession of knowledge is normally seen as legitimating his possession of power, the situated conception of power shows that there is no necessary connection between the expert knowledge possessed by the empowered agent and the structure of the power relationship itself. While the expert may *be* an authority on certain subject matters, this authority is distinguishable from the authority she comes to *have* as a result of being situated as an empowered agent. Although the normal understanding of experts makes it seem that the expert's knowledge makes the power structure in which he takes part inevitable, the situated conception of power shows that the power that accrues to the expert by virtue of his esoteric knowledge is a result of the use of his expert knowledge as the basis of a situated power relationship. It thus shows that the normal manner of legitimating such relationships is invalid since it fails to explain why the possession of esoteric knowledge legitimates the creation of the specific social structure of expertise.

Situated Power and Domination

Another advantage of the situated conception of power is that it explains how domination, which is usually conceptualized as a "macro" feature of a society, impacts upon the lives of individuals at the "micro" level. In order to demonstrate this, I shall focus upon sexism in order to show how the situated conception of power helps explain certain of its features.

In making this argument, I shall concentrate upon a specific male attitude. Although many men acknowledge the domination of women in all contemporary societies, these same men will often deny that they play any role in such domination. Not only do they not experience themselves as dominators, they claim that they do not themselves act in ways that dominate women.

Of course, feminists have argued that the fact that men have these feelings does not contradict the reality of male domination. Pointing, for example, to statistical inequalities in pay, they maintain that there is a structure of male domination despite what many men may feel about themselves.

But such a response does not explain why men feel the way they do. One way of accounting for these feelings is to say that men simply have false consciousness. One would argue that, despite what men happen to believe, they actually dominate women. They do not recognize this fact because their consciousnesses do not reflect social reality in an accurate manner.

The perils of using the idea of false consciousness are clear from the history of the Marxist use of this concept.[17] It is therefore not an adequate means of understanding the consciousness that many men have about their own roles in male domination.

The situated conception of power, however, provides an alternative means for understanding how the following two claims can both be true: that contemporary society is male-dominated and that, nonetheless, many men do not experience themselves as dominators. The situated conception of power explains this by distinguishing between the social field for specific power relationships and the power dyad itself.

In order to see that this distinction explains the workings of power in this case, let us consider a relationship between a husband and a wife in which the husband sees himself as not dominating his wife. We need to understand why it makes perfectly good sense to claim that the husband does dominate the wife in this relationship, despite his desire not to, as a result of the sexist nature of the society in which he lives.

To begin with, in claiming that society is sexist, one is claiming, among other things, that women are treated differently than men. In particular, within our society women who are not married to men have less access to many things that are normally deemed important for a fulfilled life. There are many economic situations in which single or divorced women have a much harder time gaining access to social goods than do men, be they married or single. For example, it is generally acknowledged that women have more limited opportunities in the labor market than men. When they do get jobs, their pay is only 60 percent of that men receive. There are also problems for women with sexual harassment in jobs. Further, banks and other financial institutions tend to be more stringent in their loan requirements for women. Single women, not having husbands to use as references, thus have a harder time getting loans. Such considerations point to the presence of a social structure in which single or divorced women have more difficulty gaining access to certain sorts of goods than married women.

In the terms that I have developed, all this amounts to the claim that there is a gender alignment through which nonmarried women are treated differently than men. That is, various social institutions and practices—from banks to businesses—use a woman's gender and marital status as a basis for their treatment of her. This gender alignment results in the domination of women.

In order to see this, we must acknowledge that the gender alignment, although peripheral to the nature of a particular marriage, constitutes the social field for the relationship between a husband and his wife. The situated conception of power shows why, despite the best intentions of the husband, that relationship will be one in which he has power over his wife. For when a wife considers the benefits of her relationship to her husband, she will not only be considering what that particular man is like as a husband, but she will be considering the alternatives she would have to face were she not married to him. Limiting ourselves to strictly economic factors, we can see that the social alignment will treat her differently depending upon her marital status. As a result, she gains something from the marriage and thus has reasons both to enter into it and to stay in it that transcend the particular nature of the marriage itself. It is this set of reasons, reasons that focus on the gender alignment, that constitutes the marriage relation as a form of power in our current society. The power that husbands have is not the result of their own particular intentions, though they may choose to use their power to enhance their own status in the family; it is rather the result of the situated nature of the marriage relationship itself. The general social disposition to treat women differently than men—a disposition that I have explored only superficially—functions as an alignment that constitutes the husband's power over his wife and their relationship as an example of situated power.

The situated conception of power thus provides a clear way of understanding the power that accrues to individuals when they occupy certain social roles and the power that others lose when they occupy other roles. To be a husband or a wife, a student or a teacher, is to occupy a particular social role by virtue of which one's power is constituted. The situated conception of power explains how individuals come to have a social being that transcends their own individual existence.

It is worth noting that there are features of the husband-wife relationship that are different from those in the teacher-student one. A husband does not, for example, grade his wife as a teacher does her students. Nonetheless, the situated model of power demonstrates certain important similarities in the two relationships, similarities that might not be noticed in the absence of the model. The central similarity is that a woman will have different access to things that she desires depending on her relationship to a particular man, her husband, just as a student will have depending on her relationship to her teacher. Although a teacher works to differentiate among her students on the basis of abilities, a husband is also "marking" a woman as acceptable by marrying her. This badge of respectability functions like a grade insofar as it allows married women access to different things than nonmarried women have.

Of course, not all gender domination can be explained by the situated model of power. The ways in which women think about themselves and their possibilities is not something the situated model of power attempts to explain. It does, however, show that power is exercised within particular social relationships that do not themselves seem to be the locus of power. But because of the presence of a social field in the form of a social alignment, the central dyad is made into a power relationship. As a result, the situated conception of power provides social theorists with an important means of analyzing the nature of social domination.

The Power of the Capitalist

I would now like to show the usefulness of the notion of situated power by exploring the relationship between capital and labor. Of course, this notion has been the focus of extended analysis by both liberal theorists and Marxists. It is my contention, however, that the concept of situated power provides a clear means of legitimating the claim that capitalists have power over the workers whom they employ.

The analysis of the power components of the capitalist-laborer relation combines aspects of the two types of alignments I have just discussed. In the first place, a single firm is a social institution in which the capitalist has power over the worker in a manner analogous to that in which the judge has power over the defendant. The decisions of the capitalist with regard, for example, to hiring and firing are taken by the other agents within the firm as determinative of their own practices. The laborer is hired, given work, paid, etc., all as a result of the decision by the capitalist to hire him. Within a single firm, the capitalist has a position of situated power over the worker.

However, there is more to the analysis of the power of a capitalist over one of his workers than the fact that, within the single firm in which the worker is employed, the capitalist has power. A second feature of the capitalist's power over the worker depends upon the limited set of options the worker has to achieve certain goals he has for himself and for his family without retaining the job he has been given by the capitalist.[18] The problem is to show that this aspect of the relationship between the capitalist and the worker can be understood through the model of situated power relationships.

To do this, let me outline two aspects of the capitalist alignment that will allow us to see how it constitutes the capitalist's relation to the laborer as one involving situated power. The first aspect of the alignment consists of other firms. A capitalist has power over a worker in his firm because there are not easily available employment options open to the worker. There are two reasons for this. The first is that, in some types of employment, being fired is a bad mark that other employers use as a reason not to hire a worker. The analogy to the grading case is obvious. The second is that the relatively high unemployment levels present in a capitalist society make a worker unsure of the chances of finding new employment once he has lost a job. Marx himself used the concept of the 'reserve army of the proletariat' to conceptualize this aspect of the capitalist mode of production in arguing for its structural necessity in maintaining it. My analysis also sees this aspect of the economy as playing an important role in constituting the capitalist's power over his worker.

The second aspect of the capitalist alignment that must be noted is the lack of welfare options. Since an agent's power over another depends on his ability to restrict the other's options, a capitalist's power over a worker would be greatly diminished if there were state-financed means whereby a worker could meet many of his needs and desires. It is important to the maintenance of the capitalist's power that the worker not be able to rely on such options. But this means that the welfare options available to the worker must be such that he not see them as fully acceptable alternatives to employment. And this, in turn, entails that the government not fund them in ways that would make them acceptable alternatives. This analysis shows that many institutions other than firms themselves play a role in the capitalist alignment, that alignment through which a capitalist is empowered in relation to workers.[19]

My consideration of the wage offer made by a capitalist to a worker shows how the presence of the capitalist alignment structures the options the worker is able to consider in deciding whether to accept it. The worker's action-alternatives have the structure that they do by virtue of the presence of the various facets of the capitalist alignment that result in the capitalist having power over the worker.

By focusing attention on the role that social alignments play in the maintenance of a power relationship, I have shown that the appearance of freedom in the relationship between the worker and the capitalist, which has been emphasized by liberal theory, conceals a deeper level at which power is exercised. Only because the options facing the worker have the structure that they do will the worker be willing to work for the wage he does in the conditions that he faces. This structure of alternatives is precisely what the concept of a social alignment refers to.

Subjection and Situated Power

The situated conception of power also makes an important contribution to our understanding of the very basic levels at which power operates in society. Foucault has spoken of *processes of subjection* in order to indicate that the same processes that form the individual as a "subject" of consciousness also form that individual as "subjected" to power.[20] The situated conception of power provides a means of understanding Foucault's view as part of a general theory of power in society.

In order to understand such processes, I shall focus upon power relationships that have two specific features. The first is that the subordinate agent has some desire for the items over which the alignment has control. The second is that that agent be able to affect how the dominant agent will act with regard to her. When these two features are present in a power relationship, the structure of that relationship becomes much more intentional. If, for example, a teacher were to decide arbitrarily whether or not to give a student a good grade, then, although it would still be true that the teacher had power over the student, such power would not ground a power relationship in which the student could affect how he would be treated. Only when the subordinate agent has some effect on the dominant agent's actions will the dominant agent's power have some effect on the subordinate agent's conduct or understanding.

These two features explain how such power relationships result in a process of subjection. To see this, consider the teacher-student relationship once more. First, note that the teacher-student relationship is characterized by the two additional features I just outlined. A student's access to certain items, for example jobs, is at least partially determined by the grading alignment. It is also true that a student does have a great deal of influence upon how a teacher grades him. By working harder, he will usually be able to produce better papers and examinations, the sorts of things that form the basis for the teacher's evaluation. Indeed, the point of the power relationship is precisely to get the student to adopt such a strategy. The power of the teacher is not arbitrary; it seeks to elicit actions on the part of students that affect how they will be judged by the teacher. To the extent that a student performs the sorts of actions that the teacher seeks to have him perform, such as studying and writing, he will make it more likely that he will receive a better grade from the teacher than he would have received had he not performed such actions.

The situated power relationship between a student and a teacher thus results in the student adopting certain courses of action in an attempt to affect the teacher's grading. For a student facing a teacher, the power of the teacher is located in her ability to affect his future. Because the student is aware of the functioning of the grading alignment, he understands that the grade he receives from the teacher can have a significant effect on his future career possibilities. As a result, he will do things that the teacher wants in order to satisfy her demands and thus be allowed the sorts of opportunities controled by the grading alignment.

This means that the result of the existence of such a power relationship over the subordinate agent is that he comes to adopt long-term strategies of action that are predicated upon the existence of such power relations. As a result of the existence of power relationships, the subordinate agent comes to adopt certain courses of action for the instrumental value they have in allowing him to realize his purposes. But this process is precisely one of subjection, i.e., the creation of the human agent as having desires that are adopted by the human being as his own due to his interaction with a power structure over which he has no control.

The crucial thing to recognize is that the presence of power relationships causes human beings to make choices that determine the sorts of skills and abilities they will develop. As a result, since the formation of skills and abilities is a fundamental aspect of the constitution of character, human beings become the sorts of beings they are as a result of the presence of power relationships. The situated conception of power thus provides a clear way to understand how power operates to make human beings into the sorts of beings they are by affecting their own constitution at the level of desire, skill, and ability.

Conclusion

The basic contention of the situated conception of power is that a power dyad forms only one of two important elements in most relationships of social power. The other element in such relationships is a social alignment, a structure of peripheral social agents that controls and distributes certain items in society. It is the presence of such a social alignment that constitutes the relationship between two social agents as one that involves social power.

Acknowledging the importance of alignments in the constitution of situated social power results in a very different picture of social power than that conveyed simply by focusing on the two agents who form the central dyad in a power relationship. While the place and moment of the exercise of power may well be localizable to such a dyad, this is not the case for the power relationship itself. The dyad within which power is exercised is but the point of focus of a vast field of social forces that determine the nature of such an exercise. By failing to acknowledge the existence of such a social field and its role in the constitution of a power relationship, many power theorists have failed to articulate a model of social power that adequately conceptualizes the complex structure of social practices that comprise the presence of power in the social world. The situated conception of social power rectifies this shortcoming by developing a clear picture of how such relationships are actually constituted in society.

In general then, the concept of situated power demonstrates that power is a much more pervasive feature of the social world than liberal theory maintains. By seeing the importance of social alignments in creating a set of alternatives that an individual normally encounters as given, we are able to see the importance of power relationships in structuring and reproducing society as a whole. Rather than accepting the liberal notion that power is only a peripheral phenomenon in modern societies, most of whose structures operate through the consent of those involved, the concept of situated power relations gives us a means for seeing power as a central presence in those very societies that plays an essential role in their reproduction. Such an understanding of the nature of social power is a crucial one for any critical social theory to adopt.[21]

Chapter 6

The Rhetoric of Domination

──────────── *Timo Airaksinen*

Introduction

The crudest mechanism of interpersonal domination is *coercion.* The dominant agent A presents a threat to the subordinate agent B's desires, welfare interests, or rights. B takes this into account and plans his own actions accordingly. The result that B wants to avoid is disappointment, harm, or wrong. Such a simple scenario hides some complex issues, especially the many contexts in which threats can be issued.[1] Let us distinguish among the following forms of coercion: (1) paternalistic, (2) apparent, (3) real, (4) preventive, and (5) inducive.

I shall begin by analyzing these five concepts. The issues involved show an increasing degree of complexity, leading toward the hidden issues of the practice of power and domination. By starting from some simple games of social power, one can proceed step by step toward situations in which the analytical distinctions blend in with rhetorical strategies. This can be explained by an additional, important fact: the coercive tie between agents is grounded on a conflict of interests. The agents cannot agree on some important features of their mutual situation. The emergence of the threat is the result of a deeper conflict, but more importantly, it is not the *cause* of the conflict between the agents. The agents are already unable to cooperate. They do not even try to do so. Hence I shall argue that part of their interaction must be rhetorical, with *rhetorical* being taken to mean a discourse that does not track the truth but aims at the redefinition of social roles, self-perception, and the relevant belief systems. In other words, the weaker party is led to understand some of the environmental features in a new way such that he somehow becomes the subordinate person. He cannot resist; thus, a power relation is established and the conflict seemingly disappears.[2] In other words, we proceed from an open threat to a hidden agreement concerning the direction of the domination between agents.

In sum, in cooperative contexts the parties try to establish the correctness of and the justification for their own description of the situation and its normative rules. Otherwise they cannot continue. The main premise here is that they do not agree. Thus, my final question will be about the characterization of the implicit strategies of domination, that is, the rhetoric that establishes the false (coerced) peace and agreement.

The Five Types of Coercion

Suppose that a father threatens his child with punishment if she does not go to bed early. This is a *paternalistic* case since he is thinking of her welfare, even though she protests and claims that she is being forced. The conflict between the father and the daughter is only a transient one, as can be easily shown. The father claims, with perfect justification, that if the child were more mature and better understood her own good, she would agree to go to bed and would not need to be threatened. Such a contrary-to-fact conditional proposition justifies his strategy of threats. It is indeed true that the threat is needed only because the child is unable to recognize her own good, and the conflict she claims to exist depends only on her own subjective feelings. Yet the father threatens the child, first, in the sense that she would not obey him without her recognition of the impending personal harm and, second, she in fact resents going to bed. The father intends to coerce, or to force his will upon the child.

The next type is what I call *apparent* coercion. In this case the subordinate agent not only misses the validity of any paternalistic contrary-to-fact conditional, but such a proposition need not even be mentioned. Instead, the following is suggested: If B's values, preferences, and factual beliefs were well founded and correct, he need not be coerced to act (he would act so without the threat). For example, A is a police officer who wants to persuade bank robber B to stop resisting an arrest. It is quite clear that B does not profit from obeying A. The officer does not aim at the welfare of the robber. Actually, the best choice for the robber is to escape with the money. The arrest is counter to all his current interests, except that he is afraid of the violent threat. Nevertheless, if he were to reason according to normal ethics, following also the guidelines of criminal law, he would agree that he must surrender and accept the consequences of his initial wrongdoing. As things stand now, his resistance is motivationally well founded (he anticipates a stiff sentence), although morally problematic and unjustified from the social point of view.

This type of interaction is coercive because of its structure of power, yet it is merely apparent coercion because there is a way of dissolving the conflict. The threat is real, but the underlying normative conflict remains avoidable, should the robber correct his view on ethics, law, and his own good. Of course, this is too demanding to constitute a realistic alternative. Therefore, the robber resists and the threat is justifiable.

Real coercion occurs when A both harms and wrongs B. In other words, there is no way of making the threat palatable to B, even in principle, in the sense that B could change his mind concerning the validity of some crucial contrary-to-fact condition. An example is a common robbery case: mugger A forces B to reveal the whereabouts of his money by threatening to shoot. His victim has a choice between (i) losing her money, which is a personal loss, and (ii) being shot, which is a rights violation. She can choose only between two nasty things, and we suppose that the second choice is the worst that can happen. Therefore B surrenders her money.

The point of such an example is that A wrongs B. His strategy is unjustified in the sense that no (plausible) change of the grounds of B's practical reasoning can make her agree that she should surrender the money, if she makes no mistake. In this way, the disappearance of their conflict means that B's reasoning goes somehow awry; we shall return to these irrational thoughts.

Next, let us consider *preventive* coercion. In this case A threatens B to prevent him from forming intentions he should not form. This threat is also a deterrent. B may be a perfectly law-abiding citizen who knows that should he steal he will be subject to punishment. Of course, he does not refrain from stealing because of the legal coercive threat. He knows that stealing is wrong, but he also knows that some intentions tend to be too risky and costly. One can even say that preventive threats are no real threats, simply because the context in which they are issued does not logically entail a conflict between the power-wielder and the subordinate agent. B does not resist at all. The coercion is left merely implicit, yet the threat is there. It is always possible for B to change his opinions and values, or to intend to do something that is sanctioned through the threat. And in that case, B notices that he is not free to do what he wants to do. To change his plans would be too costly. In other words, if there were a conflict, the sanction attached to certain action alternatives would work like any coercive threat.

The correct attitude toward a merely implicit threat is this: if there is no independent evidence that B is indeed prone to form sanctioned intentions, B cannot be said to be under A's coercive power. The case is analogous to the refutation of epistemic skepticism: if one has no evidence for the suspicion that one may err, one cannot be said to fail to know. Merely possible errors do not refute knowledge claims; merely possible illegitimate desires do not diminish one's freedom (because of a standing threat).

Finally, let us look at the case of *inducive* threats whose purpose is to motivate (directly) the subordinate agent. These are sometimes called "throffers," a combination of a threat and an offer.[3] A typical example would be of the form "get me some cigarettes—if you do, I'll pay you $100, otherwise I'll hurt you." The offer of a reward is backed by a genuine threat. The offeree, assuming he is a prudent, rational person in a morally innocent context, will form an intention to fetch the cigarettes. No conflict of interests or moral wrongs are mentioned, and it is accordingly incomprehensible that the offeree would resist. But if he did resist, he could also claim that he is being coerced to fetch the cigarettes. He may, for instance, insist that one must not smoke.

A more complicated but similar case is one in which B does not want to do x, but the reward offered by A is high and the punishment truly frightening. If the reward is high enough, prudent, rational B will want to do x, regardless of his initial reluctance, and so the threat becomes meaningless. Thus, only if the reward is insufficient does a conflict emerge between the two interacting parties—but this is another type of a coercive situation.

The difference between the preventive and the inducive coercion should be clear. The former entails that the subordinate agent will not do anything, even if he were to change his mind. The latter entails that the agent will do x, even if he were to change his mind. The psychological effects of such a difference are significant. The preventive case may look quite threatening because it is not at all clear that one would not steal, at least occasionally, if the background threat were missing. The agent may have no way of identifying his desires independently of that background threat. He may suspect that he is indeed prone to steal, but the threat of punishment deters him. However, in the case of inducive coercion he can maintain with perfect confidence that the threat is redundant. Going to buy cigarettes is a minor burden in comparison with the reward of $100. This is attractive. He need not even consider the case in which, contrary-to-fact, he wants to resist.

Rational Reasons and Justification

These five coercive paradigms differ in their justification from the power-wielder's point of view. The paternalistic case is easily justifiable. The only caveat is that A cannot coerce B to increase his "additive," only his "nonadditive," good. Even if B is immature with respect to her valuations and self-understanding, A should take care only of her basic welfare. A nonadditive good is similar to an aspect of health that has its normal level also as its maximum. Another example is being alive. Such a good situation cannot be increased, but it certainly can diminish. Therefore, it is perceived as valuable mostly when it is disappearing, otherwise one's attitude is that of indifference. A healthy person may not feel elated simply because he is healthy. When he is ill, however, he will miss his health dearly.

It seems that A should take care only of these nonadditive situations by means of such drastic methods as threats. Perhaps such benefits are not easily recognizable by immature people who have very little experience with the negative effects of the disappearance of the benefits. But additive goods, such as money, need not and should not be forced on even immature people by means of threats.

This simple approach to justification does not quite apply to the cases of apparent coercion. Certain differences are evident. The subordinate agent's values are genuinely different from those of A's, and therefore the paternalistic justification is impossible. B has his own values; that is, he is not merely immature, though he may miss some truths about facts and values. B genuinely and permanently disagrees with A. Therefore, A must possess solid reasons that support his decision to present a threat. He is required to support his case by some ideas of moral validity and empirical truth to which he claims he has access, unlike B. For his action to be justified, A must show that if B were better able to conduct his practical reasoning, he would consent without coercion. As things are, however, B is and remains alone with his ideas of the good and the right. The justification does not lead to a consensus. Should we worry about this? I shall return to this question.

Real coercive threats are deceptively easy to dismiss as unjustifiable. Yet no such threat position can be convincing to the victim; i.e., if he thinks that A knows he is about to wrong the victim, who knows his own good and rights. A must be willing to realize the threat against his resisting victim, and then A cannot expect to profit from their interaction. To shoot his victim without getting the money cannot look like a plausible action alternative. B may well think that A is prudent and rational and therefore will not shoot if he is firmly resisted. Shooting would no longer be profitable. Therefore, B will resist. And if A knows and predicts the outcome of such reasoning, he will never start coercing B. On the other hand, if A is imprudent, he may shoot even after getting the money from B. B's conclusion should then be that because A is unpredictable, one should not obey him. By resisting one can avoid the single worst consequence, which is both losing the money and getting shot.

All this indicates that A must have an understandable reason for coercing. In other words, A must have access to a motive that provides a reason both for presenting the threat and for realizing it against a reluctant victim. Does this not mean that the present case is like apparent coercion, supposing that A is only minimally justified in his efforts against B? I think so. To make his threat convincing A needs a good reason to make the realization of the threat worthwhile (and the useless realization of the threat against his consenting victim unattractive). Such a reason may be connected to his pride and reputation, to an established policy, or to a promise he has made to others. In any case, we have supposed that the reason is not sufficient for the justification of the threat, even if it motivates the coercer. A must have his obvious reasons for his actions.

Preventive coercion can be justified by referring to the necessity of safeguarding against the whims of people, however well informed, prudent, and moral they may appear. Of course, the retaliation and punishment must be in proportion to the possible mischief, but all of these details belong to the theory of punishment, so we need not dwell on them here. Thomas Hobbes' political philosophy illustrates the case quite nicely. People can trust neither themselves nor others to be permanently peaceloving; therefore, they need to surrender their power and rights to a sovereign who will use coercive power against them, if necessary.

The last case is inducive coercion. Here the main question is why there is a need for the threat at all. Even if inducive coercion looks redundant, innocent, and almost silly, its justification is still problematic. What is the good reason for presenting the threat if the reward itself is high enough to motivate the offeree? Alternatively, one may ask why one needs to back his offer by means of the threat, unless one suspects that the offeree is reluctant to serve him? All this hints at some hidden reasons that the offeree may mobilize against the stronger agent. And as we have already seen, the power-wielder must also have a good reason to realize the threat against the stubborn victim. It may well be that the reason he thinks he needs to issue the threat in addition to the reward is connected to the reason that makes his threat convincing (or shows why he is ready to hurt the offeree).

The discussion of coercion employs a number of contrary-to-fact conditionals. We are interested in scenarios of what might happen in the contexts in which the agents are located and, of course, to the agents themselves. The field of power is a hidden one. Efficient threats are rarely explicated. The subordinate persons have learned to anticipate them. The justification of power is in a similar way problematic: the conflict reveals a difference of normative opinions that successful threats tend to cover up. All too easily the victim is supposed to agree that he is wrong simply because he obeys.

The Conflict of Reasons

The adequacy of the model of coercive power above depends on some crucial presuppositions and premises. I have suggested that both parties are prudent and rational and that they understand what good reasons are. They have regular desires, and they aim at certain goods. The validity of some kind of moral language must also be presupposed. Both agents recognize rights and duties. They also have an idea of the good life along with its values of safety, health, and economic prosperity. Such premises make sense when both parties are supposed to understand and accept the possibility of cooperation, but perhaps not otherwise.

When the conflict cannot be dismissed, the situation must also be different; that is, the set of premises of practical reasoning must show some gaps and ruptures. The point is simple: when A threatens B, his coercive strategy is supposed to be reasonable, perhaps even morally justified; yet B cannot agree, otherwise he would need not to be coerced. The hidden disagreement may extend to any of those presuppositions listed above. Look at the simple case in which B is wrong. His ideas may look so idiosyncratic that neither A nor the audience who judges the case need take them seriously. Yet B recognizes some harms that allow A to design his threats against him, for instance physical pain. Again, coercive power, and other types of power, require that the parties use rhetoric instead of valid, rational, and truth-tracking reasoning. This follows from the existence of a conflict that entails that a moral agreement, or an interpersonal reflective equilibrium, cannot be reached and the only possibility is to argue that the other party's reasoning does not deserve to be taken seriously. The context of the exchange of ideas is now determined by the need to present a threat, and then the demand that the factual truth and rational justification must be made available is clearly out of place. On the contrary, the power-wielder supposes on the basis of his professional role, traditional rights, or the assumed urgency of the situation that he must present his threat against the subordinate person's interests, without wronging them. And he knows in advance that the other person and his supporting audience cannot accept his reasons, otherwise they would give in or cooperate in the first place. Ethics, however, aims at cooperation and the reduction of the selfish interests between people.

When cooperation becomes impossible, rational interpersonal discourse disappears. This is to say that the parties do not try to convince each other about some matters of empirical truth and normative validity, being themselves at the same time open to arguments that may shake their beliefs. The parties know that they must disagree. Of course, it does not follow that the parties would not argue any more. Certainly they will continue to inform, argue, and explain, directing their efforts to themselves in an inner soliloquy, to their own and to the other's reference group, and to their opponents. If this is not the case, the conflict has already deteriorated all the way to the use of force and violence, such as shooting guns. However, we are here talking about threats, and these typically involve speech acts. One says, "If and only if you do *not* do *x*, I shall hurt you by doing *y*." This is a complex expression that entails a large number of "felicity conditions." Their existence cannot be checked without social communication.

When one starts applying moral language the discourse is designed to lead toward the uniformity of normative opinions, so that the conflict dissolves. Of course, the stronger party may consider a threat, which presupposes that he will stop talking to the other party. He may, however, still talk to himself and his own reference group, trying to convince them of his own right reason in the case. This means that he wants to guarantee cooperation within the subgroup that is still inclined to listen.

An interesting consequence follows: once the stronger party decides that moral reasons must be provided to his own reference group to get them to agree on the justification, the subordinate person is not listened to. He is left alone and becomes a genuine victim. Alternatively, we can suppose that an impartial audience exists, so that the parties in conflict try to convince its members of their respective right to act. An external gaze must be taken care of, for instance, by providing a rhetorical veil that covers the conflict. If the parties in conflict cannot talk to each other, they can turn to the external observers whose acceptance is still available. This seems to be a fruitful way of approaching the justification of power. Yet such an audience may be only a fictional entity, one's own inner gaze, especially since it must be so impartial and independent; we shall explore this role below.

Now, the communication between the coercer and the victim is more or less rhetorical. One tries to change opinions and convince the target persons without a rational foundation. Both parties know that, in principle, they do not share those premises that alone make mutual understanding possible. In fact, communication between the parties may be impossible, and the rhetoric is therefore aimed at a neutral audience. What are the rhetorical strategies and their goals?

Rhetorical Strategies

We can illustrate the problem of rhetoric by means of the Marquis de Sade's *120 Days of Sodom*. This terrifying book is like a medieval summa of horrors, listing all possible perversions and tortures in a systematic manner. The frame is provided by the isolated castle of Silling, four libertines, four female storytellers, and several groups of servants, slaves, and victims. The storytellers provide the narratives, which the heroes put into action.[4]

We are interested in Sade's advice to his readers. If we assume that the novel is an account of a social conflict between the powerful heroes together with their allies and the helpless victims, we can also see ourselves, as the readers of those stories, as the impartial audience. The victims could then approach us with their suffering and ask our arbitration. At least the victims could think that their own desperation, as seen and felt by themselves, is a valid experience because the audience would feel the same, should they become familiar with their condition. And if their emotions are justified, their tormentors are wrong. Alas, the rhetorical approach to the case does not support the idealizing, truth-tracking theory. The reason is that no impartial audience exists, as Sade understands perfectly well. Moreover, the victims and their masters are now well defined.

The powerful heroes explain their fate to their helpless victims:

> In short: shudder, tremble, anticipate, obey—and with all that, if you are not very fortunate, perhaps you will not be completely miserable. No intrigues amongst you, no alliances, none of that ridiculous friendship between girls which, by softening the heart in one sense, in

another renders it both more ill-tempered and less well-disposed to the one and simple humiliation to which you are fated by us; consider that it is not at all as human beings we behold you, but exclusively as animals one feeds in return for their services, and which one withers with blows when they refuse to be put to use.[5]

The victims may argue that the scheme is evil simply on the basis that it first admits that they are human, capable of friendship for instance, and then denies their humanity by calling them mere animals. Not even a consistent egoist can accept this strategy of domination.

As the spokesman for the wicked heroes, Sade himself turns to his readers as follows: "And now, friend-reader, you must prepare your heart and your mind for the most impure tale that has ever been told." After this invitation he gives his advice:

> Many of the extravagances you are about to see illustrated will doubtless displease you, yes, I am well aware of it, but there are amongst them a few which will warm you to the point of costing you some fuck, and that, reader, is all that we ask of you. . . . choose and let lie the rest without declaiming against that rest simply because it does not have the power to please you. Consider that it will enchant someone else, and be a philosopher.[6]

The tales of torture, rape and murder may please some people, and Sade asks us to respect their choices. This is nothing but a rhetorical invitation to share the heroes' and Sade's point of view, and therefore to see the victims as animals. The promised enjoyment masks the relations of power.

Sade's argument in favor of the heroic position is a simple, hedonistic one: these stories will stimulate you and people like you. Let us enjoy the horrors together. We may then consider the victims' pleas for mercy as just another entertaining feature of the spectacle. The purpose of the narrative is claimed to be the entertainment of the reader. But this may presuppose that her attitude is morally neutral. Coercion neither needs justification nor can be condemned. But this is not true. On the contrary, to enjoy the stories of domination and to assume a subjectively impartial standpoint entails the rejection of the victim's role; that is, the result is partiality. This is the most extreme of those rhetorical strategies that are applied to violent power. In more modest ways, they are still constantly used.

Some additional rhetorical strategies are illustrated by R. D. Laing in his marvelous little book *Knots*. Let us look at two examples. First, the dominant person's view:

> A son should respect his father
> He should not have to be taught to respect his father
> It is something that is natural
> That's how I've brought up my son anyway.
>
> *
>
> Of course a father must be worthy of respect
> He can forfeit a son's respect
> But I hope at least that my son will respect me, if
> only for leaving him free to respect me or not.[7]

The father is able to demand respect simply by presupposing that the son will buy his rhetorical argument. If this happens, the father's inactivity is the source of his power over the son, constituted through what the father wants to call "respect," together with a whole array of ideas like what is "natural," what is education, and what "should" means. Ethics are presupposed; the son is invited to mirror the father's reasoning, and then he is trapped by the total inactivity that subordinates him. The final threat emerges: if you don't respect me, you wrong me. But certainly no one can desire this, at least if one is able to reason like the father.

Second, some positive reflections of the subordinated mind:

> What one has,
>   has been given one
> therefore everything one has
>   one is entitled to.
> The more one has
>   the better one is
>   because the more one has been rewarded
>   for being good.
> Therefore I get better and better
>   through 'making' more and more.[8]

The person's entitlements are based on the other person's acceptance or gifts. Therefore, the person may entertain the delusion of power, namely, that he really owns all he has and can grow into a better and stronger person by acquiring more entitlements. However, all this is conditional on the gift one cannot control. One's power entails an escalation of dependency. The withdrawal of rewards becomes a threat whose meaning is truly existentialist. This threat shakes the foundations of his personal constitution. Let us now check how this same type of reasoning works in coercion and explicit domination.

I shall conjecture that the coercer tries to hide the conflict; the victim wants to make it public. The coercer thinks that he is right, otherwise he could not present a recognizable threat, and his reference group agrees. In fact, they believe in the validity of the following contrary-to-fact conditional: if B were reasonable, he would agree that he is mistaken; therefore his resistance is unfounded, as he is certainly capable of drawing the right conclusion from the available premises. This move hides the conflict behind the veil of ethics. The conflict is now merely apparent since it should vanish, and so the threat should not be needed, assuming that B plays his own part right.

The second strategy used by the coercer is designed to hide the threat, while the first one covered up the conflict. This is already familiar territory. The threatening speech act depends on conditionals, so that the threat itself is dependent on the victim's decision to remain stubborn and resist. A says, "*if* you don't do x . . . ," and he may well give it a tensed reading: you still have time to think and be reasonable, agree with me, and stop resisting, so that I need not harm you. In this way the coercer is not yet threatening his victim. He is only saying that he will, if he must. Now the context of interaction becomes ambiguous. Alternatively, the speech act sounds meaningless.

The most interesting hidden case is the one in which the coercer explicates nothing, but the hidden threat has the feature that its realization is triggered by something the victim does. For example, I stand by my new car that you would like to touch, except that you know that I shall yell at you if you do so. I am not threatening you since I say nothing. I have formed no intentions in that direction. At the same time you may think that you are being unreasonably denied something you are entitled to, something that you have been able to do in the company of your friends. In this kind of rhetorical context the initial forward-looking threat is replaced by the backward-looking retaliation. The aggressiveness of the threat is now transformed into a compensation for the damage done or for the violation of a right.

In the legal context, for example, it is intolerably harsh to conceptualize a punishment as a realized threat because this entails that all citizens are indeed threatened all the time. Whatever one does and wherever one goes, the knowledge that the wrong move will bring about severe harm would be there. Instead, the language of punishments is used, which turns the time perspective upside down. One has done something that is wrong or criminal, hence the punishment. The law does not threaten you; it reacts to wrongdoing. Another way of expressing this is to say that when the criminal law uses threats, the law enforcement agency feels justified in surveying the population much more closely than otherwise. To present a threat of the form "if you do x, we punish you," it must also be able to detect the occurrences of x all over the population, in order to determine whether the threat is needed and if it works. However, if backward-looking punishments are used, the power-wielder just waits and reacts when something happens. He has no reason for surveying the population all the time.

If the threat can be called a standing threat, and if it is a fair one, coercive agents must know that it is effective. In other words, they must learn about the validity of the following contrary-to-fact condition: If we were not threatening people with fear and personal harm, they would do wrong and commit crimes. In liberal society, such control is very unpleasant. Every citizen is considered a potential criminal who is kept at bay mainly because of the efficient standing threat. It is indeed much more natural to think that the criminal law does not threaten law-abiding citizens but merely punishes criminals. And because it punishes, it also prevents crime. A law-abiding citizen does not even entertain criminal ideas. Those who are inclined to severe wrongdoing know that they cannot profit. They know about the punishment, which together with the knowledge of their inclination toward crime, tells them to avoid wrongdoing. They should constantly threaten themselves, so to speak.

My main point is that the coercer's natural rhetorical way of thinking of coercion is by trying to hide the threat. This goal is achieved by denying that the coercer is active first in surveying the opponent and then by making the decision to realize the threat. Instead, the victim is supposed to do something that triggers justified counteraction. The power-wielder does not even want to survey the victim all the time for signs of wrongdoing. On the contrary, it is the victim's own responsibility to keep in mind that if he misbehaves he must suffer for it. He is supposed to monitor himself and draw the appropriate conclusions. This strategy, whenever it can be used in full, tends to cover up the coercive reaches of social power.

The ultimate goal is to hide first, the existence of the threat, and second, its effects. An example is a prison. What you see from the outside is the prison, never its everyday reality or its inmates. Raw power and naked conflicts are covered by the wall, which only allows you to survey your own inclinations to become a prisoner and to check out the reality of punishment. You do not see the prisoners either. When they emerge from behind the walls, they are no longer prisoners. Their rehabilitation has already started, and they are at least invited to shake the old role identity. Otherwise they cannot succeed in social life, and this is an alternative that looks like a new, subtle threat, now designed to cover up the reality of power.

Perhaps this is the same conclusion that Michel Foucault reaches:

> Let me offer a general and tactical reason that seems self-evident: power is tolerable only on condition that it mask a substantial part of itself. Its success is proportional to its ability to hide its own mechanisms.[9]

Foucault also claims that "power represses sex" and that "the logic of power exerted on sex is the paradoxical logic of a law that might be expressed as an injunction of nonexistence, nonmanifestation, and silence."[10] This entails that rhetorically sexuality is power and power is sex, simply because they both share the essential feature of being hidden when they work best. Perhaps Foucault really means this, if we understand him as identifying power not only with sex, but with crime, insanity, and illness. They must be controlled by means of counterpower that normalizes them, but also, paradoxically, hides them. (Sexuality is power and sex is repressed.) At least he wants to make a distinction between law and power: "We must construct an analytics of power that no longer takes law as a model and a code."[11] This is true, but between the code of, say, criminal law and the diffuse and impersonal cultural forms of sexuality are strata of personal domination, like coercion, which are dependent both on the law model of power and its omnipresent Foucaultian counterpart. In actuality, even the law obeys the Foucaultian norms, as I have tried to show. The visible legal power is intolerable, too. It is power that is easy to perceive, true, but do we really want to see its reality?

Is it also true that some forms of repression hide their targets, which gives them all the power they have? Perhaps one can argue that the power of subordinated persons depends on this kind of paradoxical mechanism. Indeed, in social life to be powerless is a low-status position that does not call for publicity. Both the victim and the impartial audience tend to dismiss the existence of those who are victimized by threats. The victim's position is difficult. He needs publicity in order to protect himself against the excesses of power, but at the same time he cannot find the visibility attractive, simply because it means powerlessness. Moreover, this last aspect of his situation also hints at his status as the loser in some normative conflicts, or as being unjustified, irrational, and plain wrong. In this way, the victim has power when he is hidden. He is still a threat on the grounds of the following contrary-to-fact reason: if one is not controlled, one is a threat; therefore one deserves attention. And threat entails power or ability to influence and change things. Yet nobody wants this type of power: its visibility entails plain powerlessness, which is undesirable, even shameful.

My conclusion is this: A controls B, which entails that B has power. This power is realizable via making B's desires visible, which is exactly what A does not want. At the same time B knows that to make his situation visible is to make his powerlessness a public show. This is undesirable. A and B agree.

The victim's self-surveillance and fear are connected to the greater freedom of operations of those who have power. The victims are stricken by a fatal conflict, the tension between the need to publicize the threat and undeniable shamefulness of their helplessness. If they conquer the shame and make their condition public, they are able to force the power-wielder to threaten them explicitly, to survey the case himself, instead of leaving it to the inner gaze of the victim, and to assume responsibility. This tends to make the presence of threats intolerable to the public in general, including parts of the reference group of the powerful. The domination of men over women is an example: as a group, women have been able to publicize their subordination in social life and explicate the many forms of power that they have been supposed to internalize. Such a move creates two camps, women and men, and brings their conflict out in the open. The danger is the suicidal tendency involved in such an effort: women establish themselves as a different camp that has nothing to do with men. Both are free and independent, but isolated.

If the subordinated group is powerless, it may not be effective to bring the conflict into broad daylight, simply because this will make them even more powerless. This is part of what it means to be powerless. To put the same point in a different way, threats and punishments are only a thin red line that runs through a vast network of power relations, which I have called the rhetoric of domination. Conceptual and analytical study can easily reach the strict coercive side of all this. But the aspect of domination is a different matter. Power that is not efficient is not power, and power cannot be efficient if it is not distributed unevenly. Moreover, the uneven distribution, or the emergence of the powerful and the powerless, entails that the rhetoric of power flow unidirectionally. The powerful, in order to be powerful, must induce an ideology to the society. This is because we are not discussing violence here, but normative conflict, valid patterns of practical reason and convincingness of communicated messages. Therefore, the deeper aspect of power is dependent on facts such as who can see what, who is willing to recognize what, and whose aims are too costly. The powerless can hardly advertise their own position without acquiring power first.

The poor, underprivileged, handicapped, insane, elderly, criminal, and similar groups are invisible components of the affluent society. They cannot afford to publicize their condition too much, otherwise they will run the risk of losing their last vestiges of power, namely, their possibility of being a menace. They are entitled to this if they do it quietly. Otherwise, they are surveyed and dealt with by the dominant authority, which may turn out to be a legally coercive one, too. (As I explained above, such a power-wielder does not want to present genuine forward-looking threats, which are too visible and as such anxiety-ridden, disturbing, and confusing also to the powerful reference group.)

Perhaps both the powerful and the powerless are able to reach this one equilibrium point between their otherwise conflicting interests. They do not agree on it, but they act in unison—wherever the threats, their realization and effects must be hidden behind the veil of rhetoric. The powerful want domination over a given group, which means that the measures of power must be focused on the targets and not elsewhere. The general population cannot sympathize with the notion that they are potentially insane, observed and threatened with some paternalistic methods of discretion and treatment. The suspect groups must monitor themselves so that they can be threatened in the proper backward-looking, or retaliatory, manner. At the same time the powerless group knows that they can avoid the worst aspect of threats when they internalize this requirement; although they do not accept it, they just do it. The hidden, self-surveying gaze anticipates the threat and leads one to experience a hidden life of less than the full degree of self-realization. One cannot act as mean and angry as one in fact is. To bring one's own interests, values, and ideas into the open would harm both sides, the powerful as well as their victims, but it certainly harms more of those who are devoid of power. They now look like a threat to be suppressed regardless of cost. They are feared and because of the costly suppression, also hated.

In this way, in an open conflict the power-wielder may assume a new strategy: the rebellious group must be somehow stigmatized.[12]

They must be shown to have a unique feature that they do not share with other people, that is, the members of the powerful reference group. The other people need not be worried. But this achievement requires that the subordinate group be clearly stigmatized because only this creates the gap between them and others, and only this clears the newly emerging fears.

The effect of the results on the powerless tend to be catastrophic. Instead of subtle domination, based on self-surveillance and predictable punishment, the power game has changed into a new one. The key aspect is now the reification of the stigmatized people as separate objects of surveillance and constant threat. Antisemitism at its worst works like this, and attitudes toward gypsies provide another illustration. Gypsies are irresponsible vagabonds (stigma) who steal (wrong), which is why they should be kept under observation (threat) wherever they go. This explicit coercive strategy has been mobilized because they refuse to adopt the mainstream language, values, and dress code, making themselves identifiable both in terms of their appearance and values.

In terms of the strategies of domination, a subordinate group has a choice between (1) the visibility and stigma of objects of coercion and (2) invisibility and self-surveillance along with a subject's status. It is difficult to know which is the better alternative. Visibility offers some hope of changing one's status because it can be used as a point of reference when supporting political forces are mobilized. Visibility may well be a logically necessary condition for the positive change of status and power. But it may be only negligibly efficient as a condition. And invisibility can easily be taken to mean that the powerless have in fact accepted their own status. They deserve to be subordinated and are also willing to do what they can to keep the status quo intact. They survey themselves because they believe that it is right and best for them. Such a state of affairs offers practically no hope for the powerless to advance their cause.

Let us return to the discussion of one alternative way to truth about the rights and wrongs of coercion, domination, and power: the existence of an impartial audience. Indeed, much of the popular ethical rhetoric depends on the assumption of the existence of such an audience. We tend to think that the powerless may advertise their peril in front of the audience, whose opinion also matters. Does this triangular scheme work, providing the much-needed balance within the field of power?

One can argue against the popular triangular view, for instance by saying that in matters of power, the audience is always partial. They may already take a stand before they have heard both sides, the powerful and the powerless, but afterward they must do so. The external vantage point of observations and judgments is a myth. The simplest explanation of this proposition that matters of power are so important, anxiety-ridden, and far-reaching that no human audience can afford to stay apathetic. We can look back to the examples provided by Sade above to convince ourselves that impartiality is impossible.

That example shows in what sense it is true to say that when the audience faces a deep conflict, there cannot be an objective, impartial audience. Both sides invite the audience to participate in the conflict on their side, using very different rhetorical arguments to support their case. To observe a conflict is to take sides, which does not help to dissolve the conflict. On the contrary, intensification is what is achieved, but this may be the first step toward conciliation. Paradoxically, conflicts are resolved by developing them to their extreme, to the point at which something must happen, and destroying the very situation in which the conflict used to flourish. Perhaps this is what the subordinate party should think, and therefore I am personally adopting the standpoint of the powerless at this stage of my argument. The powerful may then enjoy the conflict, as it is, almost endlessly. The problem of audience is, however, difficult to evaluate. In some reasonably modest cases, it may seem that one is able to stay in the role of an impartial observer. Whether or not such a position is just another rhetorical move designed to cover up one's commitments remains an open question. Too many cases are, *prima facie*, unlike those described by Sade. Personally I feel that the concept of conflict logically entails that no neutral standpoint may exist, but this is a conjecture on my part.

Conclusion

What can and what should be done? A sociologist may suggest some remedies via cultural, political, and economic change. These things certainly change; the world is not stable. A philosopher can also spell out some implications of the definition and the logic of power. I have tried to explicate what it means to have power, focusing on its surface of strategic choices and their moral justification and taking into account the deeper aspects of the rhetorical arguments that conceal and redefine some unavoidable and essential conflicts. I have argued first that the rhetoric of domination is dismissed all too often, especially when one focuses on the analytical models of power and their exercise; and second, because coercion entails an unresolved conflict that necessitates the use of strategies that are unacceptable in any cooperative environment.

Chapter 7

The Critique of Impure Reason: Foucault and the Frankfurt School

—————————— *Thomas McCarthy*

I

Following Michel Foucault's own example, commentators have generally paid much more attention to his break with earlier forms of critical social theory than to his continuities with them. It is not surprising that a thinker of his originality, having come of age intellectually in postwar France, would eventually assert his intellectual identity in opposition to the varieties of Marxism prevalent there. But for purposes of developing a critical theory adequate to the complexities of our situation, focusing only on discontinuities can be counterproductive. In fact, viewed at some remove from the current debates, what unites Foucault with neo-Marxist thinkers is as significant as what divides them. This is particularly true of the group of theorists loosely referred to as the Frankfurt School, to whom he did not address himself in any detail. Let me begin by noting certain broad similarities between Foucault's genealogy of power/knowledge and the program of critical social theory advanced by Max Horkheimer and his colleagues in the early 1930s and recently renewed by Jürgen Habermas.[1]

1. Both Foucault and the Frankfurt School call for a transformation cum radicalization of the Kantian approach to critique. The intrinsic impurity of what we call *reason*—its embeddedness in culture and society, its entanglement with power and interest, the historical variability of its categories and criteria, the embodied, sensuous, and practically engaged character of its bearers—makes its structures inaccessible to the sort of introspective survey of the contents of consciousness favored by early modern philosophers and some twentieth-century phenomenologists. Nor is the turn to language or sign systems an adequate response to this altered view of reason; all forms of linguistic or discursive idealism rest on an indefensible abstraction from social

121

practices. To explore the "nature, scope and limits of human reason," we have to get at those practices, and this calls for modes of sociohistorical inquiry that go beyond the traditional bounds of philosophical analysis. The critique of reason, as a nonfoundationalist enterprise, is concerned with structures and rules that transcend the individual consciousness. But what is supraindividual in this way is no longer understood as transcendental; it is sociocultural in origin.

2. Correspondingly, both Foucault and the Frankfurt School reject the Cartesian picture of an autonomous rational subject set against a world of objects that it seeks to represent and, through representing, to master. Knowing and acting subjects are social and embodied beings, and the products of their thought and action bear ineradicable traces of their situations and interests. The atomistic and disengaged Cartesian subject has to be dislodged from its position at the center of the epistemic and moral universes, and not only for theoretical reasons: it undergirds the egocentric, domineering, and possessive individualism that has so disfigured modern Western rationalism and driven it to exclude, dominate, or assimilate whatever is different. Thus, the desublimation of reason goes hand-in-hand with the decentering of the rational subject.

3. More distinctive perhaps than either of these now widely held views is that of the primacy of the practical over the theoretical which Foucault shares with the Frankfurt School. A reversal of the traditional hierarchy was already proposed by Kant, only to be retracted by Hegel; it was then reinstated by the young Marx but soon faded into the background of scientific socialism. Once we have turned our attention from consciousness to culture and society, however, there is no good reason why knowledge and representation should enjoy the privilege over values and norms that Western philosophy has accorded them. Moreover, if knowledge is itself understood as a social product, the traditional oppositions between theory and practice, fact and value, and the like begin to break down, for there are practical, normative presuppositions to any social activity, theorizing included. Like other practices, epistemic practices have to be comprehended in their sociocultural contexts. In this sense, the theory of knowledge is part of the theory of society, which is *itself* embedded in practical contexts, and in rather distinctive ways. It is his recognition of the peculiarly reflexive relation of thinking about society to what is being thought about that leads Foucault to characterize his genealogy as "history of the present." Situated in the very reality it seeks to comprehend and relating the past from the practically interested standpoint of an anticipated fu-

ture, it is anything but a view from nowhere. And though Western Marxism has repeatedly succumbed to the siren calls of a scientific theory of history or a speculative philosophy of history,[2] it has usually found its way back to a similar notion of practical reflexivity. In this version of critical social theory, there is an essentially prospective dimension to writing the history of the present in which one is situated; and the projected future, which gives shape to the past, is not a product of disinterested contemplation or of scientific prediction, but of practical engagement. It is a future that we can seek to bring about.

4. With suitable changes in terminology, much of the above could also apply to philosophical hermeneutics. It too takes seriously the fact that reason, in its cognitive employment as well, is embedded in sociocultural contexts, mediated by natural languages and intrinsically related to action. It too maintains that speech and action occur against immeasurable, taken-for-granted backgrounds, which are historically and culturally variable and which can never be brought fully to conscious awareness. And yet genealogy is as distinct from hermeneutics as is critical social theory. Despite some very real differences on this point, neither wishes to leave to the participants and their traditions the final say about the significance of the practices they engage in. Both see the need for an objectifying outsider's perspective to get beyond shared, unproblematic meanings and their hermeneutic retrieval. Foucault's way of creating distance from the practices we live by is to display their "lowly origins" in contingent historical circumstances, to dispel their appearance of self-evident givenness by treating them as the outcome of multiple relations of force. From the start, critical social theory was also based on a rejection of what Marx viewed as the specifically "German ideology" and Horkheimer called "the idealist madness" of understanding ideas solely in terms of other ideas. It has insisted that the full significance of ideas can be grasped only by viewing them in the context of the social practices in which they figure, and that this typically requires using sociohistorical analysis to gain some distance from the insider's view of the participants. Genetic and functional accounts of how and why purportedly rational practices came to be taken for granted play an important role in both forms of the critique of impure reason.

5. In neither perspective, however, does this mean simply adopting the methods of the established human sciences. Both Foucault and the Frankfurt School see these as particularly in need of critical analysis, as complicitous in special ways with the ills of the present age. There are, to be sure, some important differences here, for instance, as

to which particular sciences are most in need of critique and as to how extensive critique should be.[3] But there are also a number of important commonalities in their critiques of the epistemological and methodological ideas in terms of which we have constituted ourselves as subjects and objects of knowledge. Furthermore, both are critical of the role that the social sciences and social scientifically trained "experts" have played in the process of "rationalization." They see the rationality that came to prevail in modern society as an instrumental potential for extending our mastery over the physical and social worlds, a rationality of technique and calculation, of regulation and administration, in search of ever-more effective forms of domination. Inasmuch as the human sciences have assisted mightily in forging and maintaining the bars of this "iron cage," to use Max Weber's phrase, they are a prime target for genealogical and dialectical critique.

6. As ongoing practical endeavors rather than closed theoretical systems, both forms of critique aim at transforming our self-understanding in ways that have implications. It is true that Foucault persistently rejected the notions of ideology and ideology-critique and denied that genealogy could be understood in those terms. But the conceptions of ideology he criticized were rather crude, and the criticisms he offered were far from devastating to the more sophisticated versions propounded by members of the Frankfurt School. It is in fact difficult to see why Foucault's efforts to analyze "how we govern ourselves and others by the production of truth" so as to "contribute to changing people's ways of perceiving and doing things,"[4] do not belong to the same genre. In this reading, in both genealogy and critical social theory the objectifying techniques employed to gain distance from the rational practices we have been trained in afford us a critical perspective on those practices. Making problematic what is taken for granted— for instance, by demonstrating that the genesis of what has heretofore seemed to be natural and necessary involves contingent relations of force and an arbitrary closing off of alternatives, or that what parades as objective actually rests on prescriptions that function in maintaining imbalances of power—can weaken its hold upon us. Categories, principles, rules, standards, criteria, procedures, techniques, beliefs, and practices formerly accepted as purely and simply rational may come to be seen as in the service of particular interests and constellations of power that have to be disguised to be advanced, or as performing particular functions in maintaining power relations that would not be subscribed to if generally recognized. Because things are not always what they seem to be and because awareness of this can create critical distance—because, in particular, such awareness can under-

mine the authority that derives from presumed rationality, universality, or necessity—it can be a social force for change. Whether or not this is so, and the extent to which it is so, is in the eyes of both Foucault and the Frankfurt School, not a question of metaphysical necessity or theoretical deduction but of contingent historical conditions. That is, the practical significance of critical insight varies with the historical circumstances.

If the foregoing comparisons are not wide of the mark, Foucault and the Frankfurt School should be located rather close to one another on the map of contemporary theoretical options. They hold in common that the heart of the philosophical enterprise, the critique of reason, finds its continuation in certain forms of sociohistorical analysis carried out with the practical intent of gaining critical distance from the presumably rational beliefs and practices that inform our lives. This would certainly place them much nearer to one another than to other varieties of contemporary theory, including the more influential varieties of textualism. Why, then, have the oppositions and differences loomed so large? Part of the explanation (but only part) is that the disagreements between them are no less real than the agreements. Though genealogy and critical social theory do occupy neighboring territories in our theoretical world, their relations are combative rather than peaceful. Foucault's Nietzschean heritage and the Hegelian-Marxist heritage of the Frankfurt School lead them to lay competing claims to the very same areas:

1. While both seek to transform the critique of reason through shifting the level of analysis to social practice, Foucault, like Nietzsche, sees this as leading to a critique that is radical in the etymological sense of that term, one that attacks rationalism at its very roots; whereas critical social theorists, following Hegel and Marx, understand critique rather in the sense of a determinate negation that aims at a more adequate conception of reason.

2. While both seek to get beyond the subject-centeredness of modern Western thought, Foucault understands this as the "end of man" and of the retinue of humanist conceptions following upon it; whereas critical social theorists attempt to reconstruct notions of subjectivity and autonomy that are consistent with both the social dimensions of individual identity and the situated character of social action.

3. While both assert the primacy of practical reason and acknowledge the unavoidable reflexivity of social inquiry, Foucault takes this to be incompatible with the context-transcendence of truth claims and the pretensions of general social theories; whereas the Frankfurt theo-

rists seek to combine contextualism with universalism and to construct general accounts of the origins, structures, and tendencies of existing social orders.

4. While both refuse to take participants' views of their practices as the last word in understanding them, critical social theorists do take them as the first word and seek to engage them in the very process of trying to gain critical distance from them; whereas the genealogist resolutely displaces the participants' perspective with an externalist perspective in which the validity claims of participants are not engaged but bracketed.

5. While both are critical of established human sciences and see them as implicated in weaving tighter the web of discipline and domination, Foucault understands this to be a general indictment: genealogy is not a science but an "antiscience"; whereas critical social theorists direct their critique against particular forms of social research, while seeking to identify and develop others that are not simply extensions of instrumental rationality.

6. Finally, while both see the critique of apparently rational practices as having the practical purpose of breaking their hold upon us, Foucault does not regard genealogy as being in the service of reason, truth, freedom, and justice—there is no escaping the relations and effects of power altogether, for they are coextensive with, indeed constitutive of, social life generally; whereas Frankfurt School theorists understand the critique of ideology as working to reduce such relations and effects and to replace them with social arrangements that are rational in other than an instrumentalist sense.

II

With this broad comparison as a background, I would like now to take a closer and more critical look at the radical critique of reason and the rational subject that Foucault developed in the 1970s in the context of his power/knowledge studies. For purposes of defining what is at issue between him and the Frankfurt School, I shall use Habermas' attempt to renew Horkheimer's original program as my principal point of reference.

As remarked above, Foucault's genealogical project can be viewed as a form of the critique of reason. Inasmuch as modern philosophy has understood itself to be the most radical reflection on reason, its conditions, limits, and effects, the continuation-through-transformation of that project today requires a sociohistorical turn. What have to be analyzed are paradigmatically rational *practices*, and they cannot be adequately understood in isolation from the sociohistorical contexts in which they emerge and function. Foucault is, of course, interested in the relations of power that traverse such practices and their contexts. He reminds us repeatedly that "truth is not the reward of free spirits" but "a thing of this world" that is "produced only by virtue of multiple forms of constraint."[5] Analytical attention is redirected to the rules, prescriptions, procedures, and the like that are constitutive of rational practices; to the relations of asymmetry, nonreciprocity, and hierarchy they encode; and to the ways in which they include and exclude, make central and marginal, assimilate and differentiate. This shift in focus makes us aware that there is something like a politics of truth and knowledge even at this level of analysis.[6] Irrationality, incompetence, deviance, error, nonsense, and the like get marked off in various ways from their opposites; people and practices get valorized or stigmatized, rewarded or penalized, dismissed or vested with authority on this basis. But genealogical analysis does not confine itself to the political aspects of rules and regulations *internal* to discursive practices. It also examines the *external* relations of theoretical discourses, especially the discourses of the "sciences of man," to the practical discourses in which they are applied—the discourses of psychologists, physicians, judges, administrators, social workers, educators, and the like—as well as to the institutional practices with which they are interwoven in asylums, hospitals, prisons, schools, administrative bureaucracies, welfare agencies, and the like. As soon as one tries to comprehend why a particular constellation of rules and procedures should define rational practice in a given domain, consideration of the larger sociohistorical context becomes unavoidable.

"Each society," as Foucault puts it, "has its regime of truth,"[7] and genealogy is interested precisely in how we govern ourselves and others through its production. Focusing especially on the human sciences—the sciences of which "man" is the object—he examines the myriad ways in which power relations are both conditions and effects of the production of truth about human beings. In areas of inquiry ranging from psychiatry and medicine to penology and population studies, he uncovers the feedback relations between the power exercised over people to extract data from and about them (by a variety of means, from observing, examining, and interrogating individuals to surveying and administering populations) and the effects of power that attach to the qualified experts and licensed professionals who possess and apply the knowledge thus gained. According to Foucault, the sciences of man not only arose in institutional settings structured by hierarchical relations of power, they continue to function mainly in such settings. Indeed, what is distinctive about the modern disciplinary regime, in his view, is just the way in which coercion by violence has been largely replaced by the gentler force of administration by scientifically trained experts, public displays of power by the imperceptible deployment of techniques based on a detailed knowledge of their targets. From Foucault's perspective, then, the human sciences are a major force in the disastrous triumph of Enlightenment thinking, and the panoptical scientific observer is a salient expression of the subject-centered, putatively universal reason which that thinking promotes. By tracing the lowly origins of these sciences in struggle and conflict, in particularity and contingency, in a will to truth that is implicated in domination and control, genealogy reveals their constitutive interconnections with historically changing constellations of power: "power and knowledge directly imply one another. . . . The subject who knows, the objects to be known, and the modalities of knowledge must be regarded as so many effects of these fundamental implications of power-knowledge and their historical transformations."[8]

Although Habermas agrees with Foucault in regarding truth as "a thing of this world," he distinguishes between fundamentally different cognitive approaches marked by different configurations of action, experience, and language.[9] He does this with the aim of resisting the identification of instrumental and strategic rationality with rationality *tout court*. To construe sociocultural rationalization as the growing hegemony of techniques of power and control, of domination and administration, is not so much erroneous as incomplete. That reading fails to grasp the selectivity of capitalist modernization, its failure to develop in a balanced way the different dimensions of rationality opened up by the modern understanding of the world. Because we are as much language-using as tool-using animals, the representation of reason as essentially instrumental and strategic is fatally one-sided. On the other hand, it is indeed the case that those types of rationality have achieved a certain dominance in our culture. The subsystems in which they are centrally institutionalized—the economy and government administration—have increasingly come to pervade other areas of life and make them over in their own image and likeness. The resultant "monetarization" and "bureaucratization" of life is what Habermas refers to as the "colonization of the life world."

This picture of a society colonized by market and administrative forces differs from Foucault's picture of a disciplinary society, among other ways, in targeting for critique not the Enlightenment idea of a life informed by reason, as such, but rather the failure to pursue it by developing and institutionalizing modalities of reason other than the subject-centered, instrumental ones that increasingly shape our lives. The two pictures do overlap in a number of areas. For instance, both focus on the entanglement of knowledge with power that is character- istic of the sciences of man. But Foucault regards this analysis as valid for all the human sciences, whereas Habermas wants to distinguish objectifying (e.g. behavioral) approaches from interpretive (e.g., hermeneutical) and from critical (e.g., genealogical or dialectical) ap- proaches. The interests that inform them are, he argues, fundamen- tally different, as are, consequently, their general orientations to their object domains and their characteristic logics of inquiry. From this perspective, only purely objectifying approaches are *intrinsically* geared to expanding control over human beings, whereas other approaches may be suited to extending the intersubjectivity of mutual understand- ing or to gaining reflective distance from taken-for-granted beliefs and practices.

There is broad agreement between Foucault and Habermas that the expansion of the welfare state is increasingly dependent on the generation and application of expert knowledge of various sorts. In this regard, Foucault's account of the interrelation between social in- stitutions geared to normalization and the growth of knowledge suited to that purpose parallels Habermas' account of the interconnection between the administrative colonization of the lifeworld and the rise of objectifying social science. Here too the differences have chiefly to do with how close to all-inclusive this critical perspective can claim to be. Foucault extrapolates to the human sciences in general the results of his analyses of knowledge generated in the more or less repressive contexts he singles out for attention. One consequence of this is his clearly inadequate account of hermeneutic approaches;[10] another is his inability to account for his own genealogical practice in other than action terms—it ends up being simply another power move in a thor- oughly power-ridden network of social relations, an intervention meant to alter the existing balance of forces. In the remainder of part II, I want to look more closely at two key elements of his metatheory of genealogical practice: the ontology of *power* and the representation of the *subject* as an effect of power.

Power: Ontology versus Social Theory

The differences between Foucault and Habermas are misrepresented by the usual opposition between the nominalistic particularism of the former and the abstract universalism of the latter. In his Nietzschean moments, Foucault can be as universalistic as one might like or dislike. While he insists that he wants to do without the claims to necessity typical of foundationalist enterprises, he often invokes an ontology of the social that treats exclusion, subjugation, and homogenization as inescapable presuppositions and consequences of any social practice. And while he targets for genealogical analysis social institutions that are clearly marked by hierarchies of power, his own conception of power as a network of relations in which we are all, always and everywhere, enmeshed devalues questions of who possesses power and with what right, of who profits or suffers from it, and the like. (These are questions typical of the liberal and Marxist approaches that he rejects.) What we gain from adopting this conception is a greater sensitivity to the constraints and impositions that figure in any social order, in any rational practice, in any socialization process. In this expanded sense of the term, power is indeed "a productive network that runs through the whole social body."[11] Giving this insight an ontological twist, one might then say, with Foucault, that "power produces reality, it produces domains of objects and rituals of truth,"[12] or alternatively, that "truth is not the product of free spirits" but is "produced by virtue of multiple forms of constraints."[13] It is clear, for instance, that any "regime of truth" involves privileging certain types of discourse, sanctioning certain ways of distinguishing true from false statements, underwriting certain techniques for arriving at the truth, according a certain status to those who competently employ them, and so forth. In this sense there is indeed a "political economy" of truth, as there is of any organized social activity; that insight is the principal gain of Foucault's ontologizing of the concept of power.

There are also losses incurred: having become more or less coextensive with constraint, power becomes all too like the night in which all cows are black. Welcoming or denouncing someone, putting someone at ease or into prison, cooperating with or competing with someone—these are all equally exercises of power in Foucault's conceptualization. If his aim is to draw attention to the basic fact that patterned social interaction always involves normative expectations and thus possible sanctions, this is a rhetorically effective way of doing so. But the costs for social theory of such dedifferentiation are considerable. Distinctions between just and unjust social arrangements, legitimate and illegitimate uses of political power, strategic and cooperative interpersonal relations, coercive and consensual measures—distinctions that have been at the heart of critical social analysis—become marginal. If there were no possibility of retaining the advantages of Foucault's Nietzschean move without taking these disadvantages into the bargain, we would be faced with a fundamental choice between different types of social analysis. But there is no need to construe this as an either/or situation. We can agree with Foucault that social action is everywhere structured by background expectations in terms of which we hold one another accountable, that deviations from these are sanctionable by everything from negative affective responses and breakdowns of cooperation to explicit reprimands and punishments, and that our awareness of this differential accountability is a primary source of the motivated compliance that characterizes "normal" interaction.[14] And we can agree with him that the modern period has witnessed a vast expansion of the areas of life structured by instrumental, strategic, and bureaucratic forms of social interrelation. None of this prevents us from then going on to mark the sociologically and politically crucial distinctions that have figured so centrally in the tradition of critical social theory. Nancy Fraser has stated the issue here with admirable clarity: "The problem is that Foucault calls too many different sorts of things power and simply leaves it at that. Granted, all cultural practices involve constraints. But these constraints are of a variety of different kinds and thus demand a variety of different normative responses. . . . Foucault writes as if oblivious to the existence of the whole body of Weberian social theory with its careful distinctions between such notions as authority, force, violence, domination and legitimation. Phenomena which are capable of being distinguished via such concepts are simply lumped together. . . . As a consequence, the potential for a broad range of normative nuances is surrendered, and the result is a certain normative one-dimensionality."[15]

The Subject: Deconstruction versus Reconstruction

Foucault has related on various occasions how "people of [his] generation were brought up on two forms of analysis, one in terms of the constituent subject, the other in terms of the economic-in-the-last-instance . . . "[16] As we have seen, he worked himself free of the latter by, among other things, drawing upon Nietzsche to develop a "capillary" conception of power as coextensive with the social. In working free of the former, he was able to call upon the assistance of structuralist semiotics to argue for the priority of systems of signification over individual acts thereof. Even after he distanced himself from structuralism by taking as his point of reference "not the great model of language and signs, but that of war and battle,"[17] he retained this order of priority in the form of the "regimes," the interconnected systems of discourses, practices, and institutions that structure and give sense to individual actions. From the perspective of the genealogist, the subject privileged by phenomenology is in reality not the *constituens* but the *constitutum* of history and society; and phenomenology itself is only a recent chapter in the long tradition of subjectivism. At the core of that tradition is a hypostatization of the contingent outcome of historical processes into their foundational origin—not in the sense, typically, of a conscious creation, but in the sense of an alienated objectification of subjective powers, which has then to be consciously reappropriated. This latter figure of thought is, for Foucault, the philosophical heart of the humanist project (including Marxist humanism) of mastering those forces, without and within, that compromise "man's" autonomy and thus block his true self-realization. Like Horkheimer and Adorno in the *Dialectic of Enlightenment,* Foucault sees this as inherently a project of domination, a project that defines modern Western man's domineering relation to otherness and difference in all forms.

I want to argue that Foucault's reaction to this perceived state of affairs is an overreaction. Owing in part to the continued influence of structuralist motifs in his genealogical phase, he swings to the opposite extreme of hypostatizing wholes—regimes, networks, dispositifs, and the like—against parts, thus proposing to replace an abstract individualism with an equally abstract holism. To argue that "the individual is not to be conceived as a sort of elementary nucleus, a primitive atom," it is not necessary to maintain that the individual is merely "one of the prime effects of power."[18] One might defend instead the less radical thesis that individualism is inherently linked to socialization: we become individuals in and through being socialized into shared forms of life, growing into preexisting networks of social relations. From this perspective, Foucault's claim that the individual who is an effect of power is at the same time "the element of its articulation" or "its vehicle,"[19] might be construed as advancing the common sociological view that social structures are produced and maintained, renewed and transformed only through the situated actions of individual agents. But this view entails that agency and structure are *equally* basic to our understanding of social practices, which is decidedly not Foucault's approach. He wants to develop a form of analysis that treats the subject as an effect by "accounting for its constitution within a historical framework." If this were only a matter of "dispensing with the constituent subject," of avoiding all "reference to a subject which is transcendental in relation to the field of events," the disagreement would be merely terminological.[20] It is not, however, only the constituent, transcendental subject that Foucault wants to do without; he proposes a mode of inquiry that makes *no explanatory reference* to individual beliefs, intentions, or actions. Genealogy, he advises us, "should not concern itself with power at the level of conscious intention or decision"; it should refrain from posing questions of the sort: "Who has power and what has he in mind?" The focus should instead be on "how things work at the level of ongoing subjugation, at the level of those continuous and uninterrupted processes" through which "subjects are gradually, progressively, really and materially constituted. . . . "[21] Again, if this were merely an argument for the need to *supplement* an internalist view of social practices with an externalist one, to *balance* an account of agency with an account of structure, to *integrate* a microanalysis of social practices with a structural analysis of persistent patterns of interaction, or with a functional analysis of their unintended consequences, or with an institutional analysis of the normative contexts of individual action, there would be no incompatibility in principle between genealogy and approaches operating with some concept of agency. But Foucault does not want to supplement or balance or integrate, he wants to replace. And the results of this either/or thinking are no happier here than in the traditional theories he criticizes.

There is no hope of arriving at an adequate account of social integration if the only model of social interaction is one of asymmetrical power relations and the only model of socialization is that of an intrusion of disciplinary forces into bodies. Nor can we gain an adequate understanding of most varieties of social interaction by treating agents simply as acting in compliance with preestablished and publicly sanctioned patterns—as what Foucault calls "docile bodies" or Garfinkel calls "cultural dopes." We have to take account of their own understanding of social structures and their own reflexive use of cultural resources for making sense. This is no less true of the types of setting that most interest Foucault; as Goffman and others have made so abundantly clear, interpreting social situations, understanding what is expected in them, anticipating reactions to conformity and deviance, and using this knowledge for one's own strategic purposes are also basic elements of interaction in disciplinary settings.[22] These elements open up space for differential responses to situations, the possibility of analyzing, managing, and transforming them. Furthermore, the same competence and activity of agents is required for an adequate analysis of the rule-following practices central to Foucault's notion of power-knowledge regimes. Since rules do not define their own application, rule following is always to some degree discretionary, elaborative, ad hoc. Each new application requires the agent's judgment in light of the specifics of the situation.[23]

One could go on at length in this vein. The point is simply to indicate how deeply the conceptual framework of agency and accountability is ingrained in our understanding of social practices. Foucault cannot simply drop it and treat social practices as anonymous, impersonal processes. To be sure, he does insist on the interdependence of the notions of power and resistance;[24] but he refuses to link the latter to the capacity of competent subjects to say, with reason, "yes" or "no" to claims made upon them by others. As a result, he is hard put to identify just what it is that resists; often he alludes to something like "the body and its pleasures."[25] But that only plunges us deeper into just the sorts of conceptual tangles he wants to avoid. For it is Foucault, after all, who so forcefully brought home to us just how historical and social the body and its pleasures are. When the need arises, however, he seems to conjure up the idea of a presocial "body" that cannot be fitted without remainder into any social mold. This begins to sound suspiciously like Freud's instinct theory and to suggest a refurbished model of the "repressive hypothesis" that Foucault so emphatically rejected.[26]

If treating the subject merely as "an effect of power"—which must itself then be conceptualized as a subjectless network—undercuts the very notions of discipline, regime, resistance, and the like that are central to genealogical "theory," it raises no less havoc with genealogical "practice." Who practices genealogical analysis? What does it require of them? What promise does it hold out to them? If the self-reflecting subject is nothing but the effect of power relations under the pressure of observation, judgment, control, and discipline, how are we to understand the reflection that takes the form of genealogy? Whence the free play in our reflective capacities that is a condition of possibility for constructing these subversive histories? Foucault certainly writes as if his genealogies advance our self-understanding, and in reading them we repeatedly have the experience of their doing just that. Can we make any sense of this without some, perhaps significantly revised, notion of subjects who can achieve gains in self-understanding with a liberating effect on their lives? Charles Taylor captured this point nicely when he wrote: " 'power' belongs in a semantic field from which 'truth' and 'freedom' cannot be excluded. Because it is linked with the notion of imposition on our significant desires and purposes, it cannot be separated from the notion of some relative lifting of this restraint. . . . So 'power' requires 'liberty,' but it also requires 'truth'—if we want to allow, as Foucault does, that we can collaborate in our own subjugation. . . . Because the imposition proceeds here by foisting illusion upon us, it proceeds by disguises and masks. . . . The truth here is subversive of power."[27] This metatheory, deriving from our Enlightenment heritage and shared by the Frankfurt School, seems to make better sense of Foucault's practice than his own. If that is so, we may learn more from inquiring, as Foucault himself finally did in the 1980s, how his work develops and enriches the critical tradition extending from Kant through the Frankfurt School than from insisting that it has brought it to an end.

III

In his first lecture of 1983 at the Collège de France, Foucault credited Kant with founding "the two great critical traditions between which modern philosophy is divided." One, the "analytic philosophy of truth in general," had been a target of Foucault's criticism from the start. The other, a constantly renewed effort to grasp "the ontology of the present," he acknowledged as his own: "It is this form of philosophy that, from Hegel, through Nietzsche and Max Weber, to the Frankfurt School, has formed a tradition of reflection in which I have tried to work."[28] This belated affirmation of what he calls the "philosophical ethos" of the Enlightenment signals important changes in Foucault's understanding of his critical project. In this final section, I want briefly to characterize those changes in respects relevant to our discussion, and then to examine critically their consequences for Foucault's treatments of the subject and power.[29]

Perhaps the clearest indication of Foucault's altered perception of the Enlightenment tradition can be found in his reflections on Kant's 1784 essay concerning the question "Was ist Aufklärung?"[30] He regards that essay as introducing a new dimension into philosophical thought, namely the critical analysis of our historical present and our present selves. When Kant asked "What is Enlightenment?," writes Foucault, "he meant, What's going on just now? What's happening to us? What is this period, this precise moment in which we are living? Or in other words, What are we? As Aufklärer, as part of the Enlightenment? Compare this with the Cartesian question, Who am I? As a unique but universal and unhistorical subject? For Descartes, It is everyone, anywhere, at any moment. But Kant asks something else: What are we? In a very precise moment of history?"[31] From Hegel to Habermas, Foucault continues, this question has defined a way of philosophizing that he, Foucault, has adopted as his own. What separates this way from a universally oriented "analytic of truth" is an awareness of being constituted by our own history, a resolve to submit that history to critical reflection, and a desire thereby to free ourselves from its pseudonecessities.

As I argued above, Foucault could and should have said the same of the genealogy he practiced in the 1970s; but it became clear to him only in the 1980s that his form of critique also belongs to what Taylor called the "semantic field" of enlightenment discourse. "Thought," he now tells us, "is what allows one to step back from [a] way of acting or reacting, to present it to oneself as an object of thought and question it as to its meaning, its conditions, and its goals. Thought is freedom in relation to what one does, the motion by which one detaches oneself from it, establishes it as an object, and reflects on it as a problem."[32] Freedom, in turn, is said to be the condition and content of morality: "What is morality if not the practice of liberty, the deliberate practice of liberty? . . . Liberty is the ontological condition of ethics. But ethics is the deliberate form assumed by liberty."[33] By releasing us from a state of "immaturity," critical thinking makes possible a "practice of freedom" oriented toward a "mature adulthood" in which we assume responsibility for shaping our own lives.[34]

To be sure, behind all these Kantian formulae there lies a considerably altered critical project. Foucault stresses that faithfulness to the Enlightenment does not mean trying to preserve this or that element of it, but attempting to renew, in our present circumstances, the type of philosophical interrogation it inaugurated—not "faithfulness to doctrinal elements, but rather the permanent reactivation of an attitude, that is, of a philosophical ethos which could be described as a permanent critique of our historical era."[35] Since the Enlightenment, this type of reflective relation to the present has taken the form of a history of reason, and that is the form in which Foucault pursues it: "I think that the central issue of philosophy and critical thought since the eighteenth century has always been, still is, and will, I hope, remain the question: *What* is this Reason that we use? What are its historical effects? What are its limits and what are its dangers? How can we exist as rational beings, fortunately committed to practicing a rationality that is unfortunately crisscrossed by intrinsic dangers?"[36] As noted earlier, Foucault's genealogical histories stress the local and contingent aspects of prevailing forms of rationality rather than their universality. In one way, this is continuous with Kant's linking of enlightenment and critique: when we dare to use our reason, a critical assessment of its conditions and limits is necessary if we are to avoid dogmatism and illusion. On the other hand, genealogy is a very different way of thinking about conditions and limits:

> . . . if the Kantian question was that of knowing what limits knowledge has to renounce transgressing, it seems to me that the critical question today has to be turned back into a positive one: in what is given to us as universal, necessary, obligatory, what place is occupied by whatever is singular, contingent, and the product of arbitrary constraints? The point, in brief, is to transform the critique conducted in the form of necessary limitation into a practical critique that takes the form of a possible transgression . . . criticism is no longer going to be practiced in the search for formal structures with universal value, but rather as an historical investigation into the events that have led us to constitute ourselves and to recognize ourselves as subjects of what we are doing, thinking, saying . . . it will not deduce from the form of what we are what it is impossible for us to do and to know; but it will separate out, from the contingency that has made us what we are, the possibility of no longer being, doing, or thinking what we are, do, or think. It is not seeking to make possible a metaphysics that has finally become a science, it is seeking to give new impetus, as far and wide as possible, to the undefined work of freedom.[37]

As this passage suggests, Foucault's critical histories of the "practical systems" of rationality that "organize our ways of doing things"[38] are at the same time genealogies of the subjects of these rational practices, investigations into the ways in which we have constituted ourselves as rational agents. And their point is not to reinforce established patterns, but to challenge them. Genealogy is "practical critique": it is guided by an interest in the "possible transgression" and transformation of allegedly universal and necessary constraints. Adopting an experimental attitude, it repeatedly probes the "contemporary limits of the necessary" to determine "what is not or no longer indispensable for the constitution of ourselves as autonomous subjects."[39]

Let us turn now to the two topics on which I criticized Foucault's earlier self-understanding: the subject and power. That will serve to focus my account of the theoretical shifts in his later work and to determine more precisely where they leave him in relation to Habermas.

Power Again: Strategic and Communicative Action

My criticisms of Foucault in part II turned on his one-dimensional ontology: in the world he described, truth and subjectivity were reduced in the end to effects of power. He escapes this reductionism in the 1980s by adopting a multidimensional ontology in which power is displaced onto a single axis. Referring to Habermas in his first Howison Lecture at Berkeley in the fall of 1980, he distinguishes three broad types of "techniques": techniques of production, of signification, and of domination.[40] To this he adds a fourth, namely techniques of the self, which subsequently becomes the principal axis of analysis in the second and third volumes of his *History of Sexuality*. These same four dimensions are distinguished (as "technologies") in the seminar he conducted at the University of Vermont in the fall of 1982,[41] and the first three of them are elaborated (as "relations") in the afterword (1982) to Dreyfus and Rabinow, *Michel Foucault: Beyond Structuralism and Hermeneutics*, where, referring once again to Habermas, he notes that they are not "separate domains" but analytically distinguishable aspects of social action that "always overlap" in reality.[42] By 1983 Foucault seems to have settled on a three-dimensional ontology, reminiscent of Habermas' tripartite model of relations to the objective world, to the social world, and to ourselves.

In Volume II of the *History of Sexuality*, for example, he works with a distinction between fields of knowledge, types of normativity, and forms of subjectivity, with three correlated axes of analysis: discursive practices, relations of power, and forms in which individuals recognize themselves as subjects.[43] What immediately strikes one in comparing this scheme with Habermas', is that normatively structured social relations as a matter of course are construed as relations of power. Earlier, when rules and norms constitutive of rational practices were regarded simply as technologies for "governing" and "normalizing" individuals, this is what one would have expected. But now we have to ask what has been accomplished by distinguishing the three ontological dimensions if we are still left with a reduction of social relations to power relations. Part of the answer, I think, is a shift of attention from relations of domination to strategic relations. I want to suggest, in fact, that Foucault's final ontology tends to equate social interaction with strategic interaction, precisely the equation Habermas seeks to block with his concept of communicative action.

The most elaborate explication of his later notion of power appears in Foucault's afterword to the first edition of the Dreyfus and Rabinow study. There he construes the exercise of power as "a way in which certain actions modify others," a "mode of action upon the action of others," which "structures[s] the possible field of [their] action."[44] The relationship proper to power is neither violence nor consensus, but "government" in the very broad sense of "guiding the possibility of conduct and putting in order the possible outcome."[45] Viewed in this way, says Foucault, power is "coextensive with every social relationship,"[46] for "to live in society is to live in such a way that action upon other actions is possible and in fact ongoing."[47]

Foucault's matter-of-course treatment of social relations as power relations is less startling once we realize that he now defines the latter in terms not unlike those the sociological tradition has used to define the former. What makes actions social is precisely the possibility of their influencing and being influenced by the actions and expectations of others. Under Foucault's definition, only actions that had no possible effects on the actions of others—that is, which were not social— would be free of the exercise of power. What is at stake here? Is this merely a rhetorical twist meant to sharpen our awareness of the ways in which our possibilities of action are structured and circumscribed by the actions of others? In part, perhaps, but there is also a metatheoretical issue involved. His conceptualization of social interaction privileges strategic over consensual modes of "guiding the possibility of conduct and putting in order the possible outcomes."

To see how this is so, we must first take a brief look at his distinction between power and domination. Whereas earlier, situations of domination—asylums, clinics, prisons, bureaucracies, and the like— were treated as paradigms of general power relations in the panoptical society, now they are clearly marked off as a particular type of power situation.

> When one speaks of "power," people think immediately of a political structure, a government, a dominant social class, the master facing the slave, and so on. That is not at all what I think when I speak of "relationships of power." I mean that in human relations, whatever they are—whether it be a question of communicating verbally . . . or a question of a love relationship, an institutional or economic relationship—power is always present: I mean the relationships in which one wants to direct the behavior of another. . . . These relations of power are changeable, reversible, and understandable. . . . Now there are effectively states of domination. In many cases, the relations of power are fixed in such a way that they are perpetually asymmetrical and the margin of liberty is extremely limited.[48]

Thus Foucault now distinguishes "relationships of power as strategic games between liberties" in which "some people try to determine the conduct of others" from "the states of domination . . . we ordinarily call power."[49] The idea of a society without power relations is non-

sense, whereas the reduction to a minimum of states of domination—
that is, fixed, asymmetrical, irreversible relations of power—is a meaningful political goal. "Power is not an evil. Power is strategic
games. . . . To exercise power over another in a sort of open strategic
game, where things could be reversed, that is not evil . . . The problem
is rather to know how to avoid . . . the effects of domination."[50] In short,
whereas games of power are coextensive with social relations, states of
domination are legitimate targets of political struggle aimed at freeing
up space for open strategic games. "The more open the game, the
more attractive and fascinating it is."[51]

It is difficult to judge just how far Foucault would have been
willing to take this line of thought. It leads in the end to conceptualizing social relations as strategic relations and social interaction as strategic interaction. It would be ironic indeed if his wholesale critique of
modern social theory should finally end in an embrace of one of its
hoarier forms.[52] But rather than rehearsing the familiar debates concerning game-theoretic approaches to the general theory of action, I
shall remark only on one key issue that separates Foucault from
Habermas.

There are, at least on the face of it, ways of influencing the conduct of others that do not fit very neatly into the model of strategic
games. Habermas's notion of communicative action singles out for
attention the openly intended illocutionary effects that speech acts
may have on the actions of others.[53] Establishing relations through the
exchange of illocutionary acts makes it possible for speakers and hear-
ers to achieve mutual understanding about their courses of action,
that is, to cooperate rather than compete in important areas of life.
Foucault, however, views even the consensus that results from raising
and accepting validity claims—claims to truth, rightness, sincerity, and
so forth—as an instrument or result of the exercise of power.[54] Though
he avoids any direct reduction of validity to power in his later work,
his definition of power ensures that every communication produces it:
"Relationships of communications," he writes, "produce effects of
power" by "modifying the field of information between parties."[55] Of
course, if producing effects of power amounts to no more than influencing the conduct of others, we have here a sheep in wolf's clothing.
Habermas' notion of noncoercive discourse was never intended to
refer to communication that is without effect on the behavior of others! Foucault comes closer to what is at issue between them when, in
an apparent allusion to Habermas, he criticizes the idea of dissolving
relations of power in a "utopia of a perfectly transparent communica-

tion."[56] He elaborates on this as follows: "The thought that there could be a state of communication which would be such that the games of truth could circulate freely, without obstacles, without constraint, and without coercive effects, seems to me to be Utopia."[57] This takes us back to our discussion of rational practices in part II and particularly to the idea that "truth is produced by virtue of multiple forms of constraint." As we saw there, the issue cannot be whether there are "games of truth" without the constraints of rules, procedures, criteria, and the like. And it does not seem to be whether constitutive constraints could *possibly* obligate participants in a symmetrical and reciprocal manner.[58] So the question appears to be whether what Habermas calls communication free from domination, in which claims to validity are decided on the basis of the reasons offered for and against them, can actually be realized in practice. And that seems to be a matter of more or less rather than all or nothing. If so, Habermas' idea of rational discourse would make as much sense as a *normative ideal* as Foucault's notion of a level playing field. It would be utopian only in the sense that the full realization of any regulative ideal is utopian.

The Subject Again: Autonomy and Care of the Self

Foucault's growing emphasis on the "strategic side" of the "practical systems" that organize our ways of doing things—the freedom we have to act within, upon, or against them—is not the only way in which the individual comes to the fore in his later thought.[59] His balancing of the technological with the strategic in conceptualizing power is accompanied by a shift of attention from "subjectification" via "individualizing power" to "self-formation" via "care of the self." This shift occurred between the publication of Volume I of the *History of Sexuality* in 1976 and the publication of Volumes II and III in 1984. As Foucault explains it, earlier in *Discipline and Punish* and similar writings, he had been concerned with "techniques for 'governing' individuals" in different areas of life. When he turned his attention to the genealogy of the modern subject in the *History of Sexuality,* there was a danger of "reproducing, with regard to sexuality, forms of analysis focused on the organization of a domain of learning or on the techniques of control and coercion, as in [his] previous work on sickness and criminality."[60] And this is indeed what we find happening prior to his work on Volumes II and III. In Volume I he could still describe the aim of his study as follows: "The object, in short, is to define the regime of power-knowledge-pleasure that sustains the discourse on human sexuality in our part of the world. . . . My main concern will be to locate the forms of power, the channels it takes, and the discourses it permeates in order to reach the most tenuous and individual mode of behavior."[61] In the Tanner Lectures delivered at Stanford three years later (1979), one still finds a treatment of individuality in relation to "individualizing power," that is, to "power techniques oriented toward individuals and intended to rule them in a continuous and permanent way."[62] What Foucault calls "pastoral techniques," from Christian examination of conscience and cure of the soul to contemporary methods of mental health, are analyzed there as instruments for "governing individuals by their own verity."[63] And "governmentality" apparently continued to serve as the general perspective on individualization in the years immediately following.[64]

By 1983, however, the perspective had clearly shifted. In an interview conducted by Dreyfus and Rabinow in April of that year, Foucault, hard at work on the later volumes of his *History of Sexuality*, announces that "sex is boring" and that he is interested rather in techniques of the self.[65] Clarifying that remark, he goes on to draw a clear distinction between technologies of the self geared to normalization and ethical techniques aimed at living a beautiful life.[66] What the Greeks were after, he says, was an aesthetics of existence: The problem for them was "the *techne* of life . . . how to live . . . as well as [one] ought to live." And that, he tells us, is his interest as well: "The idea of the bios as material for an aesthetic piece of art is something which fascinates me."[67] Accordingly, he now characterizes the third axis of genealogical-archeological analysis as directed not toward modes of normalizing subjectification, but toward "the kind of relationship you ought to have with yourself, *rapport à soi*, which I call ethics, and which determines how the individual is supposed to conduct himself as a moral subject of his own action."[68] Elsewhere this is described as a shift from the investigation of "coercive practices" to the study of "practices of freedom," "exercises of self upon self by which one tries . . . to transform one's self and to attain a certain mode of being."[69] And this "care of the self," which establishes a form of self-mastery, is now said to be a sine qua non of properly caring for others, that is, of the art of governing.[70]

According to Foucault, the search for an ethics of existence that was stressed in antiquity differed fundamentally from the obedience to a system of rules that came to prevail in Christianity. "The elaboration of one's own life as a personal work of art, even if it obeyed certain collective canons, was at the center, it seems to me, of moral experience, of the will to morality in Antiquity; whereas in Christianity, with the religion of the text, the idea of the Will of God, and the principle of obedience, morality took on increasingly the form of a code of rules."[71] To be sure, there are "code elements" and "elements of ascesis" in every morality, prescriptive ensembles of rules and values as well as ways in which individuals are to form themselves as ethical subjects in relation to them.[72] Nevertheless, some moralities are more code oriented, and others more ethics-oriented. In the former, the accent is on code, authority, and punishment, and "subjectivation occurs basically in a quasi-juridical form, where the ethical subject refers his conduct to a law, or set of laws, to which he must submit";[73] in the latter, the main emphasis is on self-formative processes that enable individuals to escape enslavement to their appetites and passions and to achieve a desired mode of being, and "the system of code and rules of behavior may be rather rudimentary [and] their exact observance may be relatively unimportant, at least compared with what is required of the individual in the relationship he has with himself."[74] Whereas histories of morality have usually focused on the different systems of rules and values operative in different societies or groups, or on the extent to which the actual behavior of different individuals or groups were in conformity with such prescriptive ensembles, Foucault's *History of Sexuality* focuses on the different ways in which "individuals have been urged to constitute themselves as subjects of moral conduct" and on the different "forms of moral subjectivation and the practices of the self that are meant to ensure it."[75] This choice is motivated in part by his diagnosis of the present state of morality: "If I was interested in Antiquity it was because, for a whole series of reasons, the idea of morality as disobedience to a code of rules is now disappearing, has already disappeared. And to this absence of morality corresponds, must correspond, the search for an aesthetics of existence."[76] Thus, the problem of our present and of our present selves, to which Foucault's later work is oriented, is the "ethopoetic" one of how to revive and renew "the arts of individual existence."

This certainly constitutes a major shift from his earlier emphasis on networks or fields of power in which individuals were only nodal points, and his methodological injunction to do without the subject and modes of analysis that rely on it. Both the ethical subject and the strategic subject are now represented as acting intentionally and voluntarily—within, to be sure, cultural and institutional systems that organize their ways of doing things.[77] But they are not simply points of application of these practical systems; they can critically, reflectively detach themselves from them; they can, within limits, modify them; and they can, in any case, make creative use of whatever space for self-formation they permit or provide. This model now enables us to make sense of the possibilities of resistance and revolt that Foucault always insisted are inherent in systems of power. It corrects the holistic bias we found in his work of the 1970s. The question now is whether he hasn't gone too far in the opposite direction and replaced it with an individualistic bias.

Though the later Foucault refers appreciatively to Kant's ideas of maturity and autonomy, he gives them a very different twist. In "What Is Enlightenment?," for example, his analysis of Kant's notion of *Mündigkeit* is immediately followed by a discussion of Baudelaire's attitude toward modernity: "Modern man, for Baudelaire, is not the man who goes off to discover himself, his secrets, his hidden truth; he is the man who tries to invent himself. This modernity does not 'liberate man in his own being': it compels him to face the task of producing himself."[78] In this respect, Baudelaire's attitude is Foucault's own; but it is not Kant's.[79] The representation of autonomy as aesthetic self-invention eliminates the universality at the heart of his notion—the rational *Wille* expressed in norms binding on all agents alike. This is, of course, no oversight on Foucault's part. As we saw, he distinguishes code-oriented moralities, in which a quasijuridical subject refers his or her conduct to a set of laws, from ethics-oriented moralities, in which general rules of behavior are less developed and less important than individual self-formation. There can be no doubt as to how he ranks them: "The search for styles of existence as different from each other as possible seems to me to be one of the points on which particular groups in the past may have inaugurated searches we are engaged in today. The search for a form of morality acceptable to everybody, in the sense that everybody should submit to it, strikes me as catastrophic."[80] In the context of his history of sexuality, it is Christianity that serves as the paradigm of a code-oriented morality: "The Church and the pastoral ministry shared the principle of a morality whose precepts were compulsory and whose code was universal."[81] And this, it seems to me, is what motivates the either/or approach expressed in the lines quoted above: universal morality is construed not formally but materially, that is, in a pre-Kantian manner.

Contemporary neo-Kantians treat justice and the good life as complementary, not opposed, concerns. Thus, Habermas differentiates the type of practical reasoning proper to questions of what is morally right from that concerned with what is ethically prudent.[82] When questions of justice are involved, fair and impartial consideration of conflicting interests is called for; when questions of value arise, deliberation on who one is and who one wants to be is central. Like Kant, Habermas regards matters of justice, rather than matters (specifically) of the good life or of individual self-realization, to be the proper domain of universalistic morality. This is not to say that ethical deliberation exhibits no general structures of its own; but the disappearance of value-imbued cosmologies and the disintegration of sacred canopies have opened the question, "How should I (or we, or one) live?," to the irreducible pluralism and individualism of modern life. To suppose that it could be answered once and for all, that moral theory could single out one form of life right for everyone, is no longer plausible. On that point, Habermas agrees with Foucault. For him, however, this does not eliminate the need for a general theory of a more restricted sort: a theory of justice that reconstructs the moral point of view from which competing interest- and value-based claims can be fairly adjudicated. Like Kant, Habermas understands this type of reasoning to be universal in import; however, he replaces the categorical imperative with the idea that for general norms to be valid they have to be acceptable to all those affected by them, as participants in practical discourse.

I cannot go into the details of that approach here, but enough has been said, perhaps, to indicate that Foucault's representation of universal morality, geared as it is to substantive codes, misses the point of formal, procedural models: namely, to establish a general framework of justice within which individuals and groups may pursue differing conceptions of the good or beautiful life. Although Foucault does not address himself to this most general level of morality, he too cannot do without it. When asked on one occasion if the Greek arts of existence present a viable alternative to contemporary conceptions of the moral life, he responded as follows: "The Greek ethics were linked to a purely virile society with slaves, in which the women were underdogs whose pleasure had no importance. . . ."[83] That is to say, Greek ethics were tied to unjust practices and institutions. And when asked on another occasion whether consensus might not serve as a regulative principle in structuring social relations, he replied: "I would say, rather, that it is perhaps a critical idea to maintain at all times: to ask oneself what proportion of non-consensuality is implied in such a power relation, and whether that degree of non-consensuality is necessary or not, and then one may question every power relation to that extent. The farthest I would go is to say that perhaps one must not be for consensuality, but one must be against non-consensuality."[84] And, as we have seen, Foucault proposes as a goal for political practice, the transformation of states of domination into open and symmetrical (fair?) strategic games.

In these and other contexts, it is clear that Foucault conceives the "elaboration of one's life as a personal work of art" to be limited by considerations of justice. That is the unmistakable orientation of his studies, and it is an orientation that calls for *its own* reflective elaboration: universalistic morality is not opposed but complementary to the search for a personal ethics, if that search is to be open to everyone.

The problems with Foucault's account of the practice of liberty stem from his antithetical conceptualization of individual freedom and social interaction. As any operation of the other upon the self is conceived to be an exercise of power—in which the other governs my conduct, gets me to do what he or she wants—liberty can only consist in operations of the self upon the self, in which I govern or shape my own conduct. The one-dimensional view of social interaction as strategic interaction displaces autonomy outside of the social network. There are, of course, post-Kantian alternatives to this in which individual freedom includes reasoned agreement with the norms of common life, individual identity is formed and maintained in reciprocal relations with others, and group memberships contribute to self-fulfillment. Foucault's aesthetic individualism is no more adequate to this social dimension of autonomy than was the possessive individualism of early modern political theory. The same problem turns up in a different form in his views on the relation of ethics to politics and society: "The idea that ethics can be a very strong structure of existence, without any relation to the juridical per se, to an authoritarian system, a disciplinary structure," he tells us, "is very interesting."[85] "For centuries," he continues, "we have been convinced that between our ethos, our personal ethics, our everyday life, and the great political and social and economic structures there were analytic relations, and that we couldn't change anything, for instance, in our sex life or in our family life, without ruining our economy, our democracy and so on. I think we have to get rid of this idea of an analytical or necessary link between this and other social or economic or political structures."[86] And a bit further on, he asks rhetorically: "But couldn't everyone's life become a work of art?"[87] In his earlier work, Foucault himself gave us ample grounds for answering that question in the negative under existing social, economic, and political conditions. The problem is not with "analytic and necessary links" but with de facto empirical interdependencies between structures and events at the personal and societal levels. The existence of such interconnections does not, of course, mean that "we couldn't change anything" in our individual lives without changing society as a whole. But it does mean that the conditions of individual existence, and thus the chances of making one's life into a work of art, are different at different locations in the social system. As Hans-Herbert Kögler puts it: "The sociocultural resources and opportunities for developing an autonomous personality are inequitably distributed, and this cannot be evened out by an ethical choice of self. . . . That approach leaves fully unanswered the question of how we might criticize contexts that themselves render impossible [autonomous] modes of subjectivation."[88]

Viewed from the perspective of critical social theory, Foucault's later framework of interpretation lies at the opposite extreme from his earlier social ontology of power. Then, everything was a function of context, of impersonal forces and fields, from which there was no escape—the end of man. Now, the focus is on "those intentional and voluntary actions by which men not only set themselves rules of conduct but also seek to transform themselves . . . and to make their life into an *ouvre*"—with too little regard for social, political, and economic context.[89] Neither scheme provides an adequate framework for critical social inquiry. The ontology of power was too reductive and one-dimensional for that purpose; the later, multidimensional ontology still depicts social relations as strategic relations, thus forcing the search for autonomy, so central to the critical tradition, onto the private path of a *rapport a soi*. This is not at all to deny the power and insight of Foucault's historical-critical studies; it is to question his own accounts of their presuppositions and implications. I have been arguing that his work is better understood as a continuation and enrichment of the critical-theoretical tradition. His strengths are often weaknesses of mainstream critical social theory; his nominalism, descriptivism, and historicism a counterweight to the usual emphasis on the general, the normative, and the theoretical. However universal critical theory may be at the level of concepts and principles, in pursuing its practical interest it must reach finally to the variable, contingent, "transformable singularities" that so occupied Foucault and made his work so powerful a factor in the contemporary politics of identity. In this regard, his investigations into the historical contexts in which specific "practical systems" arise and function and his studies of the formation of the moral-rational subject are a valuable complement to more global discourses about rationalization. Moreover, his relentless scrutinizing of the impositions, constraints, and hierarchies that figure in rational practices challenges critical theorists to go further than they have in detranscendentalizing their guiding conceptions of reason, truth, and freedom.

In shaping his approach, Foucault devoted himself single-mindedly to matters about which he cared a great deal. Too often his single-mindedness found expression in an either/or stance toward existing frameworks and modes of critical inquiry. I have tried to suggest that the strengths of genealogy are better viewed as complementary to those of classical critical theory. The point is not to choose between them but to combine them in constructing theoretically informed and practically interested histories of the present.

Chapter 8
More on Power/Knowledge

— *Gayatri Chakravorty Spivak*

What is the relationship between critical and dogmatic philosophies of action? By critical I mean a philosophy that is aware of the limits of knowing. By dogmatic I mean a philosophy that advances coherent general principles without sufficient interest in empirical details. Kant's warning that the Jacobins had mistaken a critical for a dogmatic philosophy and had thus brought in Terror has served generations of humanist liberals as the inevitable critique of revolutionary politics. Its latest vindication seems to be the situation of international communism. It can certainly be advanced that one of the many scripts spelling out the vicissitudes of the diversified field of the first waves of global Marxism is the consequence of the realist compromises of reading a speculative morphology as an adequate blueprint for social justice: to treat a critical philosophy as dogmatic.

Who is the ethical subject of humanism? The misadventures of international communism might teach us something about the violent consequences of imposing the most fragile part of Marx's speculations, the predictive Eurocentric scenario, upon large parts of the globe not historically centered in Europe.

To read these scripts simply as various triumphs of liberal democracy is to ignore the role of capitalism. It might be more pertinent to ask now: What is it to use a critical philosophy critically? What is it to use it ethically? Who can do so? This essay will attempt to consider these questions with reference to the word *power* in the famous opening of "Method" in *The History of Sexuality*, Volume I.[1] I will suggest: a) that it might be useful to graft the proper names of Foucault and Derrida together, although such a move would not be endorsed by either; and b) that the current critical possibility for Foucault's ethics

149

of the care of the self cannot be understood from within liberal humanism, or through calls for alternatives that remind us that they are appropriate only to liberal democracies or postindustrial societies of the North Atlantic model.[2]

Reading Foucault and Derrida Together

The lines of alignment and separation between these two names were first drawn by academic circumstance and have been redrawn authoritatively since Foucault's death by the magisterial voice of Edward W. Said, the trivializing voice of Richard Rorty, and the judicious voice of David Couzens Hoy and others.[3] A learned anthology has been compiled called *Feminism and Foucault*.[4] The rising tide of antideconstructionism among individual rights U.S. feminists has been captured in, among other texts, the chapter titled "Politics and/or Deconstruction" in Zillah R. Eisenstein's new book *The Female Body and the Law*.[5] The slash between these two proper names, Derrida/Foucault, which "emerged out of a strange revolutionary concatenation of Parisian aesthetic and political currents which for about thirty years produced such a concentration of brilliant work as we are not likely to see again for generations," marks a certain *non*-alignment: critique, denunciation, nonresponse, uneasy peace in acknowledgment of political work and, after one's death, a formal tribute by the other.[6] To speak of that impossible double name—Derrida/Foucault—is not to be able to speak *for* it, to put anything *in* that name. But perhaps one might yet be able to give in *to* both, however asymmetrically.

Let us enter the task at hand by way of the "ism" of names—nominalism—and open up once again that famous sentence: "One needs to be a nominalist, no doubt: power, it is not an institution, and it is not a structure; it is not a certain strength [*puissance*] that some are endowed with; it is the name that one lends [*prêter*] to a complex strategical situation in a particular society."[7] This provisional "naming" by the theorist is not simply to code within a given system. "This multiplicity of force relations can be *coded* . . . either in the form of 'war' or in the form of 'politics.' " The field of possible codings in principle can be indefinitely enlarged. The nominalism is a methodological necessity. One needs a name for this thing whose "mechanisms [can be used] as a grid of intelligibility of the social order." It is called "power" because that is the closest one can get to it. This sort of proximate naming can be called catachrestic.

Foucault's nominalism has been noticed by critics. David Hoy meticulously establishes the advantages gained by Foucault over his critics by his use of what Hoy calls "pragmatic nominalism."[8] Yet even in this sympathetic account a general naturalized referent for the word *power* is tacitly presupposed and, indeed, attributed to Foucault. This reference is taken for granted, for example, in such important corrective sentences as: "[Foucault's] analytics of power is not intended to tell us what power really is, but only where to look." It is as if, although Foucault's interests are not realist, he has an ontological commitment to a thing named "power." Hoy's impressive attempt, from within the North Atlantic philosophical tradition, to seize the very alienness of the French thinker trembles on the brink of subject metaphors: "Foucault thinks of power as *intentionality* without a subject. . . . " To explain Foucault's odd thinking of resistance: "to program a computer for chess, presumably *one* must include some considerations about counter-attacks."[9]

These traces of naturalized or merely systemic notions of power, present also in Irene Diamond's good, interactive take on Foucault, are what I am calling the consequences of paleonymy. The word *power* points toward what we call the empirical in the history of the language. Poststructuralist nominalism cannot afford to ignore the empirical implications of a particular name.[10]

These consequences of paleonymy are neither true to Foucault's idea of power nor untrue to them. They are functions of any subject's relationship to language. They become acutely problematic within those strategies of knowledge (*savoir*) that demand of us that academic learning (*connaissance*) should establish the claims proper to each author in the realm of the roots and ramifications of ideas.[11] I am stating the problem, not solving or denying it. Since the phrase "subject's relationship to language" might have a psychoanalytic ring to it, let me give a brief description of what I am implying by it.

A mother tongue is a language with a history (in that sense it is "instituted") before our birth and after our death, in which patterns that can be filled with anyone's "motivation" have laid themselves down. In this sense it is " 'unmotivated' but not capricious."[12] We learn it in a natural way and fill it once and for all with our own intentions and thus make it our own for the span of our life and then leave it for its other users, without intent, as unmotivated and uncapricious as we found it (without intent) when it found us. As Derrida writes, "The 'unmotivatedness' of the sign requires a synthesis in which the completely other is announced as such—without any simplicity, any identity, any resemblance or continuity—within what is not it."

Reading Foucault's nominalism by way of Derrida, I can see that although there is a "need" (Foucault's word) to be a nominalist, the nominalist still falls prey to the very problems that one seeks to avoid. This is marked by the "power is not" statements in the Foucault passage I began with. But the nominalist falls prey to them only *in a certain way*. This is not to "fail"; it is the new making-visible of a "success" that does not conceal or bracket problems. Thus, reading Foucault/Derrida, let me further propose that the bestowal of the name power upon a complex situation produces power in the general sense. The traces of the empirical encompassed by the word in the history of the language entail the so-called narrow senses of power. The relationship between the general and narrow senses spans the active articulation of deconstruction in a considerable variety of ways. As I and many others have noted, writing, trace, differance, woman, origin, parergon, gift and now, in Derrida's latest phase, such more resonant words as justice, democracy, friendship are cracked and barred in their operation by this two-sense divide. As is Derrida's habit, he does not develop a systematic description of this mode of operation. (There is, after all, no useful definition of deconstruction anywhere in Derrida's work.)

I will not go into the practical reason for this habit of elusiveness. All we need to note here is that the relationship between the two senses is never clear-cut. One bleeds into the other at all times. The relationship is certainly not that between the potential and the actual. In fact, the relationship between undecidability and the obligation and risk of deciding is something like the *rapport sans rapport* between the general and the narrow senses.[13] But it seems to me important that this curious relationship between the narrow and the general senses is what makes for the necessary lack of fit between discourse and example, the necessary crisis between theory and practice, that marks deconstruction. If we remember that such a misfit between theory and practice is the main complaint brought by nearly everyone against Foucault—indeed, it is thematized by Foucault himself as a putting aside of discourse theory in his later phase—we can see how Derrida's speculations about the general and the narrow allow us neither to look for an exact fit between theory and practice in Foucault, nor to ignore or transform the boldest bits of his theoretical writings about power. There is certainly no doubt that Foucault would have resented this way of saving his text, and it seems idle to repeat that the status of the author's resentment is not definitive, though certainly worth accounting for, in either Foucault or Derrida. As long as it is not merely an exercise in diagnostic psychobiography, I should just as certainly be interested in such an account.[14]

Nor am I substituting an excuse for an accusation. Indeed, this double gesture in Derrida is the affirmative duplicity (opening up toward plurality) that allows him to claim, most noticeably in *Limited Inc* but in fact in every text, that practice *norms* theory, that deconstruction, strictly speaking, is impossible though obligatory, and so on. I have myself argued this as the original "mistake"—not to be derived from some potential correctness—that inaugurates deconstruction. Foucault is not *in* Derrida, but Foucault joined with Derrida prevents him from being turned into a merely pragmatic nominalist or a folk hero for American feminism.

"Power" in the general sense is therefore not only a name, but a catachresis. Like all names it is a misfit. To use *this* name to describe a generality inaccessible to intended description is necessarily, as the *Oxford English Dictionary* says, to work with the risk that the word "is wrested from its *proper* meaning," that it is being applied "to a thing which it does not *properly* denote." We cannot find a proper example of it in real life by looking for it in the proper place; it must be effaced as it is disclosed.

It is this critical relationship between the general and the narrow that generally unsympathetic, strong readers such as Habermas and Richard Rorty are unable to grasp. Thus Rorty accuses Foucault's second sense of power of "a certain vacuity": "We liberal reformers [!] think that a certain ambiguity between two uses of the word 'power' vitiates Foucault's work: one which is in fact a pejorative term and the other which treats it as a neutral or descriptive term."[15] In his essay on Derrida, Habermas thinks that the asymmetrical negotiation between the narrow and the general that is the lesson of deconstruction is simply a collapsing of distinctions.[16] Quite predictably, then, Rorty decides that Foucault "refuses to separate the public and the private sphere."[17] Pushing the new pragmatism to its extreme consequences in order to give Foucault an easy out, he says that the philosophy of Foucault's final phase should simply claim the same rights of autonomy and privacy as poetry rather than ethics. "Poetry" and "rhetoric" are small words for these pragmatists and communicationists.[18] They cannot therefore grasp *this* particular rethinking of the dogmatic-critical divide. Indeed, Rorty sees the critical impulse as "a distraction from the history of concrete social engineering."[19]

Foucault's and Derrida's attention to the relationship between the dogmatic and the critical is in the wake of the *early* Heidegger, a course from which Heidegger himself swerved into a more dogmatic enterprise, following the implications of a sense of poetry and language that are different from Foucault's: a detailed analysis of the esthetic element in the conduct of life may lead to a critical appraisal of the post-Enlightenment conception of the ethical person as merely public.

> For me Heidegger has always been the essential philosopher. . . . My entire philosophical development was determined by my reading of Heidegger. . . . I think it is important to have a small number of authors with whom one thinks, with whom one works, but about whom one does not write.[20]

If for Foucault the dialogue with Heidegger is tacit, for Derrida the rememoration of Heidegger is interminable:

> More than ever, the vigilant but open reading of Heidegger remains in my eyes one of the indispensable conditions, one of them but not the least, for trying to comprehend better and to tell better why, with so many others, I have always condemned Nazism, in the horror of what, in Heidegger precisely, and so many others, in Germany or elsewhere, has ever been able to give in to it. No *immediate presentation* [a phrase in a Heideggerian recanting statement of 1942] for thought could also mean: less ease in armed declarations and morality lessons, less haste toward platforms [*tribunes*] and tribunals [*tribunaux*], even if it were to respond to acts of violence, rhetorical or other.[21]

For both Foucault and Derrida, in different ways, the ontico-ontological difference is a thinking through of the uses and limits of a critical philosophy. Their catachrestic nominalism may be trying to touch the ontic with the thought that there is a subindividual (or random, for Derrida) space even under, or below, or before (the grasp begins to falter here, but how can philosophers who will not admit that actual ethical practice is affected, indeed constituted by this, understand why it is worth trying?) the "pre-ontological Being as [Dasein's] ontically constitutive state . . . [where] Dasein *tacitly* understands and interprets something like Being."[22] Whatever the generalizing presuppositions necessary for a systematic statement or knowledge of ethics, these are the conditions within which ethics is *performed* by subjects constituted in different ways.

I will write further about this resistance to understanding as an epistemic clash. But let us now turn back to Foucault's text. The condition of possibility of power is the condition of possibility of a view-point that renders intelligible power's exercise. Robert Hurley has not done us a favor by changing the first "rendering intelligible" into "understanding," while preserving "grid of intelligibility of the *social* order." Here is the sentence: "La condition de possibilité du pouvoir, en tout cas le point de vue qui permet de rendre intelligible son exercice. . . . C'est le socle mouvant des rapports de force qui induisent sans cesse, par leur inégalité, des états de pouvoir."[23] "The condition of possibility of power, at least of the point of view that allows its exercise to be made intelligible . . . is the *moving base* of force relations that, by their inequality, incessantly *induce* states of power."

In this passage Foucault *might* be speaking of the point of view of the analysis of power as intelligible rather than the point of view of power. This too can be made to resonate with Derrida. According to Derrida, even the decision that makes the trace of the other to its origin intelligible as writing in the general sense (rather than the usual practice of ignoring the instituted trace to declare a simple origin) cannot be *finally* endorsed.[24] In our Foucaultian passage, the condition of possibility of power's intelligibility is itself such a catachrestic concept-metaphor—"a moving base"—*le socle mouvant*. The metaphor in *induire* or induce out of inequalities or differences in the magnitudes of force—not the organic "engender" as in the English ("generate" might have been better)—may be both logical and electric.[25] In both cases, this moving base of *force* fields clearly takes power quite away from the *visée* (or aimed) character of intentionality. The condition of possibility of power (or power as intelligible in its exercise)—"this moving base"—is therefore unmotivated, though not capricious. Its "origin," thus heavily framed, is in "difference," inequalities in force relations. To read this only as "our experience of power" or "institutional power" (as most people—like Walter J. Ong—read "writing" as "systems of graphic marks") is the productive and risky burden of paleonymy that must be persistently resisted as it enables practice.[26] Force is the subindividual name of power, not the place where the idea of power becomes "hollow" or "ambiguous."[27]

Why should the burden of paleonymy be resisted? Because if not, the enthusiasm of the Foucaultian can *come* to resemble the flip side of a concern for "our social infrastructure" in the interest of "quality of life, peace of mind, and the economic future."[28] This of course is precisely the element in Foucault that a Rorty would admire. And the resemblance emerges when Hoy, after emphasizing the important point that power in Foucault is productive as well as repressive, then di-

vides the necessary results into thoroughly valorized positive and negative effects.[29] (I am encouraged by the possibility of giving these adjec-
tives an electric charge.) From this it follows, for Hoy, that "the exercise
of power will invariably meet with resistance, which is the manifestation of freedom."[30]

Resistance can indeed by powerfully and persuasively coded in
the form of the manifestation of freedom, but there is no getting around
the fact that by privileging that particular coding, we are isolating a
crucial narrow sense and cutting off the tremendous unmotivated moni-
tory force of the general.

Speaking to an interlocutor who would clearly incline to such
patterns of privilege, Foucault puts the case firmly yet tactfully:

> Every power relationship implies, at least *in potentia* [and this is a
> more "rational" name on the chain of power-names—*puissance* in
> French], a strategy of struggle, in which two forces [a less "rational"
> name on the same chain] are not superimposed. . . . a relationship of
> confrontation reaches its term, its final moment . . . when stable mecha-
> nisms replace the free play of antagonistic reactions.[31]

Force is the name of the subindividual preontic substance traced
with irreducible struggle-structures in the general sense that enables
and limits confrontation. *Reading* (rather than merely quoting) Foucault, one notices the importance of the parentheses around "(and the
victory of one of the two adversaries)" that fits into the ellipsis in the
passage I have cited above. To trivialize this into mere functionalism
would, *mutatis mutandis*, put the entire materialist tradition out of
court, a consummation that Rorty et al. would not find implausible.

What does this peculiar moving base of a differentiated force field
look like? And how does the field polarize? Let us turn the page of *The
Will to Knowledge*, in which Foucault finds it possible "to advance a
few propositions." Here the distinction between the force field on the
one hand and its coming into play as power relations on the other is
unmistakable if you are on that track: "It is to be supposed that the
multiple relations of force that form themselves and play in the apparatuses of production . . . serve as support to the broad effects of cleav-
age running through the social body as a whole." "The rationality of
power"—one might have said intelligibility—" is that of often explicit
tactics which . . . finding their support and their condition *elsewhere*,
finally delineate [*dessinent*] aggregative apparatuses [*dispositifs
d'ensemble*]."[32] "Perhaps," writes Foucault, "we need to go one step
further . . . and decipher power mechanisms in terms of a strategy *im-*

manent to the relationships of force." As indicated above, this *"need* of decipherment" of the individual to calculate that the subindividual has immanent laws of motion should not be redrawn into the postindividualist register of a determinist functionalism, although perhaps the dominant Anglo-U.S. episteme can hardly avoid doing so.

The electric metaphor is particularly strong in a nearly untranslatable sentence that tries to catch the origin of resistance: "Les résistances . . . sont l'autre terme, dans les relations de pouvoir; elles s'y inscrivent comme irréductible vis-à-vis." Surely the choice here of "vis-à-vis"—a casual description of being placed facing something—over the motivated words "confrontation" or "opposition" is worth noting.[33] Mark also the curious comma between "term" and "in the relations of power." Surely this is to distinguish between "the *strategic* field of power relations" and the merely inductive force field that is its support. "Resistances" is the other term—certainly in the sense of terminal—in the field of power relations that is inscribed there as irreducibly facing. How Foucault's language is bending here to ward us off from the freedom talk of "the philosopher-functionary of the democratic state!"[34]

On the very next page Foucault cautions, under the title "Rule of Immanence," that the force field cannot be naturalized and constituted as an object of investigation. One must start from the "local foci" of power/knowledge.

If this sounds too much like the provisional beginnings celebrated everywhere in deconstruction, starting with "The Discourse on Method" in *Of Grammatology,* let me assure you that, even for a reader like me, Foucault is *not* Derrida, nor Derrida Foucault. I cannot find anywhere in Foucault the thinking of a founding violence. To quote Marx where one shouldn't, Foucault always remains within the realm of necessity (even in the clinamen to his last phase), whereas Derrida makes for the realm of freedom, only to fall on his face.[35] I would not choose between the two.

Indeed, Derrida's initial critique was in terms of Foucault's ignoring of the violence that founds philosophy. If forced into the thematic by way of reading the two together, the objection might be arranged this way:

In his earliest phase, Foucault makes the ontico-ontological difference workable too quickly, too easily. Madness, "naming" the ontic, becomes the self-consolidating other of Foucault's text, "producing" the ontological by being excluded. Continuing our somewhat forced reading, this Foucault is seen by Derrida as containing madness within the ontico-ontological difference and legitimizing Descartes' reversed position in which, instead of the inarticulable and proximate, it is the "intelligible [that is] irreducible to all . . . sensory or imaginative . . . analysis."[36] What Foucault is thought to overlook is madness as radical alterity, which must be "extinguished" after the necessary invocation of an undivided origin in which madness and the cogito are indistinguishable.[37] Foucault is as much written as writing by this tacit extinction, philosophy's hyperbole (rather than *hybris*—Foucault's word).

> Everything can be reduced to a determined historical totality except the hyperbolical project. Now, this project belongs to the narration narrating itself and not to the narration narrated by Foucault. . . . The menacing powers of madness [thus remain] the adverse origin of philosophy.[38]

This is not to obliterate the difference between philosophers. The different ways in which radical alterity is denied and negotiated maps out one history of philosophy even as it historicizes philosophy: "The historicity proper to philosophy is located and constituted in the transition, the dialogue between hyperbole and the finite structure. . . . "[39]

We must start, then, from the local foci of power/knowledge—*pouvoir/savoir.*

It is a pity that there is no word in English corresponding to *pouvoir* as there is "knowing" for *savoir. Pouvoir* is of course "power." But there is also a sense of "can-do"-ness in *"pouvoir,"* if only because in its various conjugations it is the commonest way of saying "can" in the French language. If power/knowledge is seen as the only translation of *"pouvoir/savoir,"* it monumentalizes Foucault unnecessarily. The French language possesses quite a number of these doublets. In their different ways, "laisser-faire" and "vouloir-dire" are perhaps best known to us. The trick is to get some of the homely verbiness of *savoir* in *savoir-faire, savoir-vivre* into *pouvoir* to come up with something like this: if the lines of making sense of something are laid down in a certain way, then you are able to do only those things with that something that are possible within and by the arrangement of those lines. *Pouvoir/savoir,* being able to do something, only as you are able to make sense of it. This everyday sense of that doublet seems to me indispensable to a crucial aspect of Foucault's work.[40]

Power as productive rather than merely repressive resolves itself in a certain way if you don't forget the ordinary sense of *pouvoir/savoir.* Repression is then seen as a species of production. There is no need to valorize repression as negative and production as positive. (Incidentally, this is a much "truer" view of things than most theories of ideology will produce. The notion of "interpellation" is too deeply imbricated with psychoanalysis' involvement with the laws of motion of the mind.) Let us consider a homely example that has some importance for bicultural women, women who grow up as daughters of new immigrants, women who ride the hyphen of "ethnic"-American into a different "mother tongue." We are, of course, speaking of a level still above the impersonality of the force field.[41]

Suppose the *savoir* or knowing of (exogamous) marriage in a culture for a woman is a passing from her father's protection to her husband's in order to produce women and men to perpetuate this circuit, and finally to pass under her son's protection. In terms of this *savoir,* the woman *can* (*peut* in the French, from *pouvoir*) preserve "the stability of marriage" and be loving and loved without being sexy. Suppose, on the other hand, exogamous marriage is known as the fulfillment of various kinds of interactive and creative emotive potentials in the woman. In terms of this *savoir,* the woman *can* (*peut*) seek fulfillment elsewhere if, as an individually intending subject, she feels her fulfillment thwarted. Both situations are productive, of the stability of marriage on the one hand and of the perceived freedom of woman's fulfillment on the other. Of course, pain is involved in both. But quite apart from that, there are terminals of resistance inscribed *under* the level of the tactics, sometimes explicit, with which these women fill their lives. If this seems obscure, let me invite you to think of the terminals of resistance as possibilities for reflexes of mind and activity, as an athlete has reflexes of the body to call upon. And changes in *pouvoir/savoir* can make visible the repressive elements in both situations, even through "disciplinary" means (through the Women's Studies component of the Culture Studies Collective, for example) of woman's freedom on the one hand, or of woman's right to a special role in the propagation of society on the other.[42]

One must not stop here, of course. The homely tactics of everyday *pouvoir/savoir,* the stuff of women's lives, lead not only to the governmentality of dress codes and work habits, guilt feelings, and guilt trips, but also to the delineation of the great aggregative apparatuses of power/knowledge that deploy the family as a repressive issue, day care as an alibi, and reproductive rights as a moral melodrama in national elections and policy.

Foucault insisted upon the difference between *savoir* and *connaissance,* as he did between *pouvoir* and *puissance,* the latter seen as lodged in the State or the Institution. He never wrote an *Archeologie du Pouvoir*. The reasons have been aptly thematized as a change of heart, the changing times, and the like. Yet it is also true that at the time of its writing, Foucault perceived the *Archaeology of Knowledge* (*savoir*) as a theoretical consolidation of all that had come before.[43]

There may be another theoretical reason for the absence of an archaeology of power. The differential substance of *savoir* is discourse, with its irreducible connections to language. Thus, *its* archaeology can be written. The differential substance of power is force, which does not have an irreducible connection to language. It is not even necessarily structured like a language, just as a magnetic field, which is symbolizable and not necessarily structured like a language. Writing its archaeology would entail a first step: writing *pouvoir* in terms of *savoir*. Foucault himself sometimes put this entailment somewhat more polemically, especially in his later interviews, as a turning away from mere language.

The homology I am about to draw is, strictly speaking, an imperfect homology. It is between, *puissance, pouvoir, force* on the one hand, and *connaissance, savoir, enonce* on the other. It is an imperfect homology, but it can serve as a guide to the status of *pouvoir/savoir*.

Again, English cannot quite match Foucault's distinction between *énoncé* and *énonciation*. There is the authority of the translations of *énoncé* in linguistics and semiotics—utterance, statement, etc. There is no reason to reject these translations. Yet it cannot be denied that there is in French a sense of the utter*ed*, the stat*ed*, in the simple word *énoncé*.

There can be no doubt at all that the *énoncé* as "the atom of discourse" is a catachresis. I believe this word has broken under the burden of paleonymy. This is what one camp of Foucault criticism would call the *failure* of archaeology.

All through the middle section of *The Archaeology of Knowledge* Foucault tries to be precise about the *énoncé* even as he warns us of all of its various meanings in the history of language. I think it is finally more effective that by contrast, the distinction between force and power is kept elusive. The immense effort to distinguish between the *énoncé* and discourse is impressive in its elegance, not its usefulness. If the element of the archive emerges at the end of these acrobatics as something like the field of power relations, the analogue of the force field is that "lacunary [*lacunaire*] and shredded [*déchiquetée*] . . . enunciative field," that "no place" where bits of the stated, not units but functions, cut across structures, and are rare.

Perhaps because it is *about* savoir, *The Archaeology of Knowledge* indicates the gap between practice and theory in its own rhetorical strategy. By this I do not mean the self-conscious imaginary Dialogue at the end, but rather the placing of the "Definition of the *Énoncé*" in the middle. The peculiarly abdicatory series of gestures toward the beginning of the section is noteworthy:

> I took care [*je me suis gardé*] not to give a preliminary definition of the *énoncé*. I did not try to construct one as I advanced in order to justify the naivete of my starting point. . . . I wonder whether I have not changed orientation on the way; if I have not substituted another research for my first horizon; whether . . . I was still speaking of *énoncés*. . . . Have I not varied the . . . word discourse as I shifted my analysis or its point of application, to the extent that I lost sight of the *énoncé* itself?[44]

It is by no means certain how these questions should be answered. To my mind, the paragraph marks that misfit between practice (the analysis practiced so far in the book) and theory of which I spoke in the beginning. The word "definition" itself becomes a catachresis here for, by Foucault's own rhetoric, it is not a definition that has been or can be used.

Pouvoir/savoir, then, is catachrestic in the way that all names of processes not anchored in the intending subject must be: lines of knowing constituting ways of doing and not doing, the lines themselves irregular clinamens from subindividual atomic systems—fields of force, archives of utterance. Inducing them is that moving field of shredded *énoncés* or differential forces that cannot be constructed as object of investigation. Ahead of them, making their rationality fully visible, are the great apparatuses of *puissance/connaissance.* Between the first and the second there is the misfit between the general and the narrow senses. Between the last two is the misfit that describes examples that seem not to be faithful to the theorist's argument. If read by way of the deconstructive theorizing of practice, this does not summon up excuse or accusation. This is how theory brings practice to crisis, and practice norms theory, and deviations constitute a forever precarious norm, everything opened and menaced by the risk of paleonymy. Thus, I graft the name of Foucault with Derrida's.

An Ethics Inaccessible to Liberalism

As I hope I have made clear, there is in both writers a concern with the preontological ontic level of the everydayness of the being. It is at this level that Derrida brings difference into the self-proximity of the ontic— everyday identity differed/deferred from itself by randomness and chance.[45] Foucault's concern with this level is already apparent in his early interest in Binswanger's "existential analysis."[46] This is not the place to construct an itinerary of that interest. I should like to give merely a sense of that itinerary by proposing a sentence imitating one Foucault wrote himself. Here is Foucault, writing on mental illness in 1954: "Illness is the *psychological truth* of health, to the very extent that it is its *human contradiction.*"[47] Now consider this: "*Pouvoir-savoir* is the ontophenomenological truth of ethics, to the very extent that it is its contradiction in subjecting."

Joining the proper names of Foucault and Derrida to each other, then, with the benefit of three decades of work by both philosophers after Derrida's initial criticism of Foucault, I would discover in "madness" the catachrestic name given by the early Foucault to that ontic dimension of Being that eludes Reason's ontology. I would suggest that in *Madness and Civilization* (his first "real" book) in which Foucault takes, by his own well-known account, a serious swerve away from the history of madness to the archaeology of silence, the history and the philosophy (loosely, the dogmatic and the critical) have not yet brought each other to the crisis that this new politics of practice must assiduously cultivate. Foucault is himself so brilliantly involved in the construction of the name "madness" that, at this stage, he merely betrays his own catachrestic use of it. Put another way, he is himself at once using the inaccessibility of madness (as truth of Being) as a catachresis for the *ontic*—perhaps through his on-the-job training with Heideggerian existential analysis—and is sufficiently dazzled by the paleonymic promise to make an onto*logical* commitment to madness, to want to speak it in critical speech. One could reread the summary of the book in the introduction to *The Archaeology of Knowledge* in this spirit.[48]

It is not surprising that readers have generally focused on the spectacular account of the definition and exclusion of madness rather than its definitive, intimate, inaccessible, ontic place. For in this early work there is an overriding tendency to shuttle between madness as a primordial ontic space and an ontologically displaced physicomoral condition. Yet the emphasis is certainly on "the essential unknowability of madness."[49] Because this emphasis may easily be restated as "an attempt to grasp a form of human existence entirely other than our own," it is just as certainly appropriate to notice that Derrida's chief critique is the insistence that "madness is within thought."

Within these frames, both Derrida and Foucault are interested in the production of truth. Deconstruction is not exposure of error.

Logocentrism is not a pathology. Deconstruction is "justice," says Derrida; and Foucault: "My objective . . . has been to create a history of the different modes of objectification which transform human beings into subjects." Derrida is also always on the track of the ruses of the subject centering itself in the act, in decision, in thought, in affirmation, with no hope of closure.

Yet the slash in Derrida/Foucault must be honored.

Derrida's tending of ontic "knowing" has become more and more rhetorical since the publication of *Glas* in 1974.[50] If I am right in thinking that the relationship between "folie" and "connaissance" in *Folie et déraison* is homologous to the relationship between self-proximate ontic knowing and ontological knowledge, it seems appropriate that no *ethical* position can bridge so absolute a divide.[51] The archaeology of knowledge (rather than silence) may be seen as a method that would make the divide a clinamen.[52] The articulation of *pouvoir-savoir* secures the first stage of the clinamen that makes it accessible to a sense of being. The next step, since the unquestioned, transparent ethical subject—the white, male, heterosexual, Christian man of property—has now been questioned into specificity and visibility, is to measure the plurality of ethics by researching the ways in which the subject "subjects" itself through "ability to know" (*pouvoir-savoir*). This is what it might mean to say: "Thus it is not power, but the subject, which is the general theme of my research."[53]

I am suggesting, then, that this line of ethical inquiry proceeds from the challenge of the robust Heideggerian notion of ontico-ontological difference, understood as implying onticoethical proximity and *not* neutralized, as by Heidegger himself, by way of *Dichtung* or *Lichtung*.[54]

This immense project was not realized by Foucault. He established one point: that the constitution of the modern Western subject may be through the *pouvoir-savoir* of sexuality (even this would of course be ignored by masculist ethical philosophers); but not all subjecting is done that way. In fourth-century B.C. Greece it was done through the use of pleasure in the care of the self. I am incapable of judging if Foucault was right about Greece in that period. The point here is that he follows the implications of the limits of existential analysis to come to *this* way of beginning ethical investigations. This sort of stage talk on my part is no doubt to impose a continuity. But this imposition becomes strategically necessary when, from a point of view in which the ethical subject community is *not* questioned, in which philosophy is seen as a private enterprise, in which a complete break between philosophy and citizenship (necessarily of the postimperialist or neo-colonialist liberal state), is taken as normal—from such a point of view, Foucault seems to be pushing for the poet's desire for autonomy as a general ethical *goal*.[55]

The point of my strategic and heuristic use of continuism is to emphasize that, if the ethical subject is *not* taken to be without historical, cultural, linguistic limits, then a study of its constitution(s) is the place to begin ethical investigations. According to Andre Glucksmann, any onticoethical thinking must take into account or "make appear the dissymmetries, the disequilibriums, the aporias, the impossibilities, which are precisely the objects of all commitment."[56]

Derrida too tends to the ontic, but differently, risking his disciplinary practice through the rhetoric of the everyday. His ethical concerns tend more toward a responsibility to the trace of the other than a consideration of the care of the self.[57] For Derrida, Levinas' ethics of absolute alterity has written itself upon and under the ontico-ontological difference.[58] And the being in and out of this difference has been textured by the effort to see man—the major actor—as varieties of other.[59] Foucault's last phase takes him into ground-level ethical codes of gendering.

Remember those "free boardschool shirkers" in *Finnegans Wake*, "Will, Conn and Otto, to tell them overagait, Vol, Pov and Dev?"[60] Will can and ought to—*vouloir, pouvoir*, and *devoir*. Joyce puts *savoir* out of bounds. Derrida and Foucault put *devoir* (the ethical) under scrutiny. Derrida watches out for the one who justifies practice by theory or theory by practice, compromised by both. And Foucault says in one of his last interviews:

> One did not suggest what people ought to be, what they ought to do, what they ought to think and believe. It was a matter rather of showing how social mechanisms up to now have been able to work . . . and then, starting from there, one left to the people themselves, knowing all the above, the possibility of self-determination and the choice of their own existence . . .
>
> Q[uestion]: Isn't it basically a question of a new genealogy of morals?
>
> M F[oucault]: If not for the solemnity of the title and the imposing marks that Nietzsche left on it, I would say yes.[61]

On this generalized retrospective register, "morals" and "ethics" are interchangeable. Consider another exchange, barely a year before this: "Q[uestion]: Would it be fair to say that you're not doing the genealogy of morals, because you think the moral codes are relatively stable, but what you're doing is a genealogy of ethics? A[nswer]: Yes, I'm writing a genealogy of ethics."

At this point, what we see most poignantly illustrated is the anxiety of the academic interlocutors: Tell us, you *must* be doing this? And the answer comes back, yes, yes.

This chapter may seem to be yet another entry in the debate over whether Foucault was from beginning to end an "archaeologist," or if he abandoned "archaeology" as a dead end to take up "genealogy." I have taken the position that there is an asymmetrical homology between *énoncé-savoir-connaissance* and *force-pouvoir-puissance* that has some relationship to subindividual-onticontological. Inscribed into the field of the ethical, this homology gives us a hint of how seriously Foucault pursued the role of a *critical* philosophy that was not content to assume its modernist, Eurocentric, *dogmatic* burden. Reading this way, one is struck by the specificity of Foucault's self-avowed clinamen—away from the "historical" to what in Heideggerian terminology one might call the "historial": " . . . farther and farther away from the chronological outline I had first decided on . . . to [the] analy[sis] of the flesh."[62] There is a tone of humility in beginning with other civilizations' *souci de soi*—starting with the nearest "other," Greek antiquity—rather than the arrogance of a desire for individual autonomy.

Although I was struck by this through my reading of Derrida, I have indicated that this is a different project from the possibility of the ethical within alterity and randomness implied by Derrida's work. And indeed there is here a different kind of difference worth considering for a moment.

Foucault's final focus on the relationship to the self in the experience of the flesh is a practical ontology. Transformed into reflex, such a practical ontology contaminates the ontic, but kept as code it straddles the ontico-ontological difference in a way that full-dress moral philosophies can never do: "The care of the flesh is ethically prior [*éthiquement premier*] in the measure that the relationship to the self is ontologically prior."[63] This is *pouvoir-savoir* at ground level, "the working of thought upon itself . . . as critical activity," not at degree zero.[64] This is "the soil that can nourish," this "the general form of problemization."[65] Habermas and others have thought this to be a swerve away from the subindividual level that was the most unusual aspect of Foucault's archaeogenealogy. (It is characteristic of Habermas' general epistemic block to this kind of thinking that he calls the subindividual "*supra*subjective."[66]) In actual fact, Foucault makes it clear that, although in search of the role of the ontic in the constitution of the ethical, he is now impelled to focus on another band of the discontinuous spectrum of *pouvoir-savoir;* he is not repudiating the articulation of the subindividual level: "I will call subjectivization the procedure by which one obtains the constitution of a subject, or more precisely, of a subjectivity which is of course *only one of the given possibilities of organization of a self-consciousness.*"[67] Here indeed is the consequence of that earlier position that we could only deduce: "*pouvoir-savoir* is the onto-phenomenological truth of ethics, to the very extent that it is its contradiction in subjecting."

In embracing this consequence, Foucault does indeed move away from the *mode* of the critique of humanism that Derrida inhabits even as, in renouncing mere chronological inquiry and only the particular forms of the technologies of power and strategies of knowledge, he comes closer to the younger philosopher. In this new mode, he soberly tabulates the ingredients of the ethical habit rather than running and floating with thought tangled in rhetoric, as does Derrida at the other extreme. In a way, "it is [indeed] clear how far one is from an analysis in terms of deconstruction," as Foucault says right at the end.[68] But the terrain is, in a certain way, nearer. Foucault is no longer tripping up the programs of emancipation (mostly juridicolegal and political), but instead is tracking the "practice of freedom." It is indeed clear how far he is from Derrida, who has put the *praxis* of freedom to the test by the *techne* of each act of writing. Foucault, in his final serene mood, can write: "Liberty is the ontological condition of ethics. But ethics is the deliberate [*réfléchie*] form taken by liberty."[69] The relationship between condition of (im)possibility and practice in Derrida would lead, in my understanding and formulation, to the more gymnastic "persistent critique of what one cannot not want."[70]

Our notions of political activism are deeply rooted in the bourgeois revolution from which Derrida and Foucault, descendants of 1789, have distanced themselves. A call for individual rights, national or psychosexual liberation, or constitutional agency, inscribed in a *pouvoir/savoir* deeply marked by the strategic techniques of management, cannot bring forth positive responses from them. As Foucault says, "knowing all the above, leave it to the people."[71] As Alessandro Pizzorno points out, "the 'victim' of power" for Foucault is not as he is "for Marx as for Weber, . . . the individual as such whom that structural power prevents from developing as he could have done in other conditions."[72] I suppose there is less harm in rewriting Derrida as a libertarian for the marginal or Foucault as the successful practitioner of genealogy (Godot arrived by bus, as it were) than in dismissing archaeology as nihilism, or claiming, as I heard Anthony D'Amato say at a conference in October, 1989: "The fact that a black man is rotting away in prison for a crime is simply the real world by-product of Judge Easterbrook's textbook exercise in deconstruction." I continue to think that the real usefulness of these two *is* in the lesson of their refusal to be taken in by victories measured out in rational abstractions, in the dying fall of their urge persistently to critique those dogmas for the few in the name of the many that *we* cannot not want to inhabit. By reading Foucault in Derrida, I have tried to repeat the practical lesson of history, the perennial critique: *qui gagne perd;* who wins (also) loses. "A cautious skepticism with regard to utopian politics and a neostoic almost Camusian [?] 'pessimistic activism' in the face of ultimate meaninglessness," writes Thomas Flynn, of the same lesson.[73] By reading Foucault in Derrida in the wake of a reconsideration of Heidegger, I have tried to distinguish this trajectory from the existentialist position.

This is not as mysterious or ethereal as you may think. Bearing in mind all that I have said about the narrow and general senses, let me cite an example. In September, 1989, I heard Ngugi Wa Th'iongo, the Kenyan writer and political exile, speak on "Exile and Displacement" at a panel on Third World Film in Birmingham. He spoke movingly of his sense of double exile in his own country because of its betrayal of the democratic ideal and in Britain, where he has sought *refuge,* because the worst elements in his country are collaborating with Britain. A South African from the audience asked him what he thought of recent developments toward a rapprochement in South Africa. Ngugi spoke with immense respect and support, very carefully made allowances for not being involved there, not being a savvy participant. But then he said that his greatest fear is that South Africa could fall into neocolonialism.

That is the voice of caution, raised at the moment of negotiated independence, a critique of that which one cannot not want. It is not without interest that, in explaining his final move, Foucault uses the example of decolonization:

When a colonized [*colonisé*] people tries to free itself of its colonizer, that is truly a practice [*pratique*] of liberation, in the strict sense of the word. But as we also know, this practice of liberation does not define [*définir*] the practices of liberty which will then be necessary for this people, this society and these individuals to define themselves [*se définir*] receivable and acceptable forms of their existence or of a political science.[74]

To elaborate Foucault's understanding of this double gesture into the productive unease of a persistent critique, I will move on to Mahasweta Devi.

Critical-Dogmatic in the Postcolonial Subject

Mahasweta Devi is as unusual within the Bengali literary tradition as Foucault or Derrida within the philosophical or political mainstream in France. She is not representative of Third World feminism. Thus, my risk here is to feed too easily *our* academic *pouvoir/savoir*, which would like to familiarize her singularity into an example. Virago Press wanted to docket her as an *Indian* woman writer along with Anita Desai or Bharati Mukherjee. On the other side, I have read a proposal to place her within the pantheon of great Bengali woman writers in the bourgeois tradition, merely as a "complementary voice." Once again, that conflation of episteme with nation! At this moment, to associate her with an "ism," even *feminism*, puts her singularity at risk.

Mahasweta is almost exactly the same age as Foucault, slightly older than Derrida. She too is a sometime academic; she too lived through the World War II, which for her was the prelude to the negotiated independence of India. She has seen the need for the critical watchfulness of which Ngugi spoke. Mahasweta's involvement with the Communist Party dates back nearly fifty years. Here, too, seeing a beleaguered illegal party in British India move into electoral politics has made it necessary for her to distance herself, though she is resolutely "on the left."

The real difference between Mahasweta and the two French philosophers lies in the place of woman in her texts. In terms of the narrow sense/general sense or theory/practice argument, however, a related difference is also significant. Unlike Foucault and Derrida, Mahasweta was only incidentally an academic. She is, of course, a writer of fiction, but ever since the great artificial famine of 1942, planned to feed British soldiers in the Asian theater, she has been continuously a political activist. As she has taken a distance from party politics on the left, her work has moved more and more into the area of the politics of Indian tribals and outcastes. Paradoxically, her involvement is away from the theater of armed struggle, in the arena of tribal self-development and constitutional rights. She is so involved in the immense labor of making known and helping to implement the sanctions for the tribals and outcastes written into the Indian Constitution of 1947–49 that the fine-tuning of her writing is beginning to suffer.

At the negotiated independence of the Indian subcontinent, the first Indian Constitution was written under the aegis of Lord Mountbatten and came out of what Bhikhu Parekh has recently called "the claustrophobic post-Enlightenment enclave."[75] It is Mahasweta's position as the citizen of a recently decolonized nation that puts her in a different relationship to the inheritance of 1789 than Foucault and Derrida.[76] Her position bears comparison, though it is not identical, with reproductive rights feminists in the West, who also want a share of that inheritance and write the woman's body in a normative and privative, rational juridicolegal discourse. Mahasweta must therefore persistently critique her involvement. She too is aware at some level that constitutional rights cannot take their end as an unquestioned good. I believe this critique and anxiety are staged again and again in the theater of her fiction. The fiction traffics in the untotalizable where the intending consciousness cannot be privileged. Her political activism, which is not described in the fiction, keeps its nose to a critiqued totality. The line between the two is never very clear-cut.

With this brief introduction, let me flesh out my schema a bit more. I will be repeating some of the principal arguments animating my current work.

The subject-position of the citizen of a recently decolonized nation is epistemically fractured. The so-called private individual and the public citizen in a decolonized nation can inhabit widely different epistemes, violently at odds with each other yet yoked together by way of the many everyday ruses of *pouvoir-savoir*. Literature straddling this epistemic divide cannot simply remain in the private sphere, and not only because it is at a "less-developed stage" by some "Euro"-teleology. The embarrassing myopia of a statement such as the following simply cannot see the script of the uneven epistemic violation in the decolonized theater:

> One would never guess, to read Foucault's analysis of the transformations operated in the last three centuries within European social institutions that that period has seen a considerable diminution in

suffering and an equally considerable augmentation of the chances offered to the individual to choose his life-style himself.[77]

O brave new world.

The political claims that are most urgent in decolonized space are tacitly recognized as coded within the legacy of imperialism: nationhood, constitutionality, citizenship, democracy, socialism, even culturalism. In the historical frame of exploration, colonization, decolonization—what is being *effectively* reclaimed is a series of regulative political concepts, the supposedly authoritative narrative of whose production was written elsewhere, in the social formations of Western Europe. They are thus being reclaimed, indeed claimed, as concept-metaphors for which no *historically* adequate referent may be advanced from postcolonial space. This does not make the claims less urgent. For the people who are making the claims, the history of the Enlightenment episteme is cited even on an individual level, as the script is cited for an actor's interpretation.

Feminism is also part of this heritage of the European Enlightenment. *Within* the enclosure of the heritage, it is inscribed as an "irréductible vis-à-vis" to the masculine dominant.

The space that Mahasweta's fiction inhabits is rather special, even within this specifying argument. It is the space of the subaltern, displaced even from the catachrestic relationship between decolonization and the Enlightenment, with feminism inscribed within it.

Especially in cultural critique, the event of political independence can automatically be assumed to stand between colony and decolonization as an unexamined good that operates a reversal. The new nation is run by a regulative logic derived from a reversal of the old colony from within the cited episteme of the postcolonial subject: secularism, democracy, socialism, national identity, capitalist development. There is, however, a space that did not share in the energy of this reversal, a space that had no firmly established agency of traffic with the *culture* of imperialism. Paradoxically, this space is also outside of organized labor, below the attempted reversals of capital logic. Conventionally, this space is described as the habitat of the *sub*proletariat or the *sub*altern. Mahasweta's fiction suggests that *this* is the space of the displacement of the colonization-decolonization reversal. This is the space that can become, for her, a dystopic representation of decolonization *as such*. In this context, decolonization becomes only a convenient and misleading word, used only because no other can be found.

If neocolonialism is seen only from the undoubtedly complex and important but restrictive perspective of metropolitan internal colonization or the postcolonial migrant or immigrant, this particular scenario of displacement becomes invisible. The *pouvoir-savoir* or know-it-as-this/can-do-it-as-this of the discourse of feminism is obviously counterintuitive to the inhabitants of this space, the space of Mahasweta's fiction. As she works actively to move the subaltern into hegemony, in her struggle in the field, she pushes them toward that other episteme in which the intuitions of feminism become accessible. I am not arguing a fiction/reality opposition here. The narrow and the general sense infiltrate each other, bring each other to crisis, although they are not inscribed into a continuum.

Thus, if we think back about the *pouvoir-savoir* example of mother-daughter relationships in new immigration, we can see another conjuncture of similar strands here: writer/activist, subaltern/citizen, in the same nation. Especially in the postcolonial "womanspace," this is a much more complex set of relationships than Rorty's public-private.

Mahasweta's stories are thus not about improbable awakenings of feminist consciousness in the gendered subaltern. They are also not spoken *for* them; she does not speak *as* them or *to* them. These are singular, paralogical figures of women (sometimes wild men, mad men) who spell out no model for imitation. I will mention a few that I have tried to capture in commentary and translation and a couple from my translation work in progress.

Draupadi and Jashoda are explosions from the traditional Hindu imagination of the female. In Mahasweta's stories, Draupadi stands finally fixed and naked, a figure of refusal, in front of the police officer, her breasts mangled and her vagina torn and bleeding. She is at a distance from the political activism of the male. Jashoda lies dead, her breast putrefied with cancer, a figure that blasts mothering right out of its affective coding. She is at a distance from the gradual emancipation of the bourgeois female.

Mary Oraon in "The Hunt" is the child of the violation of a tribal Christian servant-woman by the white planter who leaves the plantation at Independence. Mary is the very figure of postcoloniality, displaced to the subaltern level. At the end of "The Hunt," she has just murdered the exploitative rural contractor. Drunk on alcohol and violence, she is running along the railroad line. A half-caste, she is at a distance from the authentic ethnic.[78]

Someone not immediately involved in systemic politics is not necessarily exempt from the anxiety of being pushed into an alien, "scientific," or constitutional episteme. The philosopher-intellectual can offer nonspecific alternatives, a last-ditch hope that might inspire ecological activists in the postmodern economies (not the decolonized subaltern, for whom ancient utopias have become sites of terror under exploitation). But will those activists read literary journals, and can the aggregative apparatuses be made to listen? Michel Serres, for example, not immediately involved in what he calls the "Exact Sciences," can stage the anxiety and propose a utopian solution in the following way. First, the anxiety, here more Manichean terror:

> The terror comes, if I dare to say it, not from the fact of power, but from rightness. The thing is that science is right—it is demonstrably right, factually right. It is thus right in asserting itself. It is thus right in asserting that which is not right. Nothing is produced, no one is cured, the economy is not improved by the means of sayings, cliches or tragedies.[79]

And then the admirable solution (altogether restricted in its availability) that can, as he says, "chuck the death wish":

> I am seeking a knowledge that is finally adult. . . . The adult man is educated in a third way. Agronomist and man of the woods, savage and tiller of the fields, he has both culture and science. Criticism is fairly futile—only invention counts. This so-called adult knowledge is convinced and certain that the picture described above is full of sense.

But the anxiety still shows through, as does the binary ranking.

> Seeker, *if you need to find something* . . . take courses in the history of the sciences. . . . My hope [however] does not follow the straight road, the monotonous and dreary methodology from which novelty has fled; my hope invents the cut-off trail, broken, chosen at random from the wasp, the bee, the fly.

If you are actually involved in changing state policy on the one hand, and earning the right to be heard and trusted by the subaltern on the other, on behalf of a change that is both medicine and poison, you cannot choose the cut-off trail, declaring it as a hope when for some it has been turned into despair. And if, like Derrida and Foucault, you are a scrupulous academic who *is* largely an academic, you stage the crisis relationship between theory and practice in the practice of your theoretical production in various ways instead of legitimizing the polarization between the academic world and the real world by disavowing it, and then producing elegant solutions that will never be tested seriously either in large-scale decision-making or among the disenfranchised.

Thus, the figures of Mahasweta's fiction are at odds with the project of access to national constitutional agency for the tribal and the outcaste upon which Mahasweta is herself actively bent. This is not a contradiction, but rather the critical *rapport sans rapport* of which I spoke earlier. The most spectacular example is from "Douloti the Bountiful."[80] Here the affective, nostalgic tribal world of the young central character, a bonded prostitute, is represented with great delicacy by a lyric sentiment that is at odds with the harsh, critical collectivity of prostitutes and the armed struggle of the men in that gender-divided world. The aporia is staged *in* the fiction.

These women of Mahasweta's fiction are almost like unconnected letters in a script, neither archaic nor modern, caught neither in a past present nor on the way to a future present. They are monuments to the anxiety of their inevitable disappearance as "justice is done" and the episteme is on the way to regularization. If you consider Mahasweta's fictive and social text together, feminism becomes a necessary but misfitting name. We keep pushing her: tell us, you *must* be doing this? She will say good-naturedly—yes, yes; or being irascible and not as eager to placate as a senior academic—no.

I think now of the improbable hero of the novella I am currently translating: a pterodactyl discovered in a tribal area in the modern state of Bihar. It could not be kept alive, although the journalist and the child wanted to feed it. The look in its eyes could not be understood. The child drew its picture on the cave wall. This latest entry into that collection of figures, mute guest from an improbable and inaccessible past before the origin of paleonymy or archaeology, guardian of the margin, calling for but not calling forth the ethical antiphone, measures for me the risk of obliterating the rift between the narrow and the general in the name of a merely liberal politics.

Chapter 9

Five Faces of Oppression

———— *Iris Marion Young*

Politics is partly a struggle over the language people use to describe social and political experience. Most people in the United States would not use the term "oppression" to name injustice in this society. For a minority of Americans, on the other hand—such as socialists, radical feminists, American Indian activists, black activists, gay and lesbian activists, and others identifying with new left social movements of the 1960s and '70s—oppression is a central category of political discourse. Speaking the political language in which oppression is a central word involves adopting a whole mode of analyzing and evaluating social structures and practices that is quite incommensurate with the language of liberal individualism that dominates political discourse in the United States.

Consequently, those of us who identify with at least one of the movements I have named have a major political project: we must persuade people that the discourse of oppression makes sense of much of our social experience. We are ill prepared for this task, however, if we have no clear account of the meaning of the concept of oppression. While we commonly find the term used in the diverse philosophical and theoretical literature spawned by radical social movements in the United States, we find little direct discussion of the meaning of the concept of oppression as used by these movements.

In this chapter I offer some explication of the concept as I understand its use by new social movements in the United States since the 1960s. I offer you an explication of this concept, an unfolding of its meaning. I do not think the concept of oppression can be strictly defined, that is, corralled within one clear boundary. There is no attribute or set of attributes that all oppressed people have in common.

In the following account of oppression I reflect on the situation and experience of those groups said by new left social movements to be oppressed in U.S. society: at least women, blacks, Chicanos, Puerto Ricans, and most other Spanish-speaking Americans, Native Americans, Jews, lesbians, gay men, Arabs, Asians, old people, working-class people, poor people, and physically or mentally disabled people.

Obviously, these groups are not oppressed to the same degree or in the same ways. In the most general sense, all oppressed people share some inhibition of their ability to develop and exercise their capacities and express their needs, thoughts, and feelings. Nevertheless, reflection on the concrete uses of the term "oppression" in radical political discourse convinces me that the term refers to several distinct structures or situations. I label these with five disparate categories: exploitation, marginality, powerlessness, cultural imperialism, and violence. Before I unfold these categories, though, I need to discuss some issues of social ontology relevant to placing the concept of oppression.

New Left Revision of the Concept of Oppression

One of the reasons that many people would not use the term "oppression" to describe our society is that they do not understand the term in the same way as do radicals. In its traditional usage, which most people retain, "oppression" means the exercise of tyranny by a ruling group. Thus, many Americans would agree with radicals in applying the term to the situation of black South Africans under apartheid. Traditionally, "oppression" also carries a strong connotation of conquest and colonial domination. The Hebrews were oppressed in Egypt, and many uses of the term in the West invoke this paradigm.

Dominant political discourse may use the term to describe societies other than our own, usually communist or purportedly communist societies. Within this anticommunist rhetoric, both tyrannical and colonialist implications of the term appear. For the anticommunist, communism denotes precisely the exercise of brutal tyranny over a whole people by a few rulers, and the will to conquer the world, bringing now independent peoples under that tyranny. In dominant political discourse, it is not legitimate to use the term to describe our society because "oppression" is the evil perpetrated by the "others."

New left social movements of the 1960s and '70s, however, shifted the meaning of the concept. In its new usage, "oppression" designates the disadvantage and injustice some people suffer not because a tyrannical power intends to keep them down, but because of the everyday practices of a well-intentioned liberal society. In this new left usage, the tyranny of a ruling group over another, as in South Africa, must certainly be called oppressive. But "oppression" also refers to systemic and structural phenomena that are not necessarily the result of the intentions of a tyrant. Oppression in the structural sense is part of the basic fabric of a society, not a function of a few people's choice or policies. You won't eliminate this structural oppression by getting rid of the rulers or making some new laws, because oppressions are systematically reproduced in major economic, political, and cultural institutions. Thus, one reason that "oppression" is not commonly used to describe injustice in our society is that the prevailing political discourse does not have a place in its social ontology for structuration and social groups.

Mirroring majority political discourse, philosophical discussions of justice and injustice rarely use the term "oppression," using instead the term "discrimination" to refer to some of the injustices radicals call oppression. Even radical philosophers tend to avoid the term "oppression." Although his analysis is clearly influenced by Black Marxism and Black Power movements, Bernard Boxill, for example, consistently uses the term "discrimination" to designate the injustice that blacks have suffered and continue to suffer in U.S. society.[1] This is a symptom of the hold majority political discourse has over our thinking, perhaps especially over philosophers, who in turn help legitimate that discourse by using it and giving it technical precision. By "discrimination" I mean conscious actions and policies by which members of a group are excluded from institutions or confined to inferior positions. Discrimination is often an instrument of oppression, and discriminatory practices are certainly part of some oppressions, but the concept of oppression is neither coincident with nor reducible to discrimination.

Discrimination is a methodologically individualist concept.[2] In recent years most courts have found that there has been discrimination only if particular victims of discrimination can be individually identified, that a particular agent can be identified as responsible for discrimination, and it can be shown that the agent knew its actions or policies were discriminatory. To be sure, the concept of discrimination can make reference to groups insofar as a discriminatory policy excludes a whole class of persons from some position or activity. Even when concerning groups, however, discrimination is usually an individualist concept insofar as it presupposes an identifiable agent who discriminates, and that the sum of discrimination is the sum of discriminatory acts.

The difference between the concept of discrimination and the concept of oppression emerges most clearly with the insight that oppression often exists in the absence of overt discrimination. Though actions and policies that explicitly discriminated against members of particular groups were common in the United States not long ago and have by no means disappeared, legislation and litigation in the past twenty years have greatly lessened overt policies of discrimination against most groups, with the outrageous exception of lesbians and gay men. Socialists, feminists, antiracism activists, insist, however, that this serious reduction in overt and conscious policies of exclusion and segregation has done little to reduce the oppression that many groups have suffered and continue to suffer. This concept cites the vast and deep injustices some groups suffer as a consequence of frequently unconscious assumptions and reactions of well-meaning people in ordinary interactions, media and cultural stereotypes, and structural features of bureaucratic hierarchy and market mechanisms, in short, the normal ongoing processes of everyday life. As Marilyn Frye puts it, oppression refers to "an enclosing structure of forces and barriers which tends to be the immobilization and reduction of a group or category of people."[3]

The Concept of Social Group

Oppression refers to structural phenomena that immobilize or reduce a group. But what is a group? To be in a group is to share with others a way of life that defines a person's identity and by which other people identify him or her. Political philosophy typically has no place for a specific concept of social group. When philosophers and political theorists discuss groups, they tend to conceive them either on the model of aggregates or associations, both of which are methodologically individualist concepts. Along with Marilyn Friedman and Larry May, I think it is important to distinguish the concept of group from both aggregate and association.[4]

Liberal sentiments sometimes prompt us to assert that grouping by race, sex, religion, ethnicity, region, and so on, ought to carry no more significance than grouping by hair color, height, or the make of car we drive. Such an invocation calls for groups to be considered as mere aggregates, a classification of persons according to some attribute they share. The logic of aggregates presumes a substantial notion of the person to whom attributes are attached, and in that logical sense the person is prior to the collective. If we consider social groups as aggregates we imply that group membership does not define that person, but merely is a set of attributes, and that the collective is nothing other than the sum of the individuals with those attributes.

Political theorists tend to elide social groups more often with associations than aggregates.[5] By an association I mean a formally organized institution, such as a club, corporation, political party, church, college, union, etc. An individualist contract model of society applies to associations but not to groups. Individuals constitute associations; they come together as already formed persons and set them up, establishing rules, positions, and offices. Groups, on the other hand, constitute individuals. A subject's particular sense of history, sense of identity, affinity, and separateness, even the person's mode of reasoning, evaluating, and expressing feeling are constituted at least partly by his or her group affinities. This does not mean that persons have no individual styles or are unable to transcend or reject a group-related identity, and it does not preclude persons having many aspects that are independent of these group identities. Since the form of group differentiation in modern societies implies that a single person usually belongs to several groups, it follows that individual subjects are not unified, but multiple, heterogeneous, and sometimes perhaps incoherent.

A person joins an association, and even if membership in it fundamentally affects one's life, one does not take that association membership to define one's very identity, in the way, for example, being Navajo might. Group affinity, on the other hand, has the character of what Heidegger calls "thrownness": one *finds oneself* as a member of a group, whose existence and relations one experiences as always already having been. For a person's identity is defined in relation to how others identify him or her, and they do so in terms of groups that always already have specific attributes, stereotypes, and norms associated with them, in reference to which a person's identity will be formed. From the thrownness of group affinity, it does not follow that one cannot leave groups and enter new ones. Many women become lesbian after identifying as heterosexual, and anyone who lives long enough becomes old. These cases illustrate thrownness precisely because such changes in group affinity are experienced as a transformation in one's identity.

Despite the modern myth of a decline of parochial attachments and ascribed identities, group differentiation is endemic to modern society. As markets and administration increase the web of social interdependency on a world scale, and as more people encounter one another as strangers in cities and states, they retain and renew ethnic, locale, age, sex, and occupational group identifications, and form new ones in the processes of encounter.[6] No social group, moreover, is itself homogeneous, but mirrors in its own differentiations many of the groups in the wider society. Patterns of group differentiation are fluid, often undergoing rapid change. Before the nineteenth century, for example, homosexuality did not serve as a basis of group ascription and identification.[7]

Some writers, such as Milton Fisk, understand class as a primary example of a social group.[8] Others might be inclined to distinguish the concept of group from class on the grounds that class is a structural concept that does not include subjectivity or identity, and a group as I have defined it includes reference to identity and interaction.[9] In a way I agree with both approaches. As used in technical Marxian economic theory, the concept of class is more abstract and structural than the concept of social group. It refers specifically to a relation to the major means of production, whether one owns it and/or has major decision-making power about the movement of capital, how it is invested, and so on. Class denotes a relation to capitalist profit: who gets it, who decides who gets it and how it will be gotten, who contributes to its getting without getting it, or does none of these. These structural positions in themselves are too narrow to define social groups.

In a more colloquial and empirical sense, however, the term "class" also refers to a basis for interaction and conflict, an identity by which people recognize one another, and to that degree class names social groups as well as structural positions. The ruling class in the United States, and in most other societies, is a social group whose members tend to bond with a shared culture and world view, to have common interests, and to move within specific institutions. There is, however, no single social group of the working class correlated to that ruling class.[10] Whatever the difficulties of locating it in technical Marxian analysis, middle-class professionals and managers must be understood as a social group distinct from working-class manufacturing, clerical, and service workers and their families. Poor people, or what some theorists call the "underclass," may also constitute a social group.

Insofar as economic location and occupation significantly determine a person's self-understanding, perception of social relations and others, and insofar as such economic location in our society tends to be reproduced across generations, classes are certainly social groups in the sense I have discussed. Just how class will be defined will depend on the uses of the definition, for example, to understand the structural imperatives of accumulation or to understand the motivation of particular persons to support certain policies.

Group differentiation does not necessarily imply oppression, however; groups can exist that are not oppressed. In the United States, Catholics are a group in the sense I have discussed, but they are no longer an oppressed group. In Northern Ireland, on the other hand, Catholics are an oppressed group. Whether a group is oppressed depends on whether it is subject to one or more of the five conditions I shall discuss below. Despite the modern myth of a decline of parochial attachments and ascribed identities, I think that group differentiation is both an inevitable and desirable aspect of modern social processes. Social justice, then, requires not the melting away of differences, but institutions that promote reproduction of and respect for group difference without oppression.

I have suggested that oppression is the inhibition of a group through a vast network of everyday practices, attitudes, assumptions, behaviors, and institutional rules; it is structural or systemic. The systemic character of oppression implies that an oppressed group need not have a correlate oppressing group. While structural oppression in our society involves relations among groups, these relations do not generally fit the paradigm of one group's consciously and intentionally keeping another down. Foucault suggests that to understand the meaning and operation of power in modern society we should look beyond the model of power as "sovereignty," a dyadic relation of ruler and subject, and instead analyze the exercise of power as the effect of liberal and humanized practices of education, bureaucratic administration, production and distribution of consumer goods, medical practice, and so on. The conscious actions of many individuals daily contribute to maintaining and reproducing oppression, but those people are usually simply doing their jobs or living their lives, not understanding themselves as agents of oppression. Defining oppression as structural is an innovation of the new left usage of the term to describe our society. Many people understand oppression to refer only to a conscious tyranny of one individual or group over another and for that reason will not use the term to describe injustices in our own society.

By denying that structural oppression is perpetrated by an identifiable agent of oppression I do not mean to suggest that within this system of oppression individual persons do not intentionally do things to harm others in oppressed groups. The raped woman, the beaten black youth, the locked-out worker, and the gay man harassed on the street are victims of intentional behavior by identifiable agents. Nor do I mean to suggest that specific groups are not beneficiaries of the oppression of other groups, and thus have an interest in their continued oppression. On the contrary, for every oppressed group there is a group that is *privileged* in relation to that group.

The concept of oppression has been used among radicals since the 1960s, partly in reaction to some Marxist attempts to reduce the injustices of racism and sexism, for example, to the effects of class domination or bourgeois ideology. Racism, sexism, ageism, and homophobia, some social movements asserted, are distinct forms of oppression with their own dynamics apart from the dynamics of class, even though they might interact with class oppression. From often heated discussions among socialists, feminists, and antiracism activists in the last ten years, a consensus is emerging that many different groups must be said to be oppressed in our society, and that no group's or form of oppression can claim causal or moral primacy.[11] The same discussion has also come to understand that group differences cross individual lives in a multiplicity of ways that can entail privilege and oppression for the same person in different respects. Only a plural explication of the concept of oppression can appropriately capture these insights (cf. Maynard and Brittan, 2–8).

Accordingly, in the following sections I offer an explication of five faces of oppression as a useful set of categories and distinctions that I believe is comprehensive, in the sense that it covers all the groups said by new left social movements to be oppressed and covers all the ways they are oppressed. I derive the five faces of oppression from reflection on the condition of these groups. Because different factors, or combinations of factors, constitute the oppression of different groups, making their oppression irreducible, I believe it is not possible to have one essential definition of oppression. With the following five categories, however, the oppression of any group can be described, as well as its similarities with and differences from the oppression of other groups.

Exploitation

The central function of Marx's theory of exploitation is to explain how class structure can exist in the absence of legally and normatively sanctioned class distinctions. In precapitalist societies domination is overt and carried on through direct political means. In both slave society and feudal society the right to appropriate the product of the labor of others partly defines class privilege, and these societies legitimate class distinctions with ideologies of natural superiority and inferiority.

Capitalist society, on the other hand, removes traditional juridically enforced class distinctions and promotes a belief in the legal freedom of persons. Workers freely contract with employers, receive a wage, and no formal mechanisms of law or custom force them to work for that employer or any employer. Thus, the mystery of capitalism arises: when everyone is formally free, how can there be class domination? Why does there continue to be class distinction between the wealthy, who own the means of production, and the mass of people, who work for them? The theory of exploitation answers this question.

Profit, the basis of capitalist power and wealth, is a mystery if we assume that in the market goods exchange at their values. Marx's use of the labor theory of value, however, dispels this mystery. Every commodity's value is a function of the labor time necessary for the production of labor power. Labor power is the one commodity that in the process of being consumed produces new value. Profit then comes from the difference between the actual labor and the value of that capacity to labor that the capitalist purchases and puts to work. The owner of capital appropriates this surplus value, which accounts for the possibility of realizing a profit.

In recent years there has been considerable controversy among Marxist scholars about the viability of the labor theory of value on which this account of exploitation relies.[12] John Roemer, for example, develops a theory of exploitation that claims to preserve the theoretical and practical purposes of Marx's theory, but without assuming a distinction between values and prices and without being restricted to a concept of abstract, homogeneous labor.[13] My purpose here is not to engage in technical economic disputes, but to indicate the place of a concept of exploitation in a conception of oppression.

Marx's theory of exploitation lacks an explicitly normative meaning, even though the judgment that workers are exploited clearly has normative as well as descriptive power in Marxian theory.[14] C. B. MacPherson reconstructs the Marxian idea of exploitation in a more explicitly normative form.[15] The injustice of capitalist society consists in the fact that some people exercise their capacities under the control, according to the purposes, and for the benefit of other people. Through the institutions of private ownership of the means of production, and through markets that allocate labor and the ability to buy goods, capitalism systematically transfers the powers of some persons to others, thereby augmenting their powers. In this process of the transfer of powers, moreover, according to MacPherson, the capitalist class acquires and maintains extractive power, which gives it the continued ability to extract benefits from workers. Not only are powers transferred from workers to capitalists, but also the powers of workers diminish by more than the amount of transfer because workers suffer deprivation, a lack of control, and hence a lack of self-respect. Justice, then, requires eliminating the institutional forms that enable and enforce this process of transfer. Justice requires replacing them with institutional forms that enable all to develop and use their capacities in a way that do not inhibit, but rather enhance, others developing and using theirs.

The central insight expressed with the concept of exploitation, then, is that domination occurs through a steady process of the transfer of the results of the labor of some people to benefit others. The injustice of class division does not consist only in the fact that some people have great wealth while most people have little and some are severely deprived.[16] The theory of exploitation shows that this relation of power and inequality is produced and reproduced through a systematic process in which the energies of the have-nots are continuously expended to maintain and augment the power, status, and wealth of the haves.

Many writers have cogently argued that the Marxian concept of exploitation is too narrow to encompass all forms of domination and oppression.[17] In particular, by confining itself to examining class domination and oppression, the Marxist concept of exploitation does not contribute to an understanding of such group oppressions as sexism and racism. The question, then, is whether the concept of exploitation can be broadened to include other ways that the labor and energy expenditure of one group benefits another, thus reproducing a relation of domination between them.

Feminists have had little difficulty showing that women's oppression consists partly in a systematic and unreciprocated transfer of powers from women to men. Women's oppression consists not merely in an inequality of status, power, and wealth resulting from men's excluding women from privileged activities. The freedom, power, status, and self-realization of men is possible precisely because women work for them. Gender exploitation has two aspects, transfer of the fruits of material labor to men, and the transfer of nurturing and sexual energies to men.

Christine Delphy, for example, theorizes marriage as a class relation in which women's labor benefits men without comparable remuneration.[18] She makes it clear that the exploitation consists not in the sort of work that women do in the home, for it might be various kinds of tasks, but the fact that they perform tasks for someone else on whom they are dependent. Thus, for example, in most systems of agricultural production in the world, men take to market goods women have produced, and more often than not men receive the status and often the entire income from this labor.

With the concept of sex-affective production, Ann Ferguson identifies another form of the transfer of women's energies to men.[19] Women provide men and children with emotional care and provide men with sexual satisfaction, and as a class receive little of either from men.[20] The gender socialization of women makes us tend to be more attentive to interactive dynamics than men, and makes women good at providing empathy and support for people's feelings and at smoothing over interactive tensions. Both men and women look to women as nurturers of their personal lives, and women frequently complain that when they look to men for emotional support they do not receive it.[21] The norms of heterosexuality, moreover, are oriented around male pleasure, and consequently many women receive little satisfaction from their sexual interaction with men.[22]

Most feminist theories of gender exploitation have concentrated on the institutional structure of the patriarchal family. Recently, however, feminists have begun to theorize relations of gender exploitation enacted in the contemporary workplace and through the state. Carol Brown argues that as men have removed themselves from responsibility for children, many women have become dependent on the state for subsistence as they continue to bear nearly total responsibility for child rearing.[23] This creates a new system of the exploitation of women's domestic labor mediated by those state institutions, which she calls public patriarchy.

In twentieth-century capitalist economies, the workplaces that women have been entering in increasing numbers serve as another important site of gender exploitation. David Alexander argues that most typically feminine jobs have gender tasks involving sexual labor, nurturing, caring for a person's body, or smoothing over relations through personality.[24] In these ways, women's energies are expended in workplaces that enhance the status of, please, or comfort others, usually men; and these gender-based labors of waitresses, clerical workers, nurses, and other caretakers often go unnoticed and undercompensated.

To summarize, women are exploited in the Marxian sense to the degree that they are wage workers. Some have argued that women's domestic labor is also a form of capitalist class exploitation insofar as it is labor covered by the wages a family receives. As a class, however, women undergo specific forms of gender exploitation—ways the energies and power of women are expended, often unnoticed and unacknowledged, usually to benefit men by releasing them for more important and creative work, enhancing their status or the environment around them, or providing men with sexual or emotional service.

Race is a structure of oppression at least as basic as class or gender. Are there, then, racially specific forms of exploitation? This is different from the question of whether racial groups are subjected to intense capitalist exploitation. Racial groups in the United States, especially blacks and Latinos, are oppressed through capitalist superexploitation resulting from a segmented labor market that tends to reserve skilled, high-paying, unionized jobs for whites. There is wide disagreement about whether such superexploitation benefits whites as a group or only benefits the capitalist class, and I do not intend to resolve that dispute here.[25]

However one answers the question about capitalist superexploitation of racial groups, is it also possible to conceptualize a form of exploitation that is racially specific on analogy with the gender-specific forms I have discussed? The category of *menial* labor might provide an opening for such conceptualization. In its derivation "menial" means the labor of servants. Wherever there is racism, including the United States today, there is the assumption, more or less enforced, that members of the oppressed racial groups are or ought to be servants of those, or some of those, in the privileged group. In white racist societies this generally means that many white people have dark- or yellow-skinned domestic servants, and in the United States today there remains significant race structuring of private household service.

In the United States today much service labor has gone public: anybody can have servants if they go to a good hotel, a good restaurant, or hire a cleaning service. Servants often attend the daily—and nightly—activities of business executives, government officials, and other high-status professionals. In our society there remains strong cultural pressure to fill servant jobs—like bell hop, porter, chamber maid, bus boy, and so on—with black and Latin workers. These jobs entail a transfer of energies whereby the servers enhance the status of the served, to place them in an aristocracy—the rule of the best.

Menial labor today refers to more than service, however; it refers to any servile, unskilled, low-paying work lacking in autonomy, and in which a person is subject to orders from several people. Menial work tends to be auxiliary work, instrumental to another person's work, in which that other person receives primary recognition for doing the job. Laborers on a construction site, for example, are at the beck and call of welders, electricians, carpenters, and other skilled workers, who receive recognition for the job done. In the history of the United States, explicit racial discrimination reserved menial work for blacks, Chicanos, American Indians, and Chinese, and menial work still tends to be linked to black and Latino workers.[26] I offer this category of menial labor as a form of racially specific exploitation, only as a proposal, however, that needs discussion.

Marginalization

Increasingly in the United States, racial oppression occurs more in the form of marginalization than exploitation. Marginals are people the system of labor markets cannot or will not employ. Not only in Third World capitalist countries, but also in most Western capitalist societies, there is a growing underclass of people permanently confined to lives of social marginality, the majority of whom are racially marked—blacks or Indians in Latin America, blacks, East Indians, Eastern Europeans, or North Africans in Europe.

Marginalization is by no means the fate only of racially marked groups, however. In the United States a shamefully large proportion of the population is marginal: old people, and increasingly people who are not very old but get laid off from their jobs and cannot find new work; young people, especially black or Latino, who cannot find first or second jobs; many single mothers and their children; other people involuntarily unemployed; many mentally or physically disabled people; and American Indians, especially those on reservations.

Marginalization is perhaps the most dangerous form of oppression. A whole category of people is expelled from useful participation in social life, then potentially subject to severe material deprivation and even extermination. The material deprivation marginalization often causes certainly is unjust, especially in a society in which others have plenty. Contemporary advanced capitalist societies in principle have acknowledged the injustice of material deprivation caused by marginalization, and have taken some steps to address it by providing welfare payments and services. The continuance of this welfare state is by no means assured, and in most welfare-state societies, especially the United States, benefits are not sufficient to eliminate large-scale suffering and deprivation.

Material deprivation, which can be addressed by redistributive social policies, is not, however, the extent of the harm caused by marginalization. Two categories of injustice beyond distribution are associated with marginality in advanced capitalist societies. The provision of welfare itself produces new injustice when it deprives dependent persons of rights and freedoms that others have. If justice requires that every person have the opportunity to develop and exercise his or her capacities, finally, then marginalization is unjust primarily because it blocks such opportunity to exercise capacities in socially defined and recognized ways.

Liberalism traditionally asserts the right of all rational autonomous agents to equal citizenship. Early bourgeois liberalism made explicit that citizenship excluded all those whose reason was questionable or not fully developed and all those not independent.[27] Thus, poor people, women, the mad and the feeble-minded, and children were explicitly excluded from citizenship, and many of these were housed in institutions modeled on the modern prison: poor houses, insane asylums, schools.

In our own society the exclusion of dependent persons from equal citizenship rights is only barely hidden beneath the surface. Because they are dependent on bureaucratic institutions for support or services, old people, poor people, and mentally or physically disabled people are subject to patronizing, punitive, demeaning, and arbitrary treatment by the policies and people associated with welfare bureaucracies. Being a dependent in this society implies being legitimately subject to often arbitrary and invasive authority of social service providers and other public and private bureaucrats, who enforce rules with which the marginal must comply, and otherwise exercise power over the conditions of his or her life. In meeting needs of the marginalized, with the aid of social scientific disciplines, the welfare agencies also construct the needs themselves. Medical and social service professionals know what is good for those they serve, and the marginals and dependents themselves do not have the right to claim to know what is good for them.[28] Dependency thus implies in this society, as it has in all liberal societies, a sufficient condition to suspend rights to privacy, respect, and individual choice.

Although dependency thus produces conditions of injustice in our society, dependency in itself should not and need not be oppressive. We cannot imagine a society in which some people would not need to be dependent on others at least some of the time: children, sick people, women recovering from childbirth, old people who have become frail, and depressed or otherwise emotionally needy persons have the moral right to be dependent on others for subsistence and support.

An important contribution of feminist moral theory has consisted in questioning the deeply held assumption that moral agency and full citizenship require that a person be autonomous and independent. Feminists have exposed such an assumption as inappropriately individualistic and derived from a specifically male experience of social relations, valuing competition and solitary achievement.[29] Female experience of social relations, arising both from women's typical domestic care responsibilities and from the kinds of paid work that many women do, tends to recognize dependence as a basic human condition. Whereas in the autonomy model a just society would as much as possible give people the opportunity to be independent, the feminist model instead envisions justice as according respect and decision-making participation to those who are dependent as well as those who are independent.[30] Dependence should not be a reason to be deprived of choice and respect, and much of the oppression many marginals experience would diminish if a less individualistic model of rights prevailed.

Marginalization does not cease to be oppressive when one has shelter and food. Many old people, for example, have sufficient means to live comfortably but remain oppressed in their marginal status. Even if marginals were provided a comfortable material life within institutions that respected their freedom and dignity, injustices of marginality would remain in the form of uselessness, boredom, and lack of self-respect. Most of this society's productive and recognized activities take place in contexts of organized social cooperation, and social structures and processes that close persons out of participation in such social cooperation are unjust.

The fact of marginalization raises basic structural issues of justice. In particular, we must consider what is just about a connection between participation in productive activities of social cooperation, on the one hand, and acquisition of the means of consumption, on the other. As marginalization is increasing, with no sign of abatement, some social policy analysts have introduced the idea of a "social wage" as a socially provided, guaranteed income not tied to the wage system. Restructuring activities of production and service provision to ensure that everyone able and willing has socially recognized work to do, moreover, also implies organization of socially productive activity at least partly outside of a wage system.[31]

Powerlessness

As I have indicated, the Marxian idea of class is important because it helps reveal the structure of exploitation: that some people have their power and wealth because they profit from the labor of others. For this reason I reject the claim of some that a traditional class exploitation model fails to capture the structure of contemporary society. It is still the case that the labor of most people in the society augments the power of a few; whatever their differences from nonprofessional workers, most professional workers share with them not being members of the capitalist class.

An adequate conception of oppression, however, cannot ignore the experience of social division colloquially referred to as the difference between the "middle class" and the "working class," a division structured by the social division of labor between professionals and nonprofessionals. Rather than expanding or revising the Marxian concept of class to take account of this experience, as some writers do, I suggest that we follow Weber and describe this as a difference in *status* rather than class.[32] Being a professional entails occupying a status position that nonprofessionals lack, creating a condition of oppression that nonprofessionals suffer. I shall call this kind of oppression "powerlessness."

The absence of genuine democracy in the United States means that most people do not participate in making decisions that regularly affect the conditions of their lives and actions. In this sense most people lack significant power. Powerlessness, however, describes the lives of people who have little or no work autonomy, exercise little creativity or judgment in their work, have no technical expertise or authority, express themselves awkwardly, especially in public or bureaucratic settings, and do not command respect. Powerlessness names the oppressive situations Sennet and Cobb describe in their famous study of working class men.[33]

The clearest way for me to think of this powerless status is negatively: the powerless lack the status and sense of self that professionals tend to have. There are three aspects of status privilege that professionals have, the lack of which produces oppression for nonprofessionals.

First, acquiring and practicing a profession has an expansive, progressive character. Being professional usually requires a college education and learning a specialized knowledge that entails working with symbols and concepts. In acquiring one's profession, a person experiences progress in learning the necessary expertise, and usually when one begins practicing one enters a career, that is, a working life of growth or progress in professional development. The life of the nonprofessional by comparison is powerless in the sense that it lacks this orientation toward the progressive development of one's capacities.

Second, while most professionals have supervisors and do not have power to affect many decisions or the action of very many people, most nevertheless have considerable day-to-day work autonomy. Professionals usually have some authority over others, moreover, either over workers they supervise or over auxiliaries or clients. Nonprofessionals, on the other hand, lack autonomy, and both in their working lives and in their consumer-client lives, they often stand under the authority of professionals.

Though having its material basis in a division of labor between mental and manual work, the group division between middle class and working class designates not a division only in working life, but also in nearly all aspects of social life. Professionals and nonprofessionals belong to different cultures in the United States. The two groups tend to live in segregated neighborhoods or even different towns, not least because of the actions and decisions of real estate people. They tend to have different tastes in food, decor, clothes, music, and vacations. Members of the two groups socialize for the most part with others in the same status group. While there is some intergroup mobility between generations, for the most part the children of professionals become professionals and the children of nonprofessionals do not.

Thus, third, the privileges of the professional extend beyond the workplace to elevate a whole way of life, which consists in being "respectable." To treat someone with respect is to be prepared to listen to what they have to say or to do what they request because they have some authority, expertise, or influence.

The norms of respectability in our society are associated specifically with professional culture. Professional dress, speech, tastes, and demeanor all connote respectability. Generally professionals expect and receive respect from others. In restaurants, banks, hotels, real estate offices, and many other such public places, professionals typically receive more respectful treatment than nonprofessionals. For this reason nonprofessionals seeking a loan or a job, or to buy a house or a car, will often try to look "professional" and "respectable" in these settings. The privilege of this professional respectability starkly appears in the dynamics of racism and sexism. In daily interchange women and men of color must prove their respectability. At first they are often not treated by strangers with respectful distance or deference. Once people discover that this woman or that Puerto Rican man is a college teacher or a business executive, however, people often behave more respectfully toward her or him. Working-class white men, on the other hand, are often treated with respect until their working class status is revealed.

Cultural Imperialism

Exploitation, marginality, and powerlessness all refer to relations of power and oppression that occur by virtue of the social division of labor: who works for whom, who does not work, and how the content of work in one position is defined in relation to others. These three categories refer to the structural and institutional relations that delimit people's material lives, including but not limited to the resources they have access to, the concrete opportunity they have or do not have to develop and exercise capacities in involving, socially recognized ways that enhance rather than diminish their lives. These kinds of oppression are a matter of concrete power in relation to others, who benefits from whom, and who is dispensable.

Recent theorists of movements of group liberation, especially feminists and black liberation theorists, have also given prominence to a rather different experience of oppression, which I shall call cultural imperialism.[34] This is the experience of existing in a society whose dominant meanings render the particular perspectives and point of view of one's own group invisible at the same time as they stereotype one's group and mark it out as "other."

Cultural imperialism consists in the universalization of one group's experience and culture and its establishment as the norm. Some groups have exclusive or primary access to what Nancy Fraser calls the means of interpretation and communication in a society.[35] As a result, the dominant cultural products of the society, that is, those most widely disseminated, express the experience, values, goals, and achievements of the groups that produce them. The cultural products also express their perspective on and interpretation of events and elements in the society, including the other groups in the society, insofar as they are noticed at all. Often without noticing they do so, the dominant groups project their own experience as representative of humanity as such.

An encounter with groups different from the dominant group, however, challenges its claim to universality. The dominant group saves its position by bringing the other group under the measure of its dominant norms. Consequently, the difference of women from men, Native Americans or Africans from Europeans, Jews from Christians, homosexuals from heterosexuals, or workers from professionals becomes reconstructed as deviance and inferiority. The dominant groups and their cultural expressions are the normal, the universal, and thereby unremarkable. Since the dominant group's cultural expressions are the only expressions that receive wide dissemination, the dominant groups construct the differences that some groups exhibit as lack and negation in relation to the norms, and those groups become marked out as "other."

Victims of cultural imperialism experience a paradoxical oppression in that they are both marked out by stereotypes and rendered invisible. As remarkable, deviant beings, the culturally dominated are stamped with an essence. In contrast, the privileged are indefinable because they are individual; each is whatever he or she wants to be, they are what they do, and by their doings they are judged. The stereotype marks and defines the culturally dominated, confines them to a nature that is usually attached in some way to their bodies, and thus that cannot easily be denied. These stereotypes so permeate the society that they are not noticed as contestable. Just as everyone knows that the earth goes around the sun, so everyone knows that gay people are promiscuous, that Indians are alcoholics, and that women are good with children.

Those living under cultural imperialism find themselves defined from the outside, positioned, and placed by a system of dominant meanings they experience as arising from elsewhere, from those with whom they do not identify and who do not identify with them. The dominant culture's stereotyped, marked, and inferiorized images of the group must be internalized by group members at least to the degree that they are forced to react to behaviors of others that express or are influenced by those images. This creates for the culturally oppressed the experience that W. E. B. DuBois called "double consciousness." "This sense of always looking at one's self through the eyes of others, of measuring one's soul by the tape of a world that looks on in amused contempt and pity."[36] This consciousness is double because the oppressed subject refuses to coincide with these devalued, objectified, stereotyped visions of herself or himself. The subject desires recognition as human, capable of activity, full of hope and possibility, but receives from the dominant culture only the judgment that he or she is different, marked, or inferior.

People in culturally oppressed groups often maintain a sense of positive subjectivity because they can affirm and recognize one another as sharing similar experiences and perspectives on social life. The group defined by the dominant culture as deviant, as a stereotyped other, *is* culturally different from the dominant group because the status of otherness creates specific experiences not shared by the dominant group and because culturally oppressed groups also are often socially segregated and occupy specific positions in the social division of labor. They express their specific group experiences and interpretations of the world to one another, developing and perpetuating their own culture. Double consciousness, then, occurs because one finds one's being defined by two cultures: a dominant and a subordinate culture.

Cultural imperialism involves the paradox of experiencing oneself as invisible at the same time that one is marked out and noticed as different. The perspectives of other groups dominate the culture without their noticing it as a perspective, and their cultural expressions are widely disseminated. These dominant cultural expressions often simply pay no attention to the existence and experience of those other groups, only to mention or refer to them in stereotyped or marginalized ways. This, then, is the injustice of cultural imperialism: that the oppressed group's experience and interpretation of social life finds no expression that touches the dominant culture, while that same culture imposes on the oppressed group its experience and interpretations of social life.

Violence

Finally, many groups suffer the oppression of systematic and legitimized violence. The members of some groups live with the fear of random, unprovoked attacks on their persons or property, which have no motive but to damage, humiliate, or destroy them. In U.S. society women, blacks, Asians, Arabs, gay men, and lesbians live under such threats of violence, and in at least some regions Jews, Puerto Ricans, Chicanos, and other Spanish-speaking Americans must fear such violence as well. Violation may also take the form of name-calling or petty harassment intended to degrade or humiliate, and always signals an underlying threat of physical attack.

Such violence is systematic because it is directed at any member of the group simply because he or she is a member of that group. Any woman, for example, has reason to fear rape. The violence to which these oppressed groups are subject, moreover, is usually legitimate in the sense that most people regard it as unsurprising, and so it usually goes unpunished. Police beatings or killings of black youths, for example, are rarely publicized, rarely provoke moral outrage on the part of most white people, and rarely receive punishment.

An important aspect of the kind of random but systematic violence I am referring to here is its utter irrationality. Xenophobic violence is different from the violence of state or ruling-class repression. Repressive violence has a rational, though evil, motive: rulers use it as a coercive tool to maintain their power. Many accounts of racist, sexist, or homophobic violence try to explain it as motivated by a desire to maintain group privilege or domination. I agree that fear of violence functions to help keep these oppressed groups subordinate. I think the causes of such violence must be traced to unconscious structures of identity formation that project onto some groups the fluid, bodily aspect of the subject that threatens the rigid unity of that identity.

Conclusion

The five faces of oppression that I have explicated here function as criteria of oppression, not as a full theoretical account of oppression. With them we can tell whether a group is oppressed, according to objective social structures and behaviors. Being subject to any one of these five conditions is sufficient for calling a group oppressed. Most of the groups I listed earlier as oppressed in U.S. society experience more than one of these forms, and some experience all five.

Nearly all, if not all, groups said by contemporary social movements to be oppressed in our society suffer cultural imperialism. Which other oppressions are experienced by which groups, however, is quite variable. Working-class people are exploited and powerless, for example, but if employed and white do not experience marginalization and violence. Gay men, on the other hand, are not *qua* gay exploited or powerless, but they experience severe cultural imperialism and violence. Similarly, Jews and Arabs as groups are victims of cultural imperialism and violence, though many members of these groups also suffer exploitation or powerlessness. Old people are oppressed by marginalization and cultural imperialism, and this is also true of physically or mentally disabled people. As a group women are subject to gender-based exploitation, powerlessness, cultural imperialism, and violence. Racism in the United States associates blacks and Latinos with marginalization, even though many members of these groups escape that condition; members of these groups often suffer all five forms of oppression.

With these criteria I have specifically avoided defining structures and kinds of oppression according to the groups oppressed: racism, classism, sexism, heterosexism, ageism. The forms of group oppression these terms name are not homologous, and the five criteria can help describe how and why not. The five criteria also help show that while no group oppression is reducible to or explained by any other group oppression, the oppression of one group is not a closed system with its own attributes, but overlaps with the oppression of other groups. With these criteria, moreover, we can claim that one group is more oppressed than another, insofar as it is subject to more of these five conditions, without thereby theoretically privileging a particular form of oppression or one oppressed group.

Are there any connections among these five forms of oppression? Why are particular groups subject to various combinations of them? The answers to these questions are beyond the scope of this chapter. My project here is analytical and descriptive, not explanatory. Answering these questions is important to the theoretical project of understanding oppression. I believe they cannot be answered by an *a priori* account, however, but require a specific explanatory account of the connections among forms of oppression for each social context and for each group.

Chapter 10

The Political Economy of Contested Exchange

———— Samuel Bowles and Herbert Gintis

Introduction

Since World War II economics has shifted from being the spearhead of the left's critique of capitalism to its Achilles heel, while neoliberals and the right have come to wield economics as a powerful political weapon. Individuals in the contemporary left in the advanced capitalist countries are nearly unanimous in advocating forms of popular participation that make the exercise of power democratically accountable. Replacing capitalism with a democratic economy figures prominently in this program. Yet the left lacks a compelling account of the exercise of power in the economy, never having convincingly responded to the proposition that in a system of voluntary contractual exchanges, no agent has power over any other, simply because a buyer or seller can walk away from any transaction with impunity. Thus, the left has not effectively countered the notion that because markets provide ample opportunities for individual exit, the demand for a collective voice in economic life is misplaced.

Part of the problem, we think, may be traced to the standard microeconomic theory adopted by the contemporary left, which is incapable of modeling the exercise of economic power, is for this reason congenitally hostile to the project of economic democracy, and is in substance no different from neoclassical microeconomics.

In this chapter we present an alternative microfoundation for political economy, one that illuminates rather than obscures the democratic concerns of the left. We will argue for the rejection of the model of general competitive equilibrium due to Leon Walras, the textbook standard of neoclassical economics as well as the foundation of much neo-Marxian theory. Our objection is not the familiar, but overrated, complaint that the economy is so monopolized as to make the competitive model irrelevant or grossly misleading. Rather, we focus on a critical assumption in the Walrasian model: that conflicts of interest in the economy are resolved in contracts that are either voluntarily observed or are enforceable at no cost to the exchanging parties. The distinguished economist Abba Lerner described the treatment of conflicts of interest in the Walrasian model in this way:

> The solution is essentially the transformation of the conflict from a political problem to an economic transaction. An economic transaction is a solved political problem. Economics has gained the title of queen of the social sciences by choosing solved political problems as its domain.[1]

Exchanges may be solved political problems in which contracts are comprehensive and enforceable at no cost to the exchanging parties. We use the term "exogenous claim enforcement" to refer to this type of comprehensive, third-party (generally state) regulation of contracts; it tends to occur when the transaction is transparent in the sense that the characteristics of the goods or services exchanged are readily determined so that contractual transgressions are readily detected and redressed, often by resort to the courts.

However, when some aspect of the object of exchange is so complex or difficult to monitor that comprehensive contracts are not feasible or enforceable by a third party, exogenous claim enforcement does not pertain, and the exchange is not a solved political problem. By comparison with the transparency of the exogenously enforceable exchange, these exchanges are characterized by opacity: some aspect of the good or service exchanged is not readily determined. The two critical exchanges of the capitalist economy, the labor and the capital markets, are the archetypal examples.

In these cases, which we take to be quite general, we have a problem of *agency:* in an exchange between agents A and B, B can take actions that are harmful or beneficial to A's interests and that cannot be precluded or guaranteed by contractual agreement. Where a problem of agency exists, the de facto terms of an exchange result in part from the sanctions, surveillance, and other enforcement activities adopted by the parties to the exchange themselves. We refer to this process of regulation of the contract by the parties to the contract as "endogenous claim enforcement."

A transaction characterized by both an agency problem and endogenous claim enforcement is termed a "contested exchange." More formally, consider agent A who engages in an exchange with agent B. We call the exchange *contested* when B's good or service possesses an attribute that is valuable to A, is costly for B to provide, yet is not fully specified in a contract enforceable without cost.

Our key claim is that the most important exchanges in a capitalist economy are contested and that in these exchanges endogenous enforcement gives rise to a well-defined set of power relations among voluntarily participating agents, even in the absence of collusion or other obstacles to "perfect" competition. Power relationships unrelated to endogenous claim enforcement—state interventions in the economy or labor unions and other forms of collective action, for example—are important to the functioning of the capitalist economy; but they will not be our focus here, as their importance is commonly recognized.

Two well-known aspects of Marx's concept of labor were critical to this wedding of agency and time in economic theory. First, labor transforms nature and in the process transforms the worker and others. The labor process thus "produces" both commodities and people. Since the endogenous transformation of economic agents is irreversible and path-dependent, economic processes have an intrinsically historical character.

Second, in the labor exchange, the employer pays the worker a wage in return for the worker's formal submission to the firm's authority. The activity of work itself, as distinct from the process of exchange, is not guaranteed in the labor contract, cannot be enforced by the state or any other external party, and thus must be extracted from the worker by whatever system of control the employer may devise. The enforcement of the de facto terms of the labor contract is thus endogenous, involving a conflict of objectives between workers and employers; their capacity to carry out competing projects is thus a central determinant of the evolution of the capitalist economy.

The failure of left political economy to take seriously the issue of agency is thus at once both curious and debilitating; curious given Marx's pioneering work in the area, and debilitating given the apparent centrality of agency problems in both capitalist and other economies. It is also unnecessary, given recently developed analytical tools of post-Walrasian microeconomic analysis which, unlike the Walrasian model, focus attention on the choices of intentional actors on both sides of economic exchanges.[2]

The integration of post-Walrasian microeconomic theory with the original Marxian insights concerning the labor process provides an essential contribution to a new microfoundation for political economy, one that offers a critical perspective on the capitalist economy as well as providing some provisional insights concerning postcapitalist alternatives. The key substantive difference between our approach, which we call the theory of contested exchange, and such related strands of post-Walrasian economics as transactions cost economics is our focus both on the asymmetric power relationships arising in exchange and on the economic irrationalities entailed by endogenous enforcement in a highly unequal and hierarchical economy.

The Microfoundations of Political Economy

We take the hallmark of a microeconomic analysis to be its attention to the full range of choices facing economic agents; but by this standard the Walrasian model (and *a fortiori* the neo-Marxian adaptations of it) is simply not microeconomics, for it arbitrarily limits the range of situations in which agents optimize. If the *homo economicus* maximizes utility at the grocery store, one wonders why he does not optimize as thoroughly while deciding how hard to work for his employer or whether to default on a loan. *Homo economicus* turns out not to be The Great Optimizer he was touted to be, but a stripped-down version who obligingly declines to pursue his interest in any relationship plagued by agency problems.

By broadening the range of individual choice available to economic agents, the model we develop in the following pages yields an account of conflict and hierarchy in production and, partly as a consequence, provides a more adequate basis for the theory of collective action. By contrast, the oversocialized agent of Walrasian theory gives us an insufficiently social concept of the economy, lacking in a structure of power and bereft of opportunities for effective cooperation among agents.

Two key conclusions follow directly from this line of reasoning. First, the anonymity of exchange entails *the incompatibility of markets and discrimination,* since in a free market discriminators will incur higher costs than nondiscriminators, and hence will be driven from the market.[3] Second, there is an *absence of substantive hierarchy* since, by the nature of competitive markets, what might otherwise appear to be an authority relation (e.g., boss over worker) is in fact merely an continuously recontracted voluntary relation among equals.[4] Indeed, there is nothing in a Walrasian model suggesting that capital has even *formal* power over labor. As Paul Samuelson has noted concerning the distribution of income in a capitalist economy, "in a perfectly competitive market it really doesn't matter who hires whom; so let labor hire capital."[5]

Underlying these positions is a single critical result of the Walrasian model: the proposition that in competitive equilibrium markets clear; i.e., prices and the level of transactions in each market ensure the equality of supply and demand. We will see why this result is so important; later we will show that the market-clearing result depends on the assumption of exogenous contract enforcement and is thus a special case of quite limited relevance to the operations of a capitalist economy.

In the Walrasian model, differences in power are fundamentally absent. In an equilibrium exchange, agent B's gain from trading with A exactly equals the gain from B's next best alternative; otherwise, the assumption of competition would imply that some third agent, C, consigned to this less-desirable alternative, could have offered A a contract superior to that offered by B, in which case two of the agents (A and C) would not have implemented their optimal program, and thus the exchange between A and B would not have been an equilibrium transaction.

But if all agents are indifferent between their current transactions and their next best alternative, then markets must have cleared, for the presence of excess supply—say, of labor in the form of unemployment—would mean that employed workers are not indifferent between holding their present job and being without a job (their next best alternative); the presence of excess demand—say, for loans in the form of borrowers willing but unable to borrow more at the going interest rate—would indicate that current borrowers would prefer their current transactions to their next best alternative (going without the loans). Put differently, if markets did not clear, some agents (borrowers and workers in the above example) would be quantity-constrained (i.e., unable to transact as much as they would like to at going prices).

The Walrasian anonymity of exchange is based on the fact that all agents are indifferent between their current transactions and their next best alternative; there is no reason, therefore, to engage in long-term exchange relations, there is no possible gain to be made through strategic behavior, and the face-to-face aspect of exchange is irrelevant. Transactions take place, as it were, through a veil of prices. Paradoxically, it is because the objects of exchange are transparent that the parties to the exchange may be invisible to one another.

The apolitical conception of the economy follows directly from the above, but to show it will require introducing an important (but we think uncontroversial), *sufficient condition for the exercise of power.* Let us accept the assertion that for A to have power over B, it is sufficient that, by imposing or threatening to impose sanctions on B, A is capable of affecting B's actions in ways that further A's interests, while B lacks this capacity with respect to A.[6] Because in Walrasian equilibrium the cost to B of foregoing an exchange with A is zero (B is free to deal with C on identical terms), A cannot affect B's well-being by terminating the exchange. Thus, in the competitive equilibrium of a Walrasian economy, no sanctions may be imposed through the private actions of noncolluding agents.

Samuelson's affirmation that the locus of decision-making authority in a firm makes no difference follows trivially. For the boss has no more authority over the workers than conversely (they all have none), and there is no real decision-making authority to relocate. A worker-run firm would be constrained by competition simply to replicate the structure and functioning of the capitalist firm. By a simple extension of this argument, the traditional democratic and socialist critiques of the fragmentation of tasks, deskilling, and other aspects of work experience, technology, and the division of labor in capitalist production may be shown to be without foundation. Work may be unpleasant, but a socialist economy would offer the same unless it chose to sacrifice productive efficiency.

The unsustainability of discrimination in competitive equilibrium follows as well. If, for instance, the wages for black workers are lower than for white workers, and if the two groups are equally productive, a single nondiscriminating employer could hire the cheaper black labor, thus producing at lower cost than the discriminators and expanding at their expense. As a result, the demand for black workers would increase while the demand for white workers would decline, driving up the relative wages of the discriminated group. This process would continue until wages were equalized and hence discrimination eliminated.

Consumer sovereignty, the central normative principle of traditional economic theory, is also an unavoidable implication of Walrasian equilibrium. But we can now see that it is a peculiarly toothless kind of sovereignty. By the definition of equilibrium, the influence held by the high-income consumer does not include the power to impose sanctions. Rather it is of the behavioral form: A (the well-to-do consumer with a taste for caviar) can cause others to do what they would not have done in the absence of A's purchases (produce more caviar). A has power over none of the caviar producers, however, because each of them is indifferent between A's purchases and their next best alternative.[7]

Let us contrast these two forms of power by speaking of *command over goods and services* and *command over agents*. If we further identify two fundamental means of power as the command over violence and the command over economic resources, we can readily locate the key lacuna in the Walrasian model as a basis for a democratic political economy: its lack of a concept of command over agents based on the control of economic resources. We term this (admittedly loosely) "power in exchange," as a more adequate term must await the development of the model in the subsequent sections. Its location in a simple taxonomy of power is illustrated in Figure 1.

Figure 1
A Taxonomy of Power

		Outcome: Command Over	
		People	Goods and Services
Means: Command over	Violence	Obedience to Laws	Taxation and Transfers
	Economic Resources	Power in Exchange	Purchasing Power

As power in exchange is absent in the Walrasian model, the only power wealth confers is purchasing power. The owners of the means of production are powerful in the same way as a highly paid athlete: they have superior access to goods and services, may choose to enjoy more leisure than others, and may pass on similar advantages to their heirs. Though on a vastly different scale, the command that they exercise is no different *in kind* from that which a worker exercises when buying a cup of coffee. But this view is easily shown to be false.

Bosses and Workers: The Labor Market as a
Constitutive Contested Exchange

The relationship between boss and worker is a contested exchange in that although the worker's time can be contracted for, the amount and quality of actual work done generally cannot.[8] The relationship of borrower to lender, or of owner to the management of a firm, is a contested exchange in that although the repayment schedule of the loan or the share of income flow can be contracted for, this is not true of the actions of the borrower that determine the possibility of repayment. Exogenous enforcement will generally be absent and exchanges will be contested when there is no relevant third party (as when A and B are sovereign states), when the contested attribute can be measured only imperfectly or at considerable cost (work effort, for example, or the degree of risk assumed by a firm's management), when the relevant evidence is not admissible in a court of law (such as an agent's eye-witness but unsubstantiated experience), when there is no possible means of redress (e.g., when the liable party is bankrupt), or when the number of contingencies concerning future states of the world relevant to the exchange preclude writing a fully specified contract.

In such cases the ex post facto terms of exchange are determined by the monitoring and sanctioning mechanisms instituted by A to induce B to provide the desired level of the contested attribute.[9] We shall here analyze only one, albeit an extremely important, endogenous enforcement mechanism: *contingent renewal*. Contingent renewal pertains when A elicits performance from B by promising to renew the contract in future periods if satisfied, and to terminate the contract if not. For instance, a manager may promise a worker re-employment contingent upon satisfactory performance, or a lender may offer a borrower a short-term loan with the promise of rolling over the loan contingent upon the borrower's prudent business behavior.

The labor market is a case in point. An employment relationship is established when, in return for a wage, the worker agrees to submit to the authority of the employer. A worker's promise to bestow an adequate level of effort and care upon the tasks assigned, even if offered, is legally unenforceable. At the level of effort expected by management, work is subjectively costly for the worker to provide, valuable to the employer, and costly to measure. The manager-worker relationship thus is a contested exchange. The endogenous enforcement mechanisms of the enterprise, not the state, are thus responsible for ensuring the delivery of a particular level of labor services per hour of labor time supplied.[10]

In choosing a level of work intensity, the employee must consider both short- and long-term costs and benefits; for example, working less hard now means more on-the-job leisure now, but a higher probability of no job (and hence less income) later. To take into account this time dimension we must consider the worker's job as an asset, the value of which depends in part on the worker's effort level. We thus define the *value of employment* as the discounted present value of the worker's future income taking account of the probability that the worker will be dismissed; for obvious reasons it is an increasing function of the current wage rate. We also define the employee's *fallback position z* as the present value of future income for a person whose job is terminated—perhaps the present value of a future stream of unemployment benefits, the present value of some other job, or more likely a sequence of the two weighted by the expected duration of unemployment. Then A's threat of dismissal is credible only if the value of employment is greater than the fallback position; we define the *employment rent* or the *cost of job loss* as the difference between the two.

Employment rents are a particularly important case of the more general category, *enforcement rents*, which arise in all cases of competitively determined contested exchange under conditions of contingent renewal. Employment rents—and more generally enforcement rents—exist in a competitive equilibrium of a contested exchange. Why is this so?

A sufficiently low wage would make the job no more desirable to the worker than a spell of unemployment followed by a job search and another job. Let us call this wage at which the worker is indifferent between working and remaining unemployed the *reservation wage* and the corresponding level of labor effort the "whistle-while-you-work labor intensity." The level of the reservation wage obviously depends on the worker's relative enjoyment of leisure and work, the level and coverage of unemployment benefits, the expected duration of unemployment for a terminated worker, the loss of seniority associated with moving to a new job, and the availability of other income.

In the Walrasian model the equilibrium wage must be the reservation wage. In a contested exchange labor market, the equilibrium wage is greater than the reservation wage, since to elicit greater than whistle-while-you-work effort, A is obliged to offer a wage greater than the reservation wage, balancing the cost of paying the larger wage against the benefits associated with B's greater effort induced by a higher cost of job loss. For any given wage, the worker will determine how hard to work by trading off the marginal disutility of additional effort against the effect that additional effort has on the probability of retaining the job and thus continuing to receive the employment rent. Thus, the firm faces a *labor extraction function*, relating the level of work intensity to the wage. The equilibrium wage and effort level is thus determined by the employer, who knows the labor extraction schedule and selects the wage to maximize profits or equivalently to maximize the average effort provided per unit of wage cost. Except in the unlikely case that the whistle-while-you-work effort level is particularly high (e.g., a robotized or income-satiated worker who may be manipulated to do the employer's bidding at zero cost), the labor exchange is a contested exchange with positive employment rents and employer power.

One might charge that our representation of the labor process and labor market fails to capture important aspects of real-world capitalism. Do not the welfare state and collective bargaining offer workers some protection from job termination and a minimum living standard when unemployed? It is true that by stressing the carrot of high wages and the stick of dismissal, we detract from other possibly important aspects of the regulation of work, such as conformism, good will, and pride in work. But the degree of worker security from firing and unemployment insurance are integral parts of the model. Indeed, one of the advantages of the model is that it allows an analysis of the economic effects of the welfare state that goes considerably beyond the standard treatments of the effects of taxes and transfers on the supply of factors of production and on savings behavior.

Short-Side Power in the Production Process

Does employer A have power over worker B? Given the sufficient condition for the exercise of power, the answer is surely yes; A may use the threat of sanction to cause B to act in A's interest, but the converse is not true. First, A may dismiss B, reducing B's present value to z. Hence A can apply sanctions to B. Second, A can use sanctions to elicit a preferred level of effort from B, thus furthering A's interests. Finally, while B may be capable of applying sanctions to A (e.g., B may be capable of burning down A's factory), B cannot use this capacity to induce A to choose a different wage or to refrain from dismissing B should A desire to do so. Should B make A a take-it-or-leave-it offer to work at a higher-than-equilibrium wage or threaten to apply sanctions unless A offers a higher wage, A would simply reject the offer and hire another worker. For as we have seen in the previous section, in equilibrium there will exist unemployed workers identical to B who would prefer to be employed. Thus, A has power over B.

The employer's power is thus related to his or her favorable position in a nonclearing market. We say that the employer A, who can purchase any desired amount of labor and hence is not quantity-constrained, is on the *short side* of the market. Where excess supply exists—as in the labor market—the demand side is the short side, and conversely.[11] Suppliers of labor are on the *long side* of the market. When contingent renewal is operative and where the institutional environment is such that the threat of sanctions by the short-sider may be instrumental to furthering his or her interests, the principle of *short-side power* holds: agents on the short side of the market will have power over agents on the long side with whom they transact.[12] Long-side agents are of two types: those such as B who succeed in finding an employer and thus receive a rent that constrains them to accept the employer's authority, and those such as C who fail to make a transaction and hence are rationed out of the market. We will sometimes refer to agents such as B as long-side transactors and those such as C as quantity-constrained.

Three aspects of this result deserve to be noted. First, it might appear that A has expressed a preference for power and has simply traded away some money—the enforcement rent—to gain power. But while real world employers may act this way, it is quite unnecessary for our result: A is assumed to be indifferent to the nature of the authority relationship per se and is simply maximizing profits.

Second, it might be thought that A has intentionally generated the unemployment necessary for the maintenance of his or her short-side power. It is true that the employer's profit-maximizing strategy, when adopted by all other employers, results in the existence of unemployed workers, and that other wage-setting rules would not have this result. But we have assumed that the employer treats the level of unemployment (which figures in the determination of the workers' fallback position, z) as exogenous, for the simple reason that no employer acting singly can determine the level of aggregate employment.

Third, it may be argued that B has power over A, if not in our formal sense, then in the sense that B has the capacity to induce A to offer an employment rent over and above the amount needed to induce B to enter into the transaction. But B's advantage does not stem from B's power in the sense of a capacity that can be strategically deployed towards furthering one's interests. To see this, note that A's power to dismiss B is a credible threat, while B can put forth no credible threat whatever. Rather than attributing the fact that B receives a wage in excess of the reservation wage to B's power over A, we might better say that the employment rent derives from B's autonomy; that is, from the inability of A to determine B's level of effort without cost. The rent is a cost to A of exercising power over B.

We may summarize these results in the form of two propositions:

Proposition 1 (Short-side Power): A competitive equilibrium of a system of contested exchanges may allocate power to agents on the short side of nonclearing markets.

Proposition 2 (The Politics of Production): Those in positions of decision-making authority in capitalist firms occupy locations on the short side of the labor market and exercise power over employees.

Let us not overstate these results. First, not all contested exchanges give rise to short-side power. We analyzed an important case of contested exchange in which contingent renewal strategies of endogenous enforcement are adopted by agents on one side of the market and in which the short-side agents can make use of their advantageous short-side location. But there may be other important cases in which our sufficient condition for the exercise of power does not hold. Where no costlessly enforceable contracts can be written at all, for example, both agents may engage in endogenous enforcement activities, both may receive enforcement rents, and both may thus effectively pursue their interests by threatening to sanction the other.

Second, we have located power in the economy, but we have not shown that the exercise of this power is socially consequential. Indeed, is it not inconceivable that, while short-side agents in labor markets exercise power over long-side transactors, there is no feasible alternative institutional arrangement that would yield superior outcomes. While demonstrating this point is not trivial, we think that short-side power does make a difference in both moral and political senses.[13]

We may extract two less obvious results from the contested exchange model of the labor process and labor market. The first concerns Milton Friedman's claim that labor market discrimination and competitive equilibrium are incompatible.[14] In a contested exchange framework, disciminatory hiring practices may be an equilibrium employer strategy: paying identical workers different wages (according to race, say) will be profitable if it contributes to racial divisions that make cooperation among workers more difficult, and hence lower the cost of identifying and terminating a nonworking employee. Because all workers receive wages above their reservation wage, paying some less than others is not precluded, as it is in the Walrasian model, by the lower-wage workers' withdrawing of their labor supply. We thus have:

Proposition 3 (Divide and Rule): The competitive equilibrium of a contested exchange economy may exhibit racial, gender, and other forms of labor market discrimination among otherwise identical workers.

Our last labor market result concerns the social determination of technology, or what might be termed the shaping of the forces of production by the social relations of production.[15] The production system entailed by our model includes a production function, which describes the transformation of inputs into outputs, and a labor extraction function, which describes the manner in which the firm acquires work from employees whose time it has purchased in the labor market. Thus far we have assumed that the choice of the technologies that make up the production function is unrelated to the problems posed by the endogenous enforcement of claims arising in the labor market. But technologies differ markedly in their impact on the enforcement problem facing employers; some, like assembly lines, computerized point-of-sale terminals, or centralized word processing systems, make the detection of a laggard worker by a nonworker relatively simple, while others, like team production methods, make the production process considerably more opaque to outsiders.

Thus, the choice of technology will influence the cost of monitoring the work process and, for any given cost level, the probability that a nonworking worker will be detected. Hence a technology may be adopted not because it improves the efficiency of transforming inputs into outputs, but rather because it yields an easily monitored production process. Thus, the efficiency of a technology does not determine the course of technical change, and the choice of technique may be inefficient. This leads to:

Proposition 4 (Capitalist Technology): Where claim enforcement is endogenous, the profit-maximizing choice of production technologies will be made in light of both the efficiency with which technologies transform inputs into ouputs and their efficacy in enforcing contested claims; the resulting technologies, though cost-minimizing, will generally not be efficient.

The concept of short-side power is the key to unraveling the relation between control over economic resources and command over people, or what we earlier provisionally termed "power in exchange." But thus far we have supplied no reason for any connection between such power and the ownership of property. Exploring the relationship between wealth and power in the economy will require consideration of another contested exchange: the capital market.

Wealth and Power

What is the connection between the ownership of wealth and the exercise of economic power?[16] As we have seen, the Walrasian model implies that through the process of exchange, property rights confer on their holders no advantages other than greater consumption, leisure, or capacity to bequest made possible by, and in proportion to, the values of one's holdings; the power of wealth is purchasing power. Yet where claims are endogenously enforced the connection of wealth to power is both more extensive and less direct.

The location of agents to the short and long sides of markets (and hence the locus of economic power), as well as the division between long-siders who succeed in making transactions and those who fail, often (though not always) is related to ownership. The reason for this is straightforward: capital markets are as much arenas of contested exchange as are labor markets.

In return for a sum of money from lender A today, borrower B contracts to repay the loan, together with a specified debt service, at some given time in the future. This promise is enforceable, however, only if B is solvent at the time the repayment is called for. The borrower's promise to remain solvent is no more amenable to exogenous enforcement than is the employee's promise to supply a particular quality of work. And just as the worker will generally wish to work less hard than is profit-maximizing for the employer, the borrower will generally have an incentive to run greater risk of insolvency than would be optimal from the lender's point of view.

The credit market/labor market parallel may be extended. Just as the employer is not obliged to accept the level of work effort offered by the worker in the absence of the threat of sanctions, so the lender can devise incentives to induce more favorable performance than borrowers would spontaneously exhibit. It will generally be in the lender's interest to do so, since there is an evident conflict of interest between lender and borrower concerning the choice of risk: the profits from a high-risk, high-expected-return investment strategy accrue to the borrower, while the costs of such a strategy—a heightened chance of bankruptcy—are borne by the lender.

If the borrower's choice among investment projects involving different profiles of risk and rate of return could be contractually specified and third-party-enforced, the exchange between lender and borrower would have no need for endogenous enforcement. But this is not so. Not only are the actions of borrowers too subtle to be subjected to effective contractual specifications, but the penalties that may feasibly be imposed on a reckless borrower are limited by the borrower's exposed assets, which normally a small part of the total investment.

Given the need for endogenous enforcement, contingent renewal can be an effective strategy in the capital market, lender A promising borrower B continued access to credit so long as B performs on current obligations and gives evidence of prudent business behavior. But contingent renewal is less effective in capital markets than in labor markets. First, the sums involved in a typical business loan (and hence the

costs imposed on lenders by, say, the choice of an overly risky investment by the borrower) are orders of magnitude greater than the damage an employee can typically impose on the firm by enjoying
on-the-job leisure. Second, potential borrowers have much to gain from
misrepresenting their investment opportunities, since the discovery of
the misrepresentation is generally difficult and takes place only after
significant gains may be reaped by the borrower or possible losses
suffered by the lender. For instance, an investment project need not
have a positive expected return to be attractive to a borrower subject
only to contingent renewal since, except for reputation damage to the
borrower, it is the lender who bears the complete cost of failure. Workers, by contrast, have less to gain, since they may be quickly discovered and dismissed for poor work.

However, there is another enforcement strategy open to the lender;
namely, requiring the borrower to post collateral in order to qualify
for a loan. Since this collateral is forfeited if the borrower becomes
insolvent, the incentive incompatibility between borrower and lender,
as well as the adverse selection problem, are considerably attenuated:
a highly collateralized borrower has objectives more nearly similar to
those of the lender and has little incentive to invest in projects involving excessive risk. But collateral, by its very nature, must involve the
borrower's own wealth and cannot (except through subterfuge) itself
be borrowed without undermining the enforcement effect of the collateral requirement.

The observed relationship between the ownership of wealth and
the exercise of command in a capitalist economy thus flows from the
fact that only those who possess wealth can post collateral. The
wealthy are thus in an advantageous position to make offers characterized by reduced incentive incompatibility. We may summarize this
result in:

Proposition 5 (Money Talks): Ownership of wealth confers power on
agents by allocating them to short-side positions in contested exchange
markets.

Those who deny the connection of wealth to power, ranging from
neoclassical economists to institutionalists such as Berle and Means
and Marris, claim that in the context of perfectly competitive capital
markets, managers may hire capital in much the same way they purchase raw materials and hire labor.[17] The success of such managers
depends purely upon their entrepreneurial talents and acquired skills

in competitive survival. According to this view, such managers are in no way dependent upon the will of financial investors, any more than they are subservient to those who supply the firm with electric power or any other input. The result, of course, would be the reduction of wealth-holding to a distributional advantage with no relationship to power over such "real" economic activity as production and investment.

But hiring capital is precisely borrowing in the sense of this section. Thus, ownership of wealth is a prerequisite for favorable access to capital markets; when ownership is limited, the necessary process of borrowing imposes the possibility of sanctions on the borrower, thus critically limiting the autonomy of any but the wealthiest managers.

The ownership of wealth thus confers power, but not all forms of wealth confer equally. Only wealth that can be transferred at low cost when offered as collateral unambiguously serves to discipline potentially errant borrowers. But because labor cannot be separated from its owner and transferred to others, the promise of payments from future labor income is not third-party-enforceable. We thus have:

Proposition 6 (Forms of Wealth Matter): Different assets with equivalent present values (for example, alienable property or streams of future labor income) correspond to different positions in contested exchange markets and hence differing locations in the political structure of the capitalist economy, the differences depending on the degree to which claims on the asset must be endogenously enforced.

The existence of credit-constrained agents in the capital market and job-constrained agents in the labor market supports an important inference. Identical long-side agents will have differing incomes depending on whether they succeed in making their preferred transactions. The unemployed and the employed (possibly identical agents) have differing income levels; in capital markets, successful borrowers and the credit-constrained receive different returns on identical assets. But if identical assets yield different incomes, we must reject the designation of incomes as returns on assets. Thus we have:

Proposition 7 (Income Not a Return on an Asset): An agent's income cannot be represented as a return on the agent's asset holdings even if these are defined broadly to include skills.

We turn now from an explication of our approach to what is necessarily a provisional discussion of its implications, touching first on class and stratification theory and then (in the subsequent section) on the theory of income distribution.

Class, Stratification, and Property

Arguments concerning class structure are rarely divorced from political projects. Ours are no exception. Our conception of social stratification, like the model of contested exchange on which it is based, seeks to elucidate both the unequal incomes and the unaccountable concentrations of power generated within the capitalist economy. This focus embodies a joint commitment to democracy and to fairness. Less obviously it is motivated by the observation that the experiences of production, from alienated labor to the submission to arbitrary authority, including racial and sexual discrimination in employment, are powerful bases for mobilization of collective actors, bases of an importance possibly equal to or greater than income inequality due to differential property ownership. A model of capitalist production, even at the most abstract level, must not privilege property relationships while suppressing the exercise of power in production.

We here address three issues: the structure of class positions, the allocation of agents to class positions, and the distribution of income among class positions. Our focus on the politics of production distances this approach from recent neo-Marxian contributions, such as those of Erik Olin Wright and John Roemer, which place virtually exclusive emphasis on the distribution of wealth and income. However, we share with these contributions the affirmation that ownership is central to a theory of social stratification. By introducing short-side power and endogenous enforcement, however, we affirm that the study of class structure should concern more than the distribution of income and wealth. We reject the idea that agents are allocated to class positions solely on the basis of property, and we find the policy of redistribution (or socialization) of wealth inadequate to meet egalitarian, not to mention democratic, objectives.

Let us start with what Wright aptly calls the "embarrassment" of the middle class in Marxian theory.[18] While we have modeled just two contested exchanges (the markets for labor and capital), our analysis may illuminate the position of managers as occupying intermediate locations between capital and labor. By a manager we mean an agent possessing specialized production- and investment-related skills but lacking sufficient wealth to obtain enough credit to form a business, who is engaged to run the firm by wealth holders lacking or uninterested in exercising such skills. The contested exchange framework applies to the exchange between owners and managers, the quality and the prudence of managerial decision-making being analogous to the labor effort of the employee and the risk-taking decisions of the borrower. The manager is thus an intermediary who wields power over workers (a short-sider in the labor market) but whose actions are monitored by wealth holders (a long-sider in the market for managers).

This formulation recalls Wright's earlier insightful conception of contradictory class locations; in our terms, the position of the manager is contradictory because it is located on the short side of one market and the long side of another.[19] Managers thus have power over some agents while other agents exercise power over them. Equivalently, managers are Stackelberg leaders vis-a-vis workers and Stackelberg followers vis-a-vis owners.

Unifying the three contested markets for managers, labor, and capital we arrive at the structure of locations in the private economy described in Figure 2.

Figure 2
Contested Exchange, Short-Side Power, and Class Categories

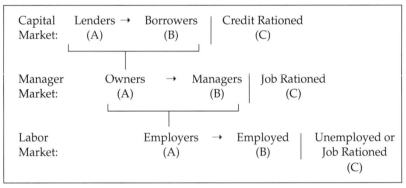

Notes: (A) indicates a short-sider, (B) a long-sider who makes a transaction, (C) a long-sider who fails to make a transaction or is forced to make a suboptimal transaction. Arrows indicate the direction of "power over."

Our approach has the attractive property of displaying the political nature of economic relationships but, because it is based on a general equilibrium model of the economy, it does not attain this goal by detracting from the competitive mechanisms accounting for the distribution of income and wealth. Moreover, by including the borrower-lender relationship as no less a determinant of distributional outcomes than the labor process and by representing labor and capital markets as interpenetrating sites of contested exchange, it explains the reproduction of capitalist class relationships in competitive markets: wealth confers power because successful borrowers emerge as employers, while workers cannot become employers or form their own firms because, lacking wealth, they are denied access to capital markets.

In addition, our perspective gives importance to the unemployed and the underemployed. This major social category is typically either assimilated in that of employed workers or is ignored altogether in class analyses based on Walrasian models in which the labor market clears. Indeed, by providing a basis for the differentiation among identical workers in competitive equilibrium (employed/unemployed, high wage/low wage) we avoid the common implication that these divisions (if they are recognized at all) are based entirely on skill differences. Finally, the contested exchange framework provides a plausible interpretation of management and entrepreneurship, categories that escape theoretical recognition in models that ignore agency problems in either work effort or risk-taking.

A possible additional contribution of the approach is its ability to model competitive economic processes in a way that illuminates the opportunities for and obstacles to collective action in capitalist economies. This may seem an intrinsically contradictory objective, for accepting (on empirical grounds) a highly competitive market framework would appear to stack the deck against collective action. Indeed, this is the case in the Walrasian model and its neo-Marxian variants, for when markets clear the rewards to collective action (and hence the possibilities of overcoming the free-rider obstacles) are very limited. While we have not used our approach to model collective action in any but the most formal ways, we believe that in comparison to other models of competitive economic processes, the contested exchange framework has several advantages.

For one, the rents identified in the model are not only enforcement instruments, they are also prizes to be won or enhanced through collective action. Collusion by one group of workers to exclude others on the basis of race, gender, or ethnic differences, for example, can increase the employment rents of this group. Moreover, as we have seen in the case of the labor market, collective action by long-side workers may enhance their economic position vis-a-vis their short-side employers and even (although we have not demonstrated this) reduce a short-side Stackelberg lender to a more symmetrically located exchange partner who must bargain with a collective of erstwhile long-siders. Finally, even our highly simplified model of the political structure of exchange in capital and labor markets may provide a framework more adequate than the Walrasian model for the analysis of similarities and differences in experience of production and exchange.

How are agents allocated to the positions in Figure 2? Recalling Proposition 5 (Money Talks), we know that both lenders and borrowers in the capital market are likely to own substantial assets in which contracts enforceable at low cost may be written. We call such people "wealthy." Recalling Proposition 6 (Forms of Wealth Matter), equally rich agents (those with similarly large expected income streams) who do not own alienable property may be credit-rationed. Credit-rationed agents in capital markets have uniformly less wealth than otherwise identical successful borrowers; failing in their attempt to obtain a loan they become short-side agents in the same market by loaning the assets they were previously willing to offer as collateral in their unsuccessful attempt to borrow.

Managers employed by owners are selected from a pool of agents with the appropriate skills, including the credit-constrained agents from the capital market. The basis for their selection does not concern us, except to observe that because the market for managers is a contingent renewal exchange, whatever characteristics the managers have, there will be identical individuals unable to find a position (or as desirable a position) as manager. Thus, agents identical in terms of organizational assets and human capital will be allocated to different positions.

Similarly, those workers who make their desired transactions (the B's) and those who are either job-rationed (occupy lower-paying secondary jobs) or unemployed (the C's) will likely differ on such grounds as skill, experience, and contacts; recalling Proposition 3 (Divide and Rule), race, gender, and other ascriptive characteristics are likely to appear as discriminators between these two groups.

A complex relationship between property and short-side power emerges. It is true, as Proposition 5 asserts, that the two are related. But we also have:

Proposition 8 (Noncorrespondence of Wealth and Power): Wealth is neither necessary nor sufficient for holding short-side power.

Property, Politics, and Income Distribution

We turn finally to the question of the distribution of income among class positions, an issue directly related to the normative orientation of our approach. Our claim here will be that contested exchange, by highlighting the political element in the economy, not only illuminates what are sometimes termed the "noneconomic concerns" of egalitarians and democrats, but also provides a more compelling account of the distribution of income.

Economists in the Walrasian tradition represent the capitalist economy as a pattern of property holdings and a set of rules governing competitive exchanges among noncolluding agents, which along with the technologically given methods of production and exogenously determined preferences of agents, determine a Pareto-optimal equilibrium set of prices and transactions. Because this equilibrium uniquely determines a distribution of income (or in some models, of income and leisure), it determines a distribution of welfare as well. The only political element in this model is the costless enforcement of property rights by the state—the protection of property and the enforcement of claims arising in exchange.

Marxists in this tradition, notably John Roemer, have effectively used this result to dramatize the determining role played by property holdings in generating the distribution of income, and to advocate a redistribution (or socialization) of property as the sine qua non of an egalitarian economic program. John Roemer writes, "If the exploitation of the worker seems unfair, it is because one thinks the initial distribution of the capital stock, which gives rise to it, is unfair."[20] It should be clear from Roemer's work that there is nothing intrinsically conservative about the distributional implications of the Walrasian model: if the distribution of income is unfair, a solution is the redistribution or socialization of assets.

In our model, by contrast, property, race, gender, and other distinctions jointly determine positions in the political structure of the capitalist economy, among which the distribution of income is determined through competitive exchange on markets that do not clear even in equilibrium. Because enforcement rents associated with such distinctions are ubiquitous and because these and other benefits may be garnered through collective action both in the economy and in the state, the model presumes neither atomistic nor collusive behavior, but rather includes both as possibilities. As our discussions of the choice of technology and divide and rule strategies reveal, neither the methods of production nor the preferences of the agents are regarded as exogenous in this model.

The state, while lacking Walrasian omnipotence, possesses distributional influence in ways precluded in the Walrasian model. State effects on the income distribution highlighted by our model, even in the simple form presented here, include the determination of the worker's fallback position through the level of unemployment and the availability of unemployment insurance, the impact of labor law and of policies concerning race and gender on the extent of cooperation among workers, the effects of bankruptcy law on the workings of the capital market, and the like.

The key difference emerging from a comparison of the Walrasian and contested exchange approaches to income distribution concerns the relative importance of property and politics. Of course, property is not absent from the contested exchange model, but its importance is mediated by the political relations among economic agents—the configuration of power and endogenous enforcement on labor and capital markets that the distribution of property supports. Indeed, one can imagine distributions of power in which the ownership of property would yield no return at all, for example, as would occur if unemployment insurance were sufficiently generous that labor could not profitably be extracted from workers (though this could hardly be a long-term reproducible solution for a capitalist economy). Similarly, politics is not absent in the Walrasian model, but its primary importance is in the state—in enforcing property rights and perhaps in taxation and transfers.

The contested exchange model holds that even under competitive conditions the redistribution of wealth is neither necessary nor sufficient as an egalitarian policy. It is not necessary because there are other ways of equalizing the distribution of income; if we are willing to assume a political movement (or state) with the power to equalize wealth, we could as well give it the power to reduce the private rate of return to zero and to devise new institutional arrangements for the allocation of credit, thereby making wealth irrelevant to the income distribution. The equalization of wealth is thus not sufficient as a distributional policy in a contested exchange economy simply because the income differences that are generated in equilibrium are not reducible to returns on differential asset holdings (Proposition 7). Since enforcement rents are major sources of inequality along with wealth differences, an egalitarian program can fruitfully address the redistribution of these benefits, for instance, through antidiscrimination policies or promotion of full employment.

Of course, equalization of property would predictably generate a more equal distribution of income and may be supported on this ground. But by itself such a redistribution would not alter the political structure of the economy and might leave the inequalities due to enforcement rents unaffected. Yet the model of the capital market as a contested exchange suggests at least one telling argument for wealth redistribution per se: it is possible that broader asset ownership will place currently credit-constrained, less-well-to-do agents (groups of workers, for example) in a position to borrow and thus to experiment with new ways of organizing production, investment, innovation, and distribution. In this respect, our criticism of the Walrasian model is not that it overstates, but rather that it misunderstands, the importance of wealth.

We close this discussion by pointing to a fundamental normative problem with the Walrasian model, one we believe is not shared by our approach. Aside from the question of fairness, other normative issues—concerning democracy or dignity in the workplace, for example—do not arise in this model because the only social relationship that it admits is competitive exchange, which under Walrasian assumptions yields Pareto-optimal allocations. Nor can one ask what kind of people this economy might produce—a question that troubled Adam Smith no less than Karl Marx—for it is a timeless system in which agents are given. Thus, within the Walrasian framework criticism of the despotic structure of production in the capitalist firm, of the fragmented and meaningless experience of the worker, or of the waste involved in managing contested exchanges in a class-divided society simply misses the mark.

Conclusion: New Directions in Political Economy

"A Marxist economic theory," wrote Adam Przeworski, "must be a political theory of the economy."[21] Przeworski was referring to a theory-building *task,* rather than an extant body of thought. In a sense, however, a political conception of the economy is nothing new. Institutional economists have long urged just this, and it is rather standard among Marxian scholars not overly impressed with Walrasian logic. But one might hesitate to term the insights flowing from such considerations a "theory of the economy."

Any novelty our approach might have lies in demonstrating the compatibility of a political theory of the economy with a competitive model of general economic equilibrium. Put somewhat differently, we have provided an economic theory that recognizes the competitive aspect of economic life but that is also noneconomistic in that it recognizes the political and cultural aspects of the economy as no less important in principle than its distributive and productive sides. The result, we hope, will be to bridge some of the distance between those who have been drawn to economistic thinking through a conviction that a theoretical understanding of the economy is important and those tending to downplay the economy because of a conviction that politics and culture matter more.

Of course, to affirm the logical coherence of the contested exchange model does not imply its empirical validity. For instance, to show that contested exchange labor markets do not clear in equilibrium is not to claim that this is the only, or even the major, reason we have unemployment (the system may, for instance, be perpetually out of equilibrium) nor does it explain the level of unemployment we have (which may perhaps be better explained by the level of aggregate demand and the average productivity of labor). A critic might well concede the coherence of the model, yet doubt its importance in understanding real capitalist societies. This is a key issue to which we cannot offer a decisive response.

However, we suspect that any framework adequate to understand the capitalist economy will be obliged to take into account that contracts do not enforce themselves, nor can they be enforced at no cost by the state; that markets, and particularly the labor market, do not clear; that agents are generally quantity-constrained; that enforcement rents are ubiquitous and the subject of political conflict both within the state and in the capitalist economy; that the economy produces people as well as goods and services; that capitalism is not simply a system of rich and poor but of bosses and subordinates as well; and that social divisions not reducible to property, such as race and gender, have an enduring importance. We take all of these attributes as descriptions of the actual workings of at least some important capitalist economies; admittedly they are rough and imprecise descriptions whose generality may be questioned.

However, some aspects of the contested exchange framework, particularly those concerning the labor process, have been subjected to extensive empirical analysis using data on the United States and the United Kingdom. While hardly conclusive, these studies strongly suggest the importance of employment rents. In the early 1980s, for example, aggregate after-tax employment rents in the United States exceeded the after-tax profits of the nonfinancial corporate business sector.[22]

We have deliberately attempted to model the capitalist economy rather than economies in general. But we cannot resist, in conclusion, suggesting several broader implications with possible relevance to building an egalitarian and democratic postcapitalist economy.

First, it is well known that markets are allocational mechanisms, promoting movements to and along an exogenously defined production possibility frontier. But markets are also disciplinary mechanisms, altering the supplies of inputs and technologies alike, and thus shifting the production possibility frontier. Just as allocative efficiency is a sensible normative standard for economic institutions, we may reasonably inquire to what extent and under what conditions markets provide efficient disciplining mechanisms.

Many critiques of market allocations concern the inefficiencies that arise in the presence of external economies and economies of scale, while arguments against state intervention often focus on the problems of the effective motivation and disciplining of economic agents in the absence of market competition. We are thus asked to choose, as it were, between the allocational irrationalities of markets and the disciplinary shortcomings of the state. But the choice may be less stark. The allocational and disciplinary aspects of markets are often thought to be inseparable, but they are not. There may be a wide range of economic arenas in which allocational inefficiencies can be significantly attenuated through tax and subsidy policies without impairing the disciplinary function of the market.[23]

The idea that markets discipline may help identify economic arenas in which markets might effectively be superseded by nonmarket mechanisms, and conversely. Rather than pointing to 'strategic sectors' or 'heavy industry' as the appropriate arena for centralized planning, one might advocate that markets be used where their allocational inefficiencies are minor or readily attenuated and where they perform an effective disciplinary function. Market discipline is likely to be most effective when the good or service in question closely approximates the Walrasian ideal of exogenous enforceability of claims, and to be least effective when significant conflicts of interest divide agents exchanging a good or service that is difficult to monitor or that for other reasons is not susceptible to exogenous enforcement.

Even where markets work imperfectly as disciplinary devices, they may be improved rather than replaced. For example, where monitoring is costly or imperfect, a case may be made for reducing the stakes of the game so that the degree of conflict of interest among exchanging parties is attenuated, thus reducing monitoring costs. This generalizes the argument that effective cooperation in the labor process may require a substantial equality of reward as a precondition.

The disciplinary aspect of markets may also illuminate the structure of power in centrally planned economies. While this structure is often implicitly assumed to be identical to the bureaucratic structures of the planning apparatus and the constituent firms, the concept of short-side power adds a distinct dimension. For reasons that need not be explored here consumer goods markets (and other goods markets as well) tend to be in chronic excess demand in centrally planned economies.[24] Thus, sellers of goods are short-siders (A's) who have power over the long-siders, who often literally wait in line to make a transaction, some succeeding (B's) and others not (C's). By contrast, goods markets in capitalist societies are often characterized by excess supply, businesses being unable to sell as much as they would like at the going price, with consumers occupying short-side positions. Thus, the location of the short side of nonclearing markets may be a key difference in the political structures and the mechanism generating inequality and securing elite control of the surplus product of capitalist and centrally planned economies.

Ironically, the importance of consumer sovereignty in a capitalist economy is more effectively argued in a contested exchange model than in the usual neoclassical framework, as argued in Herbert Gintis, "The Power to Switch: On the Political Economy of Consumer Sovereignty," in eds. Samuel Bowles, Richard C. Edwards, and William G. Shepherd, *Unconventional Wisdom: Essays in Honor of John Kenneth Galbraith* (New York: Houghton-Mifflin, 1989). In such a model the contested aspect of the consumer good is product quality, which is not contractible without cost. Because the price of such a good will exceed the marginal cost of its production in equilibrium, the seller receives a rent for each unit of the good sold.[25] Consumers can thus impose costs upon suppliers by switching to another firm; the threat of loss of patronage can discipline the supplier to maintain a high level of product quality. It might appear that consumers wield short-side power. But while the consumer A may effectively sanction the seller B by switching to another seller C and depriving B of the rent, the sanction, unless exercised collectively or by a single dominant consumer is not exercised in order to induce B to act in the interests of A, but rather to avail A of a superior supplier. Although A's interests are furthered by switching and although the switch imposes a sanction on B, the sanction is a byproduct of the switch. Thus, while its position as a long-sider in equilibrium induces the firm to improve its product quality, the consumer's action is not an exercise of short-side power in the sense of Stackelberg leadership. Consumer sovereignty is thus a structural result not attributable to any individual consumer's power over a seller.

Second, firms, not only in a capitalist setting but in any modern economy, face two crucial problems of agency: how to handle the money of outsiders and how to handle the labor of its members. We think it is insightful to see the capitalist firm as a particular solution to these two problems. Our own preliminary investigations have led us to suspect that by comparison with the currently feasible alternatives (for example, democratically run, worker-owned cooperatives or central planning) the capitalist firm is a relatively poor solution to the labor agency problem and a relatively attractive solution to the agency problem concerning credit and investment.

Among advocates of economic democracy, however, the problem of capital allocation is generally given scant attention, while the internal management of the democratic firm is the subject of a lively debate. The omission is serious in its own right and distorts the analysis of workplace democracy. Some organizational forms that might have attractive properties from the standpoint of the democratic regulation of labor (no ownership by nonmembers of the firm, for example) impinge in unfortunate ways on attractive solutions to the agency problems associated with the allocation of capital.[26]

Third, enforcement capacities are a determinant of institutional evolution. Like markets, all important economic institutions have consequences for the enforcement of claims arising from exchange. The evolution of such institutions responds to the changing technologies of enforcement no less than to the changing technologies of production and demographic shifts stressed in the standard treatment by neoclassical economic historians.[27] The workings and larger consequences of economically important institutions (schooling and the welfare state come to mind) likewise may be fruitfully analyzed from the standpoint of their effects on endogenous enforcement environments.[28]

The relationship between claim enforcement and institutional evolution suggests an extension of the Marxian theory of economic crisis: economic crises may be induced by declining profitability and stagnating investment associated with a deteriorating enforcement environment. We think that explanations based on this insight make sense of the experience of the advanced capitalist economies in recent decades more successfully than do competing models based on Keynesian (aggregate demand failure or realization crisis) or classical Marxian (rising organic composition of capital) notions.

Fourth, if claim enforcement is endogenous, economic agents cannot be exogenous. In contested exchanges it is often cost-minimizing to forgo the flexibility of spot contracting and to make and secure long-term commitments from one's trading partners. The resulting durability of exchange relationships generally gives them a face-to-face quality involving sufficiently few actors that the reciprocal effects of one's actions can be calculated and taken into account in selecting a strategy. In important exchanges one generally knows and cares about the identity of one's exchange partners.

The paradigmatic form of economic action is thus not an actor intervening in an impersonal external world (as, for example, decision-making by a price-taking firm) and interacting with other agents only through the veil of prices, but rather an intentional interaction among two or more agents. Each may have not only an *interest* in altering the capacities, trustworthiness, aggressiveness, and the like of the other agent, but also the *capacity* to do so given the long-term and nonanonymous nature of the exchange. The logic of the divide and rule strategy illustrates that the gains to be made for the employer by fostering racial sentiments arise because of the contested nature of the exchange, while the possibility of structuring labor relations to reproduce or exacerbate racism arises because workers are engaged in a long-term relationship with the firm and hence experience its labor relations as an important learning environment.

Because contested exchanges, as strategic nonanonymous relationships, are constitutive of economic agents, the relationship between constitutive and contested exchange is integral rather than elective. When claim enforcement is endogenous it is not even a useful fiction to represent exchanges as if they were between things rather than people.

Like the treatment of the economic advantages conferred by short-side power, the approach to endogenous agents suggested by the contested exchange model focuses attention on asymmetries among economic agents. Economic structures have effects on the evolution of all agents, of course, both by providing them opportunities to change or reaffirm themselves and by affecting their personal development in ways unintended and perhaps unknown to them. The contested exchange framework goes further and identifies contexts in which some agents, the holders of short-side power, have both the objective and the capacity to shape the development of other agents. Just as their Stackelberg leadership position allows short-siders the advantage of making take-it-or-leave-it offers concerning the wage or interest and collateral, short-side power may be used to make take-it-or-leave-it offers to participate in a work experience or some other environment designed to alter or affirm some preference, capacity, or other attribute of a long-side agent. Long-side agents lack this agent-making capacity for the same reason that they cannot make effective counteroffers with respect to wages, interest rates, and other more conventional economic variables.

The constitutive aspect of exchange must be added to our previously considered allocative and disciplining aspects in deciding between market and nonmarket solutions to economic problems.

Relationships among agents mediated wholly by markets militate against cooperative solutions to economic problems since each agent can always withdraw from the exchange (exit) rather than actively intervene in the interests of a collective solution (voice).[29] While the exit possibilities provided by markets are essential to their disciplinary function, the dominance of exit over voice in market relationships promotes an instrumental attitude of individuals to their social environments and thwarts the development of the collective decision-making skills on which the viability of a democratic society depends. And as we have just seen, contested exchange markets not only affect agents' preferences, they also place influence over the evolution of some agents (the long-siders) in the hands of other agents (the short-siders). The decision to use markets in a certain sphere, in short, is the decision to favor individual choice over democratic control, an issue that must be weighed along with questions of allocational and disciplinary efficacy in assessing alternative economic institutions.

The recognition of markets as learning environments suggests a reconsideration of the notion of evolutionary equilibria. If we are to use equilibrium concepts to illuminate evolutionary paths (and we think it is useful to do so), we must conceive of a joint equilibrium in which agents and rules are mutually constitutive, perhaps in complex and highly mediated ways. Thus, an adequate discussion of any alternative to capitalism must ask not only what allocations of resources and distribution of reward the proposed economic system would yield, but also how the agents making up the system would reproduce or transform the rules of the game defining it and how the game would reproduce or transform them.

Chapter 11
Power, Scientific Research, and Self-Censorship

Howard McGary

Scientists and scientific communities have a great deal of power in most societies. In the United States, scientists have played a crucial role in events that have changed the course of history, e.g., Einstein's work on special relativity. The power of the individual scientist is especially amplified in liberal democratic societies with a strong commitment to such things as individual liberty and academic freedom. However, the power of these individual scientists and their respective communities is often overshadowed in the minds of the public by the power of politicians and the heads of industry. Nonetheless, we should not underestimate the power of research scientists. Scientists have tremendous impact on many aspects of our lives: the food we eat, the air we breathe, the medicines we use to cure our ills, and the weapons we have at our disposal to resolve conflicts. It is important to realize that power takes forms other than economic and political power.

Recognizing the abuses and potential abuses of power by business persons and politicians, public interest groups and philosophers have proposed codes of ethics, guidelines, and regulations to ensure that the power of these groups stays within appropriate bounds. In some cases, laws have been passed to define and limit legally permissible uses of power. The concern that power not be used to harm innocent persons has now been extended to professions in general, e.g., doctors, lawyers, etc. Although thoughtful people recognize the value of limiting the abuses of power, many people, particularly political libertarians, are still reluctant to adopt measures that appear to infringe upon the freedom of the individual. Libertarians warn of the dangers of using the power of the state to protect unsuspecting individuals from a variety of potential harms that might result from actions of powerful persons. They argue, for example, that we should deregulate the professions rather than adding additional regulations. They argue that the market should be used to weed out those persons who don't adhere to certain standards of decency. This is not to say that they believe that professionals can do whatever they choose, but rather that clear violations of people's rights, defined in the negative sense of rights that impose duties of non-interference on others, must occur before state intervention is warranted.

Although there are differences of opinion about the extent of the role of the state in these matters, there is general agreement that these persons have the personal responsibility to exercise a certain level of moral constraint. However, research scientists, for the most part, have escaped the attention of the watch dogs of abuses of power. Research scientists have been virtually free to engage in research of their own choosing provided that their work does not involve the misuse of human subjects. But as we shall see, harm does not occur only to the subjects directly involved in the experimentation, it can also occur to innocent persons indirectly involved as a result of certain research projects and findings.

Professors Gottfredson and Ruston have put the race and I.Q. debate back in the spotlight. Gottfredson, an American,[1] and Ruston, a Canadian,[2] both contend that blacks as a group are less intelligent than whites and that blacks will thus fare poorly in any activity or task that requires a high degree of intelligence. They also conclude that it is poor reasoning to assume that, given the same opportunities, blacks and whites will do roughly the same in qualifying for careers or vocations that demand better than average intelligence.

The renewed interest in the race and I.Q. issue parallels the rise in racial hatred and violence in society in general, and on college campuses in particular. A climate of racial hatred and violence has historically fueled eugenics research. In this climate, it is not surprising to find a professor of philosophy, Michael Levin, in a letter to *American Philosophical Association Proceedings*, claiming that affirmative action programs in philosophy are unnecessary because few blacks are intelligent enough to be philosophers.[3] It is clear that race and I.Q. research is most often seen as significant in an atmosphere in which there are racial antagonisms and competition for scarce goods.

In the discussion that follows, my aims are modest. I wish to examine a common claim made by investigators of race and I.Q. that their research, even in the present climate of racial hostility and violence, does not reflect negatively on their characters. Some who hold this position claim that the search for truth is such an important value that it takes precedence over all other values, even the prevention of harm to innocent persons. On the other hand, researchers like Gottfredson reject giving such weight to the search for truth, but they still contend that their hands are morally clean when they engage in race and I.Q. research. My examination shall focus on this claim by members of the latter group.

I am not so naive as to think that all members of the second group are sincere when they make such a claim, but some may be. But what is even more important is that people of good will in general are inclined to be sympathetic to investigators if the moral nature of their actions is unclear. But if the investigators' actions are seen as morally suspect, then the general public will question the value of such investigations, even if performed with so-called good intentions. I would like to make it clear at the outset that my concern in this chapter is with moral and not legal issues, but I believe that moral disapproval can be quite effective in altering, directing, and shaping behavior.

Gottfredson in an unpublished manuscript, "Breaching Taboos: A Personal Perspective," writes: "Although much criticism of race-related research constitutes a not-so-subtle indictment of one's character, specifics are seldom spelled out." I attempt to spell out one such criticism in this paper. In the first section I set out and criticize Noam Chomsky's argument that the moral dilemma vanishes once we see that the scientific significance and social utility of projects like race and I.Q. research are slight.[4] In the second section I review the argument by Block and Dworkin that a scientist confronted with such a dilemma should voluntarily cease his investigations if they are likely to be used by others to cause serious harm.[5] Finally, I construct and reject two arguments that might be used by decent but misguided scientists who wish to defend race and I.Q. research.

I

In *For Reasons of State*, Noam Chomsky makes the following claim:

> Turning to the question of race and intelligence, we grant too much to the contemporary investigator of this question when we see him faced with a conflict of values: scientific curiosity versus social conse-quences. Given the virtual certainty that even the undertaking of the inquiry will reinforce some of the most despicable features of our society, the seriousness of the presumed *moral dilemma* [emphasis

added] depends critically on the scientific significance of the issue that he is choosing to investigate. Even if the scientific significance were immense, we should certainly question the seriousness of the dilemma, given the likely social consequences. But if the scientific interest of any possible finding is slight, then the dilemma vanishes.[6]

For some time Chomsky's remarks have troubled me. On the one hand, I share his reservations about scientists examining such hypotheses as "are whites more intelligent than blacks?" and "are blacks more intelligent than whites?" On the other hand, my allegiance to freedom of thought and expression and to the value of a person's sense of conscience leads me to doubt the validity of Chomsky's claim that once we see that the scientific significance of such examinations is slight, then the *moral* dilemma between scientific curiosity and social consequences vanishes.

Chomsky made his remarks about race and I.Q. research at a time when the views of Shockley and Jensen were receiving a great deal of attention.[7] However, two decades later, the race and I.Q. controversy is still raging. Some researchers in this country and in other democratic nations are now maintaining that race and I.Q. research is morally defensible.[8] I should say at the outset that my sympathies lie with Chomsky's position, but unfortunately arguments in support of such a position have not been totally persuasive. The arguments are enthymematic because they fail to recognize some essential ingredients that must be made explicit if a Chomskian argument is to succeed. My aim is to correct this shortcoming.

We should note that the race and I.Q. controversy should be distinguished from other cases in which the morality of certain research projects is at issue. For example, the reservations about nuclear science research are different from those about race and I.Q. research in terms of the magnitude of possible harm, the possible indiscriminate nature of the harm, and the proven benefits in spite of the possibility of great harm. As we shall see later in this chapter, the fact that race and I.Q. research involves the possibility of clearly defined groups being subjected to serious harm has a bearing on the morality of engaging in such research.

At this juncture, we should be clear about what the strong liberal position on freedom of thought and expression requires. Liberals, in the tradition of John Stuart Mill, would support the researcher's legal right to engage in the research of his choosing provided that it does not cause direct physical harm to others. We can certainly cite actual cases in which research has caused direct harm to others, so the liberal position, given Mill's harm principle, is to not allow all research unconditionally. It is also consistent with their position that researchers who engage in research that causes indirect or direct harm merit moral and social criticism. However, the liberal position is consistent with allowing people to legally engage in activities that are judged to be immoral.

On the other hand, against the liberal position, Marxists argue that individuals are not legally or morally at liberty to do things that destroy communalism. Respecting an individual's right to liberty does not license indirect physical or mental harm to others. We must be careful here and note that Chomsky is not recommending state censorship, be it from the right or the left. His point is that a scientist who engages in research that is likely to be used by others to cause indirect harm faces no moral dilemma if the social significance of the research is slight.

The alleged dilemma that Chomsky examines can be represented as a complex constructive dilemma:

P_1 If a scientist should cease potentially dangerous but insignificant research that may be used by others to cause harm, then the moral value that he assigns to individual and scientific freedom is violated.

P_2 If racists get their hands on potentially dangerous findings, they will use the findings to cause harm.

P_3 Either a scientist should not engage in potentially dangerous research if it is likely that his findings will be used by others to cause harm or racists (and others) should have the potentially dangerous findings.

∴ Either the moral value that the scientist assigns to individual and scientific freedom will be violated or racists will use his findings to cause serious harm.

Remember, Chomsky stipulates that if the race and I.Q. research has little or no value and the social consequences are negative, then the dilemma vanishes. He is probably right that if we take a current time slice, race and I.Q. research will be judged to be insignificant; but things that appear insignificant at one point may in the future prove quite significant. For example, Mendel's work on pea pods at the time was not considered to be scientifically or socially significant.[9] But as we know, his work has proven to be of great value.

In his discussion of psychology and ideology Chomsky writes:

> . . . imagine a psychologist in Hitler's Germany who thought he could show that Jews had a genetically determined tendency towards usury (like squirrels bred to collect too many nuts) or a drive towards antisocial conspiracy and domination, and so on. If he were criticized for even undertaking these studies, could he merely respond that the 'fundamental issue' is whether inquiry shall (again) be shut off because someone thinks society is best left in ignorance?[10]

Such a response is odd in the context of Nazi censorship; the issue would be clearer in present-day United States or Canada. Nonetheless, Chomsky believes that the psychologist should not maintain that he is being wronged if he is criticized for undertaking such studies.

Chomsky begins his argument by stating that a conflict of values exists between scientific curiosity and social consequences. This conflict is similar to Mill's conflict between individual freedom and the demands of utilitarianism. In both cases a dilemma exists because of a conflict between the value that a person gives to individual freedom and the value that he assigns to the prevention of harm to innocent persons. But Chomsky is quick to point out that the seriousness of the dilemma will depend upon the seriousness of the hypothesis to be explored. According to Chomsky, it would be foolish to claim that society would be left in ignorance were it not for scientific research on insignificant matters of all sorts.

This response is inviting, but it may focus on the wrong issue. It is not the knowledge to be gained that is always crucial, but the value of the scientific process itself even if it does not bear fruit. So while Chomsky may be warranted in concluding that the particular hypothesis under examination has little or no scientific significance, he may not be justified in concluding that scientific methodology also has little significance. This is hard to see in the case of the psychologist in Hitler's Germany because scientific methodology was then used to support Nazism.

A further problem with Chomsky's response is his failure to specify who is to judge the scientific and social significance of the research in question. This is a complex matter. A number of groups and their interests need to be considered. There are the public, the scientific community, legislators, and possible victims. These groups and their interests are not necessarily mutually exclusive, but their interests can and do conflict. Unfortunately, Chomsky does not give us convincing reasons for making a determination about who should be the judge. Nonetheless, I would doubt that the judgment in such cases should be left exclusively to one individual.

If I am right that the judgment of the social significance of a dangerous research project should not be left to the individual researcher, then what about the scientific significance? Is Chomsky right that this judgment should not be made exclusively by the individual researcher? I think so. But suppose we accept a Kuhnian conception of science.[11] Then during a period of 'normal science,' a project might be judged to have little or no significance merely because the majority of the scientific community rejects it. Therefore, we would be wrong in such cases to claim that the researcher has a moral obligation to refrain from pursuing his project simply because it is judged to be insignificant by his peers. Who should decide the scientific significance of a research project is no simple matter, but even with the above objection, the scientific community must be consulted. As we can see, resting one's argument on the significance of the project has its shortcomings.

Chomsky's moral argument against insignificant research projects that lead to serious social harm is consequentialist in nature, but it is not utilitarian. He does not ask the moral agent to embrace the classical act-utilitarian position that each project should be judged as morally permissible only if it is likely to produce more happiness for all affected by it than alternative projects. Nor would Chomsky recommend that the moral agent adopt modern preference utilitarianism, which judges the permissibility of a project according to whether or not it satisfies the preferences of those affected. Instead, Chomsky seeks to promote or instantiate human dignity for all and for those things that support it. I suspect that he is willing to promote this end even if the general happiness in society is reduced or if the preferences of many of those affected by the promotion of this end are not satisfied.

There is an important question that must be answered if we are to accept a Chomskian outlook. How far should one be willing to go to defend the goal of human dignity for all? Chomsky would deny that curious scientists have a moral right to engage in insignificant research that threatens human dignity. For him it is highly unlikely that insignificant research of this nature will lead to optimal social arrangements. Thus, while his approach to the issue is not utilitarian, it is close enough that it still might fall prey to the deontological criticism that it disrespects the rights of the individual scientist—in particular what some take to be an important value and perhaps a fundamental right, the right to be free. Does the scientist who chooses to continue his insignificant investigations that are likely to be used by others to cause serious harm make a morally incorrect decision?

II

Perhaps a better strategy for answering this question does not rest on the scientist's knowledge about the value of the research but focuses on whether the research, insignificant or not, creates directly harmful social consequences. The clear and present danger test in the law requires reliable evidence of a causal or statistical nature between the practice and social harm before the practice can be made illegal. In the race and I.Q. case, it is difficult to predict the actions of people who are given information of a biased or inflammatory nature; but sometimes we can be reasonably sure. When empirical evidence is available, even firm supporters of personal liberty like the American Civil Liberties Union (A.C.L.U.) have advocated limits on freedom of expression. Can we employ the reasoning in the clear and present danger test to give us some moral guidance? Will allowing research in the area of race and I.Q. create a clear and present danger?

Block and Dworkin, in their influential paper "Race, I.Q., and Inequality," state the conditions under which race and I.Q. research creates a clear and present danger. They write:

> If one believes that the media of communication are biased, either because of political considerations or because of something in the nature of the media (*Time* magazine is not likely to be willing to devote the space to the necessary clarifications even if it desired to), and that one's results will be distorted in the direction of producing harmful consequences;
>
> If one believes that the possibilities of countering such distortions are minimal (compare the force of a letter to the *Atlantic Monthly* with that of the original piece one is criticizing);
>
> If one believes the kind of research in question is burdened with methodological problems, ambiguous implications, and open to a wide range of interpretations;
>
> If one thinks it is unlikely that all sides in the disagreement will get equal access to the mass media or that, in any case, those in power will select from the ambiguous data the findings they need to rationalize their political and social programs;

If one believes that the likely benefits are minimal and the likely harms grave;

Then one has a responsibility to cease such investigations while the above circumstances obtain.[12]

Block and Dworkin appeal to consequentialist arguments as opposed to rights-based deontological ones. They believe that knowingly engaging in an activity that is likely to be used by others to cause serious harm to innocent persons is morally unjustified; on balance it creates a greater evil than renouncing the activity. But their approach and conclusions might be rejected by a scientist sympathetic to the position that there is a serious moral cost to abandoning certain strongly held values in order to promote better social consequences. The scientist who believes that she has a moral right to investigate whatever she chooses, irrespective of the consequences, is certainly engaging in a bit of fiction. Block and Dworkin make this clear, but their conditions fail to explain clearly why a scientist whose research does not cause direct harm to others has a moral obligation to cease his investigations; they obviously assume that the distinction between direct and indirect harm in these cases does not make much difference. Are they right?

Consider the scientist who wishes to engage in research that is likely to cause indirect harm. As a scientist, does he have certain moral obligations when it comes to indirect harm? Before we answer, we should be aware that the obligations of scientists vary from society to society depending upon such things as the level of technology, the abundance or scarcity of resources, and the form of government. But one thing is clear: a scientist, in any society, will have certain social obligations as a member of a particular social order. It is here that utilitarian considerations are applicable. However, as stated above, appeals to utility depend upon making judgments about the long-term consequences of research that could prove indirectly harmful. Unfortunately, these judgments are sometimes very difficult to support in a rigorous fashion. The evidence for such judgments about the consequences of indirect harm can point in opposite directions depending on how long or short the view that one takes.

An admittedly troublesome aspect of my position is the difficulty scientists face in determining when harm is to be considered "serious" harm. However, history can help us to see the serious harm that race and I.Q. research can cause. For example, in the early part of this century, there were a number of research projects that claimed that some white ethnic groups are naturally less intelligent than others.[13] These studies were used to justify immigration policies biased against certain ethnic groups. They also served as a rationale for policies that denied opportunities and needed services to members of certain ethnic groups. As you might guess, blacks were even more severely victimized because of this research. This harm was serious and quite obvious to even a casual observer. The conditions and attitudes that allowed it to occur have not changed very much, so a decent scientist has some basis for determining whether his research may be used by others to cause serious harm. The claim that a scientist must have absolute certainty in these matters is unreasonable. As Aristotle said, a discussion will be adequate if it achieves clarity within the limits of the subject matter (N.E. 1094b 13–14).[14] In some cases scientists will run into difficulties in determining whether their work will be used by others to cause serious harm, but in spite of these difficulties, judgments must be made and used to determine the nature of our moral obligations.

Sometimes we foresee and intend the consequences of our actions, but other times we do not. Decent people believe that we should feel a sense of responsibility for the harmful consequences of our intended actions and for the consequences of some actions that we did not intend, but did foresee. Block and Dworkin share this belief. For them, a scientist who does not intend his research to cause harm, but is aware that his findings are likely to be used by others to inflict serious harm, is responsible because he has failed to cease such investigations even though he knew that it was probable that his findings would be used by others to cause serious harm. The root idea here is that in "powder keg" situations a morally decent person should exercise extreme caution and self-constraint. Good intentions alone will not free one of the moral responsibility for the resulting harm.

Is it always morally indecent to knowingly engage in research that is likely to be used by others to cause serious harm? Chomsky thinks so. In the case that Chomsky cites, the researcher cannot be excused on grounds of ignorance because he must realize that harm will result from a causal process of which he is a crucial part. According to Chomsky, by continuing his research he is acting in a negligent manner; such conduct falls below the moral standard for the protection of others against unreasonable risk of harm. The crucial phrase here is "unreasonable risk."

As I have said, it is not always a simple matter to determine when risks are unreasonable, but in the race and I.Q. case Chomsky, Block, and Dworkin believe that we can speak with some certainty. Given this fact, should scientists engaging in race and I.Q. research, under the conditions described by Block and Dworkin, voluntarily cease their work because other human beings are subject to risk of harm? Some scientists are still unconvinced.

III

These scientists may persist, even though their research may be used by others to cause harm, because they believe that they don't have a duty to prevent harm to other people by curtailing activities that, in themselves, create no harm. To use terms employed by legal writers, they believe that they have a negative duty to refrain from harming others and a positive duty to aid others by protecting them from harm only if they have made some explicit or implicit agreement to do so. These scientists deny that by continuing their research they are in some indirect way morally responsible for the harm done to others. It is their opinion that even though certain negative consequences are foreseeable, this does not imply that the person who expects them and is capable of preventing them has a moral duty to do so.

Chomsky, I suspect, would reject this line of reasoning; he would claim that the scientist's belief that someone else in the causal process is morally capable of and responsible for preventing the harm is false. Chomsky does not believe that a rational person would depend upon racists in the race and I.Q. case to act in morally responsible ways.

Why does Chomsky believe that we cannot reasonably entrust material of a pernicious nature to racists? Are they mentally defective in a manner similar to persons who completely lack a conscience? It seems not. Of course, a complete answer to this question depends on an account of the agency or lack of agency of racists; lacking such an account, it would be premature to conclude that racists can never act in morally responsible ways when making decisions about the welfare of some racial groups. Thus, this would not be a position one would want to adopt even if one believes that a scientist should voluntarily cease his investigations if it is likely that his findings will be used by others (e.g., racists) to cause serious harm.

Since there is always the possibility that someone may use research findings that were intended to do good to cause pain and suffering, the scientist, as a moral agent, might maintain that it is unreasonable to hold a person responsible for these unintended consequences of his actions. Is this response correct? I think not. Perhaps a scientist would be right in claiming that he should not be held accountable for all of the unintended harmful consequences of his actions, but it is wrong to believe that he can, with good conscience, ignore entirely the unintended serious harmful consequences of his work.

Nevertheless, the idea that a person must directly cause harm in order to be responsible for the harm is a popular belief held by many concerned with legal as well as moral responsibility. Causing harm is thought to be an extension of doing harm.[15] So when there are extraneous or intervening forces that appear to break the causal chain between the agent's action and the harm done, then we must question whether agent A caused the harm. If A can't be said to have caused the harm, then we are reluctant to conclude that A is responsible for the harm done. Writing about responsibility in the law and morals, Hart and Honoré echo this point when they write:

> A throws a lighted cigarette into the bracken which catches fire. Just as the flames are about to flicker out, B, who is not acting in concert with A, deliberately pours petrol on them. The fire spreads and burns down the forest. A's action, whether or not he intended the forest fire, was not the cause of the fire: B's was.[16]

Can't the scientist, in our race and I.Q. case, argue that he is not responsible for any harm that results to blacks because he did not cause the harm? Remember, he does not use his findings to harm blacks. The harm is caused by those who misuse his findings. Isn't this similar in relevant respects to the case discussed above by Hart and Honoré? Couldn't the scientist argue that, like the case of the cigarette in the forest, his actions alone could not cause the harm?

Before we attempt to answer these questions, let us get a better picture of the moral principle that appears to lie at the heart of the scientist's reply. Let us call this principle P. Principle P says that, when another person's voluntary action intervenes with A's action and harm results because of the intervention, then A is not responsible for the harm. Does principle P justify the scientist's contention that it is morally permissible for him to engage in his research? Is this case similar enough in relevant respects to the cigarette case to make an analogy between the two plausible? Initially one might think so; however, if we explore further, we might think differently. It is true that in both cases the voluntary action of another alters the causal process such that, were it not for the interferences, the harm would never have occurred. In the words of Hart and Honoré, "it reduces the earlier action and its immediate effects to the level of mere circumstances or part of the history" rather than a cause of the harmful action.[17] But if the two cases are indeed analogous, then we may be inclined to conclude that because the scientist did not cause the harm, he is not responsible for it.

However, before we assign responsibility for the harm in either case, we must understand the background conditions. If the smoker drops the match in a very dry forest where it is common knowledge that there are people in the forest who will pour petrol on untended lighted cigarettes, then we would be warranted in concluding that the smoker is responsible for the fire even if he did not directly cause it. Likewise we must understand the background knowledge the scientist has when he decides to do race and I.Q. research. To be analogous to the smoker example, the scientist must be unaware that his research will be used to cause serious harm.

But even if we say that A is not responsible for the harm, does it follow that A's action is morally permissible? The answer to this is not straightforward. Suppose a friend of mine has a watch that he loves dearly; I also greatly admire the watch and would like to have it. Let us further suppose that my friend runs into hard times and needs money badly. If I offer to buy the watch when I could easily lend my friend the money, is my behavior morally permissible? Remember, I have not in any way caused my friend's misfortune; at worst, I have taken advantage of it.

Before we answer this question, we should distinguish morally decent behavior from good samaritanism. A good samaritan is a moral saint who goes beyond the requirements of duty, whereas a morally decent person does what moral duty requires. People are not required to be good samaritans, but they are expected to do their moral duty. Am I failing to do my moral duty when I refuse to offer my friend a loan? Does friendship require this type of behavior, or must some explicit agreement exist between friends before an obligation can be said to exist? It seems that I have a moral right not to loan the friend money even though it may seem to be the wrong thing to do. Can people have a moral right to do what is morally wrong? Some scientists may believe that they do and that this justifies their research on projects like race and I.Q.

These scientists might attempt to refute the arguments by Chomsky, Block, and Dworkin and justify their decision to continue potentially harmful research by claiming that the two propositions below are not contradictory:

1. S has a moral right to do A, where A is research on race and I.Q., and

2. S's doing A is morally wrong.

In other words, the scientist believes that a person can have a moral right to engage in his research even though it is morally wrong. Intuitively this conclusion seems incorrect, but Jeremy Waldron has argued that we should not let the linguistic awkwardness of the assertion mask the truth of the proposition.[18]

Waldron believes that the following examples serve as cases in which a person can have a moral right to do what is morally wrong:

> Someone uses all the money he has won fairly in a lottery to buy race horses and champagne and refuses to donate any of it to a desperately deserving charity.

> An individual joins or supports an organization which he knows has racist leanings, such as the National Front in the United Kingdom; he canvasses support for it among a credulous electorate, and he exercises his own vote in its favor.[19]

Waldron is careful to note that by a right he does not mean a legal right, but a moral right. For it is clear that we can have a legal right to do things that are morally wrong.

According to Waldron, moral rights give rightholders the protection to make certain decisions when alternative courses of action are available. This protection of the individual's decision-making right is not moral justification for any particular decision.[20] He also argues that the alternative courses of action open to the rightholder as a decision-maker are not restricted to ones that are either correct from the moral point of view or morally indifferent. From this he concludes that the morality that gives rise to proposition 1 is distinct from the morality that gives rise to proposition 2 because they have different functions. The morality that gives rise to proposition 1 has as its function protecting choices, while the morality that gives rise to proposition 2 guides choices. If we recognize these two kinds of morality, we can see that moral rights can protect our decision to choose actions that are morally wrong.[21]

Suppose that Waldron is right. Is this finding of any use to the scientist who wishes to morally condone the continuation of research that is likely to be used by others to cause harm? By adopting Waldron's conclusion about the function of moral rights, the scientist might conclude that he has a moral right to continue his research even though doing so is likely to cause something that is morally wrong, namely, the causing of harm to innocent persons. But if the scientist believes that this moral right justifies his action from the moral point of view, he is mistaken. The scientist cannot defend his particular choice among a range of alternative actions by appeal to his moral rights, but only his protection to make such a choice. So, although the scientist may appeal to a morality that protects his right to choose, he is wrong to think that this morality serves to justify the particular choice that he makes. Thus, Chomsky can still maintain that the scientist, as a moral agent, should recognize that he faces no moral dilemma when it comes to choosing between continuing a research project that is not of great significance and causing serious indirect harm to innocent persons.[22]

Chapter 12
Women and Power

— *Jean Baker Miller*

In recent conversations people have told me stories that raise interesting questions:

For example, a woman came up to me after a meeting and told me that she was supervisor of a large number of sales workers. She asked, "Can you tell me what to do with these women?" Then she went on to say that her company has a big meeting once a month in which all the leading sales workers are recognized individually and asked to say a few words. In the past year or so, quite a few women have been among the sales people who are recognized. The women get up and say things like, "Well, I really don't know how it happened. I guess I was just lucky this time," or "This must have been a good month." By contrast, the men say, "Well, first I analyzed the national sales situation; I broke that down into regional components and figured out the trends in buying. Then I analyzed the consumer groups, and . . . I worked very hard—overtime three-fourths of the nights this month—and . . . " The point, of course, is that the women were doing something like that too—or something in their own style that was just as effective.

Another example came my way when a woman was describing a project she initiated. She said as she starts to work, she thinks (and colleagues and friends have told her) this work might be genuinely significant and good. "Maybe I'm really onto something here," she tells herself. And immediately, almost in the same second, she says, "This is nothing," or "Everybody knows this anyhow."

Those two examples, I think, point to the question of women and power. In recent years there have emerged some writings about women and power,[1] and some meetings to consider it from several viewpoints

240

and disciplines. But if we are really going to build the kinds of institutions and personal lives that allow women to grow and flourish, I believe that we must invest much more conscious, concerted, direct attention to women and power. At the same time I believe that most of us women still have a great deal of trouble with the whole area. The only hope, it seems to me, is to keep trying to examine it together.

I am not implying that men *don't* have trouble with power (just look around the world!), but their troubles are different from those of women at this point in history. As with other major topics, I believe women's examination of power not only can illuminate issues which are important to ourselves, but also can bring new understanding to the whole concept of power. It can shed light on the traps and problems of men, perhaps illuminating those things most difficult for men themselves to discover.

I shall begin this initial consideration by reviewing some fairly common occurrences for women—analyzing them from a psychological perspective derived from clinical work.

Defining Power

There have been many definitions of power, each reflecting the historical tradition out of which it comes; also, various disciplines of study have devised their own definitions.[2] An example given in one dictionary says power is "the faculty of doing or performing anything: force; strength; energy; ability; influence . . . " and then a long string of words leading to "dominion, authority, a ruler . . . " then more words culminating in " . . . military force." I think the list reflects accurately the idea that most of us automatically have about power. We probably have linked the concept with the ability to augment one's own force, authority, or influence, and also to control and limit others—that is, to exercise dominion or to dominate.

My own working definition of power is *the capacity to produce a change*—that is, to move anything from point A or state A to point B or state B. This can include even moving one's own thoughts or emotions, sometimes a very powerful act. It also can include acting to create movement in an interpersonal field as well as acting in larger realms such as economic, social, or political arenas.

Obviously, that broad definition has to be further differentiated. For example, one may be somewhat powerful psychologically or personally but have virtually no legitimate socially granted power to determine one's own fate economically, socially, or politically. Also there's the question, "Power for what?" One may think in terms of gaining power for oneself, or one may seek influence for some general good or some collective entity.

Women's View of Power

While more precise delineations are necessary, I think it is probably accurate to say that generally in our culture, and in several others, we have maintained the myth that women do not and should not have power on any dimension. Further, we hold the notion that women do not need power. Usually, without openly talking about it, we women have been most comfortable using our powers if we believe we are using them in the service of others. Acting under those general beliefs, and typically not making any of this explicit, women have been effective in many ways. One instance is in women's traditional role, where they have used their powers to foster the growth of others—certainly children, but also many other people. This might be called using one's power to empower another—increasing the other's resources, capabilities, effectiveness, and ability to act. For example, in "caretaking" or "nurturing," one major component is acting and interacting to foster the growth of another on many levels—emotionally, psychologically, and intellectually. I believe this is a very powerful thing to do, and women have been doing it all the time, but no one is accustomed to including such effective action within the notions of power. It's certainly not the kind of power we tend to think of; it involves a different content, mode of action, and goal. The one who exerts such power recognizes that she or he cannot possibly have total influence or control but has to find ways to interact with the other person's constantly changing forces or powers. And all must be done with appropriate timing, phasing, and shifting of skills so that one helps to advance the movement of the less powerful person in a positive, stronger direction.

As a result of this vast body of experience within the family as well as in the workplace and other organizations, I think most women would be most comfortable in a world in which we feel we are not limiting, but are enhancing the power of other people while simultaneously increasing our own power. Consider that statement more closely: The part about enhancing other people's power is difficult for the world to comprehend, for it is not how the "real world" has defined power. Nonetheless, I contend that women would function much more comfortably within such a context. The part about enhancing one's own powers is extremely difficult for women. When women even contemplate acting powerful, they fear the possibility of limiting or putting down another person. They also fear recognizing or admitting the need, and especially the desire, to increase their own powers.

Frankly, I think women are absolutely right to fear the use of power as it has been generally conceptualized and used. The very fact that this is often said to be a defensive or neurotic fear is, I believe, a more telling commentary on the state of our culture than it is on women. For example, in current times one can read that women are not being strong enough or tough enough. Such statements overlook the incredible strengths that women have demonstrated all through history, and they usually refer to some comparison with men's operations in our institutions. I believe they tend to overlook a valid tendency in women—that is, the desire to enhance others' resources and to know, from actual practice and real experience, that it is an extremely valuable and gratifying life activity. On the other side of the picture, however, such statements reflect part of a truth—that women do fear admitting that they want or need power. Yet without power or something like it (which may eventually be described by another term) on both the personal and political level, women cannot effectively bring about anything.

When Women Confront Power

Now I'd like to focus on women's fears in confronting power, using individual examples to illustrate further what may have been going on in the women I described briefly at the beginning of my remarks. I will highlight some women's inner, or intrapsychic, experiences.

Power and Selfishness

Abby was a low-paid worker in the health field who sought therapy primarily because of her depression. She had spent much of her adult life enhancing her husband's and her two children's development—using her powers to increase their powers. She then started work and did an excellent job, largely because she approached her patients with the basic attitude of helping them to increase their own comfort and abilities and to use their own powers.

After much exploration, Abby recognized that she tended to become depressed not when things were clearly bad, but when she realized that she could *do* something more—for example, better understand and effectively act on a situation. She felt this especially when she wanted to act for herself. For example, she knew that she was actually better at some procedures than the doctors were—not just technically better, but *totally* better, for she helped patients feel more relaxed, more in control, and more powerful. She began to feel that she should get to do more of the interesting work, get higher pay, recognition, etc. She also realized that almost at the same moment she felt this way she became blocked by fear, then self-criticism and self-blame. This seemed to be a complex internal replica of the external conditions. The external conditions clearly blocked her advancement; she was a woman who worked in the lowest ranks of the health care hierarchy. But the internalized forces created even more complex bondage. Initially, for Abby, as for many women, there was the big fear of being seen as wanting to be powerful. This provoked notions of disapproval, but more than that, at a deeper level, evoked fears of attack and ultimate abandonment by all women and men.

Further exploration unearthed several more sticking points. One was that the prospect of acting on her own interest and motivation kept leading to the notion that she would be selfish. While she could not bear the thought that others would see her as selfish, it was even more critical that she could not bear this conception of herself. I find this theme to be extraordinarily common in women—often women in surprisingly high positions and places—and, by contrast, a rare theme in men. With this theme for Abby there usually would come the notion that she was inadequate anyhow. She felt she should be grateful that anyone would put up with her at all, and she should best forget about the whole thing.

Eventually, this inadequacy theme gave way to yet another stage in which she felt that she indeed did have powers and could use them, but doing so meant, inescapably, that she was being destructive. For Abby, this stage was illustrated by thoughts, fantasies, and dreams indicating destructiveness.

Power and Destructiveness

Another woman, Ellen, was at a different point in dealing with the same problem. She felt able to work and to think well so long as she worked on her ideas and plans in her own house. She could not bring them into the work setting. As she used to put it, "If only I could bring my inside self outside." Eventually, she said that this fear seemed to stem from the experience that as she went into the outside world or to work, immediately she became attuned to the new context, readily picking up its structures and demands. She felt she couldn't help but respond to that context and those demands.

Again, this kind of feeling is common in women, and again it reflects a very valuable quality. Historically, a woman's being attuned to and responding to her context and to the needs of everybody in it has been part and parcel of helping other people to grow and helping a family to function. Women can bring a special set of abilities to many situations because they *are* able to attune themselves to the complex realities that are operating. (This perhaps is the essence of what mental health researchers have tried to describe in characterizing mothers' contributions to infant development.)[3]

But consider the other side: Ellen felt that she could not get her own perceptions, evaluations, and judgments moving from inside her to the outside, although she had important contributions to make. To bring her ideas and actions into the outside context she had to overcome her ready tendency to be only responsive.

But that wasn't all. She felt to do so would disrupt the whole scene. In other words, she would be destructive—and that was not a way she felt she should operate.

In each person such a theme forges its specific expression from the individual's history, but the basic theme occurs regularly in many women: To act out of one's own interest and motivation is experienced as the psychic equivalent of being a destructively aggressive person. This is a self-image that few women can bear. In other words, for many women it is more comfortable to feel inadequate. Terrible as that can be, it is still better than to feel powerful, if power makes you feel destructive.

Let me emphasize this thesis: Any person can entertain the prospect of using her or his own life forces and power—individually motivated, in a self-determined direction. In theories about mental health, this is said to bring satisfaction and effectiveness. But for many women it is perceived as the equivalent of being destructive. On the one hand, this sets up a life-destroying, controlling psychological condition. On the other hand, it makes sense if one sees that women have lived as subordinates and, as subordinates, have been led by the culture to believe that their own, self-determined action is wrong and evil. Many women have incorporated deeply the inner notion that such action must be destructive. The fact that women have survived at all, I believe, is explained by the fact that women do use power all the time but generally must see it as used for the benefits of others.

Don't misunderstand me: Using one's abilities and powers for others is not bad by any means. It does become problematic for women and for men, however, when such activity is prescribed for one sex only, along with the mandate that one must not act on one's own motivation and according to one's own determinations. In most institutions it is still true that if women do act from their own perceptions and motivations, directly and honestly, they indeed may be disrupting a context that has not been built out of women's experience. Thus, one is confronted with the feeling that one must do something very powerful that also feels destructive.

Power and Abandonment

Another woman, Connie, illustrated this dramatically: She had difficulty finishing her work. But she discovered that she would become "blocked" not when she was really stuck, but when she was working well, streaming ahead, getting her thoughts in order, and making something happen. At those times she would get up from her desk, start walking around, become involved in some diversion, talk to someone, and generally get off the productive trajectory. Further exploration of why this happened led eventually to her saying that if she let herself go on when she was working well, "I'd be too powerful and then where would I be . . . I wouldn't need anyone else." For Connie, the prospect was that she would be out in some scary place. She said she would feel like some unrecognizable creature, some nonwoman. She spoke of the prospect as if it signified the loss of a central sense of identity. Her sense of identity, like that of so many women, was so bound up with being a person who *needs* that the prospect of *not needing* felt, first of all, like a loss of the known and familiar self.

On the one hand, it was an unnecessary fear. On the other hand, Connie touched on a sense that is present in many women—namely, that the use of our powers with some efficacy and, even worse, with freedom, zest, and joy, feels as if it will destroy a core sense of identity. One feature of that identity, as reflected by Connie's statement, demonstrates how deeply women have incorporated the notion, "I exist only as I need." Again, I think women are reflecting a truth that men have been encouraged to deny—that is, all of us exist only as we need others for that existence—but cultural conditions have led women to incorporate this in an extreme form. Along with it we women have incorporated the troubling notion that, as much as we need others, we also have powers and the motivation to use those powers, but if we use them, we will destroy the relationships we need for our existence.

The Troublesome Equations

With these examples I have outlined some of the inner experiences women have related to me as they confronted the issue of power. They include:

A woman's using self-determined power for herself is equivalent to *selfishness*, for she is not enhancing the power of others.

A woman's using self-determined power for herself is equivalent to *destructiveness*, for such power inevitably will be excessive and will totally disrupt an entire surrounding context.

The equation of power with destructiveness and selfishness seems impossible to reconcile with a sense of feminine identity.

A woman's use of power may precipitate attack and *abandonment;* consequently, a woman's use of power threatens a central part of her identity, which is a feeling that she needs others.

It is important to emphasize again the many sides of all of this: On the one hand, most women are keenly aware of an essential truth that we all need others, need to live in the framework of relationships, and also need to increase the powers of others through our activities. On the other hand, most women have been encouraged to experience these needs as a predominant, central, almost total definition of their personalities. And their experience tells them that change can occur only at the cost of destroying one's place in the world and one's chance for living within a context of relationships. I believe this reflects accurately the historic and cultural place, and the definition, of women.

The Challenges Ahead

The examples I have cited not only tell about individual problems but also reflect characteristics of many women. Right now I think it is important for women to recognize that we do need to use our powers. Many times, I think, women have done things that eventually proved to be destructive, often without being fully aware, because we actually felt so much pain and reluctance even to think about the topic.

Also, we need to help each other in several important ways: First, we can give sympathetic understanding to ourselves if we recognize the weight of the historic conditions that have made power such a difficult concept for most of us. Second, we can consider seriously the proposition that there is enormous validity in women's *not* wanting to use power as it is presently conceived and used. Rather, women may want to be powerful in ways that simultaneously enhance, rather than diminish, the power of others. This is a radical turn—a very different motivation than the concept of power upon which this world has operated.

Out of this, we can see that women already may have a strong motivation to approach the concept of power with a different, critical, and creative stance. Once admitting a desire and a need for power, women can seek new ways of negotiating power with others in personal life, work, and other institutions. Certainly this is a large and difficult prospect. It can appear naive or unreal even to talk this way. But the fact that it sounds unreal must not stop us. Once we recognize the undeniable truth that the world has been explained so far without the close observation of women's experience, it is easier to consider that seemingly "unreal" possibilities can become real.

There exist some obvious truths that have not been taken into account:

- Women's experience is usually not what it has been said to be.
- It is not men's experience. It does not necessarily operate on the same bases, same motivations, or the same organization of personality.
- What we find when we study women are parts of the total human potential that have not been fully seen, recognized, or valued. These are parts that have not therefore flourished, and perhaps they are precisely the ingredients that we must bring into action in the conduct of all human affairs.
- Certainly these emerging notions must be used for the benefit of women, which is reason enough to pursue them, but they must be used also for the ultimate benefit of everyone.

Chapter 13

Gender and Sexuality: Masculinity, Violence, and Domination

——————————————— *Nancy C. M. Hartsock*

Many feminists have argued that the connections of sexuality with violence and domination must be broken. They have argued that rape is not a sexual act but an act of domination and humiliation.[1] Susan Brownmiller suggests that rape, once put "within the context of modern criminal violence and not within the purview of ancient masculine codes" will be seen to fall "midway between robbery and assault."[2] Brownmiller has highlighted the extent to which power and domination are central to rape. This has been an important theoretical and political strategy for responding to the widespread view that rape is either the act of an ordinary man strangely overcome with lust or that of a maniac continually subject to excessive lust. According to this latter view, rape is an unavoidable part of human behavior due to men's overwhelming sexual desires, desires that *must* find an outlet.[3] This view focuses on sexuality, so that hostility and domination drop from view.

The question of whether pornography is erotic literature or instead involves systematic domination and degradation revolves around similar issues. Feminists have protested the violence directed at women depicted by much pornography: images of women in chains, being beaten, or threatened with attack carry the social message that "victimized women are sexually appealing" and that the "normal male is sexually aggressive in a brutal and demeaning way."[4] They have objected strongly to the prominence of "snuff films" in which the pornographic action consists largely in what is claimed to be the "on-camera" dismemberment and death of a woman.[5] What does it mean, they ask, "when men advertise, even brag, that their movie is the 'bloodiest thing that ever happened in front of a camera?' "[6] Gloria Steinem, distinguishing pornography from erotica, explicitly took over Brownmiller's point about rape. She argued, "Perhaps one could simply say that erotica is about sexuality but pornography is about power and sex-as-weapon—in the same way we have come to understand that rape is about violence, and not really about sexuality at all."[7]

Other feminists have argued against the dissociation of sexuality and power or domination. Given the power relations involved in everyday heterosexuality, they ask, "Can we really expect the realm of fantasy [and so pornography] to be free of the residues of that power struggle?"[8] Others go further and claim, "The desire to be sexual and the desire to be combative are complexly intertwined." They add that sexual relations are characterized by an exchange of power that should be made both explicit and consensual.[9] Thus, sexual connections in which relations of dominance and even force are central should not be rejected by feminists so long as these power relations are the result of the freely given consent of the parties involved.

This group has charged that some feminists are engaged in a policing of sexual practices akin to that practiced by modern Western culture as a whole, excluding all but heterosexual, procreatively oriented sexuality and refusing to recognize erotic diversity. In addition, they mistake images of sexuality with images of violence against women, with actual violence against women. They argue that theorists such as Katherine MacKinnon have confused sex with gender in arguments that "sexuality is to feminism what work is to marxism . . . the molding, direction, and expression of sexuality organizes society into two sexes, women and men."[10]

Those who argue for breaking the connections between sexuality and power have responded that these ideas (and the practices they justify) are "firmly rooted in patriarchal sexual ideology."[11] Theorists such as Audre Lorde have argued that "*even in play*, to affirm that the exertion of power over powerlessness is erotic, is empowering, is to set the emotional and social stage for the continuation of that relationship, politically, socially, and economically." She goes on to suggest that the linkage of passion to dominance/subordination is the prototype heterosexual image.[12]

The dialogue has been organized around a series of questions, including: "Are male and female sexual natures essentially different, or the product of specific historical and cultural conditions? Has women's sexuality been muted by repression, or is it wholly different from men's? Does the source of sexual danger to women lie in an intrinsically aggressive or violent male nature, or in the patriarchal conditions that socialize male sexuality to aggression and female sexuality to compliance and submission?" And "Can we act on our own behalf? Or are we purely victims. . . . ?"[13]

Both sides in what has come to be a heated debate have important insights to offer. Yet both positions are ultimately unsatisfactory. I would also argue that both these positions lead to unfortunate political alliances and strategies, but that is beyond the scope of my argument here.[14] Efforts to distinguish between erotica and degradation or violence against women face an insoluble problem. What *is* sexually exciting in the contemporary West is objectification, hostility, violence, and domination, especially but not necessarily directed against women.

This is a statement about the hegemony of phallocratic culture, not an empirical statement about a certain percentage of men and women in the societies to which I refer. There is, of course, the possibility of an "imperfect fit between hegemonic culture and lived life."[15] But it is not simply an "imperfect fit." The imperfections fall along specific lines of class, generations, religion, racial and ethnic groups, heterosexuality and homosexuality. We should recognize that like all hegemonic forms, what we see reflects and expresses the experience of the dominant group; that is, discussions of sexual excitement in general are in fact discussions of what is sexually arousing for white, heterosexual men of a certain class in a position to make their images of masculinity hegemonic. Because of the dominance of this group, their ideas gain social force.[16] I will argue, therefore, that the effort to distinguish between erotica and pornography can only fail, since this effort assumes that we can fully extract ourselves from the culture in which we live and can make independent and accurate judgments. However, those who have taken the position that sexuality in general cannot be separated from power relations and involves exchanges of power and combat have ignored the gender-specific nature of these connections in contemporary culture. They have failed to recognize that sexuality as defined by the institutions and apparatus of cultural hegemony is a specific type of masculine sexuality. This sets limits on, though does not necessarily completely define, the sexual desire and practices of many groups of people. Indeed, opposition to sexuality culturally constructed in this way has emerged even among those whose gender, race, class, and sexual identity would seem to ally their experience of sexual desire with the culturally dominant pattern.

Given that sexuality is determined by a complex mix of factors (unconscious, biological, social, cultural), my point is not to argue for the construction of an alternative "feminist sexuality," but rather to engage in a cultural critique of masculine power as it operates in the field defined by sexuality. We need a more adequate understanding of sexuality in order to work for change. One important task is the analysis of the sexuality in the contemporary West that is tied to hostility and domination on the one hand, and definitions of masculinity on the other.

Sexuality and Society

We must begin with a few words about what is meant by sexuality. Definitions of what is to be included often cover many aspects of life. For example, Freud included but did not clarify the interrelationships among such various things as libido (the basic tendency to live and reproduce), the biological attributes of being male or female, sensuality, masculinity and femininity, reproductive behavior, and intense sensations in various parts of the body, especially the genitals.[17] And Jeffrey Weeks, summarizing our culture's understanding of sex, argues that in our society "sex has become the supreme secret," which is at the same time the 'truth' of our being. It defines us socially and morally. Moreover, the common understanding of sexuality treats it as a "supremely private experience," which is at the same time "a thing in itself."[18]

My own reading of the literature suggests that in contrast to these definitions, we should understand sexuality not as an essence or set of properties defining an individual or as a set of drives and needs (especially genital) of an individual. Rather, we should understand sexuality as culturally and historically defined and constructed. Anything can become eroticized, and thus there can be no "abstract and universal category of 'the erotic' or 'the sexual' applicable without change to all societies."[19] Rather, sexuality must be understood as a series of cultural and social practices, meanings, and institutions that both structure and are in turn structured by social relations more generally. Thus, "sex is relational, is shaped in social interaction, and can only be understood in its historical context. . . . "[20]

Because a number of theorists have argued for this position in a number of different contexts, it seems unnecessary to go into detail here, but I will merely state that I subscribe in a general way to their arguments.[21] At the same time, because sexuality is commonly seen as rooted in human nature, it is relevant to add here a reminder about the continuing significance in my work of the essentially Marxian assumption that human activity or practice constructs an historical and constantly changing human nature and, thus, a set of historically specific and changing sexual practices and relations. It is worth reiterating this point here since in much of the literature on sexuality, possibilities for systematically changing human nature and for changing the dynamics of sexual excitement remain unaddressed; one wonders about the extent to which many theorists hold to a view of human nature as unchanging at least in this area.[22]

Hostility and Sexual Excitement

If sexuality is a social and historical construction, how has contemporary Western culture shaped it? There is a surprising degree of consensus that hostility and domination as opposed to intimacy and physical pleasure are central to sexual excitement.[23] The work of Robert Stoller is central to understanding these connections.[24] Stoller contends that in our culture, "putting aside the obvious effects that result from direct stimulation of erotic bodily parts it is hostility—the desire, overt or hidden, to harm another person—that generates and enhances sexual excitement. Thus, erotic excitement must be understood as only one component of sexual excitement—others are triumph, rage, revenge, fear, anxiety, risk."[25] Moreover, he contends, "the same dynamics, though in different mixes and degrees, are found in almost everyone, those labeled perverse and those not so labeled."[26] He suggests as well that if researchers of sexual excitement look closely they will discover that "permutations of hostility will be found far more frequently than is acknowledged today"; to underline this point, we should note that he chose the term "hostility" rather than power or aggression to indicate that "harm and suffering" are central to sexual excitement.[27] As Stoller outlines it, the mechanisms that construct sexual excitement rest most fundamentally on fetishization and on the dehumanization and objectification of the sexual object. And these are associated with the debasement of the object and the construction of mystery, risk, illusion, and a search for revenge. The sexual object is to be stripped of its humanity: the focus is on breasts, buttocks, legs, penises, not faces. Or an inanimate object, an animal, or a partial aspect of a human such as a breast or penis is given the personality taken from the object. These are the ways fetishization as a means for creating sexual excitement can go far beyond the clinical cases in which the fetishism is obvious. It is present in the widespread practice of treating people as though they were only organs or functions.[28]

Given our stated cultural ideals, one would not expect to find hostility at the center of sexuality. Why not intimacy, warmth, or physical pleasure? But Stoller is not alone in finding hostility in sexual excitement. A wide variety of theorists have commented on the relation of hostility and anger to sexual excitement. For example, Kinsey noted that "the closest parallel to the picture of sexual response is found in the known physiology of anger."[29] Or consider a psychologist's note that sex can be a power weapon and that "in general it has far more intimate relationships with dominance feeling than it has with physiological drive."[30] And Kate Millett has commented that in some literary sources "the pleasure of humiliating the sexual object appears to be far more intoxicating than sex itself."[31]

Nor are references to the relation between sexual excitement and hostility limited to passing comments. These links are at the center of philosopher/pornographer George Bataille's theory and fiction. As he describes it, "sexual activity is a form of violence." And the desire of the "potential killer in every man" to kill relates to the taboo on murder in the same way that the desire for sexual activity relates to the various prohibitions on it. Killing and sexual activity share both prohibitions and religious significance. Their unity is demonstrated by religious sacrifice since the latter:

> is intentional like the act of the man who *lays bare,* desires and wants to penetrate his victim. The lover *strips* the beloved of her identity no less than the bloodstained priest his human or animal victim. The woman in the hands of the assailant is *despoiled* of her being . . . loses the firm barrier that once separated her from others . . . is *brusquely laid open* to the violence of the sexual urges set loose in the organs of reproduction; she is *laid open* to the impersonal violence that overwhelms her from without.[32]

Note the use of the terms "lover" and "assailant" as synonyms and the presence of the woman as victim.

Issues of sexuality and hostility appear as well in the context of analyses of racism. Thus, one writer notes that the practice of linking apes, African-Americans and Jews with the mythological satyrs "reveals that there are sensitive spots in the human soul at a level where thought becomes confused and where sexual excitement is strangely linked with violence and aggressiveness. . . . "[33] And another writer, in the context of an argument about the connections between racial hostility and sexuality, makes a fairly detailed case that "the gratification in sexual conquest derives from the experience of defilement—of reducing the elevated woman to the 'dirty' sexual level, of polluting that which is seen as pure, sexualizing that which is seen as unsexual, animalizing that which is seen as 'spiritual.' "[34]

In the context of these statements it is not surprising to encounter a commonsense view that sex is dangerous and violent.[35] Nor should we be surprised to find hostility and violence deeply ingrained in language itself: the best-known of the vulgar sexual verbs comes from the German *flicken*, meaning "to strike"; similar violent verbs are present in Latin, Celtic, Irish, Gaelic, and so forth. Consider also other English terms such as "screw" and "bang."[36]

The hostility Stoller analyzes is fueled in part by danger and the construction of risk. Childhood traumas, frustrations, and dangers are turned into risks in which there is a more clearly calculable outcome, and in which the degree of risk can be carefully controlled. The risk, then, is experienced as excitement, the childhood trauma recreated as adult sexual script. But this can only happen if the risk is simulated and the danger not too extreme.[37]

The dynamic of undoing childhood traumas and frustrations, Stoller argues, is central to the construction of sexual excitement. And while hostility is embedded in a number of social institutions and practices (e.g., humor), Stoller argues that the hostility in sexual excitement grows out of traumas and frustrations intimately connected with and threatening to the development of masculinity or femininity. He has, of course, much company in his position that these practices are continuing attempts to undo childhood traumas and frustrations that threatened the development of masculinity or femininity.[38] He concludes that sadomasochism has to be seen as a central feature of *most* sexual excitement and that the desire to hurt others in revenge for having been hurt is essential for most people's sexual excitement all the time, but not all people's excitement all the time.[39]

While I find his analysis very useful, I want to differentiate my position from his by also stressing the importance of adult experience. Rather than simply repeating scripts established early in life, we can to some extent modify them as adults. And rather than simply arguing that experiences in infancy produce sexual dynamics of hostility, I want to argue that our society has configured sexuality in such a way that this is the culturally hegemonic result; that is, it represents a culturally "normal" sexuality. Tracing all the influences that produce this result would be very difficult, but certainly more is involved than issues of infancy.

Given the weight of evidence, both scholarly and popular, one can see how the effort to separate erotica from pornography and sexuality from violence can gain little analytical ground. While the separation of sexuality from hostility or violence is an essential political goal, at present efforts to distinguish erotica from pornography amount to blindness to a cultural reality that systematically superpositions them. Desire as domination, sexuality as hostility, must be recognized as the culturally hegemonic forms in which sexuality is constructed.

Some feminists have criticized Stoller's account of these dynamics. Kathleen Barry states that his argument about how hostility is infused into sexuality removes responsibility from the actors, who are in most cases males. As she sums up his position, he is arguing that the fetish is created to right past wrongs; thus, when a woman is being raped, the rapist is not really raping her but rather is fetishizing her to right the past wrongs of being denied sexual intercourse with his mother. One can see, she adds, how this explanation plays into myth that black men rape to right the wrongs of racial injustice, or lower-class men to right past or present wrongs of poor working conditions.[40] Moreover, Stoller's work leads to the conclusion that "sexual violence simply can't be helped—it's nature—as said Sade, as said Freud, now says Stoller . . . "[41]

There are really two issues here: the responsibility of those who commit violent acts against another and the question of whether sexual violence is inevitable. On each point, Stoller's writing gives some support to Barry's reading. Yet I think her dismissal of his insights goes too far: as I read him, Stoller is analyzing a cultural tradition of violence he neither endorses nor supports. While he puts far too much responsibility for producing "normal heterosexuals" on mothers, I do not read him as saying that rapists should not be held responsible for their acts. In addition, he explicitly raises the question of whether hostility is a real universal or is simply ubiquitous, i.e., whether gross hostility is not necessary but only usual.[42] He argues as well that it is probably not inevitable, even if universal, that people debase their sexual objects. And he proclaims himself disappointed that sexual pleasure in most people depends on neurotic mechanisms. Finally, he suggests in a hopeful tone that perhaps there is a continuum toward less use of hostility in sexual excitement. Especially in the range of "the normative," Stoller believes there may be both hostility and affection and capacity for closeness. At the far end of the continuum, he suggests, there may be a small group of contented and secure people who are not so frightened by intimacy that they must fetishize the other person.[43] Still, Barry's view that Stoller sees the dynamic of hostility as inevitable does gain support from the fact that Stoller seems to see no way to avoid the dynamic of hostility; she also notes that his views put him at odds with those who see sex as a cultural and historical phenomenon (although from the text it is unclear what she means by this) and that he titles his last chapter, "The Necessity of Perversion."[44] Stoller's more recent work, *Observing the Erotic Imagination*, makes these charges even less plausible. Here he turns his attention to the question of which erotic behaviors are not perverse. His suggestion that nonperversion is not defined by the "anatomy used, the sex of the participants, its theater elements, or its aesthetics but by our acceptance of the selfhood, the humanness, of those we might need" seems to give much more play to possibilities for social construction, for moral rather than scientific issues, as he puts it.[45]

Andrea Dworkin objects to Stoller's work on other grounds. She accuses Stoller of arguing that sexual sadism is manifested in both males and females. Women too are sadists, she quotes Stoller as saying. Thus, he justifies men's abuse of women because women too are "formidable" sadists, despite the fact that it is not socially or historically self-evident."[46] As she puts it, "The sexual philosophers, like the pornographers, need to believe that women are more dangerous than men or as dangerous as men so as to be justified in their social and sexual domination of them."[47] Moreover, she argues, Stoller mistakes female suffering for female triumph. Belle's fantasies (Belle is the pseudonym of the female patient on whom Stoller bases much of his theorization of sexual excitement) are those in which she is ostensibly in the control of brutal, powerful men who try to dominate her but (in Stoller's view) cannot enslave her.

Instead, he should have seen these sexual images as symbolic of a larger sexual reality in which she is "used, trapped, humiliated, angry, and powerless to change the values of the men who devalue her." But Stoller holds that Belle chooses "sexual masochism because through it she triumphs over men whom ultimately she controls because she is the provocation to which they respond. This is an expression 'of her own oversexed nature.' She wants it, they all do."[48]

Once again Stoller's text lends support to Dworkin's charges. He was clearly unaware of the lack of choices available to most women and far too unquestioning of the cultural institutions and apparatuses of male supremacy (e.g., he takes the cultural meanings of the penis for granted, describing it as "aggressive, unfettered, unsympathetic, humiliating").[49] There may be, however, a deep theoretical disagreement between Dworkin and Stoller. The latter sees not just female masochism, but all masochism, from another point of view as expressing sadism and power.[50] Whatever their differences on this point, how-ever, Stoller comes to a conclusion very similar to Dworkin's own: "antagonism is established in male sexual thought as a key element in sexual excitement."[51]

Dworkin's claim that Stoller attempts to assimilate male and fe-male sexual behavior misreads what I consider to be one of the most intriguing and interesting aspects of his work—the existence of impor-tant but admittedly unexamined gender differences in sexual behavior and sexual excitement, differences that allow me to read Stoller as supportive of my own contention that what is culturally defined as sexuality for us is masculine sexuality, a masculine sexuality that does not grow from or express the lives of women. This reading is sup-ported by his more recent work, in which he recognizes the impor-tance of gender differences and argues that while themes of hostility are present in "women's movies," and "women's novels," the dynam-ics are different. Men's pornography does not depict relationships among people whereas women's does.[52] The area in which these dif-ferences emerge is what he terms "perversion."

Masculinity, Perversion, and Normality

I should note that Stoller would probably not agree with the use I have made of his arguments. In particular, we part company over the meaning to be attached to, and the behaviors to be described as per-versions in his earlier work, although his more recent work is much less concerned with 'normality' and 'deviance.' He defines perversion as "the erotic form of hatred," a fantasy either acted out or restricted to a daydream of doing harm. It is a fantasy motivated by hostility—the wish to do harm, not by simple aggression or forcefulness.[53] In a refinement of this definition, he adds that "the activity is perverse . . . if the erotic excitement depends on one's feeling that one is sinning."[54]

He adds:

> The more gross the hostility, the less the question that one is dealing with perversion. Murder that sexually excites, mutilation for excite-ment, rape, sadism with precise physical punishments such as whipping or cutting, enchaining and binding games, defecating or urinating on one's object—all are on a lessening scale of conscious rage toward one's sex object, in which an essential purpose is for one to be superior to, harmful to, triumphant over another. And so it is also in the non-physical sadisms like exhibitionism, voyeurism,

dirty phone calls or letters, use of prostitutes, and most forms of promiscuity."[55]

It is important to note here that the psychological dynamics of perversion do not differ importantly from those Stoller has identified as typical of sexual excitement. Hostility, fetishization, and dehumanization figure centrally in both perverse and 'normal' sexual excitement.[56] While he attempted to distinguish these sexualities in his earlier work, he seems now to have concluded that these categories are more polemical than scientific.

Stoller found two interesting puzzles in his work on perversion. First, he continually ran into the problem that, by his definition in which hostility is central to perversion, a great deal (perhaps even most) of contemporary normal heterosexual sexual activity must be labeled perverse. Thus, he notes that we face the risk of finding that there is very little sexual behavior that does not have a touch of the perverse. He attempts to draw back from this position, however: Wouldn't this ruin the meaning of the term perverse he asks? And he complains that "the idea of normality crumbles" if one notes the ubiquity of sexual pathology in heterosexuals who are supposed to be the "normals."[57] One must deal, then, with behavior that is not aberrant in a statistical sense.

Stoller is not alone in finding this difficulty. The scholars at the Institute of Sex Research also found something similar. Dworkin calls attention to a statement from *Sex Offenders: An Analysis of Types*. "If we labelled all punishable sexual behavior as a sex offense, we would find ourselves in the ridiculous situation of having all of our male histories consist almost wholly of sex offenders. . . . The man who kisses a girl in defiance of her expressed wishes is committing a forced sexual relationship and is liable to an assault charge, but to solemnly label him a sex offender would be to reduce our study to a ludicrous level."[58]

This last quotation points to the second puzzle Stoller found in his work but did not analyze. Why, he asks, is perversion (i.e., gross hostility or eroticized hatred) found more in males?[59] He also raises several other important, related questions. He wonders whether "in humans (especially males) powerful sexual excitement can ever exist without brutality also being present," and he asks, "Can anyone provide examples of behavior in sexual excitement in which, in human males at least, disguised hostility in fantasy is not a part of potency?" And given that psychoanalysis explains why women are as perverse as men, why has it not explained why they are not?[60]

His own analysis in *Sexual Excitement* follows this pattern; as he himself notes, he has not dealt with the issue of how women are unlike men rather than like them in the construction of sexual excitement.[61] In addition, Stoller wonders why women neither buy nor respond to pornography as intensely as men (he defines pornography by the presence of a victim) and begins to ask whether the question itself is wrong. Women, Stoller argues, do buy "masochistic" but "romantic" and "unsexual" stories; thus, he suspects, the definition of pornography hinges on what is pornography for men.[62] The romantic, masochistic stories women buy raise another problem as well for Stoller: Why, he asks, given these fantasies, do so few women practice sadomasochism.[63]

Thus, Stoller's account suggests that what we treat as sexuality and sexual excitement is a gendered masculine sexuality and masculine sexual excitement.[64] He himself makes this argument explicit in his more recent work. He argues that the fact that perversion is more common among men than women is not a simple counting error and holds that women are not less perverse because they do not dare to be. He adds that in almost all cultures there is a tendency to tie sexual performance more to masculinity than femininity.[65]

The masculinity of sexual practices can be strikingly confirmed in a variety of areas: ordinary language and popular assumptions, social psychology, and literature. The language that describes the institution our society places at the center of acceptable human sexuality, heterosexual intercourse, focuses exclusively on the experience of the man. As Janice Moulton has put it, "sexual intercourse is an activity in which male arousal is a necessary condition, and male satisfaction, if not also a necessary condition, is the primary aim . . . (whereas) female arousal and satisfaction, although they may be concomitant events occasionally, are not even constituents of sexual intercourse."[66] While the polite language is one of symmetry, the vulgar language presents quite a different picture; e.g., "If he fucked her, it does not follow that she has fucked him."[67] And the conceptual baggage of even the polite language is such that intercourse formally begins when the male's primary focus for sexual stimulation is inserted in the vagina and ends with male orgasm. Given this conceptual baggage, Moulton is led to wonder why "anyone ever thought the female orgasm had anything to do with sexual intercourse, except as an occasional and accidental co-occurrence." As she notes, "Sometimes the telephone rings, too."[68]

The assumptions implicit in common language take more explicit forms as well. Feminist writers have commented widely on the popular assumption that what is referred to as the sex drive is a male sex drive.[69] Feminists have also noted that "It was not very long ago that the notion of being sexual *and* being female was outrageous." Others have lamented the "total lack of images of women being motivated by sexual desire."[70] These assumptions appear as well in more professional contexts populated by sex researchers, educators, clinicians, and social workers. One feminist report from such a conference noted that "sex" was the term for heterosexual sex and it required "genital contact, male erection, and penetration."[71]

Sociological studies support both the fundamental masculinity of "sex-drive" ideas and their connections with dynamics of hostility and domination. One study of "corner boys" indicates that the "maximization of sexual pleasure clearly occurs for these boys when there is a strong component of conquest experience in the sexual act" and goes on to suggest that "without the conquest, the act is less gratifying."[72]

Kate Millet, analyzing the work of Normal Mailer, finds similar dynamics. She argues that sex for Mailer is a "thrilling test of self" (the self defined as an "athletic 'hunter-fighter-fucker' "). "Little wonder," she states, "that Mailer's sexual journalism reads like the sporting news grafted onto a series of war dispatches." On reading the work of Henry Miller, she concludes, "the pleasure of humiliating the sexual object appears to be far more intoxicating than sex itself."[73] And Charles Stember underlines her point that, indeed, "for men it is a vital part of the sex act, not an added attraction."[74]

Thus, we can state with some confidence that the culturally produced dynamics of hostility that structure sexual excitement correspond to a hegemonic masculine sexuality that depends on defiling or debasing a fetishized sexual object. Let me once again stress that I am focusing my attention on the dominant cultural practices.

Given this evidence, then, those who discuss sexual pleasure and desire without attending to gender differences and without recognizing that our culture has constructed sexuality in such a way that it carries a masculine gender have made an important error. We must recognize that sexuality in our culture is a power relation in which hostility, violence, and domination play central roles. This is not to say that those who argue that a nongendered sexuality must or should involve power relations are simply male-identified. This would be simplistic. Rather, it is to say that what our culture has made of sexuality expresses the experience of the ruling group—a group marked by its gender, race, economic status, and heterosexuality. And because of this hegemony, this masculine experience sets the dynamics of the social relations in which all parties are forced to participate—women as well as men, men who refuse masculinity as well as those who attempt to attain it.

Thus, the understanding of sexuality as involving power relations but not carrying a masculine gender must be seen as a kind of masculinist ideology that on the one hand expresses the experience and dominance of men, and on the other structures real sexual relations for women as well as men. It cannot, then, be dismissed as simply false. This should not be surprising. One should expect that in the cultural construction of sexuality, as in the development of moral judgment, the need for achievement, and so forth, it is the experience of the ruling gender that defines the terms and structures the content.[75]

Thus, we must insist that we face a gendered power relation based in what our culture has defined as sexuality. This does not change the fact that these dynamics are more typical of men than women and correspond to men's rather than women's experience.

If these are the dynamics of 'normal' heterosexual excitement, we can begin to understand both the existence of rape and rape fantasies and the depiction of violence against women for purposes of arousing sexual excitement. If we cannot distinguish between sexuality and hostility, pornography and erotica, should we then conclude that sexuality is inseparable from violence against women, that sex *is* masculine and violent? And therefore feminists should simply stay away from sex? If hostility is so omnipresent—for men, and given our culture, women too—is there any escape? (Note that the patient with or on whom Stoller worked out his theory of sexual excitement was a woman.)

The Nature of Eros

In order to move the discussion onto new and hopefully more productive ground, I propose to reformulate issues of sexuality under the heading of eros. Such a reformulation will allow me to put forward a broader understanding of the variety of forms taken by sexuality in our culture and to include the sexual meanings of issues and institutions that are not explicitly genitally focused. Finally, recasting the issue in these terms can clarify and refine the central dynamics of sexual excitement and thus aid in tracing the association of sexuality with virility, violence, and death. In addition, such a reformulation can provide a space to develop an understanding of sexuality that need not depend on hostility for its fundamental dynamic.

Three distinct though not necessarily separate aspects of eros emerge from my reading of the psychological literature.[76] The first is represented by Freud's definition of eros as "the desire to make one out of more than one."[77] This desire may take a narrowly genital form or other, sublimated forms. Freud suggests, and Marcuse agrees, that the inhibition of the direct aims of sexual impulses and their subjugation to the control of "higher psychical agencies, which have subjected themselves to the reality principle" (i.e., the repression of eros) is required for the development of civilization.[78] And thus one should expect to find a number of sublimated forms of eros.

The second aspect of eros turns on the role given to sensuality and bodily concerns in social life. Historically, various societies of Western civilization have found little place for this aspect of eros in public life as traditionally understood. Plato, for example, was one of the first to reject it as unworthy of a citizen's concern due to the bad effects of uncontrolled appetites—likened in the *Republic* to being at the mercy of "a raging and savage beast of a master." He argued that if the soul were in proper order, the body would be well taken care of, and therefore was due special concern.[79]

Creativity and generation—whether intellectual creativity in philosophy and art, physical work on the substances of nature, or the generation of children through sexual relations—emerge as the third aspect of eros. Some psychologists have pointed to pleasure in the 'effortful achievement of purpose' as fundamental to what makes us human. They have suggested that only when these pleasures take pathological forms can sublimation (and the civilization on which it depends) occur.[80] Freud concurs, at least to some extent, when he argues:

> No other technique of the conduct of life attaches the individual so firmly to reality as laying the emphasis on work; for his work at least gives him a secure place in a portion of reality, in the human community. The possibility it offers of displacing a large amount of libidinal components, whether narcissistic, aggressive, or even erotic, on to professional work and on to the human relations connected with it lends it a value by no means second to what it enjoys as something indispensable to the preservation and justification of existence in society . . . if it is a freely chosen one . . . it makes possible the use

of existing inclinations. . . . And yet, as a path to happiness, work is not highly prized by men.[81]

Marx's great achievement, from this perspective, was to open the possibility of a society in which the majority of people need not be driven to work only under the press of necessity. This is the society to which Marcuse refers when he suggests the possibility of "non-repressive sublimation."[82] In this case, sexuality would not be blocked or deflected from its object, but rather in attaining its object, transcend it. Under these conditions, Marcuse argues that sexuality could tend to grow into eros in a broader sense through what he terms the resexualizing of work. He argues that this may become a real possibility, thus eroticizing the body as a whole. These then are some important features of the third aspect of eros, the pleasure derived from acting in the world.[83]

These then—the making of one out of more than one, sensuality in a broad sense, and finally, the pleasure of competent activity—all represent the aspects of eros. It is important to note that by reformulating the issues in terms of eros we can both clarify the underlying issues sexuality involves and also make it possible to envision a social construction of eros in which hostility does not play such a central role.

But in a world of hostile and threatening others, each aspect of eros takes a repressive rather than liberating form, one that points toward death rather than life. For example, the desire for fusion with another can take the form of domination of the other. Sensuality and bodily pleasures can be denied, and the third aspect of eros, creativity and generation, can also take forms of domination both in the world of work, where creative activity becomes alienated labor, or in reproduction, in which the creation of new life becomes either disembodied or recast as death.

These dynamics can be most fruitfully analyzed in pornography, since there we see detailed schemas for creating sexual excitement. In addition, this extensive industry illustrates how what may appear to be a series of individual actions and decisions are in fact structured and limited by society as a whole. My point here is to underline the dynamics of cultural hegemony.

Because I have taken the position that it is analytically ineffective to attempt to distinguish erotica from pornography, I here propose to use as a working definition Robert Stoller's useful statement that pornography requires hostility and the presence of a victim. For Stoller, no victim, no pornography. He adds, however, several important qualifications: nothing is pornographic until the observer's fantasies are added. And with the addition of these fantasies, several hostile dynamics may take place: voyeurism is the most apparent, sadism is the second, and masochism, or identification with the depicted victim, is the third.[84] Moreover, all pornography has in common a construction of risk and an evocation of danger surmounted. Thus, for Stoller there is no nonperverse pornography, i.e., "sexually exciting matter in which hostility is not employed as a goal." Finally, pornography will be loathsome to the person responding to it. Stoller here refers not only to forbidden sensuality but also to the observer's fears that hostility will be released.[85] All of these factors are part of the definition.

The fantasies of sexual excitement that appear in pornography so defined are most importantly structured by the dynamic of reversal/revenge; as a result, each aspect of eros takes a repressive form that points toward violence and death. The specific dynamics of reversal/revenge depend on infant and childhood experience since the traumas of childhood are memorialized in the details of sexual excitement; the fantasies that produce sexual excitement recreate the relationships of childhood by trying to undo the frustrations, traumas, and conflicts.[86] The traumas recreated in sexual excitement are, Stoller hypothesizes, memorials to childhood traumas aimed at sexual anatomy or masculinity or femininity, i.e., at gender identification. Moreover, he suggests, sexual excitement will occur at the moment when adult reality resembles the childhood trauma, the anxiety being re-experienced as excitement.[87]

Reversal/revenge (my term) is the major shift that allows anxiety to take the form of pleasure, i.e., a reversal in the positions of the actors in order to convert the trauma into revenge. In men, Stoller suggests, this dynamic of reversal/revenge leads to perversion (and, more generally in the light of his later work, to sexual excitement) constructed out of rage at giving up the early identification with the mother and concomitant ecstasies of infancy, the fear of failing to differentiate oneself from the mother, and a need for revenge on her for putting one in this situation.[88] This dynamic of reversal/revenge rooted in childhood trauma means that revenge fantasies can be expected to be most often directed against the mother. Stoller notes that to the degree that a child feels he has been debased, he will as an adult reverse this process in fantasy to create sexual excitement.[89] The sexual fantasies of pornography, then, can be read as patterned reversals of the traumas of childhood and as adult (male) revenge on the traumatizer. These dynamics structure each aspect of eros in specific ways. Some are clearest in pornography itself. Others emerge with greater clarity in the work of those Dworkin has termed the "sexual philosophers," such as Mailer and Bataille.

Fusion, Community, and the Death of the Other

In pornography, the desire for fusion with another takes the form of domination of the other, which leads to the only possible fusion with a threatening other: when the other ceases to exist as a separate, and for that reason threatening, being. Insisting that another submit to one's will is simply a milder form of the destruction of discontinuity in death since in this case one is no longer confronting a discontinuous and opposed will, despite its discontinuous embodiment. This need to destroy the other is directly connected with childhood experience. Stoller argues that sexuality and intimacy can threaten (especially) "one's sense of maleness" and that this risk is at the same time a source of sexual excitement.[90] Pornography, then, must reduce this danger to a titillating risk if sexual excitement is to be created.

In order to reduce the danger of fusion or intimacy, pornography substitutes control. Susan Griffin, in her analysis of the major themes that motivate what she terms "the pornographic mind" argues that the idea that a woman might reject a man appears at the heart of the culture of pornography.[91] The problem, she notes, is that when a woman rejects a man, he must face the reality that he does not control her. Thus, in pornography issues of control are central to the creation of sexual excitement. One finds the importance of controling women repeated at length: the woman is controled, mastered, and humiliated.[92] One can remark as well the consistency of advertisements for sexual dolls in men's magazines. The makers argue that their products are better than real women because they will never say no.

The dynamic of conquest and the thrill of obtaining control by overcoming a resistant will are epitomized in the figure of Don Juan, for whom excitement and gratification come not from sensual pleasure and intimacy but rather from overcoming the resistance of a woman: "Easy women do not attract him."[93] Kathleen Barry has commented on more extreme forms of this dynamic and cites passage from several stories in which women are "bound, gagged and tied into positions which render them totally vulnerable and exposed."[94]

Fetishism is a second and related move to avoid fusion and intimacy with another. Rather than concentrating on the pleasure of overcoming the will of another, fetishism avoids confronting the will by fantasizing the other as a thing rather than a human being, treating a body part as a substitute for the person, or even dispensing with the human being altogether.[95] A woman's "thingness" can also be created through her reduction to an image. The mildest of heterosexual male pornography is represented by a massive industry producing photographs of nude women that reduce the real women to images on the page, "imprison" them on paper, thereby rendering them powerless to threaten the viewer.[96] One should view Griffin's account of Hugh Hefner's own practices in this light. Hefner, she argues, was fascinated with images as opposed to experience. He lived in a world made up of images he could control; Griffin suggests that his control over the images allowed him both to keep a safe distance from reality and real women and to believe that he could control this reality.[97]

The reality of women as fellow human beings can also be avoided by forbidding them to speak. Griffin notes that "a morbid fear of female speech" is central to pornography and that "even the sexual action, in pornography, seems to exist less for pleasure than to overpower and silence women."[98] And her analysis of *The Story of O* takes note that the heroine is silenced: one of the first rules at Roissy is not to speak to another woman, and then later, not to speak at all.[99]

The dynamics of control and fetishization are both well illustrated by the photograph "Beaver Hunters," described by Andrea Dworkin. The naked woman in the picture, tied like a dead animal to the front of a jeep, has been hunted, subdued (the caption states that the hunters "stuffed and mounted their trophy as soon as they got her home," thus playing off and highlighting the suggestion that the woman was killed) and displayed as a trophy of conquest.[100]

Third, erotic fusion and intimacy take forms structured by reversal/revenge. And here the infantile roots of the fear of intimacy are more clearly visible. Griffin points tellingly to the importance in pornography of the image of

> . . . a woman driven to a point of madness out of the desire to put a man's penis in her mouth. So that finally, by this image, we are called back: this image reminds the mind of another scene, a scene in which the avidity to put a part of the body into the mouth is not a mystery. Here is a reversal again. For it is the infant who so overwhelmingly needs the mother's breast in his mouth, the infant who thought he might die without this, who became frantic and maddened with desire, and it was his mother who had the power to withhold.[101]

The dynamic of reversal/revenge also occurs in a variety of cultural myths in which the man struggles against dangerous women.

One example of this struggle is that between Samson and Delilah, about which Griffin argues, "not only is male freedom based on female silence, but a man's life depends on the death of a woman." She finds this theme in the modern novel as well; for example, in Norman Mailer's *An American Dream*, in which the protagonist is described as a victim who acted in self-defense when he killed his wife. "It was as if killing her, the act had been too gentle. I had not plumbed the hatred where the real injustice was stored."[102]

And of course this is not just fiction. Lawrence Singleton, convicted of raping and cutting off the hands of a teenage girl, considered that it was he, not she, who was kidnapped and threatened. In his mind, the roles were reversed and he was the victim. "Everything I did," he said "was for survival."[103] Given this kind of hostility, ability to reverse roles, and deep needs for revenge, one can begin to understand why watching a woman tortured or dismembered on camera can be sexually exciting. Perhaps she should be seen as a sacrificial victim whose discontinuous existence has been succeeded in her death by "the organic continuity of life drawn into the common life of the beholders."[104]

Shameful Sensuality: The Denial of the Body

The second aspect of eros can also take a repressive form—the denial of sensuality and bodily pleasures. While this may initially strike the reader as an odd claim to make about literature and photographs intended to produce sexual and thus presumably physical excitement, the generation of this excitement relies on the experience of the body as shameful. And the source of this shame can be found in childhood experience. One psychologist has commented that, "The loathing and disgust that we felt for what we cannot help being interested in is our homage to the reasons we had for burying the interest."[105]

In pornography, the body—usually a woman's body—is presented as something that arouses shame, even humiliation, and the opposition of spirit or mind to the body (the latter sometimes referred to as representing something bestial or nonhuman) generates a series of dualities. Griffin captures the essence of this experience of the body when she argues that "speaking to that part of himself (the pornography) wishes to shame, he promises, 'I'm going to treat you like something that crawled out of the sewer.' "[106]

Pornography is built around, plays on, and obsessively recreates these dualities. The dichotomy between "spiritual love" and "carnal knowledge" is recreated in the persistent fantasy of transforming the virgin into the whore. She begins pure, innocent, fresh, even in a sense disembodied, and is degraded and defiled in sometimes imaginative and bizarre ways.[107] Dworkin has traced some of the connections between sexuality and "dirt/death" in similar ways.[108] Transgression is important here since forbidden practices are being engaged in. The violation of the boundaries of society breaks its taboos. Yet the act of violating a taboo, of seeing or doing something forbidden, does not do away with its forbidden status. Indeed, in the ways women's bodies are degraded and defiled in the transformation of the virgin into the whore, the boundaries between the forbidden and the permitted are simultaneously upheld and broken.[109] Put another way, the obsessive transformation of virgin into whore simply crosses and recrosses the boundary between them. Without the boundary, there could be no transformation at all; without the boundary there to violate, the thrill of transgression would disappear.

The sexual excitement a strip tease produces can be viewed as similar in form. It only works to produce sexual excitement because the exposed body is considered shameful and forbidden. The viewer is seeing something he is not entitled to see, something forbidden and potentially dangerous because it might have the power to change or transform him. Griffin suggests that our culture believes that the sight of a woman's flesh can turn a man into a rapist, and presumably can make him do other things as well.[110] One finds the same view of the (female) body as loathsome, humiliating, and even dangerous in a stripper's comment that one of several styles of producing sexual excitement in strip tease is "hard," that is, emphasizing the dark, hard lines of constraint provided by women's clothing, constraint of an aggressive female sexuality: "It is as if the notion of sexual woman were so overwhelming that she had to be visibly bound."[111]

Loathing for the body, in the sense that bodily needs and desires are humiliating, appears in another form in pornography in the contrast between the man's self-control and the woman's frenzied abandon. It is consistently a woman who is, as Griffin puts it, "humiliated by her desire, her helplessness, and materiality."[112] These issues of control and humiliation are clear in *The Story of O.* The speech O receives her first night at Roissy is one in which the men are portrayed as fully in control of their bodies. Thus, she is told that while their costume "leaves our sex exposed, it is not for the sake of convenience . . . " and that what is done to her is "less for our pleasure than for your enlightenment." Thus, they make clear that while they make use of her, they are independent and do not need her.[113] This insistence on independence and control on one side and a victim humiliated by her own desires on the other appears frequently.[114] The presence of a victim, one who submits in fact, requires another who remains in control, who, one author suggests, establishes selfhood by controlling the other.[115] The fact that it is the woman whose body is in control of the other and the woman who is humiliated by her desires and materiality records the reversal/revenge of infant and childhood experience.

The theme of succeeding by ignoring/overcoming the feelings of the body is related to the fear and loathing of the body. Thus, Griffin can argue that Don Juan, the "femme fatale," and de Sade share the quality of being unfeeling, an unfeelingness that allows them to be "powerful and free," yet leads at the same time to feelings of numbness.[116] In pornography, feeling is conquered by projecting emotions onto the victim, who is humiliated by bodily appetites, by being reduced to the status of a feeling body, and in "snuff" films to a literal corpse.

Thus, sensuality and bodily concerns, the second aspect of eros, take negative forms. They become entangled with the movement toward death—what Griffin has termed the death of feeling as well as the death of the body. Griffin is right to point out that the denial of the body is in part due to the fact that it is a reminder of mortality and therefore of death itself.[117] Indeed, as she argues in her excellent and innovative analysis of the Oedipus myth, knowledge of the body *is* knowledge of death. She holds that Oedipus' association with flesh comes from the fact that he grew up away from his father (and therefore, Griffin claims, closer to nature and the body). More importantly, though, his knowledge of the body represents knowledge of his mortality. It was this that allowed him to answer the riddle of the Sphinx: "What walks on four legs in the morning, two in midday, and three in the evening?" As Griffin points out, he can answer the riddle with "man" because he knows that he was once a vulnerable infant and will one day require a cane to aid him in the weakness of age.[118]

One should note that denial/loathing of the body also carries important racial dimensions. Subjugated races tend to be seen as more defined by their bodies, as dirty, as having racial smells, etc. Susan Griffin's *Pornography and Silence* takes note of these connections by devoting substantial attention to antisemitism.[119]

Generation, Creativity, and Death

The third aspect of eros, that of creativity and generation, can also take the form of domination and death. We have noted how each aspect of eros as constructed by pornography involves death: fusion with another requires the death (or at least submission) of the other; bodily feelings are denied because the fact of our existence as embodied beings reminds us that we are mortal. In this context, it should not surprise us that issues of creativity, generation, and reproduction are reformulated in ways that link them to death.[120] These linkages appear to some extent in pornographic stories and photographs but are more clearly stated by those Dworkin has identified as sexual philosophers.

Dworkin has described an instance of these links in a genre she terms the "pornography of pregnancy." She argues that this pornography, both in pictures of pregnant women and in the accompanying text, stresses the "malevolence" of the female body, "its danger to sperm and especially its danger to the woman herself." In this vision, the "pregnancy is the triumph of the phallus over the death-dealing vagina." She notes as well that the transformation of the virgin into whore is present as well, since the pregnancy is evidence of lack of virginity.[121] Thus, reproduction comes to be linked with danger and even death. Historically, of course, reproduction did have important connections with death. It is perhaps significant that a writer like Norman Mailer recognized these connections when he noted that sexual intercourse had lost its gravity (in part?) because pregnancy had ceased to be dangerous.[122]

French philosopher/pornographer George Bataille makes even clearer connections between eros and death and reformulates even reproduction itself as death. He argues that there is a "profound unity of these apparent opposites, birth and death." (Bataille is in good company: Aristotle too argued that whatever comes into being must pass away.) Yet despite their unity, Bataille gives primacy to death and argues that one must recognize a "tormenting fact: the urge towards love, pushed to its limit, is an urge toward death."[123] Moreover, reproduction is connected to continuity, but the continuity is defined by death. Indeed, "death is to be identified with continuity, and both of these concepts are equally fascinating. This fascination is the dominant element in eroticism."[124] Reproduction itself, seen from this perspective, is better understood as death: the new entity formed from the sperm and ovum bears in itself the "fusion, fatal to both, of two separate beings."[125] One can see here the traces of some of the roots of this view in childhood experience and the threat to identity posed by fusion: the erotic fusion of the sexual connection not only threatens death but indeed requires it. The danger is not simply a risk to be run but is, at some level, inevitably fatal.

The separation of generation and reproduction from life takes a second, more indirect, form as well: sexuality and sexual activity are portrayed in pornography as profoundly distanced from the activities of daily life. The action in pornography takes place in what Griffin has termed "pornotopia," a world outside of real time and space, where no one worries about doing dishes or changing diapers, and women enjoy rape, bondage, and humiliation. The distance from the real world structured by daily necessities is aptly symbolized by Griffin's description of Hugh Hefner's house: "His house has no windows. Nothing unpredictable or out of his control can happen to him there. Sunrise makes no difference. . . . Food emanates from a kitchen supplied with a staff day and night. . . . (And) as if one layer of protection (or distancing) were not enough, his bedroom contains another self-sufficient and man-made world, with a desk, and food supplies, and a bed which is motorized so that it not only changes positions but also carries him about the room"[126]

This transformation of creative activity and generation into negative forms is not limited, of course, to sexuality but occurs in other areas of society as well. Some of the clearest examples occur in the world of work. There, what could have been empowering and creative activity in conjunction with external nature becomes alienated labor in industries that pollute and destroy both their natural surroundings and the minds and bodies of those who labor, not a development of physical and mental capacities but a destruction of both.

Alternatives to Violence and Domination

Beneath the polite language of sexual reciprocity we have uncovered not only one-sided relations of domination and submission, but also dynamics of hostility, revenge, and a fascination with death. These are the negative forms taken by eros, forms that in our culture define masculinity: intimacy and fusion with another pose such deep problems that they require the domination of the other or control of the actions of the other, reducing the presumably threatening person to a nonentity with no will of its (her) won. Fetishism provides a second solution to the problem of intimacy: the other who presents the possibility (or threat) of erotic fusion produces such fright that she (since in most cases it is a woman) must be reduced to two-dimensional images or even a set of body parts to make it safe enough to pleasurably fantasize her victimization. And even in fantasy she must be silenced, reduced to a being without feelings or speech.

As for the second aspect of eros, in its negative, masculine form our existence as embodied beings does not open possibilities for sensual and physical connections with others but comes to stand as a loathsome reminder of our mortality that must be excised as much as possible from existence. Virility requires the denial of the body and its importance, whether this takes the form of control of the body of another or the portrayal of the man in heterosexual male pornography as complete master of his own body and the woman as totally at the mercy of his desires. The third aspect of eros is also given negative form. Creativity and generation become instead a fascination with death, and even reproduction is reformulated as concerned with death rather than life. Issues of daily life and necessity, as reminders of mortality and materiality, must be avoided.

Why are virility and domination so intimately connected? The key structuring experience can now be seen as the fear of ceasing to exist as a separate being because of the threat posed by a woman. These fears are expressed clearly in the institutionalized masculine sexual fantasies as depicted in pornography. Intimacy with a woman is so dangerous that she must be reduced to a nonentity or made into a thing. The body, constituting a reminder of loathsome mortality, must be denied and repressed. The whole man is reduced to the phallus; bodily feelings are projected onto the woman who is reduced to a body without a will of her own. And in sexual fantasy and philosophy about sexual fantasy, creativity and generation take the form of a fascination with death.

The feelings of the body, because they are reminders of materiality and worse, mortality, reminders that one will one day cease to exist, must be rejected and denied. And because to be born means also to die, reproduction and generation are either understood in terms of death or are appropriate to men in disembodied form. Over and over, then, the fear of ceasing to exist is played out.

If sexuality in our culture is institutionalized as heterosexual masculine sexuality, where can we look for alternatives? I believe that women's experience does not contain an alternative sexuality, since that experience does not take place outside the confines of hegemonic culture. But one can find in women's lives intimations and echoes of a different world, a world in which the erotic can be constructed as "an assertion of the life-force of women."[127] We are only at the beginning of the construction even of alternative visions. Yet as a beginning, two disparate literatures seem particularly promising: research on maternal sexuality and the current debate about sexuality within the feminist movement; the one concerned with sexuality as it appears in reproduction, the other with sexual excitement and sexual pleasure.

Maternal sexuality is particularly interesting since it has generally been held to be nonexistent and therefore remains culturally constructed as asexual. Perhaps one might say that this is a feminine sexuality since sexuality and maternity, like sexuality and femininity, are generally held to involve a contradiction. Here the work of Niles Newton is very useful. She argues that if one looks at the three "intense interpersonal reproductive acts" available to women—coitus, parturition, and lactation, one finds marked correlations and interrelationships.[128] Yet despite her documentation of a systematic series of similarities between childbirth and sexual excitement, and between breast-feeding and coital orgasm, most women in our culture do not perceive these experiences as sexual. Some of those few women who have reported sexual feelings in nursing also reported feeling guilty about those feelings. In the case of breast-feeding, researchers who probed beyond the conventional answers did find a substantial percentage of mothers who reported that they enjoyed the experience, but who described their enjoyment as not specifically sexual, but rather as feelings of tenderness and closeness.[129]

The inhibition of the sensual pleasures of breast-feeding may, Newton suggests, be similar to those that make birth orgasm rare in our culture: mother and infant are separated in the hospital, and rules about duration and timing of each sucking period are frequently enforced, Newton notes, "by persons who usually have never successfully breast fed even one baby." She concludes that "probably most people in our society would be willing to concede that we would cause coital frigidity if we prescribed the act only at scheduled times and laid down rules concerning the exact number of minutes intromission should last."[130]

The belief in our culture is that good mothers have no sexual feelings in relation to children, despite the fact that there is general agreement in the psychological literature that the early mother-child relationship should be erotic for the child.[131] What is less generally appreciated is that breast-feeding can be considered to be a reciprocal or symmetrical activity that does not involve the mother alone, but also the infant. Unlike coitus, this experience can be more persuasively characterized as an "equal opportunity experience."[132] These experiences, bodily, sensual, creative in the large sense of the term, suggest that women's lives may be able to incorporate eros without insisting that the only fusion with another lies in the death of the other; without, for that matter, insisting that isolation or fusion are the only options.

Contemporary arguments about the nature of a feminist sexuality have so far produced little more than polarization.[133] Yet these arguments both raise the issue of what sexual woman might look like and also illustrate how eros, even in negative forms, poses different problems for women than for men. Because of masculine hegemony, one would expect that women's sexual excitement too would depend on hostility and transgression, and women's writings about sexuality indicate that this is true. But even among feminists whose sexual excitement has been characterized as deeply structured by masculinist patterns, there is some evidence to support the contention that women are less perverse than men, i.e., that women's sexual excitement depends less than men's on victimization and revenge. Thus, one finds even in fictional, autobiographical, and political statements of lesbian proponents of sadomasochism echoes of different experiences. In terms of eros one finds that in fusion with another, empathy with the partner receives far more attention than separation from the other by means of domination and submission.[134] Rather than treating the body as a loathsome reminder of mortality whose needs must be projected onto the body of another, the rejection of the body takes the form of a need for permission to enjoy the pleasures of the flesh without guilt or responsibility.[135] Ironically, given the current controversy, one can compare these dynamics and issues to Anne Snitow's descriptions of the heroine's submission to greater force in Harlequin romance novels.[136]

Creativity and generation seem to play a small role in the fantasies described by Samois members. One finds little evidence of a fascination with death. The negative form of this aspect of eros appears only indirectly in the separation of sexuality from daily life activity. It is perhaps significant that this aspect too is shared by the sexual dynamics of Harlequin romances.[137] In sum, research in these two areas suggests that women are indeed less perverse than men, that even the forms of eros that appear to take forms similar to the dominant masculine forms take less dangerous forms for women.

Neither of these literatures provides an alternative vision. Moreover, the construction of alternative sexualities is more than a vision. It would require the real power of women to define and socially construct their own sexuality. And this, of course, would require an important shift in power relations.

Chapter 14

Masculine Identity and the Desire for War:
A Study in the Sickness of Power

 *Roger S. Gottlieb*

It is now a well-known that the current world supply of nuclear weapons is capable of destroying, at the very least, the vast majority of human beings. The full use of these weapons could mean the elimination of all human life. Even a comparatively limited nuclear exchange would probably cause the destruction of all societies and most of the population in the northern hemisphere and would have unforeseeable ecological effects.

It is also clear that nuclear weapons can be understood as *instruments* designed to serve human interests. The threat of nuclear war continues a pattern of aggression and self-defense deeply embedded in human social life. Collective violence to achieve the aims of a group has been used throughout virtually all of recorded human history.

It is ironic that were these weapons actually to be used, they could end up destroying the humans whose interests they are supposedly designed to serve. Nevertheless, their existence (though not their actual use) has aided in the pursuit of particular goals. The *threat* of the use of nuclear weapons has been part of American foreign policy over the last four decades. It has been instrumental in a number of situations in dictating Soviet response to U.S. interests. Simultaneously, the counterthreat of Soviet nuclear power has constrained the actions of the United States in its foreign policy (for example, in its conduct of the Vietnam war).[1] Within each of the contending superpowers, there are economic and bureaucratic interests in the production, sale, and administration of nuclear weapons. People make money producing them, become respected for designing them, and establish careers planning their use. Nuclear weapons, then, are partly the products of concrete and specifiable human interests, interests that are 'rational' only in the very limited sense of being part of the accepted, socially sanctioned structure of conscious motivations of advanced industrial societies.

In this chapter I will examine another facet of the nuclear threat: nuclear holocaust not as a means—either irrational or rational—to the accomplishment of some end, but as an end in itself. I will suggest that nuclear holocaust is desired by some people for its own sake. This suggestion, let me emphasize, is not meant to replace the explanations sketched above, but to supplement them.

The hypothesis I will put forward here can be stated briefly: the overwhelming destruction that would be caused by a nuclear war holds some attraction for people with a highly developed masculine identity. This attraction arises because some of the very mechanisms of social organization and personality structure by which masculine elites generate and maintain social and personal power lead to a kind of unconscious distress, a basic sickness of power. The psychic solution for that distress is sought blindly, without awareness, in cataclysmic destruction. While there are more familiar and accessible reasons for the existence of nuclear weapons and the threat of their use, the magnitude of folly surrounding nuclear weapons requires that we search for other reasons as well, reasons that are somewhat darker, more obscure—and more speculative. My arguments are therefore tentative and are intended to initiate rather than complete a discussion.

Three Aspects of Masculine Identity

With the rise of the women's movement, not only women but also men have become objects of study. Male culture and personal identity, no longer represented as universal norms for human beings, can now be understood and criticized as particular forms of thought, feeling, and social practice. These forms embody particular strengths and weaknesses, characteristics all the more significant because it is masculine identity that dominates the public space of social life. That domination—the masculine prerogative and burden of power—is central to culturally constructed masculinity and the attraction of nuclear war.

Two aspects of masculine identity—competitiveness and the need to prove oneself as a man—bear an obvious relation to war. As the ultimate competition for the ultimate stakes, nuclear war is an exaggerated version of a form of consciousness that sees all human interactions as defined by winning and losing. Similarly, nuclear war is an extreme form of other dangerous or destructive activities (violent sports, personal combat, mountain climbing) in which potential injury and the confrontation with death are measures of masculinity. Killing and being killed, threatening others and risking death, standing tall and refusing to blink—these measures of personal fearlessness celebrate masculine power from the gang wars of ghetto streets to the tension-riddled encounters of heads of states. With nuclear war on the agenda, masculine power raises the game to its highest level: "I am not only willing to kill you and to die myself, but to annihilate the world. Match my courage, or submit to my power."

While competitiveness and the need to prove oneself are essential to the masculine desire for war, they have received extensive attention already.[2] In addition, while masculine passions of competition and proving oneself are clearly endemic among the power elites who manage world politics, the dominant ideology of expertise that justifies political power appeals as much—perhaps more so—to seemingly more impersonal and passionless styles of thought and selfhood. My focus here, therefore, is on three other aspects of masculine identity—rationalization, professionalization, and commodification—and on how they are manifested in the male-dominated scientific, technical, and political elites that create and sustain nuclear terror.

These three principles have long been recognized as essential determinants of advanced capitalist society. As I will define them, they are also essential to the contemporary bureaucratic state (e.g., the Soviet Union). More recently, these principles have been identified as key constituents of forms of personal identity that are culturally male. They dominate a public space that, as opposed to the private, has been relegated to the control and activity of men.[3] I will take for granted here the extensive literature that defines the nature, importance, and maleness of these principles and focus on how they contribute to a specifically masculine desire for nuclear war.[4] Throughout the discussion it will be taken for granted that these three principles are among the essential sources of masculine social power in modern society. The mastery of these principles—both in reality and ideologically—helps distinguish the largely male, largely white, social elites from women and minorities. These principles produce both social and technical control, which, however, comes at an enormous cost in sickness both for those who wield the power and for those who are subject to it.

I am using the term "rationalization" in the sense developed by Weber and Lukacs: the process of understanding and controling the social and natural world in technical and bureaucratic terms. Rationalization divides reality into increasingly smaller subsystems, each of which is then subjected to rational (scientific, nontraditional, professionalized) forms of inquiry and administration. This limited rationality has the goal of making each of these subsystems increasingly calculable, predictable and controllable. Rationalization produces enormous, but necessarily limited, success. Our rationalized modern society has typically lost all sense of the interrelation of the various subsystems or the ends of the system as a whole. As a consequence, social life as a totality, including our relations with the natural world, becomes increasingly irrational and bizarre. For instance, extremely sophisticated forces of production are part of economies still subject to the business cycle and to highly unjust distributions of wealth. Enormous success in agriculture coexists with a social inability to adequately feed segments of the population of even advanced nations. The achievements of modern industry and transportation systems threaten to make the natural world uninhabitable.

Professionalization is a form of consciousness and practice in which human beings are divided, in Jurgen Habermas' words, into the "social engineers and the inmates of closed institutions."[5] Professionalization turns on the capacity of certain subjects (the professionals) to conceptualize and treat other people (the patients)[6] as objects. Essential to this process is the denial of the Self in the Other. The patient is seen as a collection of subsystems of performance and effect, subject to measurement, testing, and diagnosis. While pity may arise, empathy and compassion—feeling with and feeling for the Other—are ruled out. Moreover, the forms of knowledge and the activities of the subject—the professional—are themselves represented as stemming from an impersonal and objective rationality, determined by theories and goals that are universal rather than partial, based in reason rather than emotion, the product of health and normality rather than disease and abnormality. In professionalization, relations with other living beings are such that neither subject nor object is really alive: the subject is the embodiment of depersonalized reason; the object is the product of forces that escape the awareness of all but the professional. If the paradigm for rationalization is the relation between industrial production and the economic system, the paradigm for professionalization is in medicine (including psychiatry) and biological research.

Commodification is the transformation of human productive and relational capacities into activities whose central goal is exchange. As the economy becomes increasingly commodified, more and more of human action and consciousness is experienced under its model. Not only work in the public sphere, but leisure, love, play, and creativity come to be seen only as means to the acquisition of some product (material good or social position) for which they can be exchanged. Normative evaluations of those consequences are excluded; or, rather, the only possible normative evaluation is found in the realm of exchange. People work and act for money, prestige, and success. Personal fitness is measured not in the experience of health, but in how many minutes (seconds/tenths of a second) it takes to run a mile. Sexual exploits are measured in a scale of conquests, not in terms of the immediate and noncalculable pleasures of intimacy.

Marxian analysis of the commodification of capitalist society is well known. A similar analysis for bureaucratic state societies (e.g., the Soviet Union) is perhaps less familiar. Acquaintance with such societies, however, suggests that commodification, in the sense I have described, is equally present in them, though it obviously does not take the form of separate and competing capitals striving for expanded reproduction.

Rationalization, professionalization, and commodification are essential constituents of the nuclear terror. That terror is based in enormously complex and 'successful' technical systems for the delivery of weapons of mass destruction. It is thus a striking example of rationalization. Tens of thousands of individuals master separate parts of the overall system: supplying raw materials for the production of bombs; choosing among prospective enemy sties for targets; mastering the routine of firing the weapons; designing guidance systems for intercontinental missiles; calculating the effects of nuclear explosions. In each case the totality of the nuclear terror is divided up into smaller and smaller subsystems, and individuals participating in those subsystems do so without conceptualizing the whole which that mastery helps from. Through rationalization, they are unable to understand the whole for the madness it is. Yet they too will die if the process reaches its designated conclusion.

Professionalization contributes to the nuclear terror by making possible consciousness and practice that deny the effects of nuclear war. The language of nuclear strategists dehumanizes the enemy and denies the reality of the effects of nuclear war on ourselves. The everyday existence of the Other—children on the way to school, women buying groceries, men in bathtubs—becomes a set of numerical abstractions: body counts, megakills, population density, kill ratio, etc. The life-world of humanity becomes subject to a detached rationality that simply calculates. Empathy for the experience of the Other is impossible. It is also impossible to feel for oneself. The nuclear rationalizers leave their offices, silos, and command posts and return to comfortable homes, barking dogs, and laughing children. The nuclear madness puts all this in a bracket of despair, poised on the brink of a simple computer error or a sequence of political follies. Through professionalization, the masters of the process are able to detach from this prospect—from the manner in which their own activity puts their wives, children, homes, and communities in danger.

Finally, commodification turns the activities and roles that contribute to nuclear terror into means for the economic, political, or career advancements of the agents involved. Actions here are not experienced as threatening the existence of human life, but as producing an income, a research grant, a villa on the Black Sea, or a higher military rank. The immediate gratification that comes from serving the machine turns away any thought of that machine's ultimate purpose. The flip side of the professional's denial of feelings and the blindness to totality of rationalization is a pathetic slavery to immediate gratification that denies any ultimate meaning or effect to one's acts.

In what sense are rationalization, professionalization, and commodification essentially *masculine*? Don't they have a logic of their own apart from gender? I cannot completely answer these questions here but will simply point out that the political and cultural triumph of these three go hand-in-hand with the development of the modern sex-gender system in which the home-bound wife, separated from the public world of politics and commodity production, is matched against the publicly oriented husband. In modernized societies the capacities to cooperate, share feelings, and be sensitive to others' emotional states (without paternalizing them) are typically left to women. Men's inability to manifest these capacities is connected to their identification with the soulless forms of rationalization, professionalization, and commodification. But since even the most professionalized of men retain relational needs, the modern, bourgeois fantasy of adult autonomy is built on the denial of men's dependence on their mothers, wives, secretaries, and whores. The traits that men shed to become 'real' men are still needed—they are provided by women. Without the hidden truth of women's relational skills, men would not be able to deform their own characters into the molds of rationalization, professionalization, and commodification. As always in master-slave relations, femininity is the 'hidden truth' of masculinity.[7]

The Desire for War

I have described how three aspects of masculine identity contribute to the nuclear terror. My description so far, however, has not shown the connection between masculine identity and the *desire* for war. As described above, rationalization, professionalization, and commodification can be understood as products of developments such as the rise of industrial society, capitalism, and male-dominated professional and bureaucratic elites. From Horkheimer to Foucault, from feminist theory to deconstruction, from the critique of the medical model in psychology to the critique of the instrumental attitude toward nature, the practices and principles bound up in rationalization, professionalization, and commodification have been dissected as unjust sources of social power. Yet in our discussion so far, the nuclear threat is and the nuclear holocaust may be among their consequences, but are not outcomes to which the principles are explicitly directed.

How then is nuclear war an end to be desired, and not simply an instrument or a consequence of policy?

Rationalization, professionalization, and commodification are more than forms of human identity with disastrous consequences for social life. They are also distortions of the personality that inevitably lead to a kind of systematic madness on the part of those who manifest them. Masculine identity is not only destructive, it is self-destructive. This self-destructiveness, in turn, has now reached the very brink of its ultimate form: the desire for nuclear war.

To support this point I will suggest, but not argue for, the claim that each of the three principles of masculine identity—rationalization, professionalization and commodification—involves the repression of 'natural' human needs or desires. These include the need for totality, for empathic, emotionally based human interidentification, and for meaningful, nonalienated labor. By calling these needs natural I do not mean to suggest that they are biological in origin. Rather, I mean that they are generated (and frustrated) by the current state of social life. It is the repression of these needs in masculine identity that makes nuclear war an object of masculine desire. Clearly this desire is unconscious in the sense of being inarticulate and suppressed.

Human beings may be thought of as complex systems of needs and capacities. In theory, we can distinguish our needs and capacities for love, work, and play, and our material, intellectual, emotional, and spiritual lives. Yet such distinctions do not describe a series of fragmented, abstract capacities or interests. It is the same person who eats, makes love, designs electronic circuits for guidance systems, and watches a football game. It is a unitary center of experience and moral responsibility, a particular selfhood, who adapts his (the male pronoun is used intentionally) generalized needs and capacities to these different social contexts.

(I realize that in the current intellectual climate of antiessentiallism and deconstruction these are highly controversial claims. This is clearly not the place to argue for them in any extended way. I would simply make the following point: to the extent that no unitary selfhood exists, that the self is simply the constructed outcome of systems of power and discourse, there is no possibility of serious ethical reflection—or political action—on dilemmas such as the nuclear terror. Any serious discussion of these matters—i.e., a discussion that is not merely an intellectual exercise but hopes to have some possible practical implications—must take for granted that humans are, at least potentially, moral and political subjects.)

Corresponding to this unitary center of selfhood is a unitary world, a 'totality' of interdependent causes and effects, actions and experiences, in which the self unfolds. Rationalization represses this unitary selfhood and its capacity to totalize, that is, to comprehend and relate to the social and natural world as a whole. It fractures persons into disconnected subsystems, forbidden to make or incapable of making intellectual and emotional connections among different parts of a unitary life. In the sphere of work, rationalization denies what is necessarily felt as true: that one's labor affects not only this or that limited end, but the nature and quality of productive or economic life as a whole. The artificially constricted consciousness engendered by rationalization thus involves the denial of what we know to be true: that we are not simply 'doing our job.' " Rather, we are contributing to a totality. Simultaneously, however, the practice of rationalization demands that we reject the totality we have created: that totality cannot be ours, for our knowledge, expertise, and labor have been adapted only to this particular subsystem. The totality becomes, then, that which we know but deny knowing; that which we yearn for but reject; that which we need but cannot have; and that for which we cannot acknowledge our need. As a consequence, the totality becomes a center of profound ambivalence, an object of love and hate. Nuclear war, in turn, represents the final totality: the incomparable flowering and destruction of totality. It is an act so enormous and so overwhelming that it breaks through the rationalized subsystems of everyday existence. And it is the last totality, the end of that which is the center of so much ambivalence, desire, and dread.

Professionalization requires the repression of feeling. As a learning process, it entails mastery of the denial of recognition of the Other as like oneself. But human beings have a natural (in the sense I have defined) and necessary capacity to recognize the Other. Without such recognition we would not learn a language, develop relational capacities and superegos, or even understand fictional narratives. To professionalize oneself is thus to erase or suspend this necessary capacity. Recognition of the feelings of the Other are the crucial danger to the professionalized ego. But since those feelings cannot really be denied, what is left is the denial of feelings in the professionalized ego itself. The consequence is, in Kierkegaard's phrase, "a disorder of feelings, a disorder consisting in not having any."[8] But human beings *are* emotional, *do* recognize the Other, and naturally respond to the similarity or connection between themselves and those with whom they are in relation. Like totality, feelings and even the life of both Self and Other become objects of both desire and fear. We do feel and want to feel more. Simultaneously, we want to deny our feelings and those of others. As a consequence, there arises the desire to obliterate feelings, all feelings. For this end nuclear war possesses an inevitable attraction. No longer will the professionalized ego be threatened by a human recognition that could undermine its chosen sense of stability. No longer will it have to confront the desired and forbidden emotional vulnerability. The ultimate threat to the professionalized ego—that it will feel or see its feelings reflected in another—will have been removed. All that is living, human, partial, and subjective will have been eliminated. The world will be left unthreatening because the world will be dead.

Commodification, as the Marxist tradition has shown, turns objectification into alienation. The products of human labor no longer possess inherent value or meaning.[9] They are tokens of exchange. But labor is a, perhaps *the*, central category of human action and experience. When labor is embodied only in exchange value, work for exchange becomes the model of human activity as such. A paradigm of delayed gratification, of infinite substitutability, comes to dominate not just labor, but also human relationships and play. Since all action becomes modeled on the instrumentality of producing for the wage that will buy some other thing, true enjoyment of anything becomes increasingly difficult to achieve. Perhaps this is only another way of saying that the desire for commodities and the commodification of desire cannot produce human fulfillment. As labor becomes nothing but money, so sex, love, family, and fun turn into ciphers for other things: quantifiable place-holders for a final gratification that is always to be the result of the next exchange. What we do becomes simply an indication of what we can buy. And an endless and unprofitable round of transactions indefinitely postpones happiness. In such a world, a natural desire finally to accomplish something definite and complete arises. We seek to see the reality of our labor in a product so irrevocable that the cycle of labor and postponed fulfillment is ended forever. That is exactly what nuclear weapons are: the last commodities, ones that will insure—by the power of their effects—that we *have* accomplished something and that the waiting will be over forever.

Power

Rationalization, professionalization, and commodification are all forms of power, and their current manifestation indicates a desperate sickness of power. Rationalization gives mastery, even if over a tiny subsystem of social or natural reality and at the cost of inserting that subsystem into an irrational context. He who rationalizes understands— or at least can predict and control—the behavior of others and of the limited and local aspects of the social system. Professionalization gives the professional power over the patient: the prestige of objective reason, the status of a (supposedly) impersonal self. The more our personal needs or the limited perspectives of a particular social group are disguised as a universal Reason, the more we can dictate the diagnosis and control of those who are 'merely' particular, limited persons. Commodification gives us the power of money: to use our resources to command those of others.

The nuclear terror is also essentially about power. Perhaps the most compelling relation between masculine identity and the desire for war is simply that masculine desire or need to manifest power in as extreme and destructive a form as possible.

Various explanations have been offered for the masculine drive for power. Some writers have claimed that it stems from men's inability to give birth, to create out of their bodies another life. Others have argued that mother-monopolized childrearing practices create a psychological dynamic leading to masculine styles of power.[10] In a limited sense, of course, power is also simply its own reward, as it confers status and privilege on those who wield it. To the extent that a social world posits certain possessions as goods and makes them available to the powerful, it is not surprising that those who *can* achieve power try to do so.

Whatever the validity of these explanations, it is now widely accepted that in our gender system much of masculine power is devoted to destructive ends. Correspondingly, there is an unconscious desire to use nuclear weapons. This suppressed relish stems from the same impulse as that of the schoolboy who (as I once did) pours boiling water on an anthill just to see what will happen; of an Ahab who seeks to "strike through the mask" at a natural world whose only crime was resisting his attempts to kill it for profit; of a grown man who watches a violent sporting event with the only partially hidden hope that someone will die; of a male eroticism that in rape, pornography, and much of 'normal' sex fuses hostility and sexuality, 'love' and domination. Despite all the public protestations to the contrary, I believe that there is a hidden lust to use nuclear weapons, to see just how overwhelming our power can be, to flourish male power in the face of a universe that has condemned us to creative impotence—and, it might be added, to flourish male power in the face of an awakening female gender no longer so accepting of male domination: the mushroom clouds will be so enormous; the explosion so overwhelming; the consequences so catastrophic.

Scientific knowledge is power—to create new machines, to find out how things work, to take apart an organism to find its hidden secrets. It seems that the most masculine of books are the ones in which the hero goes out and kills something and then writes about how interesting it all is. But what could be more interesting than the destruction of the world? What could possibly prove as convincingly the enormous success of our knowledge and the technical powers we have generated from it? As professionalization and commodification make the torture of laboratory animals routine and allow researchers to take for granted that they have the right to do virtually anything to wild animals (e.g., shoot them with tranquilizers and implant radioactive tracers to follow their migrations) in the pursuit of 'knowledge,' so the use of nuclear weapons will be the final experiment, the last research project. Will we really have a nuclear winter? Will anyone survive? Will the ozone layer be destroyed? Will insects mutate into something fascinating? How interesting it will all be. Of course, in reality no one will be around to observe the experiment or collate the results. But that is all right, for as professionals there are no persons here now—only the disinterested servants of the impersonal Reason.[11]

Hope?

I have painted the bleakest of pictures. If even a fraction of what I have said is true, then the dominant structure of masculinity turns our societies toward the end of human life. Is there hope?

I believe there are ground for responses other than despair. Masculine identity is more than the homogeneous negativities of rationalization, professionalization, and commodification, or the use of these in the maniacal pursuit of destructive power. Caring and creativity, love and joy are also accessible to men. They rape women but also love them. They send their children to die in wars but also father and protect them. They love the Earth even as they destroy it. Most important: the very sickness of power that makes nuclear war attractive in some ways oppresses the vast majority of men and poisons the lives of those who manifest it in the most extreme ways. As workers, blacks, Jews, homosexuals, and members of the third World, men can also be 'feminized' by the dehumanizing structures of modern masculine power. It is these facts that offer at least some hope and suggest that the fulfillment of masculine identity may not be the destruction of the Earth but the transformation of men into persons who no longer repress themselves and threaten to extinguish the future.

Postscript

This chapter was written before the recent lessening in the confrontational and suicidal relations between the superpowers. While we all have cause to rejoice over recent developments, I believe the argument here remains relevant for three reasons.

First, because even if the nuclear threat were to pass away forever, it would still be of great importance to ask: how could the human race have managed to coexist with it for so long?

Second, because we see a persistent commitment to defense budgets, nuclear weapons, and the need for military power on the part of many in our government. Not all are rushing toward a 'peace dividend.' Some will only move in that direction kicking and screaming. Why?

Third, and perhaps most important: while the nuclear crisis may have abated somewhat, the environmental crisis continues to escalate. Is there any relation between the two? Are the diseases of masculine identity that created the arms race also present in some form in our tendency to threaten our own ecosystem?

Whatever the state of international relations, if my arguments here shed light on any of these three issues, they will join what is perhaps the most important conversation—and call to action—of our time.

NOTES

Notes to Introduction

1. James Agee and Walker Evans, *Let Us Now Praise Famous Men: Three Tenant Families* (Boston: Houghton Mifflin Co., 1939–41). Future references to this text will be given parenthetically.

2. Similarly, Evans' photographs focus upon whites, with African-Americans appearing only in one.

3. I would like to thank Roger Gottlieb and Ed Royce for their helpful criticisms of earlier versions of this introduction.

Notes to Chapter 1

1. Spinoza, *Ethics*, Book IV, Definition 8, in *The Collected Works of Spinoza*, tr. Edwin Curley (Princeton: Princeton University Press, 1985), Vol. I, 547.

2. Thomas Hobbes, *Leviathan* (Cambridge, England: Cambridge University Press, 1935), Part I, Chapter 10, 54.

3. George Meredith, "An Essay on Comedy," in Wylie Sypher, ed. *The Meanings of Comedy* (New York: Doubleday, 1956). Percy Bysshe Shelley, *A Defense of Poetry* (Indianapolis: Bobbs-Merrill, 1904).

4. Cf. A. O. Rorty, "Imagination and Power," in *Mind in Action* (Boston: Beacon Press, 1988).

5. Linda Burns, Naomi Chazan, Theodore Draper, Jay Rorty, and Richard Schmitt graciously and patiently discussed these tangled topics with Buff and Rebuff.

Notes to Chapter 2

I have learned a good deal about power from friends and critics, particularly Jeffrey Isaac, Steven Lukes, Donald Moon, and Felix Oppenheim. The present essay is a considerably shortened and somewhat revised version of Chapter 4 of my *Transforming Political Discourse* (Oxford: Blackwell, 1988).

1. Herbert Simon, *Models of Man* (New York: Wiley, 1957), 4.

2. Anthony Giddens, *The Constitution of Society* (Berkeley and Los Angeles: University of California Press, 1984), 283.

3. George Eliot, *Middlemarch* (Harmondsworth: Penguin, 1965), 111.

4. See my *Transforming Political Discourse* (Oxford: Blackwell, 1988), Ch. 4, especially 81–86.

5. Simon, *Models of Man*, 5.

6. See, inter alia, Robert Dahl, "The Concept of Power," *Behavioral Science* 2 (July, 1957):201–15, specif. 202; "Cause and Effect in the Study of Politics," in *Cause and Effect*, ed. Daniel Lerner (New York: Free Press, 1965), 75–98, esp. 88; "Power," in *International Encyclopedia of the Social Sciences*, ed. David L. Sills (New York: Macmillan-Free Press, 1968), Vol. XII, 405–15, specif. 410; James G. March, "An Introduction to the Theory and Measurement of Influence," *American Political Science Review* 49 (June, 1955):431–51, specif. 437; Felix E. Oppenheim, *Dimensions of Freedom* (New York: St. Martin's Press, 1961), 40–41; Andrew S. McFarland, *Power and Leadership in Pluralist Systems* (Stanford, Calif.: Stanford University Press, 1969), 3.

7. Robert Dahl, *Modern Political Analysis* (Englewood Cliffs, N.J.: Prentice-Hall, 1963), 41.

8. See my "Models of Power: Past and Present," *Journal of the History of the Behavioral Sciences* 11 (July, 1975):211–222 and "Power, Causation and Explanation," *Polity* 8 (Winter, 1975):189–214.

9. Dahl, for instance, suggests that power, influence, rule, and authority are "serviceable synonyms": "The Concept of Power," 201.

10. Simon, *Models of Man*, 7.

11. Dorwin Cartwright, *Studies in Social Power* (Ann Arbor: University of Michigan Press, 1959), 7. See also Dahl, "The Concept of Power," 204; McFarland, *Power and Leadership*, 10.

12. See, for example, Dahl, "The Concept of Power," 202.

13. Again see, *inter alia*, Dahl, "The Concept of Power," 204; William Riker, "Some Ambiguities in the Notion of Power," *American Political Science Review* 58 (June, 1964), 341–49; McFarland, *Power and Leadership*, 9.

14. For further discussion and a critique of the aforementioned series of claims, see my "Power, Causation and Explanation."

15. Peter Bachrach and Morton S. Baratz, "Two Faces of Power," *American Political Science Review* 56 (1962):451–60; and the elaboration of their views in "Decisions and Nondecisions: An Analytical Framework," *American Political Science Review* 57 (1963):641–51; and *Power and Poverty* (New York: Oxford University Press, 1970), Part I.

16. Lukes, *Power: A Radical View* (London and New York: Macmillan, 1974), 26.

17. Ibid., 34–35.

18. Lukes, "Power and Authority," in *A History of Sociological Analysis*, ed. Tom Bottomore and Robert Nisbet (New York: Basic Books, 1978), 669.

19. Lukes, *Power*, Chapter 6.

20. See John Gaventa, *Power and Powerlessness: Quiescence and Rebellion in an Appalachian Valley* (Urbana, Ill.: University of Illinois Press, 1980).

21. These criticisms are made by Felix E. Oppenheim, *Political Concepts: A Reconstruction* (Chicago: University of Chicago Press, 1981), 51. They are anticipated, if not countered satisfactorily, in Lukes, *Power*, 32–33.

22. David West, "Power and Formation: New Foundations for a Radical Concept of Power," *Inquiry* 30 (March, 1987):137–54.

23. John Gray, "Political Power, Social Theory, and Essential Contestability," in *The Nature of Political Theory*, ed. David Miller and Larry Siedentop (Oxford: Clarendon Press, 1983), 75–101, esp. 94–101.

24. See, for example, the discussion of power in Nancy C. M. Hartsock, *Money, Sex and Power* (London: Longman, 1983), Ch. 9, and her essay in the present volume.

25. For an attempt to link a typology of "persuasive communications" or speech-acts with power, influence, and other concepts, see my "Power, Causation and Explanation," 211–12.

26. Peter Winch, "The Idea of a Social Science," in *Rationality*, ed. Bryan R. Wilson (Oxford: Blackwell, 1970), 9–10.

27. Hannah Arendt, "On Violence," in *Crises of the Republic* (New York: Harcourt Brace Jovanovich, 1972), 142–43.

28. Hannah Arendt, *The Human Condition* (Chicago: University of Chicago Press, 1958), 200–205.

29. Arendt, "On Violence," 143.

30. Ibid., 140.

31. Arendt, *Human Condition*, 200.

32. Lukes, *Power*, 28–31, 59.

33. Arendt, "On Violence," 143.

34. For an explication of Hegel's "master-slave dialectic," see my "Two Concepts of Coercion," *Theory and Society* 8 (January, 1978): 97–112. On the affinities between Heidegger's and Arendt's understanding of 'power,' see Fred Dallmayr, *Polis and Praxis* (Cambridge, Mass.: M.I.T. Press, 1985), chapter 3.

35. Brian Fay, *Critical Social Science* (Ithaca, N.Y.: Cornell University Press, 1986), 130.

36. Jürgen Habermas, "Hannah Arendt: On the Concept of Power," in *Philosophical-Political Profiles*, transl. Frederick G. Lawrence (Cambridge, Mass.: M.I.T. Press, 1983), 173.

37. Ibid., 174.

38. Ibid., 175.

39. Ibid., 176.

40. Ibid., 183.

41. Ibid.

42. Jürgen Habermas, "Warheitstheorien," in *Wirklichkeit und Reflexion* (Pfullingen: Neske, 1973), 239.

43. The "realism" to which I refer here should not be confused with two other species of realism. I do not refer to political realism of the *Realpolitik* variety espoused by Henry Kissinger and other "realists." Nor do I refer to the view, defended by some philosophers of science, that scientific theories represent ever-closer approximations to reality. The sort of metascientific realist to whom I refer may, but need not, be a realist of the latter sort.

44. See Rom Harré, "Powers," *British Journal for the Philosophy of Science* 21 (1970):81–101; and Rom Harré and E. H. Madden, *Causal Powers* (Totowa: Rowman and Littlefield, 1975). For early and admittedly sketchy attempts to link the realists' non-Humean view of causation with alternative ways of thinking about political power, see my "Power, Causation and Explanation," especially 209, 213–14; and "Two Concepts of Coercion." For a more systematic and sophisticated treatment, see Jeffrey C. Isaac, *Power and Marxist Theory: A Realist View* (Ithaca, N.Y.: Cornell University Press, 1987), particularly Part I.

45. See Russell Keat and John Urry, *Social Theory as Science* (London: Routledge & Kegan Paul, 1975); Roy Bhaskar, *A Realist Theory of Science* (Atlantic Highlands, N.J.: Humanities Press, 1978); Peter T. Manicas, "On the

Concept of Social Structure," *Journal for the Theory of Social Behaviour* 10 (1980):65–82; and *A History and Philosophy of the Social Sciences* (Oxford: Blackwell, 1987).

46. The following points are adapted and summarized from Isaac, *Power and Marxist Theory*, Chapters 2 and 3, and "After Empiricism: The Realist Alternative," in *Idioms of Inquiry*, ed. Terence Ball (Albany, N.Y.: State University of New York Press, 1987), Chapter 8.

47. One need not, however, be a realist in order to be a relationalist. On ontological relationalism, see my "Two Concepts of Coercion."

48. Jeffrey C. Isaac, "Beyond the Three Faces of Power: A Realist Critique," *this volume*, 46.

49. Ibid., 47.

50. Isaac, *Power and Marxist Theory*, 5.

51. Michel Foucault, *Power/Knowledge*, ed. Colin Gordon (New York: Pantheon, 1980), 183–84. Further observations on power as exercised in specific social settings are to be found in his *Discipline and Punish: The Birth of the Prison*, transl. Alan Sheridan (New York: Random House, 1979); *The History of Sexuality*, transl. Robert Hurley, Vol. I (New York: Random House, 1978); and "Space, Knowledge, and Power," in *The Foucault Reader*, ed. Paul Rabinow (New York: Pantheon, 1984), 239–56.

52. Foucault, *Power/Knowledge*, 119.

53. This point is made in a particularly graphic and grisly way in the opening scene (for it is indeed that, rather than a conventional introduction) of *Discipline and Punish*.

54. Michel Foucault, "The Subject and Power," Afterword to Hubert L. Dreyfus and Paul Rabinow, *Michel Foucault: Beyond Structuralism and Hermeneutics*, 2nd en. (Chicago: University of Chicago Press, 1983), 208; *Power/ Knowledge*, 106.

55. Foucault, "The Subject and Power," 213–16.

56. Foucault, *Power/Knowledge*, 119.

57. Foucault, "The Subject and Power," 212.

58. Foucault, *Power/Knowledge*, esp. Chapters 3 and 9.

59. See James Farr, "Marx's Laws," *Political Studies* 34 (Spring, 1986):202–22; and Isaac, *Power and Marxist Theory*, Chapter 4.

60. Foucault, "The Subject and Power," 218.

61. Ibid., 218.

62. Ibid., 220.

63. Ibid., 222.

64. Ibid., 225. For an excellent critique, see Nancy Fraser, "Foucault on Modern Power: Empirical Insights and Normative Confusions," *Praxis International* 1 (October, 1981):272–87.

Notes to Chapter 3

1. Robert A. Dahl, "The Behavioral Approach in Political Science: Epitaph for a Monument to a Successful Protest," *American Political Science Review* 58 (December, 1961):767.

2. Ibid., 764.

3. David Easton, *A Systems Analysis of Political Life* (New York: Wiley, 1965), 7; see also his "Alternative Strategies in Theoretical Research," in *Varieties of Political Theory*, ed. Easton (Englewood Cliffs, N.J.: Prentice-Hall, 1966).

4. Adam Przeworski and Henry Teune, *The Logic of Comparative Social Inquiry* (New York: Wiley-Interscience, 1970), 18. For a similar view of scientific theory, see Robert T. Holt and John E. Turner, eds., *The Methodology of Comparative Research* (New York: Free Press, 1970).

5. Cf. Rom Harré, *Principles of Scientific Thinking* (London: Macmillan, 1970); and Roy Bhaskar, *A Realist Theory of Science*, 2nd Ed. (Atlantic Highlands, N.J.: Humanities Press, 1978). For a defense of this label and of the position that it denotes, see Bas C. Van Fraassen, *The Scientific Image* (Oxford: Clarendon Press, 1980).

6. Karl R. Popper, *The Open Society and its Enemies*, Vol. I (Princeton, N.J.: Princeton University Press, 1966), 32.

7. Karl R. Popper, *The Logic of Scientific Discovery* (London: Hutchinson, 1959, and New York: Harper & Row, 1968), 59–60.

8. See, in addition Popper, Carl Hempel's *Aspects of Scientific Explanation* (New York: Free Press, 1965), especially 364–67. As Holt and Turner write: "Typically, the [scientific] hypothesis involves a predicted relationship between at least two variables and takes the general form of 'If A, then B.' " Holt and Turner, *Methodology*, 6.

9. See, for example, Herbert A. Simon, "Notes on the Observation and Measurement of Political Power," *Journal of Politics* 15 (1953), 500–16; and James G. March, "An Introduction to the Theory and Measurement of Influence," *American Political Science Review* 49 (1955), 431–51.

10. Robert A. Dahl, "Power," in *International Encyclopedia of the Social Sciences*, Vol. 12 (New York, 1968), 407.

11. Ibid., 418.

12. Robert A. Dahl, "The Concept of Power," *Behavioral Science* 2, no. 3 (July, 1957):203–4.

13. Robert A. Dahl, "Cause and Effect in the Study of Politics," in *Cause and Effect*, ed. Daniel Lerner (New York: Free Press, 1965), 94.

14. Dahl, "The Concept of Power," 203–4.

15. Nelson Polsby, *Community Power and Political Theory* (New Haven, Conn.: Yale University Press, 1980), 5–6.

16. Robert A. Dahl, "A Critique of the Ruling Elite Model," *American Political Science Review* 58 (1958):463–64.

17. Cf. Peter Bachrach and Morton Baratz, "The Two Faces of Power," *American Political Science Review* 56 (1962):942–52, and "Decisions and Nondecisions: An Analytic Framework," *American Political Science Review* 57 (1963):632–42. These essays are reprinted in the authors' *Power and Poverty* (New York: Oxford University Press, 1970).

18. Bachrach and Baratz, *Power and Poverty*, 43–44.

19. Ibid., 44.

20. Polsby, *Community Power*, 208, emphasis added. See also Raymond Wolfinger, "Nondecisions and the Study of Local Politics," *American Political Science Review* 65 (1971), 1063–81, for a similar criticism. For an interesting critique of the positivism that Polsby/Wolfinger fall into, and a defense of the possibility of discovering covert decisions of Bachrach and Baratz's sort, see Frederick Frey's "Nondecisions and the Study of Local Politics: A Comment," *American Political Science Review* 65 (1971), 1081–1101.

21. Bachrach and Baratz, *Power and Poverty*, 19.

22. Ibid., 46.

23. Geoffrey Debnam, "Nondecisions and Power: The Two Faces of Bachrach and Baratz," *American Political Science Review* 69 (September, 1975), 889–900.

24. Polsby, *Community Power*, 190.

25. Steven Lukes, *Power: A Radical View* (London: Macmillan, 1974), 22–23.

26. Steven Lukes, "Power and Authority," in *A History of Sociological Analysis*, ed. Tom Bottomore and Robert Nisbet (New York: Basic Books, 1978), 669.

27. Lukes, *Power: A Radical View,* 27.

28. Ibid., 41.

29. Ibid., 22–25.

30. Ibid., 27.

31. Ibid., 34–35. This view of interests, as Lukes acknowledges, has been developed by William E. Connolly, "On 'Interests' in Politics," *Politics and Society* 2, no. 4 (Summer, 1972). This conception owes much to the work of Jürgen Habermas, particularly his *Knowledge and Human Interests* (Boston: Beacon Press, 1968). Lukes explicitly links himself to the idiom of critical theory in a later paper, "On the Relativity of Power," in *Philosophical Disputes in the Social Sciences,* ed. S. C. Brown (Sussex and New Jersey: Harvester and Humanities, 1979), 267. It is therefore curious that in a more recent paper he rejects Habermas' (and his own earlier) transcendental conception of objective interest, opting instead for a Weberian subjectivism in many ways akin to Polsby. See Steven Lukes, "Of Gods and Demons: Habermas and Practical Reason," in *Habermas: Critical Debates,* ed. John B. Thompson and David Held (Cambridge, Mass.: M.I.T. Press, 1982). This is an issue on which Lukes shows some confusion. For a critique, see Michael Bloch, Brian Heading, and Phillip Lawrence, "Power in Social Theory: A Non-Relative View," in Brown, *Philosophical Disputes,* 243–60.

32. See Steven Lukes, "Power and Structure," in *Essays in Social Theory,* ed. Steven Lukes (London: Macmillan, 1977).

33. See Lukes, "Power and Authority," 635; "Relativity of Power," 263–64.

34. Lukes, *Power: A Radical View,* 31.

35. James March, "The Power of Power," in *Varieties of Political Theory,* ed. David Easton (Englewood Cliffs, N.J.: Prentice Hall, 1966), 67–68. As he writes: "The measurement of power is useful primarily in systems that conform to some variant of the force model [i.e., behavioral compliance]. . . . If I interpret recent research correctly, the class of social-choice situations in which power is a significantly useful concept is much smaller than I previously believed."

36. On "conventionalism," see Russell Keat and John Urry, *Social Theory as Science* (London: Routledge and Kegan Paul, 1975). See also Harold I. Brown, *Perception Theory, and Commitment: The New Philosophy of Science* (Chicago: University of Chicago Press, 1977). Indispensable is Imre Lakatos and Alan Musgrave, eds., *Criticism and the Growth of Knowledge* (London: Cambridge University Press, 1970).

37. See Harré, *Principles;* Bhaskar, *Realist Theory;* and Keat and Urry, *Social Theory.*

38. See Rom Harré and E. H. Madden, *Causal Powers* (New Jersey: Rowman and Littlefield, 1975).

39. Bhaskar, *Realist Theory,* 51.

40. Stephen Toulmin, *Foresight and Understanding* (New York: Harper Torchbooks, 1961), 75.

41. Quoted in Gerald Holton, "Mach, Einstein, and the Search for Reality," *Daedalus* 97 (Spring, 1968), 636–73.

42. See Roy Bhaskar, *The Possibility of Naturalism: A Philosophical Critique of the Contemporary Human Sciences* (Sussex: Harvester Press, 1979). See also my "Realism and Social Scientific Explanation: A Critique of Porpora," *Journal for the Theory of Social Behaviour* 13, no. 3 (October, 1983), 301–08.

43. See Peter T. Manicas, "On the Concept of Social Structure," *Journal for the Theory of Social Behaviour* 10, no. 2 (1980), 65–82.

44. See Anthony Giddens, *New Rules of Sociological Method* (New York: Basic Books, 1976), 121; and Bhaskar, *Possibility of Naturalism,* 39–43. Giddens has further developed this notion of structure in *Central Problems of Social Theory* (Berkeley: University of California Press, 1979), and *A Contemporary Critique of Historical Materialism* (Berkeley: University of California Press, 1981).

45. On transformation see Bhaskar, *Possibility of Naturalism,* 42–45; Giddens has called the process of the constitution and transformation of social structures "structuration." See his "On the Theory of Structuration," in *Studies in Social and Political Theory,* ed. Anthony Giddens (New York: Basic Books, 1977).

46. Giddens, *New Rules,* 160.

47. See Hannah Feneichel Pitkin, *Wittgenstein and Justice* (Berkeley: University of California Press, 1972), 264–86.

48. Jack Nagel, *The Descriptive Analysis of Power* (New Haven, Conn.: Yale University Press, 1975), 175.

49. My point here is not that the debate has failed to stimulate inquiry. It is simply that most of the research done on power, even by Dahl and Bachrach and Baratz, does not strictly conform to the standards of empiricism. Two studies that attempt to "operationalize" the concepts discussed are Matthew Crenson, *The Un-Politics of Air Pollution* (Baltimore, Md.: Johns Hopkins University Press, 1971), and John Gaventa, *Power and Powerlessness: Quiescence and Rebellion in an Appalachian Valley* (Urbana: University of Illinois Press, 1980). I would argue, however, that neither book does operationalize its purported method, and that the success of these works is due to their abandonment of a concern with methodology.

50. See Peter T. Manicas and Arthur N. Kruger, *Logic: The Essentials* (New York: McGraw-Hill, 1976), 34–38, on real definitions.

51. I am here building upon an important essay by Terence Ball, "Power, Causation, and Explanation," *Polity* 8, no. 2 (Winter, 1975), 189–214. See also his "Models of Power: Past and Present," *Journal of the History of the Behavioral Sciences* (July, 1975), 211–22; and his "Two Concepts of Coercion," *Theory and Society* 15, no. 1 (January, 1978), 97–112.

52. See "Power," *Oxford English Dictionary* (Oxford: Clarendon Press, 1933), 1213; see also Pitkin, *Wittgenstein and Justice*, 274–79.

53. Rom Harré, "Powers," *British Journal of the Philosophy of Science* 21 (1970):85.

54. The following discussion draws heavily from Chapter 3 of my *Power and Marxist Theory: A Realist View* (Ithaca, N.Y.: Cornell University Press, 1987).

55. Giddens, *Central Problems*, 93.

56. See Peter Abell, "The Many Faces of Power and Liberty: Revealed Preference, Autonomy, and Teleological Explanation," *Sociology* 11, no. 1 (January, 1977), 3–24; K. Thomas, "Power and Autonomy: Further Comments on the Many Faces of Power," *Sociology* 12, no. 2 (May, 1978), 332–35; and G. W. Smith, "Must Radicals Be Marxists? Lukes on Power, Contestability, and Alienation," *British Journal of Political Science* 11 (1978), 405–25.

57. See particularly Polsby, *Community Power*, 223–24.

58. See Erik Olin Wright, *Classes* (London: Verso, 1985).

59. For a fine recent discussion of this, see Joel Rogers and Joshua Cohen, *On Democracy* (London: Penguin, 1984).

60. See C. Wright Mills, *The Sociological Imagination* (London: Oxford University Press, 1956).

61. See particularly Roy Bhaskar, *Scientific Realism and Human Emancipation* (London: Verso, 1986).

62. See Jürgen Habermas, *Knowledge and Human Interests*, and his "On Systematically Distorted Communication," *Inquiry* 13 (1970), 205–18.

63. On this dualism in Habermas, see Quentin Skinner's "Habermas's Reformation," *The New York Review of Books* (October 1, 1982), 35–39; on Lukes' failings in this regard, see Ted Benton, "Objective Interests and the Sociology of Power," *Sociology* 15, no. 2 (May, 1981), 161–84.

64. See George Lukács, *History and Class Consciousness* (Cambridge, Mass.: M.I.T. Press, 1971). The same problem can be found in Ralf Dahrendorf's *Class*

Conflict in Industrial Society (Stanford, Calif.: Stanford University Press, 1959), 175–79; I have criticized Benton on this in my "On Benton's 'Objective Interests and the Sociology of Power': A Critique," *Sociology* 16, no. 3 (August, 1982), 440–44.

65. On this problem within classical Marxism, see Svetozar Stojanovic's excellent *In Search of Democracy in Socialism: History and Party Consciousness* (New York: Prometheus Books, 1981); also Norman Geras, "The Controversy About Marx and Justice," *New Left Review* 150 (March–April, 1985), 47–88.

66. See Robert A. Dahl, *Polyarchy* (New Haven, Conn.: Yale University Press, 1971); *Dilemmas of Pluralist Democracy* (New Haven, Conn.: Yale University Press, 1982); *Who Governs?* (New Haven, Conn.: Yale University Press, 1959). For the argument that Dahl does not employ his own methodology in his actual research, see Peter Morriss, "Power in New Haven: A Reassessment of 'Who Governs?' " *British Journal of Political Science* 2 (1972).

67. See Michele Barret's synthetic discussion in *Woman's Oppression Today* (London: Verso, 1981).

68. Karl Marx and Freidrich Engels, "The Communist Manifesto," in *The Marx-Engels Reader,* ed. Robert C. Tucker, 1st ed. (New York: Norton, 1969), 347.

69. See my *Power and Marxist Theory,* Part II.

70. C. Wright Mills, *The Power Elite* (London: Oxford, 1956), 4–5.

71. Harold Lasswell and Abraham Kaplan, *Power and Society* (New Haven, Conn.: Yale University Press, 1950), x–xv.

72. David Easton, *The Political System* (New York: Knopf, 1953).

73. David Easton, "The Political System Besieged by the State," *Political Theory* 9, no. 3 (August, 1981):316.

74. Bob Jessop, *The Capitalist State* (New York: New York University Press, 1982), 221. For a good summary of recent arguments about the state, see Martin Carnoy's *The State and Political Theory* (Princeton, N.J.: Princeton University Press, 1984).

Notes to Chapter 4

1. M. Taylor, *Anarchy and Cooperation* (London: Wiley, 1976).

2. See J. von Neumann and O. Morgenstern, *Theory of Games and Economic Behaviour* (Princeton: Princeton University Press, 1953), for the classical account of game theory, and J. W. Friedman, *Oligopoly and the Theory of Games*

(Amsterdam: North-Holland, 1977); R. Axelrod, *The Evolution of Cooperation* (New York: Basic Books, 1984); J. Maynard Smith, *Evolution and the Theory of Games* (Cambridge: Cambridge University Press, 1982); Kreps, et al., "Rational Cooperation," *Journal of Economic Theory* 27 (1982):245–52, for more recent developments.

3. See R. Dahl, "The Concept of Power," *Behavioural Science* 2 (1957):201–15; S. Lukes, *Power: A Radical View* (London: Macmillan, 1974); and J. W. Thibaut and H. H. Kelley, *The Social Psychology of Groups* (New York: Wiley, 1959), for recent accounts.

4. T. Wartenberg, *The Forms of Power: From Domination to Transformation* (Philadelphia: Temple University Press, 1990).

5. The first part of this claim cannot be defended here for reasons of space; for the second, see Wartenberg's book, in particular Chapter 5.

6. Compare W. Balzer, C. U. Moulines, and J. D. Sneed, *An Architectonic for Science* (Dorecht: Reidel, 1987), Chapter 4 for the notion of theory-nets, and Chapter 6 for the "reduction" claim.

7. This becomes more clear when the individuals are seen in the broader context of an institution. Compare W. Balzer, "A Basic Model for Social Institutions," *Journal of Mathematical Sociology* 16 (1990).

8. See F. Mosteller and P. Nogee, "An Experimental Measurement of Utility," *Journal of Political Economy* 51 (1951):371–404, for an example.

9. Von Neumann and Morgenstern, *Theory of Games and Economic Behaviour*, 49.

10. J. S. Wentzel, *Elemente der Spieltheorie* (Leipzig: Teubner, 1964), 6. Translation is mine.

11. G. Owen, *Spieltheorie* (Berlin: Springer, 1971), 1. Translation is mine.

12. Wartenberg, *The Forms of Power*. The following definitions are taken from that book with minor variations.

13. Compare my paper on social institutions, "A Basic Model for Social Institutions."

14. Compare Wartenberg, *The Forms of Power*. I have merged his notions of control and change into that of intentional change in order to avoid a discussion of "control." We think that intentional change, though apparently weaker, covers all important aspects.

15. See Wartenberg, *The Forms of Power*. It may be noted that *bribery* also can be included in this list, though it is not treated by Wartenberg.

16. Compare Balzer, Moulines, Sneed, *An Architectonic for Science*, Chapter 6, for accounts of the intertheoretical relations mentioned.

17. P. Feyerabend, "Problems of Empiricism," in *Beyond the Edge of Certainty*, ed. R. G. Colodny (Englewood Cliffs, N.J.: Prentice-Hall), 145–260. See in particular 227, note 19.

18. This definition is a straightforward and natural generalization of my account in "On Incommensurability," in *Imre Lakatos and Theories of Scientific Change* eds. K. Gavroglu, et al. (Dordrecht: Kluwer), 287–304.

19. T. Kuhn, *The Structure of Scientific Revolutions* (Chicago: University of Chicago Press, 1970).

Notes to Chapter 5

1. Brian Fay, *Critical Social Science* (Ithaca, N.Y.: Cornell University Press, 1987), 120. My emphasis.

2. I want to stress that both the example that I am using and the model that I am developing are necessarily abstract. In order to see how situated power works, both at a theoretical level and in terms of the example of grading, I shall abstract from various other features of the concrete situation in which teachers and students find themselves in order to focus my attention upon the manner in which a set of social relationships external to the teacher-student relationship constitutes that relationship as a power relationship.

3. There are institutions of higher education like Hampshire College that evaluate rather than grade their students. I leave out of consideration how such a divergence affects the power between students and teachers. The teacher-student relationship that I am discussing here is the standard one in American higher education.

4. Fay, *Critical Social Science*, 120.

5. Fay's use of "causal outcome" in his definition of power is also problematic. My telling you that today is a holiday may have as a causal outcome a change in your actions, but this does not mean that I have exercised power over you.

6. Previous social theorists have talked about "anticipatory reaction" in this context. See Carl J. Friedrich, *Man and His Government: An Empirical Theory of Politics* (New York: McGraw-Hill, 1963), Chapter 11, for an elaboration of this concept. The problem with this concept is that it describes the existence of such power as dependent solely upon the subordinate agent.

7. What counts as a low grade will depend on both the student's perceptions and desires. A student who believes that a "B – " is a sign of intellectual failure will react differently to that grade than one who sees it as a sign of success. Although the meaning of grades is not subjective, there is a subjective factor in the assessment of them.

8. Let me stress once again that I have abstracted from the purely evaluative aspect of the grade and am considering it solely as a social measure of a student's success. Compare my earlier separation of evaluation as a universal feature of teaching relationships with grading as a particular means of evaluation.

9. I use quotation marks to indicate that although I have used language that implies that the peripheral agents intentionally cooperate with the empowered agent, power can be constituted without such intentions playing a part in them. Agents who use the grades received by a student as a reason for giving or denying her access to items they control are not thereby intending to give the teacher power over the student. Rather, their use of the grade has this effect without their explicitly intending it to. In this sense, my account of power conceptualizes it as nonintentional: An agent can have power over another agent without the intentional assistance of other agents; only a structure of differential response is necessary as a basis for the existence of a situated power relationship.

10. It is worth mentioning that the act of evaluation can ground the teacher's power in ways other than that upon which I am focusing. A student who desires to learn a skill from a teacher will experience the teacher as powerful because the teacher is able to measure how well the student has learned the skill. My point is that this type of power can be analytically distinguished from the power the teacher has as a result of the social role that a grade plays.

11. It is in this context that I would place Freud's notion of introjection. Freud's use of this concept is geared to the idea that the structure of the individual's consciousness is a reflection of certain relationships of power in the external world.

12. My description should make it clear that I have in mind the situation of certain minority groups in this country and that the source of this problem is not the educational system.

13. David Hume, *A Treatise of Human Nature,* ed. L. A. Selby-Bigge (Oxford: The Clarendon Press), 312. Hume's use of authority as the basis of the ascription of power, though not used in a contemporary sense, raises certain problems that I shall simply pass over. William McBride called my attention to this feature of Hume's claim.

14. David Hume, *Enquiry on Human Understanding,* 2nd Ed., ed. L. A. Selby-Bigge (Oxford: The Clarendon Press, 1902), Section VII, Part I, 69.

15. *Webster's Seventh New Collegiate Dictionary* (Springfield, Mass.: G. & C. Merriam Co., 1963), 22.

16. All the claims made in this discussion should be read as including a *ceteris paribus* clause.

17. I discuss this issue in my "Marx, Class Consciousness, and Social Transformation," *Praxis International* 2 (1982):52–69.

18. I follow Marx here in privileging the male worker and presume him to head a family.

19. For a more thorough development of the role of relations of power in the employment relation, see Samuel Bowles and Herbert Gintis, "Structure and Practice in the Labor Theory of Value," *The Review of Radical Political Economics* 12:4 (Winter, 1981):1–26. In my discussion, I omit their insightful consideration of the problems of actually extracting labor from the laborer. See also their contribution to this volume for a different account of such power.

20. See, for example, Michel Foucault, *The History of Sexuality, Volume 1: An Introduction,* trans. Robert Hurley (New York: Pantheon, 1978).

21. It is worth noting that the situated conception of power is not itself free of certain problematic assumptions about power made by social theorists. In particular, it treats power in a synchronic rather than a diachronic manner. For a discussion of a more dynamic model of power, see my *The Forms of Power: From Domination to Transformation* (Philadelphia: Temple University Press, 1990), Chapter 8.

Notes to Chapter 6

1. See T. Airaksinen, *The Ethics of Coercion and Authority* (Pittsburgh: The University of Pittsburgh Press, 1988). I have not introduced the idea of coercive circumstances in this paper in order to keep the discussion more manageable; see my "An Analysis of Coercion," *Journal of Peace Research* 25 (1988), 213–227.

2. For the problems of the conventional sociological theories of power, see A. Kernohan, "Social Power and Human Agency," *Journal of Philosophy* 86 (1990), 712–726. My general line of argument in *The Ethics of Coercion and Authority* agrees with Kernohan's negative conclusions on p. 726.

3. For some additional aspects of threats and offers, see M. Häyry and T. Airaksinen, "Elements of Constraint," *Analyse und Kritik* 10 (1988), 32–47.

4. The Marquis de Sade, *120 Days of Sodom,* trans. A Wainhouse and R. Seaver (New York: Grove Press, 1966).

5. Ibid., 251.

6. Ibid., 252–53.

7. R. D. Laing, *Knots* (New York: Vintage Books, 1972), 4.

8. Ibid., 40.

9. Michel Foucault, *The History of Sexuality, Vol. I: An Introduction,* trans. R. Hurley (New York: Vintage Books, 1980), 86. See also A. Kontos, "Domination: Metaphor and Political Reality," in *Domination,* ed. A. Kontos (Toronto: University of Toronto Press, 1975), 211–228.

10. Foucault, *The History of Sexuality,* 84, 85.

11. Ibid., 90.

12. See Erving Goffman, *Stigma* (Englewood Cliffs, N.J.: Prentice-Hall, 1963).

Notes to Chapter 7

1. See Horkheimer's inaugural lecture (1931) as Director of the Institut für Sozialforschung, "The State of Contemporary Social Philosophy and the Tasks of an Institute for Social Research," in ed. S. Bronner and D. Kellner, *Critical Theory and Society* (New York: Routledge, 1989), 25–36, and his contributions to the *Zeitschrift für Sozialforschung* from the early 1930s, some of which have been collected in Horkheimer, *Critical Theory* (New York: Herder and Herder, 1972) and Horkheimer, *Selected Essays* (Cambridge: M.I.T. Press, forthcoming). Habermas' renewal of this program is elaborated in *The Theory of Communicative Action,* Vols. I and II (Boston: Beacon Press, 1984, 1987). The comparison that follows would look quite different if its reference point were the version of critical theory developed by Horkheimer and Adorno in the 1940s, particularly in their *Dialectic of Enlightenment* (New York: Continuum, 1972), which is very close in spirit to the genealogy of power/knowledge Foucault practiced in the 1970s. It is that period of Foucault's work, by far the most influential in the English-speaking world, that is the other point of reference for the comparison in this section. The ethic of the self, which he developed in the 1980s, will be discussed in part III. I will not be dealing with the first phase(s) of his thought, which came to a close around 1970–71 with the appearance of "The Discourse on Language," printed as an appendix in *The Archeology of Knowledge* (New York: Harper, 1972), 215–37, and "Nietzsche, Genealogy, History," in *Language, Countermemory, Practice* (Ithaca: Cornell University Press, 1977), 139–64).

2. This includes the early Horkheimer.

3. The differences are as great among the various members of the Frankfurt School at the various stages of their careers.

4. M. Foucault, "Questions of Method," in *After Philosophy,* eds. K. Baynes, J. Bohman, T. McCarthy (Cambridge, Mass.: M.I.T. Press, 1987), 100–17, here 112.

5. M. Foucault, "Truth and Power," in Foucault, *Power/Knowledge* (New York, 1980), 109–33, here 131.

6. The application of sociological and ethnographic approaches to the natural sciences has led to similar conclusions.

7. Foucault, "Truth and Power," 131.

8. M. Foucault, *Discipline and Punish* (New York: Vintage Books, 1979), 27–28.

9. See J. Habermas, *Knowledge and Human Interests* (Boston: Beacon Press, 1971); for his development of the ideas that follow, see *The Theory of Communicative Action,* Vol. II.

10. He seems later to have adopted a more positive attitude toward hermeneutics when that was called for by his desire to appropriate—rather than merely to objectify—Greek and Roman texts on the care of the self. In a note on p. 7 of Volume Two of Foucault, *The History of Sexuality, The Use of Pleasure* (New York: Pantheon, 1985), he characterizes his approach in classically hermeneutic terms: "to examine both the difference that keeps us at a remove from a way of thinking in which we recognize the origin of our own, and the proximity that remains in spite of that distance which we never cease to explore."

11. Foucault, "Truth and Power," 119.

12. Foucault, *Discipline and Punish,* 114.

13. Foucault, "Truth and Power," 131.

14. Cf. Harold Garfinkel, *Studies in Ethnomethodology* (Cambridge, England: Polity Press, 1984).

15. N. Fraser, "Foucault on Modern Power: Empirical Insights and Normative Confusions," in Fraser, *Unruly Practices* (Minneapolis: University of Minnesota Press, 1989), 17–34, here 32.

16. Foucault, "Truth and Power," 116.

17. Ibid., 114.

18. Foucault, "Two Lectures," in *Power/Knowledge*, 78–108, here 98.

19. Ibid., 98.

20. Cf. Foucault, "Truth and Power," 117.

21. Foucault, "Two Lectures," 97.

22. See Erving Goffman, *Asylums* (Harmondsworth: Penguin, 1961).

23. See John Heritage, *Garfinkel and Ethnomethodology* (Cambridge, England: Polity Press, 1984), 103–34.

24. See, for instance, Foucault, *The History of Sexuality*, Vol. I, (New York: Vintage, 1978), 94–96.

25. Ibid., 157.

26. For a discussion of this problem, see David Michael Levin, *The Listening Self* (London and New York: Humanities Press, 1989), 90ff.

27. Charles Taylor, "Foucault on Freedom and Truth," in *Foucault: A Critical Reader*, ed. David Hoy (Oxford and New York: Blackwell, 1986), 69–102, here 91–93.

28. A revised version of part of the lecture was published as "The Art of Telling the Truth," in Michel Foucault, *Politics, Philosophy, Culture* (New York: Routledge, 1988), 86–95, here 95. Foucault sometimes writes as if the analytic of truth in general—that is, the traditional concerns with knowledge, truth, reality, human nature, and the like—should be abandoned as a lost, but still dangerous, cause. At other times, he represents it as a still viable research orientation, which, however, he chooses not to pursue. See, for example, "The Political Technology of Individuals," in *Technologies of the Self: A Seminar with Michel Foucault*, eds. L. H. Martin, H. Gutman, P. H. Hutton (Amherst: University of Massachusetts Press, 1988), 145–62, here 145. In either case, the fact that he pursues his "ontology of the present and of ourselves" separate from any (explicit) "analytic of truth" constitutes a major difference from Habermas, whose diagnosis of the present is linked to a continuation of the critical project Kant inaugurated with his three *Critiques*. I will not be able to explore that difference here.

29. In emphasizing the changes in Foucault's self-understanding in the 1980s, I am taking issue with commentators who stress the continuity with earlier work, usually by treating Foucault's later *redescriptions* of it as accurate accounts of what he was "really" up to at the time. The frequent (and varied) redescriptions he offers are, in my view, better read as *retrospectives* from newly achieved points of view. Foucault himself was often quite open about the changes. See, for instance, the three interviews conducted in January, May, and June of 1984: "The Ethic of Care for the Self as a Practice of Freedom," in *The Final Foucault*, eds. James Bernauer and David Rasmussen (Cambridge,

Mass.: The M.I.T. Press, 1988), 1–20; "The Concern for Truth," in *Politics, Philosophy, Culture,* pp. 255–267 (on p. 255 he says "I changed my mind" after the publication of Volume I of *The History of Sexuality*); and "The Return of Morality," in Foucault, *Philosophy, Politics, Culture,* 242–54 (where he says essentially the same thing on pp. 252–53). From his published writings, see for instance the introduction to Foucault, *The Use of Pleasure,* especially "Modifications," 3–13. I find this straightforward acknowledgment of a "theoretical shift" hermeneutically more satisfactory than any of the attempts to read his earlier work as if it had been written from the perspective of the 1980s. For an overview of the development of Foucault's thought and the distinctive features of the last phase, see Hans-Herbert Kögler, "Fröhliche Subjektivität. Historische Ethik und dreifache Ontologie beim späten Foucault," in *Ethos der Moderne— Foucault's Kritik der Aufklärung,* eds. E. Erdmann, R. Forst, A. Honneth (Frankfurt: Campio, 1990). For a somewhat different view, see Arnold I. Davidson, "Archeology, Genealogy, Ethics," in *Foucault: A Critical Reader,* 221–33.

30. Translated as "What Is Enlightenment?," in *Kant on History,* ed. Lewis White Beck (New York: Bobbs-Merrill, 1963), 3–11. Foucault's fullest treatment can be found in a posthumously published text with the same title, in *The Foucault Reader,* ed. Paul Rabinow (New York: Pantheon, 1984), 32–50. In the 1980s he repeatedly expressed his appreciation of Kant's essay. In addition to the text just cited, see his afterword, "The Subject and Power," to Hubert Dreyfus and Paul Rabinow, *Michel Foucault: Beyond Structuralism and Hermeneutics* (Chicago: The University of Chicago Press, 1982), 145–62, here 145; and "Structuralism and Poststructuralism: An Interview with Michel Foucault," *Telos* 55 (1983): 195–11, here 199, 206.

31. Foucault, "The Subject and Power," 216.

32. Foucault, "Polemics, Politics, and Problematizations," in *The Foucault Reader,* 381–90, here 388. Compare Foucault's remark in the introduction to Volume II of the *History of Sexuality* that the object of those studies is "to learn to what extent the effort to think one's own history can free thought from what it silently thinks, and so enable it to think differently" (9).

33. Foucault, "The Ethic of Care for the Self as a Practice of Freedom," 4.

34. The concept of "mature adulthood" (Kant's *Mündigkeit*) is discussed in Foucault's "What Is Enlightenment?," 34–35 and 39. Dreyfus and Rabinow deal with this topic in "What Is Maturity? Habermas and Foucault on 'What Is Enlightenment?,' " in *Foucault: A Critical Reader,* 109–21. But their representation of Habermas' position is misleading on key points, e.g., as regards his views on "*phronesis,* art, and rhetoric" (111), on authenticity (112), and on reaching agreement (119–20).

35. Foucault, "What Is Enlightenment?," 42; see also Foucault, "The Art of Telling the Truth," 94–95.

36. Foucault, "Space, Knowledge, and Power," in *The Foucault Reader,* 239–56, here 249.

37. "What Is Enlightenment?," 45–46. Foucault sometimes takes a line closer to Habermas', for instance when he explains that "singular forms of experience may perfectly well harbor universal structures," in the original preface to *The History of Sexuality,* Volume II, in *The Foucault Reader,* 333–39, here 335. But characteristically he immediately goes on to say that *his* type of historical analysis brings to light not universal structures but "transformable singularities" (ibid.). As we saw in part II, it nevertheless relies on an interpretive and analytic framework comprising universalistic assumptions about the structure of social action. As I shall elaborate below, the same holds for his later investigations as well, but the framework has been altered in important respects.

38. Foucault, "What Is Enlightenment?," 48.

39. Ibid., 43. Foucault explicitly gives preference to "specific" and "partial" transformations over "all projects that claim to be global or radical" and "any programs for a new man" (46–47). Compare Habermas' remarks in *Knowledge and Human Interests,* 284–85. There are many similarities between the Foucault of "What Is Enlightenment?" and the earlier Habermas, who pursued "an empirical theory of history with a practical intent." Cf. my account of this phase of Habermas' thought in *The Critical Theory of Jürgen Habermas* (Cambridge, Mass.: The M.I.T. Press, 1978), Chapters 1, 2, and 3.

40. Unpublished manuscript, 7. He is apparently referring to the scheme Habermas proposed in his inaugural lecture at Frankfurt University in 1965 (printed as the appendix to *Knowledge and Human Interests,* 301–17) and subsequently altered. On p. 313 Habermas characterized his three dimensions of analysis as labor, language, and domination (*Herrschaft*).

41. Martin et al., eds., *Technologies of the Self,* 18–19. It is clear, however, that he has not yet fully disengaged from the power ontology, for all four types of technologies are said to be "associated with" domination, and he characterizes his new field of interest as "the technologies of individual domination." See note 64 below.

42. Foucault, "The Subject and Power," 217–18.

43. Foucault, *The Use of Pleasure,* 4. A version of this appears in his discussions with Dreyfus and Rabinow at Berkeley in April, 1983, "On the Genealogy of Ethics: An Overview of Work in Progress," in *The Foucault Reader,* 340–72, here 351–52. It is elaborated in the original preface to Volume II, 333–39, as a distinction between fields of study, sets of rules, and relations to self.

44. Foucault, "The Subject and Power," 219, 221.

45. Ibid., 221.

46. Ibid., 224.

47. Ibid., 222.

48. Foucault, "The Ethic of Care for the Self as a Practice of Freedom," 11–12. This interview, conducted in January of 1984, was twice reworked and edited by Foucault before he authorized its publication. The formulations that appear are thus no mere accidents of the occasion. See *Freiheit und Selbsorge*, eds. H. Becker, et al. (Frankfurt: Materials, 1985), 7, 9.

49. Ibid., 19. The categories of power, domination, and strategy are of course used earlier as well, but not with the same meanings. In Volume I of *The History of Sexuality*, for instance, "states of power" are said to be generated by virtue of the *inequality* of force relations (93), and power is said to be exercised in *nonegalitarian* relations (94); "major dominations" arise as the hegemonic effects of wide-ranging cleavages that run through the social body as a whole (94), while strategies are embodiments of force relations (93, with example on 104–105).

50. Ibid., 18.

51. Ibid., 20.

52. Foucault's three-part definition of "strategy" in "The Subject and Power," 224–25, is conventional enough. It is said to designate: a) means-ends rationality aimed at achieving some objective; b) playing a game with a view to gaining one's own advantage; and c) the means to victory over opponents in situations of confrontation.

53. See "What Is Universal Pragmatics?," in Habermas, *Communication and the Evolution of Society* (Boston: Beacon Press, 1979), 1–68, esp. 59–65, and Habermas, *The Theory of Communicative Action*, Vol. I, 273–37.

54. See Foucault, "The Subject and Power," 220.

55. Ibid., 218.

56. Foucault, "The Ethic of Care for the Self as a Practice of Freedom," 18.

57. Ibid., 18.

58. See Foucault's discussion of the "morality that concerns the search for truth" in "Polemics, Politics, and Problematizations," 381–82, in which he describes what are essentially symmetric conditions among dialogue partners. See also his account of the role that communication with others played in the care of the self, in *The History of Sexuality*, Volume III (New York: Random House, 1986), 51–54. The reciprocity of helping and being helped by others

that he describes there hardly accords with his official view of social relations as strategic relations.

59. Foucault draws a distinction between the "strategic" and "technological" sides of "practical systems" in, for instance, "What Is Enlightenment?," 48.

60. The original preface to *The History of Sexuality*, Vol. II, 337–39.

61. Foucault, *The History of Sexuality*, Vol. I, 11.

62. Foucault, "Omnes et Singulatim: Towards a Criticism of Political Reason," in *The Tanner Lectures on Human Values*, Vol. II, ed. Sterling McMurrin (Salt Lake City: The University of Utah Press, 1981), 225–54, here 227.

63. Ibid., 240.

64. For example, in his Howison Lectures delivered at Berkeley the next fall (1980), he describes his project as an investigation of the historical constitution of the subject that leads to the modern concept of the self (manuscript, Lecture I, 4), and goes on to say that he is focusing on "techniques of the self" by which "individuals effect a certain number of operations on their own bodies, on their souls, on their own thoughts, on their conduct" (I, 7). Though he clearly distinguishes such techniques from "techniques of domination," they have to be understood precisely in relation to them (ibid.). The "point of contact" between the two is government: "When I was studying asylums, prisons, and so on, I insisted too much on the techniques of domination . . . But that is only one aspect of the art of governing people in our societies. . . . [Power] is due to the subtle integration of coercion technologies and self technologies. . . . Among [the latter], those oriented toward the discovery and formulation of the truth concerning oneself are extremely important." (I, 8) Accordingly, in the closing passage of his lectures, he asks rhetorically whether the time has not come to get rid of these technologies and the sacrifices linked to them (II, 20). In the first part of "The Subject and Power," 208–16, which was delivered as a lecture at the University of Southern California the following fall (1981), the way in which we turn ourselves into subjects is described as an element in the "government of individualization" (212). At the same time, however, Foucault notes the increasing importance of struggles against "forms of subjection" exercised through "individualizing techniques" (213), the shaping of individuals to ensure their integration into the modern state (214). And he concludes with a line that could serve as the epigraph of his last studies: "The political, ethical, social, philosophical problem of our days is not to try to liberate the individual from the state and from the state's institutions, but to liberate us both from the state and from the type of individualization which is linked to the state. We have to promote new forms of subjectivity through the refusal of this kind of individuality which has been imposed on us for several centuries" (216). In an outline of his 1980–81 course at the Collège de France, "Subjectivité et vérité," which dealt with the materials of

the final volumes of *The History of Sexuality*, Foucault locates the care of the self at the crossroads of the history of subjectivity and the analysis of forms of governmentality. Studying its history enables him "to take up again the question of 'governmentality' from a new point of view: the government of self by self in its articulation with relations to others," M. Foucault, Résumé des cours 1970–82 (Paris, 1989), 134–36.

65. Foucault, "On the Genealogy of Ethics," 340. The subordination of his interest in sexuality as such to a broader problematization of techniques of self-formation is clearly stated in those volumes. It is, he writes, with sexual behavior as a "domain of valuation and choice" and with the ways in which "the individual is summoned to recognize himself as an ethical subject of sexual conduct" that the later studies are concerned (II, 32). Thus, his analyses of "prescriptive discourses" about diatetics, household management, erotics, and so forth focus on the modes of subjectivation presupposed and nourished in the corresponding practices. Very briefly, the genealogy of "desiring man" as a self-disciplined subject" is Foucault's key to the genealogy of the "subject of ethical conduct" (II, 250–51); and this is itself an element in a more comprehensive "history of truth" (II, 6). Similarly, in analyzing *parrhēsia*, or truth-telling, in antiquity, Foucault conceives of the genealogy of the parrhesiastic subject, the truth-teller, as part of the "genealogy of the critical attitude in Western philosophy," M. Foucault, *Discourse and Truth: The Problematization of Parrhēsia*, transcription by Joseph Pearson of a seminar given at the University of California, Berkeley, in the fall of 1983, 114. These connections suggest the continuing relevance of Foucault's work to what I referred to as the critique of impure reason.

66. Ibid., 341.

67. Ibid., 348.

68. Ibid., 352.

69. Foucault, "The Ethic of Care for the Self," 2–3.

70. Ibid., 6–7. The connections between governmentality, care of the self, and strategic interaction are suggested on pp. 19–20 of the same interview: " . . . in the idea of governmentality I am aiming at the totality of practices by which one can constitute, define, organize, instrumentalize the strategies which individuals in their liberty can have in regard to each other. It is free individuals who try to control, to determine, to delimit the liberty of others, and in order to do that, they dispose of certain instruments to govern others. That rests indeed on freedom, on the relationship of the self to self and the relationship to the other." On the relation between self-mastery and the mastery of others in antiquity, see Foucault, *The History of Sexuality*, Volume II, 73ff.

71. Foucault, "An Aesthetics of Existence," in *Philosophy, Politics, Culture*, 47–53, here 49. Foucault's later studies abound in comparisons between ethi-

cal practices in antiquity and in Christianity. See, for example, *The History of Sexuality*, Vol. II, 92, 136–39, and Vol. III, 68, 140ff., 165, 235ff. These comparisons, so patently unfavorable to Christianity, bespeak Foucault's own commitment to an ethopoetics of existence. In my view, an analysis of the evaluative presuppositions underlying Foucault's last works—which are ostensibly constructed in a nonevaluative, descriptive mode—would reveal them to be more or less the ones he openly espoused in the lectures, interviews, and methdological asides of the last period. In neither phase should the absence of explicit value *judgments* in his sociohistorical studies obscure the presence of implicit value *orientations* underlying them. (Compare Weber's distinction between *Werturteile* and *Wertbeziehungen*.) But the large gap between the avowed and the actually operative frameworks of evaluation in the 1970s (see the essay by Nancy Fraser cited in note 15 above) was considerably closed in the 1980s.

72. Foucault, *The Use of Pleasure*, 25–26.

73. Ibid., 29.

74. Ibid., 30.

75. Ibid., 29.

76. Foucault, "An Aesthetics of Existence," 49. See also "On the Genealogy of Ethics," 343, and "The Concern for Truth," 262–63.

77. Foucault, *The Use of Pleasure*, 10.

78. Foucault, "What Is Enlightenment?," 42.

79. Nor, for that matter, is it Socrates', Plato's, or Aristotle's. There is more than one way to take issue with Foucault's notion of an ethics of self-invention. I will be stressing Kant's connection of autonomy to a rational will, but problems could also be raised from the standpoint of the ethics of community, character, virtue, and the like.

80. Foucault, "The Concern for Truth," 253.

81. Foucault, *The Use of Pleasure*, 21.

82. See Habermas, *Moral Consciousness and Communicative Action* (Cambridge, Mass., 1990) and Habermas, *The Theory of Communicative Action*, Vol. II, 92–111.

83. Foucault, "On the Genealogy of Ethics," 44. The masculinist and dominative orientation of Greek ethics is stressed throughout Volume II of *The History of Sexuality*. See, for example, 69–77, 82–86, 146–51, and 215–25.

84. Foucault, "Politics and Ethics: An Interview," in *The Foucault Reader*, 373–80, here 379.

85. Foucault, "On the Genealogy of Ethics," 348.

86. Ibid., 350.

87. Ibid., 350.

88. "Fröhliche Subjektivität," Unpublished Manuscript, 29.

89. Foucault, *The Use of Pleasure*, 10. To be sure, the studies of self-formative processes in Volumes II and III of *The History of Sexuality* do view classical practices of the self in their sociocultural contexts. But Foucault is himself opposed to the shaping of individuals to fit societal contexts, be it as citizens of the Greek polis or of the modern state. As he conceives it, the practice of the self is a practice of liberty precisely insofar as it frees self-formation from such functional contexts. The question of whether this is compatible with any type of social order is left largely open, as is that of the new types of community to which it could give rise. These are of course very important questions for *social* movements struggling to change *socially* imposed identities and to have those changes *legally* and *institutionally* secured. I am indebted to Michael Kelly for a discussion of this point.

Notes to Chapter 8

1. Michel Foucault, *The History of Sexuality*, trans. Robert Hurley (New York: Vintage, 1980), Vol. 1. The particular title of this volume is *The Will to Knowledge*. I will occasionally refer to the book by that title. All translations, from this and other French texts, have been modified when necessary.

2. Ernesto Laclau and Chantal Mouffe's provocative and influential *Hegemony and Socialist Strategy: Towards A Radical Democratic Politics*, trans. Winston Moore and Paul Cammack (London: Verso, 1985) must be counted among these.

3. For the academic circumstances, see Didier Eribon, *Michel Foucault* (Paris: Flammarion, 1989), 144–47. Roy Boyne, *Foucault and Derrida: The Other Side of Reason* (London: Unwin Hyman, 1990) sees Foucault's entire subsequent project as a considered response to Derrida's early critique, going beyond the published reply, which was confined to "the sociological phenomenon of academic disputations" (88).

4. Irene Diamond and Lee Quinby, eds. *Feminism and Foucault: Reflections on Resistance* (Boston: Northeastern University Press, 1988).

5. Zillah R. Eisenstein, *The Female Body and the Law* (Berkeley: University of California Press, 1988), 6–41.

6. Edward Said, "Michel Foucault, 1926–1984," in ed. Jonathan Arac *After Foucault: Humanistic Knowledge, Postmodern Challenges* (New Brunswick: Rutgers University Press, 1988), 1–2.

7. Foucault, *History of Sexuality*, 93. The two following passages are also on this page.

8. Ed. David Couzens Hoy, *Foucault: A Critical Reader* (London: Blackwell, 1987), 135. The following passage is on the same page.

9. Ibid., 128, 136. Emphasis is mine.

10. For a different and most interesting sense of nominalism, see Etienne Balibar, "Foucault et Marx. L'enjeu du nominalisme," in *Michel Foucault: Philosophe* (Paris: Seuil, 1989), 74–75.

11. To compile a responsible balance sheet of the two bodies of thought, to bring about an articulation, is a somewhat different enterprise. For a consideration of Foucault's politics from a deconstructive point of view, see Tom Kennan, "I. The 'Paradox' of Knowledge and Power: Reading Foucault on a Bias," *Political Theory* XV.i (Feb., 1987): 5–32. For a broader articulation, see Boyne, *Foucault and Derrida*. This book came to my attention after I had completed the initial draft of this chapter. Although I cannot agree with many of the details of interpretation in it, I am in general sympathy with Boyne's careful attempt at articulation. By contrast, my chapter does not offer a survey but rather moves outward in irregular circles from one sentence in Foucault. I should perhaps refer the reader also to an earlier text relating Foucault and Derrida: Gayatri Chakravorty Spivak, "Can the Subaltern Speak?," in *Marxism and the Interpretation of Culture*, eds. Larry Grossberg and Cary Nelson (Urbana: University of Illinois Press, 1988), 271–311.

12. Jacques Derrida, *Of Grammatology*, trans. Spivak (Baltimore: Johns Hopkins University Press, 1976), 47. The rest of the citations in this paragraph are from the same passage.

13. Jacques Derrida, "Force of Law," trans. Mary Quinaire, paper presented at conference on "Deconstruction and the Possibility of Justice," Cardozo School of Law, Yeshiva University, Oct. 1989.

14. Boyne's sense of "reason-in-general" in Derrida is much more localized than my own reading of the general and the narrow.

15. Richard Rorty, "Moral Identity and Private Autonomy," *Foucault philosophe*, 388.

16. Jürgen Habermas, *The Philosophical Discourse of Modernity*, trans. Frederick Lawrence (Cambridge: M.I.T. Press, 1987), 185–210. I have discussed this at length in the last chapter of *Master Discourse, Native Informant: Deconstruction in the Service of Reading* (Harvard University Press, forthcoming).

17. Rorty, "Moral Identity," 390.

18. Although Habermas is more respectful toward Foucault, he puts him with Derrida in his insistence that Foucault is too "literary," *Modernity,* 238.

19. Richard Rorty, "Habermas and Lyotard on Postmodernity," in *Habermas and Modernity,* ed. Richard J. Bernstein (Cambridge, M.I.T. Press, 1985), 173.

20. The discussion of the Heideggerian swerve begins in Derrida, "The Ends of Man," in *Margins of Philosophy,* trans. Alan Bass (Chicago: University of Chicago Press, 1982) and continues throughout his work with many clinamens. The Foucault passage on Heidegger is from "Final Interview," trans. Thomas Levin and Isabelle Lorenz, in *Raritan* V.i (Summer, 1985), 8. It is characteristic of Habermas' strong misreading of Foucault that he sees the connection with Heidegger, articulates it as yet another failure to use German material, contrasts Foucault yet once again with Adorno who did so much better along this line, and finally diagnoses the Heidegger connection as an irritating affinity for Foucault to acknowledge! (Habermas, *Modernity,* 256–57.) It is beyond the scope of this chapter to engage with Pierre Bourdieu's account of the Heideggerian trajectory itself in *The Political Ontology of Heidegger,* trans. Peter Collier (Cambridge: Polity Press, forthcoming). In note 42 I will suggest that Foucault's published critique of Derrida did not match his final wisdom about the uselessness of mere polemic. Here I am obliged to say that, in trivializing Foucault's silence, Derrida withholds from him the patience that he otherwise prescribes: "Impatience is never justified. It should incite one to take one's time and to submit oneself to what is not self-evident, without avoiding it," introduction to Philippe Lacoue-Labarthe, *Typography: Mimesis, Philosophy, Politics,* trans. Christopher Fynsk (Cambridge: Harvard University Press, 1989), 15. Derrida's rhetoric at the end of the dismissive footnote on page 17 of the same essay can describe both Foucault's treatment of Heidegger and Derrida's treatment of Foucault within "a kind of film of the French philosophical scene in this quarter-century. To be deciphered: again the avoiding of the unavoidable." These matters should caution us about the inhibiting script of our own academic scene implicated in our own philosophicopolitical production rather than the correct line of Foucault/Derrida. I thank Sonu Shamdasani of the Freud Museum for bringing this note to my attention.

21. Jacques Derrida, "*Comment Donner Raison?* 'How to Concede, With Reasons?,' " *Diacritics* XIX.3–4 (Fall-Winter, 1989):8. This is no place for undertaking a commentary on Derrida's turning of Heidegger. As of this writing, Herman Rapaport, *Heidegger and Derrida: Reflections on Time and Language* (Lincoln: University of Nebraska Press, 1989) is perhaps the most recent extended publication on this.

22. Martin Heidegger, *Being and Time,* trans. John Macquarrie and Edward Robinson (New York: Harper and Row, 1962), 39; emphasis mine.

23. Michel Foucault, *La volonte de savoir* (Paris: Gallimard, 1976), 122.

24. This pervasive suggestion in Derrida begins to appear as early as "Structure, Sign, and Play, in the Sciences of Man," in *The Structuralist Controversy*, eds. Richard Macksey and Eugenio Donato (Baltimore: The Johns Hopkins University Press, 1970).

25. Jean Baudrillard is excited by the electric metaphor and understands the need for catachresis in his *Forget Foucault* (New York: Semiotext(e), 1987), 33ff. But he is so intent on proving the superiority of his own idea that the real is forgettable, that he seeks to demolish Foucault's notion of power by complaining that there *is* no such example of power to be found in reality!

26. Walter J. Ong, *Orality and Literacy: the Technology of the Word* (New York: Methuen, 1982).

27. Rorty, "Moral Identity," 388.

28. *The Common Good: Social Welfare and the American Future* (New York: Ford Foundation, 1989), 2.

29. Hoy, "Power, Repression," in *Foucault*, ed. Hoy, 142–43.

30. Ibid., 139.

31. Michel Foucault, "The Subject and Power," in *Michel Foucault: Beyond Structuralism and Hermeneutics*, eds. Hubert L. Dreyfus and Paul Rabinow (Chicago: University of Chicago Press, 2nd ed., 1983), 225.

32. For a detailed discussion of these aggregative apparatuses, see Gilles Deleuze, "Qu'est-ce qu'un dispositif," in *Foucault philosophe*, 185–93.

33. Habermas' casual inattention is nowhere more marked than in his bulldozing of this passage, with no reference: "In his later studies Foucault will . . . comprehend power as the interaction of warring parties, as the decentered network of bodily, face-to-face confrontations, and ultimately as the productive penetration and subjectivizing subjugation of a bodily opponent" (*Modernity*, 255).

34. Francois Ewald (of Richard Rorty), "Compte rendu des discussions," *Foucault philosophe*, 39ff.

35. Karl Marx, *Capital*, trans. David Fernbach (New York: Viking-Penguin, 1981), Vol. 3, 959. I have presented an interpretation of this passage in terms of Marx's theory of practice in *Master Discourse*.

36. Jacques Derrida, "Cogito and the History of Madness," in *Writing and Difference*, trans. Alan Bass (Chicago: University of Chicago Press, 1978), 49; word order rearranged for coherent citation.

37. Although Hegel is not mentioned in Derrida's essay, this extinction may be dramatized in the break between the Absolute Necessity of Being and

the beginning of Determinate Being in Hegel's *Science of Logic,* trans. A. V. Miller (New York: Humanities Press, 1969), 108–109.

38. Derrida, "Cogito," 57–58, 61.

39. Ibid., 60. Was Foucault right or wrong in rapping Derrida on the knuckles in his well-known response, "My Body, This Paper, This Fire," trans. Geoff Bennington, *Oxford Literary Review* IV.i (Autumn, 1979)? Let the more mature Foucault provide the answer: "There are the sterilizing effects: Has anyone ever seen a new idea come out of a polemic? And how could it be otherwise, given that here the interlocutors are incited, not to advance, not to take more and more risks in what they say. . . . " "Polemics, Politics, and Problemizations," in *The Foucault Reader,* ed. Paul Rabinow (New York: Pantheon, 1984). Derrida's point is not really about dreams and madness. But Foucault has a lot at stake in dreams. For the reader of the exchange, it remains interesting that Foucault's avowed origin is in the decipherment of dreams; Michel Foucault and Ludwig Binswanger, *Dream and Existence,* trans. Forrest Williams and Jacob Needleman, a Special Issue from *Review of Existential Psychology and Psychiatry* XIX.i, 1984–85. The end is also with a book of dreams: *The Care of the Self* opens with Artemidorus' *Interpretation of Dreams.*

40. I believe this to be so much an ordinary-language aspect of the doublet that most French interpretations simply take it for granted. See, for example, *Foucault philosophe,* 61, 65, 95–96, 207. Deleuze's book, *Foucault,* trans. Sean Hand (Minneapolis: University of Minnesota Press, 1988) comes alive if this is kept in mind.

41. For relevant discussions in the later Foucault, see "The Ethic of Care for the Self as a Practice of Freedom," in *The Final Foucault,* ed. James Bernauer and David Rasmussen (Cambridge: M.I.T. Press, 1988), 114, 122–23, 130. At this point the ontico-ontological *difference* has been rewritten as an entry way: "I have tried to know [*savoir*] how the human subject entered into games of truth"; *pouvoir-savoir* rendered into "how games of truth can put themselves in place and be linked to relationships of power" (ibid., 112, 127). And Foucault cautions about the burden of paleonymy: "The word 'game' can lead you into error: when I say 'game,' I say an ensemble of rules for truth-production [*je dis un ensemble de règles de production de la vérité*]."

42. This fits the U.S. case. Looking forward to my last section, let me simply remind the reader that the possibilities within a feminist pedagogy of the oppressed in decolonized areas are of course much more complicated.

43. Michel Foucault, *The Archaeology of Knowledge and the Discourse on Language,* trans. A. M. Sheridan Smith (New York: Pantheon, 1972), 15ff. The next passage is on p. 119.

44. Ibid., 79–80.

45. For a staging of this see Derrida, "My Chances/*Mes Chances:* A Rendezvous with Some Epicurean Stereophonics," in *Taking Chances: Derrida, Psychoanalysis, and Literature,* eds. Joseph H. Smith and William Kerrigan (Baltimore: The Johns Hopkins University Press, 1984).

46. Michel Foucault and Ludwig Binswanger, *Dream and Existence,* trans. Forrest Williams and Jacob Needleman, *Review of Existential Psychology and Psychiatry* XIX.i (1984–85). "To study forms of experience in this way—in their history—is an idea that originated with an earlier project, in which I made use of the methods of existential analysis in the field of psychiatry and in the domain of 'mental illness' " (Preface to the *History of Sexuality,* Vol. 2, in Rabinow, *Foucault Reader,* 334). At that earlier stage, Foucault conceived of his project in Husserlian terms. But the lineaments of the thematic—of making the constitutive rupture workable—that I have been at pains to disclose are straining through. "Phenomenology has managed to make images speak; but it has given no one the possibility of understanding their language.... The dream is situated in the ultimate moment in which existence is still its world: once beyond, at the dawn of wakefulness, already it is no longer its world.... Analysis of a dream starting from the images supplied by waking consciousness must precisely have the goal of bridging that distance between image and imagination.... Thus is the passage from anthropology to ontology, which seems to us from the outset the major problem of the analysis of Dasein, actually accomplished" (Foucault and Binswanger, 42, 59. 73). With benefit of hindsight, one can see the way clear from the rarefied *énoncé* of the *Archaeology* to the ethical self-constitution of the final phase: "The dream is not meaningful only to the extent that psychological motivations and physiological determinations interact and cross-index in a thousand ways; on the contrary, it is rich by reason of the poverty of its objective context [English translation unaccountably has "content" here].... Cultural history has carefully presented this theme of the ethical value of the dream" (Ibid., 44, 52).

47. Quoted in Eribon, *Foucault,* 94.

48. Foucault, *Archaeology,* 16.

49. Boyne, *Foucault and Derrida,* 32; the next passages are from 35, 70. I have quoted these three passages from Boyne to demonstrate his feeling for the readings, though not necessarily for their philosophical moorings and unmoorings.

50. Jacques Derrida, *Glas,* trans. John P. Leavey, Jr., and Richard Rand (Lincoln: University of Nebraska Press, 1986).

51. Michel Foucault, *Folie et déraison: Histoire de la folie a l'âge classique* (Paris: Plon, 1961).

52. "I did not want to make the history of that language; rather the archaeology of that silence" (Ibid., v).

53. Dreyfus and Rabinow, *Michel Foucault,* 209.

54. See Derrida, "The Ends of Man." Dreyfus can make the case for a substantive affinity between Heidegger's Being and Foucault's power by rendering Heidegger into what I shall later call the Anglo-U.S. episteme and by refusing to "read" all the passages from Foucault that he cites, in "De la mise en ordre des choses," in *Foucault philosophe.*

55. This point of view is to be found in Rorty, "Moral Identity."

56. Andre Glucksmann, "Le nihilisme de Michel Foucault," in *Foucault philosophe,* 389.

57. Jacques Derrida, "The Politics of Friendship," *Journal of Philosophy* LXXV.11 (November, 1988):632–44. This is an abridged version of a longer, unpublished paper, "Of Friendship, Of Democracy." See also Introduction to Lacoue-Labarthe, *Typography.*

58. Jacques Derrida, "Violence and Metaphysics," in *Writing and Difference,* 79–153.

59. In view of Derrida's intense concern for "the sign 'man' " since "The Ends of Man," Boyne's note 18 on *Foucault and Derrida,* 89, is surprising. Major Derrida texts inspired by this concern are *Glas* and *The Post Card,* trans. Alan Bass (Chicago: University of Chicago Press, 1986). On the latter, see Gayatri Chakravorty Spivak, "Love Me, Love My Ombre, Elie," in *Diacritics* XIV.iv (Winter, 1984).

60. James Joyce, *Finnegans Wake* (New York: Viking, 1969), 51.

61. Dreyfus and Rabinow, *Foucault,* p. 240. The earlier passage is from Foucault, "An Aesthetics of Existence," in John Johnston, tr. *Foucault Live: (Interviews, 1966–84)* (New York: Semiotext(e), 1989), p. 312, 310–311.

62. Preface to *History of Sexuality,* Vol. II, 339.

63. "Ethic of care," 118.

64. Ibid., 256.

65. Rabinow, *Foucault Reader,* 389.

66. Habermas, *Modernity,* 256. Thus, I must read Thomas Flynn's account of the change in Foucault's last lectures as, strictly speaking, a displacement upon the constituted subject where it *is* the agent of truth-telling rather than simply a changeover to "the subject as the 'agent' of truth-telling"; Thomas Flynn, "Foucault as Parrhesiast, His Last Course as the College de France," in *The Final Foucault,* eds. James Bernauer and David Rasmussen, 79–80. Flynn's lovely essay can take this reading on board. As he writes: "It is clear that Foucault continued to respect these 'structuralist' concepts as he insisted that

we 'rethink the question of the subject.' . . . He was not growing soft on subjectivism"; Flynn, "Parrhesiast," 225.

67. Foucault, "Final Interview," 12. Emphasis mine. The following quote is from 22.

68. Foucault, "Polemics," in Rabinow, *Foucault Reader,* 389.

69. Foucault, "Ethic of Care," 115.

70. For (im)possibility, see Gayatri Chakravorty Spivak, *In Other Words: Essays in Cultural Politics* (New York: Methuen, 1987), 263, 308, n. 81. For "persistent critique of what you cannot not want," see Spivak, "The Making of Americans, the Teaching of English, and the Future of Culture Studies," in *New Literary History* (forthcoming) and Spivak, "Remembering the Limits: Difference, Identity, and Practice," in *Socialism and the Limits of Liberalism,* ed. Peter Osborne (London: Verso, forthcoming). Flynn signals the final shift as follows: "What is at issue is not a 'testing' of one's life once and for all but an on-going practice, a certain style of life"; Flynn, "Parrhesiast," 219. In the model I derive from Derrida, it is the testing itself that is an askew, ongoing, practical counterpoint, employing all the subterfuges of any serious *techne.* After this writing, I read Derrida's introduction to *Typography.* The "gymnastics" of the "cannot not" are recited there in the motif of "rhythm," "pirouette," more cryptically "desistance." Following this route, or falling into this abyss, the opposition between "critical" and "dogmatic/positive" will itself be an indefinite double bind. My work, as a rule, honors this in the breach (or the abyss) and remains "after" the "mistake" (de)constituting politics.

71. Against Habermas' feeling that for Foucault, "the politics that has stood under the sign of the revolution since 1789 has come to an end" (*Modernity,* 282), or Rorty's that Foucault's "remoteness . . . reminds one of the conservative who pours cold water on hopes for reform, who affects to look at the problems of his fellow-citizens with the eye of the future historian" (Rorty, "Habermas and Lyotard," 172) is the final Foucault's counterpointed distance: "We have a subject who was endowed with rights or who was not and who, by the institution of a political society, has received or has lost rights. . . . On the other hand, the notion of governmentality allows one, I believe, to set off the freedom of the subject and the relationship to others, i.e., that which constitutes the very matter of ethics"; Foucault, "Ethic of Care," 131.

72. Pizzorno, "Foucault et la conception libérale de l'individu," *Foucault philosophe,* 238.

73. Flynn, "Parrhesiast," 227.

74. Foucault, "Ethic of Care," 113–14.

75. Bhikhu Parekh, "Identities on Parade," *Marxism Today* (June, 1989):27.

76. I cannot go here into the considerable difference in historicopolitical inscription of our two philosophers. Suffice it to say that as a Sephardic Jew growing up in North Africa, Derrida is not exactly a participating member in the colonial enterprise.

77. Rorty, "Moral Identity," 387.

78. Mohasweta Devi, "Draupadi," "Breastgiver," in Gayatri Chakravorty Spivak, *In Other Worlds: Essays in Cultural Politics* (New York: Methuen, 1987). A discussion of "The Hunt" is to be found in Spivak, "Who Claims Alterity?," in eds. Barbara Kruger and Phil Mariani, *Remaking History* (Seattle: Bay Press, 1989).

79. Michel Serre, "Literature and the Exact Sciences," *Substance XVIII.ii (1989):*4. The subsequent passages are from 6, 23.

80. Devi, *Imaginary Maps,* trans. Spivak (New York: Routledge, Chapman and Hall, forthcoming).

Notes to Chapter 9

1. Bernard Boxill, *Blacks and Social Justice* (Totowa, N.J.: Rowman and Allenheld, 1984).

2. Marlene Fried, "The Invisibility of Oppression," *The Philosophical Forum* XI, no. 1 (1979):18–29.

3. Marilyn Frye, "Oppression" in *The Politics of Reality* (Trumansburg, N.Y.: The Crossing Press, 1983), 1–16.

4. Marilyn Friedman and Larry May, "Harming Women as a Group," *Social Theory and Practice,* 11, no. 2 (1985):207–234.

5. Peter French, "Types of Collectivities and Blame," *The Personalist* 56 (1975):160–69.

6. Cf. Jeffrey Ross, Introduction to *The Mobilization of Collective Identity,* eds. Ross and Cottrell (Lanham, Md.: University Press of America, 1980); also, Joseph Rothschild, *Ethnopolitics* (New York: Columbia University Press, 1981).

7. Dennis Altman, *The Homosexualization of America* (Boston: Beacon Press, 1982).

8. Milton Fisk, *Ethics and Society* (New York: New York University Press, 1980), Part I.

9. E.g., Nicos Poulantzas, *Classes in Contemporary Capitalism* (London: Verso Books, 1975).

10. Cf. Manuel Castells, *The Economic Crisis and American Society* (Princeton, N.J.: Princeton University Press, 1980), 138–61.

11. See Roger Gottlieb, *History and Subjectivity* (Philadelphia: Temple University Press, 1987).

12. See R. P. Wolff, *Understanding Marx* (Princeton, N.J.: Princeton University Press, 1984).

13. John Roemer, *A General Theory of Exploitation and Class* (Cambridge: Harvard University Press, 1982).

14. Alan Buchanan, *Marx and Justice* (Totowa, N.J.: Rowman and Allenheld, 1980).

15. C. B. MacPherson, *Democratic Theory: Essays in Retrieval* (Oxford: Clarendon Press, 1973), especially Chapter III.

16. Cf. Buchanan, *Marx and Justice*, 44–49; Nancy Holmstrom, "Exploitation," *Canadian Journal of Philosophy*, VII, no. 2 (1977):353–69.

17. Anthony Giddens, *A Contemporary Critique of Historical Materialism* (Berkeley: University of California Press, 1981), 242; Arthur Brittan and Mary Maynard, *Sexism, Racism and Oppression* (Oxford: Basil Blackwell, 1984), 93; Raymond Murphy, "Exploitation or Exclusion?" *Sociology* 19, no. 2 (May, 1985):225–43; Herbert Gintis and Samuel Bowles, *Capitalism and Democracy* (New York: Basic Books, 1986).

18. Christine Delphy, *Close to Home: A Materialist Analysis of Women's Oppression* (Amherst: University of Massachusetts Press, 1984).

19. See her "Women as a New Revolutionary Class" in *Between Labor and Capital*, ed. Pat Walker (Boston: South End Press, 1979) and "On Conceiving Motherhood and Sexuality: A Feminist Materialist Approach" in *Mothering: Essays in Feminist Theory*, ed. Joyce Trebilco (Totowa, N.J.: Rowman and Allenheld, 1984).

20. Cf. Brittan and Maynard, *Sexism*, 142–48.

21. Barbara Easton, "Feminism and the Contemporary Family," *Socialist Review* 39 (May/June 1978):11–36.

22. Rhonda Gottlieb, "The Political Economy of Sexuality," *Review of Radical Political Economy* 16, no. 1 (1984):143–65.

23. Carol Brown, "Mothers, Fathers and Children: From Private to Public Patriarchy" in *Women and Revolution*, ed. Lydia Sargent (Boston: South End Press, 1981), 239–68; cf. Ellen Boris and Peter Bardaglio, "The Transformation of Patriarchy: The Historic Role of the State" in *Families, Politics and Public*

Policy, ed. Irene Diamond (New York: Longman, 1983), 79–93; Kathy Ferguson, *The Feminist Case Against Bureaucracy* (Philadelphia: Temple University Press, 1984).

24. David Alexander, "Gendered Job Traits and Women's Occupations" (Ph.D. Dissertation, University of Massachusetts, 1987).

25. Michael Reich, *Racial Inequality* (Princeton, N.J.: Princeton University Press, 1981).

26. Al Symanski, "The Structure of Race," *Review of Radical Political Economy* 17, no. 4 (1985):106–20.

27. Gintis and Bowles, 1986.

28. Nancy Fraser, "Women, Welfare, and the Politics of Need Interpretation," *Hypatia: A Journal of Feminist Philosophy* 2, no. 1 (Winter, 1987):103–22; Ferguson, *The Feminist Case,* 1984, Chapter 4.

29. Carol Gilligan, *In a Different Voice* (Cambridge, Harvard University Press, 1982); Marilyn Friedman, "Care and Context in Moral Reasoning" in *Moral Dilemmas: Philosophical and Psychological Issues in the Development of Moral Reasoning,* ed. Carol Harding (Chicago: Precedent, 1985).

30. Virginia Held, "A Non-Contractual Society" (paper given at Conference on Feminist Moral, Legal and Political Theory, University of Cincinnati, November, 1986).

31. Claus Offe, *Disorganized Capitalism: Contemporary Transformation of Work and Politics* (Cambridge: M.I.T. Press, 1986), Chapters 1–3.

32. Max Weber, "Classes, Status Groups and Parties" in *Weber: Selections in Translation,* ed. W. G. Runciman (Cambridge: Cambridge University Press, 1978), 43–64; David Beetham, *Max Weber and the Theory of Modern Politics* (Oxford: Polity Press, 1985), 79–82.

33. Richard Sennet and Jonathan Cobb, *The Hidden Injuries of Class* (New York: Vintage Books, 1972).

34. Maria C. Lugones and Elizabeth V. Spelman, "Have We Got a Theory for You! Feminist Theory, Cultural Imperialism and the Demand for 'The Woman's Voice,' " *Women's Studies International Forum* 6, no. 6 (1983):573–81.

35. Nancy Fraser, "Social Movements vs. Disciplinary Bureaucracies: The Discourses of Social Needs," CHS Occasional Paper #8 (Center for Humanistic Studies, University of Minnesota, 1987), 1–37.

36. W. E. B. DuBois, *The Souls of Black Folks* (New York: Signet, 1903, 1969).

Notes to Chapter 10

1. Abba Lerner, "The Economics and Politics of Consumer Sovereignty," *American Economic Review* 62 (1972):259.

2. For reasons that will become clear in our concluding section, we think that what we term "post-Walrasian economics" marks a significant break with the neoclassical tradition, though whether or not to call these economists "neoclassical" seems of purely terminological interest. See, in particular, Joseph Stiglitz, "The Causes and Consequences of the Dependence of Quality on Price," *Journal of Economic Literature* 25 (March, 1987):1–48; George Akerlof and Janet Yellen, *Efficiency Wage Models of the Labor Market* (Cambridge: Cambridge University Press, 1986); Oliver Williamson, *The Economic Institutions of Capitalism* (New York: The Free Press, 1985); Louis Putterman, "On Some Recent Explanations of Why Capital Hires Labor," in *The Economic Nature of the Firm*, ed. Putterman (Cambridge: Cambridge University Press, 1986); Gregory Dow, "The Function of Authority in Transaction Cost Economics," *Journal of Economic Behavior and Organization* 8 (1987):13–38; and our own contributions to this literature: Herbert Gintis, "The Nature of the Labor Exchange and the Theory of Capitalist Production," *Review of Radical Political Economics* 8 (1976):36–54; Samuel Bowles, "The Production Process in a Competitive Economy: Walrasian, Neo-Hobbesian, and Marxian Models," *American Economic Review* 75,1 (March, 1985):16–36; Samuel Bowles and Herbert Gintis, "The Inefficiency and Competitive Survival of the Capitalist Firm," Department of Economics Working Paper 1989–6 (University of Massachusetts, May, 1989); and Samuel Bowles and Herbert Gintis, "Power and Wealth in a Competitive Capitalist Economy," Department of Economics Working Paper 1989–10 (June 1989). In this last paper, we comment on post-Walrasian economic theory, its varieties, its relationship to neoclassical economics, and our relationship to it.

3. Milton Friedman, *Capitalism and Freedom* (Chicago: University of Chicago Press, 1962), 109–10.

4. Armen Alchian and Harold Demsetz, "Production, Information Costs, and Economic Organization," *American Economic Review* 62 (December, 1972):777.

5. Paul Samuelson, "Wages and Interest: A Modern Dissection of Marxian Economics," *American Economic Review* 47 (1957):894.

6. This is obviously not a necessary condition for A to have power over B in the ordinary (plural) senses of the term. Our conception of power is relational (characteristic not of an individual, but of a relationship among individuals) and interest-based (rather than behavioral). This conception of power as a dyadic relation between agents may at first glance appear too narrow to include such central forms of power as the ability to set the decision-making

agenda facing agents—Peter Bachrach and Morton Baratz, *Power and Poverty: Theory and Practice* (New York: Oxford University Press, 1970)—or the capacity to influence agents' preferences and conception of their interests—Steven Lukes, *Power: A Radical View* (London: Macmillan, 1974). However, we show that in general economic equilibrium and agenda-setting power (e.g., control of the decision-making structure of the enterprise) flow from power in our more limited sense. And as will become clear, what we somewhat loosely term an interest-based concept of power does not preclude, but rather illuminates, the endogenous formation of preferences. We treat these questions at greater length in Bowles and Gintis, "Power and Wealth in a Competitive Capitalist Economy."

7. The purchasing power conferred by a high income thus would be termed "power" according to Dahl's well-known definition: "A has power over B to the extent that he can get B to do something that B would not otherwise do"; Robert A. Dahl, "The Concept of Power," *Behavioral Science* 2 (1957):202–203. Yet according to our usage, which stresses sanctions as integral to the exercise of power, this is not power over these other agents who, by the implementation of their optimal equilibrium-defining programs, are on the margin indifferent to exactly which services they provide or to whom they are provided, and who therefore are not subject to sanctions by any of their trading partners.

8. For a more complete treatment of the theory of contested exchange and its political implications, see Samuel Bowles and Herbert Gintis, "Contested Exchange: New Microfoundations for the Political Economy of Capitalism," *Politics and Society* (June, 1990), 165–222.

9. We refer to these as enforcement mechanisms or strategies rather than adopting the broader term "transaction costs." Transaction costs, as used by Williamson (*The Economic Institutions of Capitalism*), pertain to much more than enforcement of claims arising in contested exchanges; in any case the distinction between transaction costs and production costs cannot be made coherent when production technologies are selected with their enforcement capabilities in mind. (We avoid the term "enforcement costs" for the same reason.) Our analysis is limited to the case in which enforcement problems are present on only one side of the exchange. By addressing cases in which one side of the exchange provides a monetary payment (for which the costs of monitoring are assumed to be zero), we set aside the more general problem of 'bilateral endogenous enforcement,' in which both parties to exchange exercise strategic power. See Masahiko Aoki, *The Co-operative Game Theory of the Firm* (London: Clarendon, 1984).

10. The following arguments are developed in a more complete manner in Bowles, "The Production Process in a Competitive Economy," Herbert Gintis and Tsuneo Ishikawa, "Wages, Work Discipline, and Unemployment," *Journal of Japanese and International Economies* 1 (1987):195–28, and Bowles and Gintis,

"Contested Exchange: New Microfoundations for the Political Economy of Capitalism."

11. More generally, the short side of an exchange is located where the total amount of desired transactions is least: the demand side if there is excess supply and the supply side if there is excess demand. See Jean-Pascal Benassy, *The Economics of Market Disequilibrium* (Orlando: Academic Press, 1982).

12. We have explored the implications of democratic accountability in Samuel Bowles and Herbert Gintis, "The Power of Capital: On the Inadequacy of the Conception of the Capitalist Economy as 'Private,' " *Philosophical Forum* xiv, 3–4 (Spring–Summer, 1983), and Herbert Gintis, "Financial Markets and the Political Structure of the Enterprise," *Journal of Economic Behavior and Organization* 1 (1989):311–22, and "The Principle of External Accountability in Financial Markets," in *The Firm as a Nexus of Treaties,* Masahiko Aoki, Bo Gustafsson, and Oliver Williamson (New York: Russell Sage, 1989).

13. Note that being on the short side of a nonclearing market does not in itself ensure that an agent has short-side power. Since such a market does not clear, short-sider A can indeed impose sanctions on long-sider B. However, A need not have the ability to use this capacity in any way to affect B's behavior.

14. For a development of this theme, see Gintis, "The Nature of the Labor Exchange"; James Devine and Michael Reich, "The Microeconomics of Conflict and Hierarchy in Capitalist Production," *Review of Radical Political Economics* 12,4 (Winter, 1982):27–45; Samuel Bowles and Herbert Gintis, "The Marxian Theory of Value and Heterogeneous Labor: A Critique and Reformulation," *Cambridge Journal of Economics* 1 (1977):173–92; and Samuel Bowles, "The Production Process in a Competitive Economy: Walrasian, Neo-Hobbesian, and Marxian Models," *American Economic Review* 75,1 (March, 1985):16–36.

15. Stephen Marglin, "What Do Bosses Do?," *Review of Radical Political Economics* 6 (1974):60–112.

16. We define wealth as property rights in assets for which exogenously enforceable contracts may be written; thus, land, buildings, and money are wealth, a college degree or even a skill is not. We will consider 'human capital' forms of wealth presently.

17. Adolph A. Berle and Gardiner C. Means, *The Modern Corporation and Private Property* (New York: Macmillan, 1932); Robin Marris, *The Economic Theory of "Managerial" Capitalism* (New York: The Free Press, 1963).

18. Erik Olin Wright, "What Is Middle about the Middle Class?," in *Analytical Marxism,* ed. John Roemer (Cambridge: Cambridge University Press, 1986), 116.

19. Erik Olin Wright, "Class Boundaries in Advanced Capitalist Societies," *New Left Review* 98 (1976). In more recent work Wright has criticized the

contradictory class location framework because, among other things, "it tends to shift the analysis of class relations from exploitation to domination" and thus to favor "the 'multiple oppressions' approach to understanding society"; Wright, "What is Middle about the Middle Class?," 116–17. Yet we do not see exploitation and domination as competing concepts, having argued in Samuel Bowles and Herbert Gintis, *Democracy and Capitalism: Property, Community, and the Contradictions of Modern Social Thought* (New York: Basic Books, 1986), Ch. 4, that exploitation is a form of domination that cannot be defined independent of the political relations among agents. Nor do we believe that racial or gender oppression reduces to class oppression or that class phenomena have any explanatory priority in principle over other forms of domination.

20. John Roemer, *Free to Lose* (Cambridge: Harvard University Press, 1988), 54.

21. Adam Przeworski, *Capitalism and Social Democracy* (Cambridge: Cambridge University Press, 1985), 234.

22. The studies in question involve the measurement of the cost of job loss, the relationship between the cost of job loss on the one hand and strike incidence (a direct measure of labor intensity) and the rate of change of labor productivity on the other, the relationship between the workers' fallback position and movements in the real wage and the profit rate, and even movements in United States monetary policy. See James Rebitzer, "Unemployment, Long Term Employment Relations, and Productivity Growth," *Review of Economics and Statistics* 69,4 (November, 1987):624–35; Juliet B. Schor, "Does Work Intensity Respond to Macroeconomic Variables? Evidence from British Manufacturing, 1970–1986," *Harvard Institution of Economic Research, Discussion Paper #1379* (April, 1988); Samuel Bowles, David Gordon, and Thomas Weisskopf, *Beyond the Waste Land: A Democratic Alternative to Economic Decline* (New York: Doubleday, 1983); "Hearts and Minds: A Social Model of U.S. Productivity Growth," *Brookings Papers on Economic Activity* 2 (1983); "Power and Profits: The Social Structure of Accumulation and the Profitability of the Postwar U.S. Economy," *Review of Radical Political Economics* 18, 1,2 (1986):132–67; "Business Ascendancy and Economic Impasse: A Structural Retrospective on Conservative Economics, 1979–1987," *Journal of Economic Perspectives* 3,1 (Winter, 1989):107–34; *After the Wasteland: A Democratic Economy for the Year 2000* (Armonk, N.Y.: M. E. Sharpe, 1990); Juliet B. Schor and Samuel Bowles, "Employment Rents and the Incidence of Strikes," *Review of Economics and Statistics* 64,4 (November, 1987):584–91; Francis Green and Thomas Weisskopf, "The Worker Discipline Effect: A Disaggregative Analysis," *Review of Economics and Statistics* LXXII, 2 (May 1990), 241–49; and Gerald Epstein and Juliet Schor, "Macropolicy in the Rise and Fall of the Golden Age," in *The Rise and Fall of the Golden Age: Lessons for the 1990's*, ed. Stephen Marglin (Oxford: Oxford University Press, 1989). We doubt that the strong support for the contested exchange framework evident in these studies of the United States would be forthcoming for all capitalist economies. Empirical support for capital rationing in the in-

ternational economy is presented in Gerald Epstein and Herbert Gintis, "An Asset Balance Model of International Capital Market Equilibrium," in *Financial Openness and National Autonomy*, eds. Tariq Banuri and Juliet B. Schor (Oxford: Oxford University Press, forthcoming).

23. This defense of an activist state-planning function in a market environment may appear similar to arguments for the selective use of markets, as in Oskar Lange and Fred M. Taylor, *On the Economic Theory of Socialism* (Minneapolis: University of Minnesota Press, 1938). It differs, however, by stressing the disciplinary as well as the allocative aspect of markets.

24. Janos Kornai, *The Economics of Shortage* (New York: North Holland, 1980).

25. Price may exceed marginal cost in addition because firms face downward-sloping demand curves, are sales-constrained due to aggregate demand failures, or for other reasons. See Gintis, "The Power to Switch."

26. For instance, under reasonable conditions we would expect worker-run firms in a market economy to be superior in terms of productive efficiency, but to choose investment projects involving a socially suboptimal degree of risk-taking. See Gintis, "Financial Markets and the Political Structure of the Enterprise" and "The Principle of External Accountability in Financial Markets."

27. Here Douglass North's recent work *Structure and Change in Economic History* (New York: Norton, 1981) represents a major contribution to the post-Walrasian theory of institutional structure and evolution, while his earlier work is closer to the Walrasian tradition. See also Margaret Levi, *Of Rule and Revenue* (Berkeley: University of California Press, 1988).

28. Failure to analyze the effect of schooling on the labor market enforcement environment was our main critique of human capital theory in Samuel Bowles and Herbert Gintis, "The Problems with Human Capital Theory," *American Economic Review* 65,2 (May, 1975):74–82, and *Schooling in Capitalist America: Educational Reform and the Contradictions of Economic Life* (New York: Basic Books, 1976). On the effect of the welfare state on enforcement environments see Samuel Bowles and Herbert Gintis, "The Crisis of Liberal Democratic Capitalism," *Politics and Society* 11 (1982):51–93, "The Welfare State and Long-Term Economic Growth: Marxian, Neoclassical, and Keynesian Approaches," *American Economic Review* 72,2 (May, 1982):341–45, and Schor and Bowles, "Employment Rents and the Incidence of Strikes."

29. This theme is developed using a repeated prisoner's dilemma game in Samuel Bowles, "Mandeville's Mistake: The Moral Autonomy of the Market Reconsidered," University of Massachusetts Economics Department Working Paper (1990), and Albert Hirschman, *Exit, Voice, and Loyalty* (Cambridge: Harvard University Press, 1970).

Notes to Chapter 11

1. The controversy over Dr. Linda S. Gottfredson's work on race and I.Q. illustrates that this is still a live issue. Dr. Gottfredson is Associate Professor of Education Studies at the University of Delaware.

2. The psychologist J. Philippe Ruston of the University of Western Ontario supports the idea of a racial hierarchy in intelligence with Asians as the most intelligent race, whites next most intelligent, and blacks the least intelligent. It is worth noting that the research on race and I.Q. by Gottfredson, Ruston, and Schockley was all supported by the controversial Pioneer Fund. According to its charter, one purpose of the fund is to give financial support to "Children . . . descended predominately from persons who settled in the original 13 states prior to the adoption of the Constitution."

3. *Proceedings and Addresses of the American Philosophical Association* 63, No. 5 (1990):62–63.

4. Noam Chomsky, *For Reasons of State* (New York: Random House, 1973).

5. N. J. Block and Gerald Dworkin, "I.Q., Heritability, and Equality," in *The I.Q. Controversy,* eds. Block and Dworkin (New York: Random House, 1976), 410–540.

6. Ibid., 361.

7. See A. R. Jensen, *Genetics and Education* (New York: Harper & Row, 1972), 69–204, and "How Much Can We Boost IQ and Scholastic Achievement?," *Atlantic Monthly* (September 1971):43–64; W. Shockley, "Dysgenics, Geneticity, Raceology: A Challenge to the Intellectual Responsibility of Educators," *Phi Delta Kappan* (January, 1972):297–307.

8. See, for example, Linda S. Gottfredson, "Societal Consequences of the g Factor in Employment," *Journal of Vocational Behavior* 29, No. 3 (1986):379–410; J. E. Hunter, "Cognitive Ability, Cognitive Attitudes, Job Knowledge, and Job Performance," *Journal of Vocational Behavior* 29, No. 3 (1986):340–62; A. R. Jensen, "g: Artifact or Reality?," *Journal of Vocational Behavior* 29, No. (1986):301–31; R. L. Thorndike, "The Role of General Ability in Prediction," *The Journal of Vocational Behavior* 29, No. 3 (1986):332–39.

9. Hugo Iltis, *Life of Mendel,* trans. Eden and Cedar Paul (New York: W. W. Norton and Co., 1932), esp. the preface and Chapter 8.

10. Chomsky, *For Reasons of State,* 360.

11. Thomas Kuhn, "The Structure of Scientific Revolutions," *Foundations of the Unity of Science,* Vol. 2, No. 2 (1970).

12. Block and Dworkin, *I.Q.,* 517–18.

13. Leon J. Kamin, "Heredity, Intelligence, Politics, and Psychology: II," in Block and Dworkin, *I.Q.*, 376–81.

14. Aristotle, *Nicomachean Ethics*, trans. Martin Ostwald (New York: Bobbs-Merrill Co., 1966).

15. See Hart and Honoré, *Causation in the Law*, 2nd Ed. (Oxford: Oxford University Press, 1985), 73.

16. Ibid., 74.

17. Ibid., 73.

18. Jeremy Waldron, "A Right to Do Wrong," *Ethics* 92, No. 1 (1981):21–39.

19. Ibid., 21.

20. Ibid., 35.

21. Ibid., 37.

22. I am grateful to Gerald Dworkin, Mary Gibson, Douglas Husak, William Lawson, Walton Johnson, and the late Irving Thalberg, Jr., for their comments and criticisms of earlier drafts of this chapter.

Notes to Chapter 12

1. See, for example, Elizabeth Janeway, *Powers of the Weak* (New York: Alfred A. Knopf, 1980).

2. See, for example, David C. McClelland, *Power: The Inner Experience* (New York: Irvington, 1979).

3. Donald W. Winnicott, *Playing and Reality* (New York: Basic Books, 1971).

Notes to Chapter 13

1. Susan Griffin, *Rape: The Power of Consciousness* (New York: Harper & Row, 1979); Andrea Medea and Kathleen Thompson, *Against Rape* (New York: Farrar, Strauss and Giroux, 1974); Heidi Hartmann and Ellen Ross, "Comments on 'On Writing the History of Rape,' " *Signs* III, 4 (Summer, 1978):931–35.

2. See Susan Brownmiller, *Against Our Will* (New York: Simon and Schuster, 1975), 423–24. My own view is that it is more an assault than a robbery, the latter term being too bound up with an exchange mentality.

3. See, for example, Medea and Thompson, *Against Rape*, 32. See also Brownmiller's conversations with reporters in Vietnam, in *Against Our Will*, 87–118.

4. *Women Against Violence Against Women* Newsletter (June, 1976): 1.

5. "Snuff" films claim not only to depict a woman's death and dismemberment, but also as one of the selling points of the advertising that the actress is really killed on camera. See Beverly La Bell, "Snuff—the Ultimate in Woman-Hating," in *Take Back the Night*, ed. Laura Lederer (New York: Morrow, 1980).

6. Editors *Aegis* (November/December, 1978):3.

7. Gloria Steinem, "Erotica and Pornography: A Clear and Present Difference," in *Take Back the Night*, 38.

8. Paula Webster, "Pornography and Pleasure," *Heresies* 12 (1980):49–50.

9. For the quotation, see Virginia Barker, "Dangerous Shoes, or What's a Nice Dyke Like Me Doing in a Get-up Like This," *Coming to Power*, ed. Samois Collective (Palo Alto: Up Press, 1981).

10. For these countercharges, see Samois, *Coming to Power*, and Gayle Rubin, "Thinking Sex," in *Pleasure and Danger*, ed. Carol Vance (Boston: Routledge and Kegan Paul, 1984). The statement from MacKinnon is from "Feminism, Marxism, Method and the State: An Agenda for Theory," *Signs* 7, No. 3 (Spring, 1982):515–16.

11. This is the stated purpose of a collection of feminist essays, *Against Sadomasochism* eds. Robin Ruth Linden, Darlene R. Pagano, Diana E. H. Russell, Susan Leigh Star (East Palo Alto: Frog in the Wall Press, 1982). Similar arguments have been made about butch-femme relationships and role-playing.

12. Audre Lorde and Susan Leigh Star, "Interview with Audre Lorde," in *Against Sadomasochism*, 68, 70.

13. Carol Vance, "Pleasure and Danger: Toward a Politics of Sexuality," *Pleasure and Danger*, 2, 6–7.

14. See, for example, Jeffrey Weeks' critique of the antipornography movement, *Sexuality and Its Discontents* (London and Boston: Routledge and Kegan Paul, 1985), 236.

15. Joan Cocks, *The Oppositional Imagination* (New York: Routledge, 1989), 157. She discusses a number of different bodily/erotic possibilities despite the dominance of phallocratic culture.

16. This says several things: 1) They do not represent all 'our' ideas or the ideas and experiences of the rest of us; 2) they of necessity become to different extents 'our' ideas; and 3) to say these are the dominant views does not make statements about the lived experience of sexuality. See, for example Cocks, *The Oppositional Imagination*, and Vance, *Pleasure and Danger*, 17.

17. Robert Stoller's restatement of Freud, in *Perversion* (New York: Pantheon, 1975), 12–14.

18. Jeffrey Weeks, *Sex, Politics, and Society* (Essex, U.K.: Longman, 1981), 12.

19. This argument is made in much more depth by Robert Padgug, "Sexual Matters," *Radical History Review* 20 (Spring–Summer, 1979), quoted material from 11. I should note that while his case is similar to mine, he does not focus as much as I do here on the effects of structured social relations. Nor am I using his definition of *praxis* as "language, consciouness, symbolism and labor" since that strikes me as too compartmentalized.

20. Weeks, *Sex, Politics, and Society*, 12. Weeks gives a series of factors to be taken as guidelines in studying sexuality: he includes the kinship and family system, economic and social changes, changing forms of social regulation, the political moment, and the existence of cultures of resistance.

21. See especially Jeffrey Weeks' discussion of the different strategies of investigating sexuality in "Sex, Politics, and Society," 1–18; *Radical History Review*, Special Issue on Sexuality No. 20 (Spring/Summer, 1979); Sherry B. Ortner and Harriet Whitehead, "Accounting for Sexual Meanings," in *Sexual Meanings: The Cultural Construction of Gender and Sexuality*, eds. Sherry Ortner and Harriet Whitehead (New York: Cambridge University Press, 1981), 1–27; Adrienne Rich, "Compulsory Heterosexuality and Lesbian Existence," *Signs* V, No. 4 (Summer, 1980), 631–60; Ann Ferguson, Jacquelyn Zita, and Kathryn Pyne Addelson, "On Compulstory Heterosexuality and Lesbian Existence: Defining the Issues," *Signs* VII, No. 1 (Autumn, 1981), 158–99.

22. One can find these assumptions in, for example, Amber Hollibaugh and Cherrie Moraga, "What We're Rolling Around in Bed With," *Heresies* 12 (1981), 58–62; Paula Webster, "Pornography and Pleasure," *Heresies* 12 (1981), 48. Webster does not state that masculinity and femininity are social constructions, but at the same time argues that the images one gets in pornography are at least demystifying and that our fantasies can be used to map the zones of arousal, thus accepting unquestioningly the erotic conventions of our culture. See also Barbara Lipschutz, "Cathexis," in *What Color Is Your Handkerchief?* (Berkeley, Calif.: Samois, 1979), 9. One of the basic problems that appears in much of this feminist literature is what while authors state that they see sexuality as a cultural creation, they often go on to argue in ways that suggest that changing one's sexuality is an impossibility: one must simply accept it. But if sexuality is a social relation and is culturally and historically specific, then those who are committed to changing other social relations must include sexuality as one of the dimensions of existence open to change.

23. See, for example, Andrea Dworkin, *Intercourse* (New York: Free Press, 1987), 170–94, and Jeffrey Weeks, *Sexuality and Its Discontents*, 61–72.

24. I should note at the outset that I have many difficulties with the positions he takes; I note them here in part to indicate that the points of his that I use are just that and not an endorsement of the position he puts for-

ward. In particular, I oppose his unquestioning acceptance of the existence of the vaginal orgasm—Robert Stoller, *Sexual Excitement: The Dynamics of Erotic Life* (New York: Pantheon, 1979), 88, and *Perversion* (New York: Pantheon, 1975), 23; his stress on the centrality of maternal responsibility in producing "normal" heterosexuals—*Perversion*, 138, 154, 161; and his account of how people become homosexuals—e.g., *Perversion*, 153. Nor do I share his concerns: I do not believe homosexuality should be considered either a perversion or a diagnosis, nor am I interested in the psychological origins of gender identity; see *Perversion*, xvi, 199ff. At times as well, Stoller's discussion is marred by a masculine understanding of the world, e.g., his statement that "it is hard to imagine a little girl, confronted with this task, who would not envy boys and their aggressive, penetrating, hedonistic, arrogant, unfettered, God-granted, antisocial, unsympathetic, humiliating penis"—*Sexual Excitement*, 74. Thus, he seems to accept without question the social and cultural meanings associated with the penis.

25. Stoller, *Sexual Excitement*, 26.

26. Ibid., 6.

27. Ibid., 23, 76.

28. See Stoller, *Perversion*, 8, 59, *Sexual Excitement*, 8.

29. Andrea Dworkin, *Pornography: Men Possessing Women* (New York: W. B. Putnam's Sons, 1979), 182, quoting Alfred C. Kinsey, Wardell B. Pomeroy, Clyde E. Martin, and Paul H. Gebhard, *Sexual Behavior in the Human Female* (Philadelphia: W. B. Saunders and Co., 1953), 705. She adds that the reference indicates that this physiology is true of both males and females. Her own style of presentation suggests that she does not believe this to be true.

30. A. H. Maslow, "Self-Esteem (Dominance-Feeling) and Sexuality in Women," *Journal of Social Psychology* 16 (1942):291, quoted by Stember, 145.

31. Charles H. Stember, *Sexual Racism* (New York: Harper and Row, 1976), 150, quoting Kate Millet, *Sexual Politics* (New York: Doubleday, 1970), 304.

32. George Bataille, *Death and Sensuality* (New York: Arno Press, 1977), 90. The italics are mine.

33. O. Mannoni, *Prospero and Caliban* (New York: Praeger, 1964), 111, quoted by Stember, 164.

34. Stember, 149. The gender dimensions of this statement are not accidental, nor is the notion of pollution. See also Dworkin, *Intercourse*, 174–79.

35. See the immediate following discussion in Deirdre English, Amber Hollibaugh, and Gayle Rubin, "Talking Sex: A Conversation on Sexuality and Feminism," *Socialist Review* 58 (July–August, 1981):52.

36. Barbara Lawrence, "Four-Letter Words *Can* Hurt You," in *Philosophy and Sex*, eds. Robert Baker and Frederick Elliston (Buffalo, N.Y.: Prometheus Books, 1975), 32.

37. Stoller, *Perversion*, 7, 105–109, *Sexual Excitement*, 18–21.

38. Ibid., xii. This is a common psychoanalytic position; see also Ann Snitow, "Mass Market Romance: Pornography for Women Is Different," *Radical History Review* 20 (Spring/Summer, 1979):153.

39. Stoller, *Sexual Excitement*, 113.

40. Kathleen Barry, *Female Sexual Slavery* (New York: Avon Books, 1979), 230. These myths have been important tools of white and male domination, and have provided important ideological supports for lynching.

41. Ibid., 233.

42. Stoller, *Sexual Excitement*, 23, 33, respectively.

43. Ibid., 13, 35, 31, respectively.

44. See also Stoller, *Perversion*, 208.

45. Robert Stoller, *Observing the Erotic Imagination* (New Haven: Yale University Press, 1985), 3, 43.

46. Dworkin, *Pornography*, 135.

47. Ibid., 136.

48. Ibid., 151.

49. Stoller, *Sexual Excitement*, 74.

50. Ibid., 124. See also Stoller, *Perversion*, 58 where Stoller argues that the masochist is never really a victim because she or he never really relinquishes control.

51. Dworkin, *Pornography*, 158.

52. Stoller, *Imagination*, 35–40.

53. Ibid., 4.

54. Ibid., 7.

55. Ibid., 56.

56. One can compare Barry's definition of perversion as "not just that which is wrong, bad, or evil, but that which distorts, devalues, depersonalizes, warps, and destroys the person as she or he exists in time and space. It involves destruction of the human being in fact. Accordingly . . . sexuality that is

fostered through the arrested male sex drive which objectifies, forces, and violates, whether it is heterosexual or homosexual, is perversion." Objectification itself, she argues, is perversion. (See Barry, *Female Sexual Slavery,* 266.)

57. See Stoller, *Perversion,* 97, xvii, respectively.

58. Paul Gebhard, John H. Gagnon, Wardell B. Pomeroy, and Cornelia V. Christenson, *Sex Offenders: An Analysis of Types* (New York: Harper and Row, 1965), 6, cited in Dworkin, *Pornography,* 52 (italics mine).

59. Stoller, *Perversion,* 9.

60. Ibid., 88 and 135ff, 98, respectively.

61. Stoller, *Sexual Excitement,* 220–21.

62. Stoller, *Perversion,* 89–91.

63. On this point, Stoller seems to subscribe to the idea/argument that sexuality is a social construction when he notes that female masochism should be expected to be related to women's power in a particular culture and states that masochism should not at all be considered a biological drive; *Sexual Excitement,* 119, 122.

64. This in and of itself should not be surprising. McClellan's work, since redone by Matina Horner, on need for achievement, or Lawrence Kohlberg's work on the stages of moral development, since redone by Carol Gilligan and Susan Freeman, provide two important examples of other areas in which this has been true.

65. Ibid., 35–37.

66. Janice Moulton, "Sex and Reference" in *Philosophy and Sex,* eds. Robert Baker and Frederick Elliston (Buffalo, N.Y.: Prometheus Books, 1975), 34–45.

67. Ibid., 36.

68. Ibid., 36.

69. See Barry, *Female Sexual Slavery,* 255ff, where she cites a number of authors in support of her point.

70. Amber Hollibaugh, "Talking Sex," *Socialist Review* 58 (July–August, 1981):46. Dierdre English laments the "total lack of images of women being motivated by sexual desire," Ibid., 53.

71. Carole Vance, "Gender Systems, Ideology, and Sex Research: An Anthropological Analysis," *Feminist Studies* VI, 1 (Spring, 1980):133. See also Weeks, *Sex, Politics, and Society,* 3, where he notes that among those who see sex as a driving force, it is held to be basically male, and to have a firmly heterosexual orientation.

72. William F. Whyte, "A Slum Sex Code," *American Journal of Sociology* 49 (July, 1943):27, cited in Stember, 146.

73. Kate Millet, *Sexual Politics* (New York: Doubleday, 1970), 327, cited in Stember, 146.

74. Stember, 150.

75. My point here is identical in form to Marx's point that the ideology of the ruling class expresses the dominant material relations in the form of ideas, and that this ideology (and the institutions that support it) structures the existence of the dominated classes as well.

76. I should note that my definition here differs from that of others who have used the term. Stoller uses the term as a narrower reference than "sexuality." Thus, he argues that most of what we label sexual excitement has many different parts, only one of which can be characterized as erotic excitement. The others include triumph, rage, revenge, fear, anxiety, and risk. (*Sexual Excitement*, 26.) In contrast I take eros to be the more inclusive term. Nor is my definition the same as that put forward by Susan Griffin, who states "The very force of eros, the very brilliance of vitality, the irrepudiability of feeling, that eros cannot be reasoned out of existence . . . "; Susan Griffin, *Pornography and Silence* (New York: Harper and Row, 1981), 77.

77. Sigmund Freud, *Civilization and Its Discontents,* trans. Joan Riviera (Garden City, N.Y.: Doubleday, 1958), 57. Freud, however, does not recognize the possibility of making one out of more than two.

78. Ibid., 42–43.

79. Plato, *Republic* I: 329c and III: 403d, respectively, in *The Collected Dialogues of Plato,* trans. Paul Shorey (Princeton: Princeton University Press, 1978). All references to dialogues are from this collection unless otherwise noted. In this context, the uniqueness of Marx's contribution to political thought is marked by the centrality of the place given to human sensuous experience, one indicating a respect for rather than devaluation of the body, with all its needs and failings. What could be more explicit than his critique of Feuerbach's materialism for not conceiving of reality itself as "human sensuous activity"? "Thesis I," in *The Marx-Engels Reader,* 1st Ed., ed. Robert Tucker (New York: W. W. Norton and Co., 1972), 143.

80. See Dorothy Dinnerstein, *The Mermaid and the Minotaur* (New York: Harper and Row, 1976), 140. Note her discussion of Norman Brown's *Life Against Death* (Middletown, Conn.: Wesleyan University Press, 1959), 135–51. See also Herbert Marcuse, *Eros and Civilization* (Boston: Beacon Press, 1955).

81. Freud, *Civilization and Its Discontents,* 21.

82. Marcuse, *Eros and Civilization,* 211.

83. Ibid., 220, 222. I differ with him on the possibilities for a resexualized work since it seems that the pleasure of acting on the world is in itself an erotic one.

84. Stoller, *Perversion*, 64–65.

85. Ibid., 86, 91, respectively.

86. Ibid., 4, 80; Stoller, *Sexual Excitement*, 77.

87. Stoller, *Perversion*, 105.

88. Ibid., 99. I should note that Stoller makes this point in the context of an argument that perversion "may be a gender disorder in the development of masculinity." On this point, see my argument in Chapter X of *Money, Sex and Power: Toward a Feminist Historical Materialism* (New York: Longman, 1983).

89. Ibid., 119; Stoller, *Sexual Excitement*, 13.

90. Stoller regards this as a tentative hypothesis (*Sexual Excitement*, 21). He notes in *Perversion* that the perversion is a fantasy that is a defensive structure raised to preserve pleasure and that perversion arises as a way of coping with one's gender identification (xiv, xii, respectively). The stress on gender differentials occurs in *Observing the Erotic Imagination*, 34–36.

91. See Griffin, *Pornography and Silence*, 144. I have relied heavily on her description of the major themes to be found in contemporary pornography, but I have many fundamental and important disagreements with her. I do not believe that the problems we face can be traced to the pornographic *mind*. Nor do I believe that pornography endangers our lives because action begins in the mind and then moves to reality. Rather, I hold that what endangers our lives is the same social structure that produces pornography as well as other attacks on humanity. Griffin misses the importance of institutions, in part because she focuses on the mind. Thus, she can hold that the pornographer cuts off the heads of nature, and others grow, and for this reason the violence must accelerate. In addition, I am not concerned as Griffin is to address questions of whether the pornographer is a revolutionary of the imagination or whether pornography is catharsis—worthy subjects, but not my own. Nor do I think pornography is fundamentally rooted in religion (as she claims, p. 16). Nor do I share the mysticism that invades her work; e.g., her references to "sacred image of the goddess, the sacred image of the cow, the emblematic touch of divinity in the ecstasy of the sexual act . . . " (71). I find her elevation of the heart as an organ between mind and appetite difficult to accept (81). Why not the liver? I found myself asking. The heart as a model for feeling is a cultural, not universal, construction. I list this variety of disagreements to indicate my various difficulties with her analysis and to indicate that as with Stoller's work, points are being taken over and used in my own framework of analysis. I should note in addition that I found it extremely difficult to trans-

late Griffin's account into my own terms. Thus, the footnote references to *Pornography and Silence* should be seen as references to the parts of her work in which I found the material I make use of and to places where her work highlighted issues for me, not as references to arguments she has made, unless clearly indicated as such.

92. Ibid., 34.

93. Stoller, *Perversion*, 57.

94. Barry, *Female Sexual Slavery*, 208–209.

95. Se Griffin, *Pornography and Silence*, 41, 49; Stoller, *Perversion*, 133.

96. Stoller, *Perversion*, 133.

97. Griffin, *Pornography and Silence*, 122–23.

98. Ibid., 89, 90.

99. See Griffin's chapter on silence, Ibid., 201–50.

100. Dworkin, *Pornography*, 25–26.

101. Griffin, *Pornography and Silence*, 61. Griffin's point here is echoed by Stoller, who underlines that the major way for looking to be sexually exciting is for the man to believe he is acting sadistically and revengefully on an unwilling woman (*Perversion*, 108–109).

102. Griffin, *Pornography and Silence*, 91, quoting Normal Mailer, *An American Dream* (New York: Dell, 1965), 9.

103. See Amands Spake, "The End of the Ride," *Mother Jones* (April, 1980). The quotation is from 40. This case set off much public outrage, and when Singleton was released from prison a number of communities protested when they discover he was a resident.

104. George Bataille, *Death and Sensuality*, 91. See 91ff for a more complete account of the commonalities of sexual activity and ritual sacrifice.

105. Dinnerstein, *The Mermaid and the Minotaur*, 135.

106. Griffin, *Pornography and Silence*, 24–28, 59.

107. For an analysis of how this works, see Angela Carter, *The Sadeian Woman* (New York: Pantheon, 1978), 38–77; and for a very different analysis, more similar to that put forward here, see Griffin, *Pornography and Silence*, 21–25. See also Dworkin's synopsis of Bataille's *Story of the Eye* with the (to me) odd centrality of egg fetishism—a proof, if one is needed, that anything can be eroticized (*Pornography*, 167–75).

108. Dworkin, *Intercourse*, 169–94.

109. See Jessica Benjamin, "The Bonds of Love: Rational Violence and Erotic Domination," *Feminist Studies* VI, 1 (Spring, 1980):154.

110. Griffin, *Pornography and Silence*, 30. See also the discussion of the power dynamics of strip tease from the stripper's point of view: if the show is going well, the stripper is in complete control. Seph Weene, "Venus," *Heresies* 12 (1980):36–38.

111. Ibid., 37. The other types she mentions are "soft and powerless," "not-a-woman," and "rich." It is interesting to note that each of these ways of producing sexual excitement relies on a move away from dailiness.

112. Ibid., 64.

113. Benjamin, "The Bonds of Love," 157. The quotation she takes from Pauline Reage, *The Story of O*, trans. S. d'Estree (New York: Grove Press, 1965), 15–17.

114. Griffin gives a number of examples: *Pornography and Silence*, 64–66, 68.

115. Benjamin, "The Bonds of Love," 155.

116. Ibid., 56–48. Griffin analyzes *The Story of O* as an account of how O "unlearns all the knowledge of her body" (219ff). But it should instead be read, I believe, as a series of ever-increasing attacks on the body and more precisely, the will of another.

117. Ibid., 29.

118. Ibid., 132–38. See also the Apollo story in Aeschylus' *Oresteia*, ed. G. Thomson (New York: A. M. Hakkirt, 1966), which is an attempt to deny this.

119. See also Dworkin, *Intercourse*, 49–53, 176–77.

120. Griffin makes a seemingly similar but in fact different point. She argues that pornography contains three levels of death—the links of death with sex, the fear of the body, and the death of self-image. See *Pornography and Silence*, 32.

121. Dworkin, *Pornography*, 222. The account of the photographs and stories appears on 217–23.

122. Dworkin, *Pornography*, 54, citing Norman Mailer, *Prisoner of Sex* (Boston: Little, Brown, 1971), 126.

123. Bataille, *Death and Sensuality*, 42. While Adrienne Rich acknowledges the sometimes violent feelings between mothers and children, she quite clearly does not put these at the heart of the relation; Adrienne Rich, *Of Woman Born* (New York: Norton, 1976).

124. Bataille, *Death and Sensuality*, 13.

125. Ibid., 14. See also 101.

126. Griffin, *Pornography and Silence*, 123. She uses this description to make the point of the obsessive need for control.

127. Audre Lorde, "The Master's Tools Will Never Dismantle the Master's House," in *This Bridge Called My Back*, eds. Cherrie Moraga and Gloria Anzaldua (Watertown, Mass.: Persephone Press, 1981), 99.

128. Niles Newton, "Interrelationships Between Sexual Responsiveness, Birth, and Breast Feeding," in *Contemporary Sexual Behavior*, eds. Joseph Zubin and John Money (Baltimore: The Johns Hopkins University Press, 1971), 95.

129. Ibid., 83. The preceding paragraphy summarized 80–83.

130. Ibid., 84.

131. Susan Weisskopf, "Maternal Sexuality and Asexual Motherhood," *Signs* V, 4 (Summer, 1980): 770.

132. The quoted phrase is Janice Moulton's, from "Sex and Reference." I am indebted to Sarah Begus for pointing this out to me.

133. See, for example, Gayle Rubin, "The Leather Menace: Comments on Politics and S/M," in *Coming to Power*, ed. Samois; for other views, see *Off Our Backs* XII, 6 (June, 1982).

134. See Pat Califia, "Feminism and Sadomasochism," 32; Amber Hollibaugh and Cherrie Moraga, "What We're Rollin' Around in Bed With," *Heresies* 12 (1980): 60; Pat Califia, *Sapphistry* (Tallahassee, Fl.: Naiad Press, 1980), 124, 125, 128.

135. For example, Pat Califia's statement that "most of us feel some guilt or shame about being sexual (*Sapphistry*, 131). See also Sarah Zoftig, "Coming Out," 88, 93; Pat Califia, "Jessie," 167; Gayle Rubin, "The Leather Menace," 215; and Sophie Schmuckler, "How I Learned to Stop Worrying and Love My Dildo," 98–99; all in *Coming to Power*.

136. Anne Snitow, "Mass Market Romance," 151.

137. Ibid., 151.

Notes to Chapter 14

1. See the discussion by E. P. Thompson in *Protest and Survive*, ed. E. P. Thompson (New York: Monthly Review Press, 1980).

2. For example, see Helen Caldecott, *Missile Envy* (New York: William Morrow, 1984), and Nancy Hartsock, *Money, Sex and Power: Toward a Feminist Historical Materialism* (Boston: Northeastern University Press, 1983).

3. As principles directing social life and supporting class, racial, and gender privilege, rationalization, professionalization, and commodification are unequally distributed among men. They are most consistently found, I believe, in the same (essentially male) elite that produces and controls nuclear weapons. It is also the case that women are not completely exempt from these principles. However, as recent writings on female psychology and moral theory have shown, women's social position within the sex-gender system enables them to maintain forms of consciousness and action determined by principles of a type fundamentally different from those that structure the male world. See, for instance, Jean Baker Miller, *Toward a New Psychology of Women* (Boston: Beacon, 1975); Nancy Chodorow, *The Reproduction of Mothering* (Berkeley: University of California Press, 1978); Ann Ferguson, "Sex and Work: Women as a New Revolutionary Class in the United States," in *An Anthology of Western Marxism: From Lukacs and Gramsci to Socialist-Feminism,* ed. Roger S. Gottlieb (New York: Oxford University Press, 1989); and Carol Gilligan, *In a Different Voice* (Cambridge: Harvard University Press, 1983).

4. The sources for my discussion of rationalization, professionalization, and commodification and the male drive for power include the general theoretical perspectives of Lukacs, Marx, Sartre, and Nietzsche; Andrea Dworkin's *Pornography: Men Possessing Women* (New York: Perigee, 1979) and Susan Griffin's *Pornography and Silence* (New York: Harper, 1981), two accounts of male identity and pornography; Michel Foucault's and R. D. Laing's many discussions of psychiatry and medicine; Suzanne Arms' account of male domination and childbirth in *Immaculate Deception* (Boston: Houghton-Mifflin, 1975); the Frankfurt School's general critique of instrumental rationality; and Nancy Hartsock's summary of feminist writings on male sexuality in *Money, Sex and Power.*

5. Jürgen Habermas, *Theory and Practice* (Boston: Beacon Press, 1973), 271.

6. I use the term "patients" rather than "clients" because I believe that professionalization in general is modeled on the treatment of the ill by modern medicine.

7. I do not want to suggest that I have provided a thorough analysis of rationalization, professionalization, and commodification. The logic of these forms is not exhausted by their relation to gender. But without analyzing the relations between them and gender, we cannot fully understand either.

8. Soren Kierkegaard, *Concluding Unscientific Postscript* (Princeton: Princeton University Press, 1968), 175.

9. Women are also subject to commodification. Yet as the bearers of emotional life in our sex-gender system, they are less dominated by it than are men; or, at least, more emotionally conflicted about being subject to it.

10. On childbirth, see Arms, *Immaculate Deception.* On the effects of female parenting, see Chodorow, *Reproduction.*

11. For an analysis of the Holocaust that bears some similarity to the analysis of nuclear terror presented here, see Richard Schmitt, "Murderous Objectivity: Reflection on Marxism and the Holocaust," in *Thinking the Unthinkable: Meanings of the Holocaust,* ed. Roger S. Gottlieb (New York: Paulist Press, 1990).

SELECTED BIBLIOGRAPHY

Abell, Peter. "The Many Faces of Power and Liberty: Revealed Preference, Autonomy and Teleological Explanation." *Sociology* 11 (1977):3–24.

Airaksinen, Timo. "Coercion, Deterence, and Authority." *Theory and Decision* 17 (1984):105–17.

———. *The Ethics of Coercion and Authority.* Pittsburgh: University of Pittsburgh Press, 1988.

———. "Hegel on Poverty and Violence." In *Economic Justice: Private Rights and Public Responsibilities,* edited by Kenneth Kipnis and Diana T. Meyers, pp. 42–58. New Jersey: Rowman & Allanheld, 1985.

Arendt, Hannah. *On Violence.* New York: Harcourt Brace Jovanovitch, 1969–70.

———. "What Is Authority?" In *Between Past and Future: Eight Exercises in Political Thought.* Harmondsworth: Penguin, 1954.

Bachrach, Peter, and Baratz, Morton S. "Decisions and Non-decisions: An Analytical Framework." *American Political Science Review* 57 (1963):641–51. Reprinted in Bell, Roderick, et al., eds., *Political Power: A Reader in Theory and Research,* pp. 100–109. New York: Free Press, 1969.

———. "Two Faces of Power." *American Political Science Review* 56 (1962):947–52. Reprinted in Bell, Roderick, et al., eds., *Political Power: A Reader in Theory and Research,* pp. 94–99. New York: Free Press, 1969.

Balbus, Issac. "Ruling Elite Theory vs. Marxist Class Analysis." *Monthly Review* #23 (May, 1971):36–46.

Ball, Terence. "Authority and Conceptual Change." In *Authority Revisited, NOMOS XXIX,* edited by John W. Chapman and J. Rolland Pennock. New York: New York University Press, 1987.

———. "Marxian Science and Positivist Politics." In *After Marx,* edited by Terence Ball and James Fair, pp. 253–260. Cambridge: Cambridge University Press, 1984.

———. "Models of Power: Past and Present." *Journal of the History of the Behaviorial Sciences* 11 (July, 1975):211–22.

————. "Power, Causation and Explanation." *Polity* (1975):189–214.

————. "Two Concepts of Coercion." *Theory & Society* 15 (Jan., 1978):97–112.

Barnes, Barry. *The Nature of Power.* Urbana and Chicago: University of Illinois Press, 1988.

Barry, Brian. *Power and Political Theory: Some European Perspectives.* London: John Wiley, 1976.

Bartky, Sandra Lee. "Toward a Phenomenology of Feminist Consciousness." *Social Theory and Practice* 3:4 (Fall, 1975):425–39.

Bell, Roderick; Edwards, David V.; and Wagner, R. Harrison, eds. *Political Power: A Reader in Theory and Research.* New York: Free Press, 1969.

Bernstein, Richard J. *Beyond Objectivism and Relativism: Science, Hermeneutics, and Praxis.* Philadelphia: University of Pennsylvania Press, 1983.

Blau, Peter. *Exchange and Power Social Life.* New Brunswick: Transaction Books, 1986, 2nd Edition.

Bloch, Michael; Heading, Bryan; and Lawrence, Philip. "Power in Social Theory: A Non-Relative View." In *Philosophical Disputes in the Social Sciences,* edited by S. C. Brown, pp. 243–75. Atlantic Highlands, N.J.: Humanities Press Inc., 1979.

Bourdieu, Pierre. *Outline of a Theory of Practice,* translated by Richard Nice. Cambridge: Cambridge University Press, 1977.

Bowles, Samuel, and Gintis, Herb. "Structure and Practice in the Labor Theory of Value." *The Review of Radical Political Economics* 12:4 (Winter, 1981):1–26.

Braybrooke, David. "Two Blown Fuses in Goldman's Analysis of Power." *Philosophical Studies* 24:6 (November, 1973):369–77.

Card, Claudia. "Oppression and Resistance: Frye's Politics of Reality." *Hypatia* 1:1 (Spring, 1986):149–66.

Cartwright, Dawn, ed. *Studies in Social Power.* Ann Arbor: University of Michigan Press, 1959.

Charlesworth, James C., ed. *Contemporary Political Analysis.* New York: The Free Press, 1967.

Chodorow, Nancy. *The Reproduction of Mothering: Psychoanalysis and the Sociology of Gender.* Berkeley: University of California Press, 1978.

Chomsky, Noam, and Foucault, Michel. "Human Nature: Judgement versus Power." In *Reflexive Water: The Basic Concerns of Mankind,* ed. Fons Elders, pp. 135–97. Oregon: Souvenir Press, 1974.

Connolly, William E. "Discipline, Politics, and Ambiguity." *Political Theory* 11:3 (August, 1983):325–41.

———. "Modern Authority and Ambiguity." In *Authority Revisited, NOMOS XXIX,* edited by John W. Chapman and J. Rolland Pennock. New York: New York University Press, 1987.

———. "Taylor, Foucault, and Otherness." *Political Theory* 13:3 (August, 1985):365–76.

———. *The Terms of Political Discourse.* Princeton: Princeton University Press, 1974 and 1983.

Dahl, Robert. "The Behaviorial Approach in Political Science: Epitaph for a Monument to a Successful Protest." *American Political Science Review* 55 (1961):763–72.

———. "The Concept of Power." In Bell, Roderick, et al., *Political Power: A Reader in Theory and Research,* edited by Roderick Bell, et al., pp. 79–93. New York: Free Press, 1969.

———. "A Critique of the Ruling Elite Model." In *Political Power: A Reader in Theory and Research,* edited by Roderick Bell, et al., pp. 36–41. New York: Free Press, 1969.

de Jouvenal, Bertrand. *On Power: Its Nature and the History of its Growth.* Boston: Beacon Press, 1945.

Dietz, Mary G. "Citizenship and Maternal Thinking." *Political Theory* 13:1 (February, 1985):19–38.

Domhoff, William. *Who Really Rules: New Haven and Community Power Re-Examined.* Santa Monica: Goodyear Publishing Co., 1978.

Emmet, Dorothy. "The Concept of Power." *Proceedings of the Aristotelian Society* (1953):1–25.

Fay, Brian. *Critical Social Science.* Ithaca: Cornell University Press, 1987.

Foucault, Michel. *Discipline and Punish.* New York: Vintage, 1975.

———. "Governmentality." M/f: *A feminist journal* 3 (July, 1979):5–21.

———. *The History of Sexuality Volume 1: An Introduction,* translated by Robert Hurley. New York: Pantheon, 1978.

———. "Is It Useless to Revolt?" *Philosophy and Social Criticism* 8:1 (Spring, 1981):3–9.

———. "Omnes et Singulatim: Towards a Criticism of Political Reason." In *Values,* edited by Sterling M. McMunim, pp. 225–55. (Salt Lake City and Cambridge: Utah Press and Cambridge University Press, 1981.

———. "The Political Function of the Intellectual," translated by Colin Gordon. *Radical Philosophy* 17 (Summer, 1977):12–14.

———. *Power/Knowledge: Selected Interviews and Other Writings 1972–1977*, edited by Colin Gordon. New York: Pantheon, 1980.

French, John R. P., and Raven, Bertrand. "The Bases of Social Power." In *Studies in Social Power*, edited by Dawn Cartwright, pp. 118–49. Ann Arbor: University of Michigan Press, 1959.

French, John R. P., and Synder, Richard. "Leadership and Interpersonal Power." In *Studies in Social Power*, edited by Dawn Cartwright, pp. 150–67.Ann Arbor: University of Michigan Press, 1959.

Friedrich, Carl J. "Authority, Reason, and Discretion." ed. Friedrich, *Authority, NOMOS I*, pp. 28–48. Cambridge: Harvard University Press, 1958.

———. *Man and his Government: An Empirical Theory of Politics*. New York: McGraw-Hill, 1963.

Gallie, W. B. "Essentially Contested Concepts." *Proceedings of the Aristotelian Society* (1956):167–98.

Giddens, Anthony. *Central Problems in Social Theory: Action, Structure and Contradiction in Social Analysis*. Berkeley and Los Angeles: University of California Press, 1979.

———. *The Constitution of Society*. Cambridge, England: Polity Press, 1984.

———. " 'Power' in the Recent Writings of Talcott Parsons." *Sociology: The Journal of the Brittish Sociological Association* 2:3 (September, 1988):257–72.

Goldman, Alvin I. "On the Measurement of Power." *The Journal of Philosophy* LXXI:8 (May 2, 1974):231–52.

———. "Power, Time, and Cost." *Philosophical Studies* 26:3/4 (November, 1974):263–70.

———. "Toward a Theory of Social Power." *Philosophical Studies* 23:4 (June, 1972):221–67.

Habermas, Jürgen. "Hannah Arendts Begriff der Macht." In *Philosofisch-politische Profile*, pp. 228–48. Frankfurt: Suhrkamp, 1981.

———. *Knowledge and Human Interests*. Boston: Beacon Press, 1971.

———. *The Philosophical Discourse of Modernity*, translated by Fredrick Lawrence. Cambridge: M.I.T. Press, 1987.

———. "Taking Aim at the Heart of the Present." In *Foucault: A Critical Reader*, edited by David Couzens Hoy, pp. 103–108. Oxford: Basil Blackwell, 1986.

———. *The Theory of Communicative Action, Volume I: Lifeworld and System: A*

Critique of Functionalist Reason, translated by Thomas McCarthy. Boston: Beacon Press, 1987.

Harsanyi, John C. "Measurement of Social Power, Opportunity Costs, and the Theory of Two-Person Bargaining Games." In *Political Power: A Reader in Theory and Research,* edited by Roderick Bell, et al., pp. 226–38.

Hartsock, Nancy. *Money, Sex, and Power: Towards a Feminist Historical Materialism.* New York and London: Longman, 1983.

Hegel, G. W. F. *Phenomenology of Spirit,* translated by A. V. Miller. Oxford: Oxford University Press, 1977.

Hindess, Barry. "Power, Interests, and the Outcomes of Struggles." *Sociology* 16:4 (November, 1982):498–511.

Homans, George Caspar. *Social Behavior: Its Elementary Forms.* New York: Harcourt, Brace & World, 1961.

Hoy, David. "Power, Repression, Progress: Foucault, Lukes, and the Frankfurt School." In *Foucault: A Critical Reader,* pp. 123–47. Oxford: Basil Blackwell, 1986.

Issac, Jeffrey C. *Power and Marxist Theory: A Realist View.* Ithaca and London: Cornell University Press, 1987.

Kliemt, H. "A Philosophical View of Power." In *Power, Voting, and Voting Power,* edited by Manfred L. Holler, pp. 52–64. Heidelberg, Germany: Physica-Verlag, 1981.

Korpi, Walter. "Developments in the Theory of Power and Exchange." *Sociological Theory* 3:2 (Fall, 1985):31–45.

Kuykendall, Elanor H. "Toward an Ethic of Nurturance: Lucy Irigaray on Mothering and Power." In Trebilcot, Joyce, ed., *Mothering: Essays in Feminist Theory,* edited by Joyce Trebilcot, pp. 263–74. Totowa, New Jersey: Rowman & Allanheld, 1983.

Laclau, Ernesto. "The Specificity of the Political: The Poulantzas-Miliband Debate." *Economy and Society* 4 (1975):87–110.

Laswell, Harold, and Kaplan, Abraham. *Power and Society.* New Haven, Conn.: Yale University Press, 1950.

Lively, Jack. "The Limits of Exchange Theory." In *Power and Political Theory: Some European Perspectives,* edited by Brian Barry, pp. 1–13. London: John Wiley, 1976.

Livesay, Jeff. "Normative Grounding and Praxis: Habermas, Giddens, and a Contradiction within Critical Theory." *Sociological Theory* 3:2 (Fall,1985):66–76.

Luhmann, Niklaus. *Trust and Power: Two Works.* New York: John Wiley, 1979.

Lukes, Steven. *Power: A Radical View.* London and Basingstoke: Macmillan, 1974.

———. "Perspectives on Authority." In *Authority Revisited,* edited by John W. Chapman and J. Rolland Pennock, pp. 60–75. New York: New York University Press, 1987.

———. "Power and Authority." In *A History of Sociological Analysis,* edited by Tom Bottomre and Robert Nisbet, pp. 633–76. New York: Basic Books, 1978.

———. "Power and Structure." In *Essays in Social Theory,* pp. 3–23. New York: Macmillan, 1977.

———, ed. *Power.* Oxford: Basil Blackwell, 1986.

Macpherson, C. B. *Democratic Theory: Essays in Retrieval.* Oxford: Oxford University Press, 1973.

Martin, Biddy. "Feminism, Criticism, and Foucault." *New German Critique* 27 (February, 1982):3–30.

Miliband, Ralph. "The Capitalist State: Reply to Nicos Poulantzas." *New Left Review* 59 (1970):53–60.

———. "Political Action, Determinism, and Contingency." In *Political Power and Social Theory,* Vol. 1, edited by Maurice Zeitlin, pp. 1–19. Greenwich, Conn.: JAI Press, 1980.

———. "Poulantzas and the Capitalist State." *New Left Review* 82 (1973): 83–92.

Miller, Alice. *Thou Shalt Not Be Aware: Society's Betrayal of the Child.* New York: New American Library, 1984.

Mills, C. Wright. *The Power Elite.* Oxford: Oxford University Press, 1956.

Minson, Jeff. "Strategies for Socialists? Foucault's Conception of Power." *Economy and Society* 9:1 (February, 1980):1–43.

Mintz, Beth, and Schwartz, Michael. *The Power and the Structure of American Business.* Chicago: University of Chicago Press, 1985.

Morgenthau, Hans J. "Love and Power." In *The Restoration of American Politics,* Vol. III of *Politics in the Twentieth Century.* Chicago: University of Chicago Press, 1962.

Morris, Meaghan, and Patton, Paul, eds. *Michel Foucault: Power, Truth, Strategy.* Sydney: Feral Publications, 1979.

Morriss, Peter. "The Essentially Uncontestible Concepts of Power." In *The Fron-*

tiers of Political Theory, edited by Michael Freeman and David Robertson, pp. 198–232. New York: St. Martin's Press, 1980.

——. *Power: A Philosophical Analysis.* New York: St. Martin's Press, 1987.

Nozick, Robert. "Coercion." In *Philosophy, Politics, and Society (Fourth Series),* edited by Peter Laslett, W. G. Runciman, and Quentin Skinner, pp. 101–35. Oxford: Oxford University Press, 1972.

Parenti, Michael. *Power and the Powerless.* New York: St. Martin's Press, 1978.

Parsons, Talcott. "Authority, Legitimation, and Political Action." In Carl Friedrich, ed., *Authority, NOMOS I,* pp. 197–221. Cambridge: Harvard University Press, 1958.

——. "On the Concept of Political Power." In *Political Power: A Reader in Theory and Research,* edited by Roderick Bell, et al., pp. 251–84. New York: Free Press, 1969.

——. *Politics and Social Structure.* New York: Free Press, 1969.

Pitkin, Hannah. *Wittgenstein and Justice.* Berkeley, Los Angeles, and London: University of California Press, 1972.

Polsby, Nelson W. *Community Power and Political Theory.* New Haven, Conn.: Yale University Press, 1980.

Poulantzas, Nicos. "The Capitalist State: A Reply to Miliband and Laclau." *New Left Review* 95 (1976):63–83.

——. Political *Power and Social Classes.* London: New Left Books, 1973.

——. "The Problem of the Capitalist State." *New Left Review* 58 (1969):67–78.

——. *State Power, Socialism,* translated by Patrick Camiller. London: New Left Books, 1978.

Przeworski, Adam. "Material Bases of Consent: Economics and Politics in a Hegemonic System." In *Political Power and Social Theory,* Vol. 1, edited by Maurice Zeitlin, pp. 21–66. Greenwich, Conn.: JAI Press, 1980.

Riker, William. "Some Ambiguities in the Notion of Power." In *Political Power: A Reader in Theory and Research,* edited by Roderick Bell, et al., pp. 110–19. New York: Free Press, 1969.

Russell, Bertrand. *Power.* New York: W. W. Norton, 1983.

Sampson, Ronald V. *The Psychology of Power.* New York: Pantheon Books, 1966.

Tambiah, S. J. "The Magical Power of Words." *Journal of the Royal Anthropological Institute* 3 (1968):175–208.

Taylor, Charles. "Connolly, Foucault, and Truth." *Political Theory* 13:3 (August,

1985):377–85.

———. "Foucault on Freedom and Truth." In *Philosophy and the Human Sciences*, pp. 152–84. Cambridge: Cambridge University Press, 1985.

Thomas, K. "Power and Autonomy: Further Comments on the Many Faces of Power." *Sociology* 12 (1978):332–35.

Trebilcot, Joyce, ed. *Mothering: Essays in Feminist Theory.* Totowa, N.J.: Rowman & Allanheld, 1983.

Truman, David. "The Implications of Political Behavior Research." Social Science Research Council *Items* 5 (1951):37–39.

Wartenberg, Thomas E. "Beyond Babies and Banners: Towards an Understanding of the Dynamics of Social Movements." *New Political Science* 14 (Winter, 1985–6):157–71.

———. "The Forms of Power." *Analyse & Krittik* 10 (1988):3–31.

———. *The Forms of Power: From Domination to Transformation.* Philadelphia: Temple University Press, 1990.

Weber, Max. *Wirtschaft und Gesellschaft: Grundriss der Verstehenden Soziologie.* Tübingen: J. C. B. Mohr, 1985.

West, David. "Power and Formation: New Foundations for a Radical Concept of Power." *Inquiry* 30 (March, 1987):137–54.

Wrong, Dennis. *Power: Its Forms, Bases, and Uses.* Oxford: Blackwell, 1979.

Young, Iris. "Is Male Gender Identity the Cause of Male Domination?" In *Mothering: Essays in Feminist Theory,* edited by Joyce Trebilcot, pp. 129–46, Totowa, N.J.: Rowman & Allanheld, 1983.

Zimmerman, David. "Coercive Wage Offers." *Philosophy and Public Affairs* 10:2 (Spring, 1981):121–45.

NOTES ON CONTRIBUTORS

Timo Airaksinen, Professor of Philosophy at the University of Helsinki, has published widely in ethics, epistemology, and the history of philosophy. He is the author of *The Ethics of Coercion and Authority* (Pittsburgh: University of Pittsburgh Press, 1988) and *Of Glamour, Sex, and De Sade* (Wakefield, N.H.: Longwood Academic Press, 1991).

Terence Ball is Professor of Political Science at the University of Minnesota. He is the author, most recently, of *Transforming Political Discourse* (Oxford and New York: Blackwell, 1988) and the coauthor (with Richard Dagger) of *Political Ideologies and the Democratic Ideal* (New York: Harper-Collins, 1991). He is currently working on a book about environmental ethics and obligations to future generations.

Wolfgang Balzer, Professor at the Seminar for Philosophy, Logic, and the Theory of Science at the University of Munich, is a leading figure in the 'structuralist' approach to the philosophy of science. He has published several books in German and many articles in international journals, mostly on topics in the philosophy of science.

Samuel Bowles and Herbert Gintis are Professors of Economics at the University of Massachusetts at Amherst. Their previous collaborations include *Schooling in Capitalist America* (New York: Basic Books, 1976) and *Democracy and Capitalism* (New York: Basic Books, 1986).

Roger S. Gottlieb is Professor of Philosophy at Worcester Polytechnic Institute. He is the author of *History and Subjectivity: The Transformation of Western Marxist Theory* (Philadelphia: Temple University Press, 1987). He has edited books on Western Marxism, the Holocaust, and contemporary spirituality.

Nancy Hartsock is Associate Professor of Political Science and Women's Studies at the University of Washington. She is the author of *Money, Sex, and Power: Towards a Feminist Historical Materialism* (New York and London: Longman, 1983; Northeastern University Press, 1984). She is currently working on a book titled *Post-Modernism and Political Change.*

351

Jeffrey C. Isaac is Associate Professor of Political Science at Indiana University. He is the author of *Power and Marxist Theory: A Realist View* (Ithaca and London: Cornell University Press, 1987). He is currently completing a book on Hannah Arendt and Albert Camus.

Thomas McCarthy is Professor of Philosophy at Northwestern University. He is the author of *The Critical Theory of Jürgen Habermas* (Cambridge: M.I.T. Press, 1978) and the editor of the M.I.T. Press Series *Studies in Contemporary German Social Thought*. His most recent work is *Ideals and Illusions: On Reconstruction and Deconstruction in Contemporary Social Theory* (Cambridge, Mass.: The M.I.T. Press, 1991).

Howard McGary is Associate Professor of Philosophy at Rugers University. He has published essays on a variety of topics in African-American philosophy, ethics, and social philosophy. He is the coauthor of *Between Slavery and Freedom: Philosophy and the American Slave Experience* with Bill Lawson. He is currently working on the topic of liberalism and moral conflict.

Jean Baker Miller, M.D., is a Clinical Professor of Psychiatry at Boston University School of Medicine and Director of Education at the Stone Center, Wellesley College. She has written *Toward a New Psychology of Women* (Boston: Beacon Press, 1976, 2nd Ed., 1987) and edited *Psychoanalysis and Women* (Baltimore: Penguin, 1973), as well as numerous articles on depression, dreams, and the psychology of women.

Amelie Oksenberg Rorty is Professor of Philosophy at Mount Holyoke College and the Matina Horner Distinguished Visiting Professor at Radcliffe College. Her recent book *Mind In Action* was published by Beacon Press (1988). Among the books she has edited are *Perspectives on Self-Deception* with Brian McLaughlin (Berkeley and Los Angeles: University of California Press, 1988) and *Essays on Aristotle's Poetics* (Princeton: Princeton University Press, forthcoming).

Gayatri Chakravorty Spivak is Professor of English and Comparative Literature at Columbia University. She is the translator of Jacques Derrida, *Of Grammatology* (Baltimore: The Johns Hopkins University Press, 1976) and the author of *In Other Words* (New York and London: Methuen, 1987).

Thomas E. Wartenberg is Associate Professor of Philosophy at Mount Holyoke College. Aside from his recent book, *The Forms of Power: From Domination to Transformation* (Philadelphia: Temple University Press, 1990), he has published widely in the history of philosophy and social theory.

Iris Marion Young is Associate Professor of Public and International Affairs at the University of Pittsburgh. She is the author of *Justice and the Politics of Difference* (Princeton: Princeton University Press, 1990) and *Throwing Like A Girl and Other Essays in Feminist Philosophy and Social Thought* (Bloomington: Indiana University Press, 1990).